D0897611

POETIC
CONFIGURATIONS

POETIC
CONFIGURATIONS

Essays

in

Literary History

and

Criticism

Lowry Nelson, Jr.

The Pennsylvania State University Press
University Park, Pennsylvania

Library of Congress Cataloging-in-Publication Data

Nelson, Lowry, Jr.
    Poetic configurations : essays in literary history and criticism /
Lowry Nelson, Jr.

        p.   cm.
    Includes bibliographical references and index.
    ISBN 0-271-00800-8
    1. Poetry—History and criticism.   2. Criticism.   I. Title.
PN1136.N38   1992
809.1—dc20   91-3690
                                                  CIP

It is the policy of The Pennsylvania State University Press to use acid-free paper for
the first printing of all clothbound books. Publications on uncoated stock satisfy the
minimum requirements of American National Standard for Information Sciences—
Permanence of Paper for Printed Library Materials, ANSI Z39.48–1984.

Especially for
P. M. Pasinetti and René Wellek

CONTENTS

PREFACE

I have long acknowledged to myself that the essay is my preferred form. My ideal in that form is to combine fresh insight, thorough scholarship, wide relevant reference, criticism within a coherent concept of literature, and urbanity of style. I hope, in this volume, that I have, at least in part, met these goals. My scope is very broad and I think properly so. The general continuity in Western poetry is usually appreciated as an unexamined datum. One way to exemplify it would be to compile a sort of narrative catalogue of names and works and influences that could fill volumes with much superficiality: a history of lyric poetry in the Western tradition. My choice here has been to make soundings, to be selective and specific, to draw larger connections, to juxtapose, and also, in the more theoretical essays at the beginning and the end, to assert the "comparative" and "readerly" perspectives. The essays are arranged as chronologically as possible to honor often overprized continuity (which holds the danger of forcing and falsifying) and inevitable discontinuity (which can be appraised only in some chronological frame). Of my readers I naturally expect a love of poetry and wide reading in it, a desire for new experience, and an openness toward the whole Western tradition. Translations are given for most of the texts quoted; where there are none I think I have supplied sufficient paraphrase. In my notes and elsewhere I have cited quite a number of scholar-critics and given specific sources for the reader's convenience. Any direct indebtedness has been explicitly and gratefully acknowledged. Many of the poems and poets I discuss are so famously standard and the commentary on them is so voluminous that to contemplate even select bibliographies in handbook style would seem to me pretentious and foolhardy.

To the friends who have sustained me over the years with their graceful erudition, their good counsel, and their affection I choose to give private thanks. With public or, as it were, published gratitude I thank the Penn State Press for their hospitality, particularly in the person of Philip Winsor.

ACKNOWLEDGMENTS

The following are reprinted in revised form in this volume:

"The Rhetoric of Ineffability: Toward a Definition of Mystical Poetry," *Comparative Literature* 8 (1956), 323–36.

"Baudelaire and Virgil: A Reading of 'Le Cygne,'" *Comparative Literature* 13 (1961), 332–45.

"The Fictive Reader and Literary Self-Reflexiveness," in *Disciplines of Criticism,* ed. Peter Demetz, Thomas Greene, and Lowry Nelson, Jr. (New Haven: Yale University Press, 1968), 173–91.

"Leopardi First and Last," in *Italian Literature: Roots and Branches,* ed. Giose Rimanelli and K. J. Atchity (New Haven: Yale University Press, 1976), 333–62.

"The Matter of Rime: Sonnets of Sidney, Daniel, and Shakespeare," in *Poetic Traditions of the English Renaissance,* ed. Maynard Mack and George deF. Lord (New Haven: Yale University Press, 1982), 123–42.

"Giambattista Vico e Gaspare Gozzi, Critici di Dante," in *Vico/Venezia,* ed. Cesare De Michelis and Gilberto Pizzamiglio (Florence: Olschki, 1982), 301–15.

"*Translatio Lauri:* Ivanov's Translations of Petrarch," in *Vyacheslav Ivanov: Poet, Critic and Philosopher,* ed. Robert L. Jackson and Lowry Nelson, Jr. (New Haven: Yale Center for International and Area Studies, 1986), 162–89.

"Defining and Defending Comparative Literature," in *The Comparative Perspective on Literature,* ed. Clayton Koelb and Susan Noakes (Ithaca: Cornell University Press, 1988), 37–47.

INTRODUCTION

An old tradition, first fully shaped in eighteenth-century England, in effect distinguishes three modes of contemplating poetry: theory, criticism, and historical understanding. For long periods before and since one or another of those modes has held the ascendant over the rest. At times, as in the Renaissance, as well as now, guises of theory have courted and commanded attention by asserting that literature should follow precept or that literature, as part of general discourse, makes impossible pretense to cognitive autonomy and emotive meaning. The precarious realm of aesthetics—ever inadequate to account for creativity, fantasy or imagination, the perception of beauty and form, and the positing of fiction and play for their own sake—seems hardy and persistent enough in daily experience but notoriously vulnerable to arbitrary prescription on the one hand and to epistemological or even ontological dismantling on the other. Criticism in the past has often been considered a practical activity of discernment that, according to usage and consonant with etymology, purports to characterize and evaluate the finished products of literature and to set them somewhere in a canon shared or disputed by critic and public. Presumably the critic performs his task by adducing principles and arguments and fitting them to particular works. He may, after attaining some authority or prestige, simply rely on his standing or his sponsors to pass summary judgment, or he may become a general cultural commentator, or he may cultivate a private, associative personality in print. If the published critic achieves a certain status or fame he does so not only by the depth and skill of his formulations but also by the interest and taste of his public, which is made up of both "common readers" and fellow critics in or out of academia. Aside from the putative glamor of such titles as "critic" or "intellectual," surely every attentive intelligent reader is a critic and intellectual (to use those terms), whether or not he registers in durable documentary form his perceptions, principles, and arguments. Critics of record, so to say, are those who have the gift and discipline of formulating and preserving their views. A proper history of criticism must consider the forgotten and the unglamorous just as it must reconsider the touted and the famous. A critic may be disposed to decry history and historical perspective; he may flout or disregard historical considerations in the name of present concerns. But if he is indeed a critic of record he inevitably slips into categorizations and groupings that, even in a brief span of time, become historical counters to be played on the widening field of the past. Primacy or originality are not in themselves guarantees of excellence or even interest. Yet present claims and present achievements can be adequately appreciated only through knowledge of what has been claimed and achieved in the past. The past may be a fragment of archaic Greek poetry found in the sands of Egypt or today's poem in the *New Yorker*. Historical awareness and historical meaning are part of reflective daily life. Even the inveterate *laudator temporis acti* is actively engaged in an evaluation of the present. Simply pitting the past against the present is, however, a prejudicial practice that can only foster a false or trivial dichotomy between "modernism" and "passéism." Those terms are polemical and temporary rather than freely contemplative. Privileging the past is hardly more interesting than privileging the present. Given literature and the language of its expression as institutions or traditions of expectation and given the almost limitless resources of retrieval we now have, surely it is both our duty and our pleasure to know the past as part of the present. The older positivism has had its day: the achievements of nineteenth-century literary and linguistic scholarship understandably induced a self-congratulatory headiness and for a time seemed to justify an obsession with discovery of origins, verifiability of facts, and methodical establishment of texts. In the process, so much was recovered and preserved and set in place, as printed "working tools," that even those who scorn the most enlightened scholarly formulations of the nineteenth century can make use of the texts and the apparatus even as a sort of playground of curiosities and quaint surprises. But, of course, those working tools and the assumptions on which they were fashioned are in constant need of repair and revision, indeed of reconception.

Part of the ebullience and rowdiness of late twentieth-century culture (in its broadest sense) is the play of ideologies, pursued for the "ideas" and also meretriciously for the prestige. Exhibitionism and promotional competition, rather than care and urbanity, are too often encountered in public, academic, and publishing life. Ambitions of frenetic modernity and habits of faded modernism almost obscure the essential interdependence of literary theory, criticism, and history. These realms are, to their detriment, often pursued quite separately and capriciously. Theory nowadays often borrows concepts or slogans from psychoanalysis, from Marxism, from existential philosophers (Nietzsche, Heidegger, and their heirs and epigones), and from the more austere formulations of linguists and semioticians. The combinations and recombinations competing for attention drive in two main directions: toward a general formulaic poetics based on linguistic theory (Saussure to Jakobson) and on rhetoric (a revived study of tropes), and toward general psychological or cultural appropriations of literature to idiosyncratic and syncretic attempts at synthesis either on a ground of philosophy or on a vast spectrum of anthropology conceived as the *sciences de l'homme.* In practical criticism, which must be based on some sort of attentive reading or apprehension of aesthetic objects, we witness a welter of attempts to set works in large schemes of human activity and to show how they inevitably and repetitively exemplify, say, the insoluble dilemmas of expressing meaning, polemical focus on class or sex, varieties of biographical and psychological determinism, or simply aleatory caprice of words on a page. In the process, older methods and doctrines are first caricatured and then impugned. As much criticism is usually behind the times, it often attempts still to exploit notions, now quite ancient, expressed in the famous essays and manifestoes of modernism and its parent symbolism. Programmatically outrageous snook-cocking, as with the futurists, formalists, dadaists, and surrealists, has belatedly been adopted by some as their method and claim to novelty. In the process, a fructifying sense of history and simply some objective and detailed knowledge of the past have been abandoned by many as irrelevant or unknowable or readily revisable or even, with touching naïveté, as fully and inertly preserved in archives and reference works. The richness and peculiarity of the past can thus be misconstrued out of relative ignorance or out of false assurance that it can be pillaged at random for some casual contemporary use. In the midst of this methodological turmoil, which is perhaps more notorious than representative, there continue to be serious attempts, in theory, criticism, and history, to preserve the integrity of the aesthetic object and to consider its status in the whole range of human experience past and present. Meanwhile myriads of odd "readings" and joiner's "theories" make their way through the press.

Theory without example is gray. Example without theory is mere motley. These essays on poetry attempt to honor consistently the claims of example and of theory and to interpret poems through historical understanding and, above all, aesthetic criticism. They are arranged in an order that roughly accommodates chronology and theoretical emphasis. Eight of them, as will be noted, have been published elsewhere and are here revised and updated.

"Defining and Defending Comparative Literature," published in a most heterogeneous collection called *The Comparative Perspective on Literature: Approaches to Theory and Practice* (1988), attempts to survey the welter and, at the risk of appearing "reactionary" to some, affirms the centrality of literature as comprising integral works of art. "To Express the Inexpressible" is introductory and inductive in exploring some ordinary and literary uses of language. Recently composed, it generalizes matters proposed in "The Rhetoric of Ineffability in Mystical Poetry," which is the first of the essays in this volume to have been written (published in *Comparative Literature* in 1956). The two together thus reflect a continuing view that poetry is irreducible either to language in general or to formal and theoretical prescription. If the second essay is concerned with borderline instances near the edge of indeterminacy, it does not thereby argue that cleverness of technique or depth of sentiment can make a good poem. "The Kind of Early Lyric," taking seriously the usefulness of considering the lyric as a genre, makes a long and occasionally bumptious sweep through history up to Petrarch. A similar matter—when and how did Western vernacular poetry begin?—is treated in the essay "Conditions of Provensal Poetry," which reevaluates the hoary notion of "origins" or "beginnings" and makes some claim for originality, genius, and value. "Cavalcanti's Centrality in Early Vernacular Poetry," adapted from my edition of the poet (1986), sees Guido as the first truly great Italian poet, inheritor of the great lyric tradition, and no mere precursor of the younger Dante who called him his "first friend." "Close Reading of Lyric Poetry" attempts to answer a question I have not seen posed elsewhere: When did close, integral, critical reading of *whole* poems begin? Historically, the great early Provensal poets and their successors in Sicily and northern Italy set the fashion and discipline of rime for much Western lyric poetry, and that, with English Renaissance examples, is the subject of "The Matter of Rime" (published in the jubilee volume for Louis L. Martz). "Civic Poetry" sketches a perennial though oddly fated thematics that has generally been shunned or unrecognized in English literature, and so it seems appropriate to stress some English instances. Recovering and understanding past art for the present are exemplified in "Vico and Gozzi as Innovators in Poetic Criticism." Though the instance is not primarily lyric, nor indeed was their epoch propitious to lyric, still the momentous example of recovering and understanding greatness foreshadows our own inheritance and possible appreciation of the past from a present perspective. Out of the lyric paucity of the eighteenth century came a mode of contemplative poetry that was indeed pan-European, as exemplified in the Russian Lomonosov, at the very beginning of postmedieval Russian literature, as well as in the far more familiar Wordsworth and Leopardi: "Bottomless Soundings" returns in a different key to the preoccupations of the second and fourth essays. The historical burden is carried along in the single poetic career of Giacomo Leopardi, who traced his own peculiar trajectory as argued in "Leopardi First and Last" (published originally in *Italian Literature: Roots and Branches,* the jubilee volume for Thomas G. Bergin). "Baudelaire and Virgil: A Reading of 'Le Cygne'" (published in *Comparative Literature* in 1962) discusses a prime example of literary allusion. Baudelaire's poem, because it incorporates a whole episode from the *Aeneid,* is not therefore an exercise in poet's angst or simply another case of "metapoetry"; rather it gains from that allusion—which is, if anything, an act of homage—great richness in its vast and particularized survey of exile and captivity. That is one means whereby literature remains a living institution and a living and shared experience through art. "*Translatio Lauri:* Ivanov's Translations of Petrarch," published in *Vyacheslav Ivanov: Poet, Critic and Philosopher* (1986), considers two critical matters. First, it grapples with the difficulty of comparing and evaluating the translations of one great poet by another. Second, it focuses on the vast achievement of Russia's greatest symbolist poet in incorporating the European Renaissance into Russian literature, which had none. The last essay, "The Fictive Reader and Literary

Self-Reflexiveness" (published in 1968), is, I think, the first to foreground readers as participants in the "performance" of the literary work of art: readers obviously have a part in what I call the rhetorical situation, and they find their role written in the text.

1

DEFINING AND DEFENDING COMPARATIVE LITERATURE

I

In the simplest and best formulation, Comparative Literature is nothing other than the study of literature. My notion of literature is that it is an art; that its productive human faculty is conveniently called imagination; that its works must be considered in their individual integrity and also in groupings by national and international traditions, movements, periods, and genres; and that its theory and mode of existence belong under the philosophical heading of aesthetics. In Aristotelian and Kantian terms, to which I largely subscribe, literature is purposive without purpose, that is, it is goal seeking (to fulfill its wholeness, form, or the implications of its subject matter) and yet does not have its goal in practical or moral activity or in the proofs of logic, epistemology, and metaphysics. Such a view avoids the triviality of art for art's sake and also the grandiosity of literature as world saving and inclusive of all verbal discourse. Likewise, the prime effect of literature is "disinterested pleasure"—a complex of both thought and feeling that a text arouses by its artistry and not by its practical, partisan, or historically illustrative usefulness. Once the prime object and the prime attitude toward it are established—and only then—it is possible to view literature as an institution and its study as one of the many human pursuits that by their humanity are all intricately interrelated. Literary works can be seen as documents in history, psychology, anthropology, and philosophy; they are often made to be part of music, social doctrine, and even propaganda and ritual. Or conversely, those nonliterary disciplines may, with care, use literary works as subsidiary texts or as documents or as evidence. Such interchange can often be illuminating all round, so long as literary scholars keep their grasp on their own object of study and maintain a reasoned concept of its wholeness or integrity. What in my own work I have found indispensable, along with primary aesthetic response, is a continually hard-won sense of history and social context. But history is not simply what we know of the past; it is also how our living in the present—as part of continuing history—clarifies and "perspectivizes" the past. Similarly, to read a previously unread work of literature also deepens or even changes our sense of literary art and its possible classifications. A lifetime is insufficient for reading and knowing enough. What is essential is to keep a double perspective in these matters: to know all one humanly can of the past and to see history as including one's own necessary and inescapable present. For me the best lesson is that in Greek mythology the Muses are the daughters of Memory.

In this straight summary fashion I express my views concerning the study of literature at the risk of seeming peremptory or simplistic. I can be blunter in the negative. Comparative Literature is *not* a specialty; it is simply a convenient traditional designation for the whole study of the whole of literature so far as one's mind and life can stretch. True, the word *literature* in the phrase *Comparative Literature* refers to the *study* of literary works, but that is a now archaic meaning that can be tolerated in conventional usage. It is far simpler, of course, to say that one reads literary works as a prime or an adopted or a chosen purpose in life. The academic, professional, or private terminology may well follow from that direct statement, yet it must be scrutinized often for adventitious conno- tations. For instance, I would insist that a critic is not a special species: any experienced and reflective reader who renders a coherent judgment is thereby a critic. The purpose of literary study is not immediately to relate literature to some other pursuit but rather, first and foremost, to under- stand and appreciate, to perceive, enjoy, and evaluate works of literature in their artistic integrity and aesthetic interrelatedness. Such an emphasis does *not* presume to deny social, national, temporal, biographical, or even private associations that may prove interesting, instructive, provocative, illuminating, or personally precious. It merely seeks to assert a first principle or essential priority that would seem almost self-evident if there were not currently so clamorous a bazaar in which, competing for attention, are many celebrity egos, the familiar isms in newfangled garb, an assortment of panaceas and aporias, any number of peccadillos and perversions that bear watching, and uncountable pages coming prematurely into print.

As a new decade begins, a seeming turn in time may be sufficient pretext for reflecting on the general state of literary study (a phrase equivalent, for my purposes, to Comparative Literature) and for asserting some perspectives in the current welter. Literature, literary study, and literary theory have an intertwined genealogy, such that the lone reader may welcome reassurance that poets and fiction writers do indeed make art works and not velleitous swatches of texts, that those who discourse *about* art perform a different function (unseemly if it is exploitative or competitive), and that good and original theorists of literature are historically very much rarer than fine poets and fiction writers. In saying that literature is an art and not merely a semiotic product, one sets it in the realm of aesthetics and not epistemology or logic or metaphysics. Yet the shortcomings of traditional aesthetics may discourage the amateur literary philosopher, who often ends up as a frantic loner, an impulsive joiner, an eclectic, or a purveyor of vigorously misplaced rigor.

II

What is now institutionalized as Comparative Literature has, of course, a pedigree that can be variously traced—back to Aristotle, perhaps, who considered all there was in the way of tragedy and derived a theory of a "perfected" or fulfilled genre; back to the Alexandrians, who preserved and treasured their ancient past and made a strangely new literature on the foundations of the old; back to the Romans, who then had two venerable traditions to experience and from which to make literature even more strangely new in their own way; back to the middle Middle Ages when the remote classical past was only spottily known and when its casual or respectful teaching could conveniently be assimilated to rhetoric and at the same time become a model (Walter's *Alexandreis*), a subtext (Henric van Veldeke's *Eneit*), or even perhaps an antimodel (new Latin and newer vernacular poetry) in a momentous process to continue in barely charted ways into the Renaissance. All along, such preceptors or theorists as Aristotle, Horace, Longinus, Geoffroi de Vinsauf, and Dante considered literature, in effect, to be what there was to hand, irrespective of language or nationality, and even more, the practitioners of literature, for the most part silently, chose their array of inherited exemplars to "imitate" (the least understood of terms) in an international process of making over into something else, as the German Wolfram refashioned the French Chrétien or the English Chaucer refashioned the Italian Boccaccio. In this respect Dante, with his survey of the known "national" literatures in the *De vulgari eloquentia*, emerges as the broadest "comparatist" up to his time. Yet what is most momentous is not theoretical pronouncement but the continuing practice of practicing authors in constituting for themselves a creatively chosen and multifarious tradition without any prescribed or predictable bounds. And that practice will of course continue through subsequent ages.

An intensely explicit or self-conscious program was created by the theory and practice of the Romantics (from the Schlegels and Mme. de Staël to Franz Bopp, Friedrich Schelling, Coleridge, and Hegel), who collectively founded a vast canon of literature, a general science of "philology," and, almost paradoxically, a basis for a *national* literature seen in its separate development from primitive roots to luxuriant foliage. In effect the old system of genres was overturned, and especially prized were the romance and the novel and the subjective meditative poem; "exotic" literatures were explored and smaller national literatures were founded; by "imitation," translation, and reportage (especially in the great magazines of the time) a new sense of the vastness and variety of world literature became possible. On the model of the natural sciences and of all-explaining philosophical systems, some pioneers of literary history and literary theory, basing themselves on the enormous continuing labors of antiquaries and scholars, were emboldened to write sweeping histories of national or regional literatures (Simonde de Sismondi, George Ticknor, Hippolyte Taine, Francesco De Sanctis) and to essay general propositions about literature as a whole and its differentiation according to national character, tradition, taste, and even climate. Such a situation made it possible to sketch theories of literatures compared, or, on the analogy of *anatomie comparée, littérature comparée* and eventually Comparative Literature, *vergleichende Literaturgeschichte,* etc. The terms had various fates that have been informatively explored, yet only in the last two generations has some concept of Comparative Literature been institutionalized, practiced, and propagated. That concept or focus of attention is rightly under constant discussion and in dispute; at the same time, by apparent paradox, it is taken for granted as a field.

One plausible way of simplifying the state-of-things-now is to declare that literature (in the sense of imaginative or artistic literature) needs no qualifying adjective, that standing by itself it can, like physics or economics or philosophy, be understood as a field of study corresponding to a certain human activity or realm of experience and restricted only by the degree of skill, sensibility, and longevity of the student. The skills would be those of an attentive and thoughtful reader who habitually reads and reflects on many texts in several languages. The sensibility required is harder to characterize summarily and uninvidiously. Surely it should include an open and responsive mind, a capacity to exercise a "willing suspension of disbelief . . . that constitutes *poetic* faith," and an experienced aesthetic taste. Because of its medium, language, literature of all the arts is most subject to distortion and misapprehension. The blind and color-blind are unfortunately incompetent to experience painting, the deaf and tone-deaf to experience music; yet many with analogous disabilities undertake to study and judge literature and to construct theories that pervert its nature. Literature occasionally attracts those who lack skill and sensibility and those who wish above all to *do* something with it, that is, to use it for some nonaesthetic purpose without being able to understand its nature. Attention is thereby drawn away from the literary or imaginative aesthetic object and is brought to focus on external typologies, general intellectual history, linguistics, and various philosophical or political or religious schemes and systems of belief. Thus the object or subject matter of literary study becomes diffuse and obscured, and in keeping with the spirit of now superannuated modernism, literary study seems stymied by being displaced to its farthest frontiers, which vaguely border on an infinity of other human or humane pursuits. One may indeed sense that any connection is possible and that anything goes if it gets attention.

Through its very medium the integrity of literature in general or of a particular work is precarious. A text, like a fabric, can be pulled apart and made to serve other than "intended" purposes. A lovely fabric can be used as a rag or incorporated into pulp for making paper. A literary text, given that all words are to some extent polysemous, may be perversely made to bear any meaning of any word or may be used to "document" some ideological or philosophical point. The analogy of literary work to fabric is limited because of the latter's necessary materiality and can be made only by a prevalent misuse of etymology. More to the point would be an analogy to painting or to music or to other works of art. A painting may be retouched or even destroyed and a piece of music may be transposed, played slower than indicated, or cast from a "classical" into a "popular" style. Indeed, a painting or a score may have a cultic or even propagandistic origin. Yet even within such changes of functionality or intention, some works and versions may be judged better than others and may be said to possess aesthetic qualities perceivable even by those unaware of the original or its original function. The sorting out of motives and uses is clearly a difficult matter: the same objects may be perceived and discussed under greatly differing aspects. Yet, the *literary* study of literature must obviously be grounded in some fundamental acknowledgment of aesthetic or artistic or imaginative qualities. It is based upon certain capacities of the human mind that, for some or for many, possess central experiential importance. Such capacities and their exercise and gratification, even if, unfortunately, not universal, seem to me the essentials of literary study and, therefore, the foundation and prerequisite of Comparative Literature. Otherwise the jig is up and it's better to go into some other line of business.

Upholding the aesthetic integrity of the literary work of art may seem either obvious or untenable: obvious and therefore to be taken for granted or untenable in that aesthetics as a whole is suspected of lacking rigor or proof, in that Comparative Literature has so often or even traditionally been occupied with matters external to art, in that literary scholarship does not officially require a capacity for appreciative aesthetic response. But literary studies are always perilously exposed to assimilation to such other pursuits as philosophy or politics or psychology and to the ancillary activities of establishing texts or constructing typologies or illustrating rhetorical terms. If the essential value of literature is abandoned because it seems difficult to defend, then its appreciators are depreciated and its prestige, so often meretriciously traded on, diminishes for all concerned, including the traders. Indeed, for many, the very value of life is involved. For some, no calamity would ensue, and in fact an obscenely egalitarian urge might be satisfied. It is unlikely, however, that no more authors would aspire to create further fictions on which they and their readers set aesthetic and even moral value.

III

One looks to modern philosophy for aid, if not comfort, in sorting out the issues of art. My impression is that philosophers for some time now have been most successful in logic; in social, political, and legal theory; in ethical speculation; and in discourse about the physical world (philosophy of science). Two large realms where it is difficult for me to see successful activity are hermeneutics (including philosophy of language) and general aesthetics. In hermeneutics, the territory staked out is impossibly vast, covering as it does the whole subject matter of the three Kantian *Critiques* (not to mention a whole library of quick fixes), and the method is excessively dependent on restricted and inexpert language theory. In general aesthetics, since Ernst Cassirer, Suzanne Langer, and Nelson Goodman, little attempt has been convincingly made to incorporate and accommodate literature in a system or theory of the arts. The large systems most common currently seem to be the familiar derivatives of Marxism, psychoanalysis, and linguistics—often combined in varying ad-mixtures or wholly housed under the capacious circus tent of semiotics. Such arrangements have the effect of degrading or dismissing the aesthetic function and value especially of literature, which, as a language art, can be insidiously assimilated or exploited to serve other than aesthetic purposes. In comparison, artistic expression in stone or metal, in paint, in body movement, or in consciously produced and modulated sound, is much less "common" and is generally restricted to a situation of assumed aesthetic expectation. If we were to pursue an evenhanded aesthetics of all art, we might be justified in considering literature, despite its highly diffuse medium of language, as also existing in an integral or circumscribed condition that presupposes aesthetic expectation. Then, just as we would not turn over sculpture to the geologist, painting to the interior designer, or music to the acoustician, so we would not surrender literature to the ideologue, the psychologist, the preacher, the linguist, the rhetorician, the cultural historian, or the antimetaphysical meta-metaphysician.

My plaint or complaint concerns general aesthetics and literature's place within it along with the other arts. Most attentive readers, I presume, make aesthetic assumptions: coherence, purposiveness or "form," correct-ness (in grammar and idiom according to tone or level), interest, pleasure, and a whole list of other qualities that may or may not be present or fulfilled in a given work. At the same time there are those nowadays who nurse an exacerbated sense that we should question such qualities and lay them bare by attempting to demonstrate their imperfect or even impossible fulfillment, by adducing extreme or borderline cases or exceptions to disprove any rule or norm, and by transferring interpretation from the realm of art to biographical or ideological or general linguistic explanations. In the process, the notion of text becomes almost as generic as the notion of textile, the notion of literary performance or enactment becomes diluted in Noam Chomsky's elementary contrastive set of competence/performance (a version of Saussure's *langue/parole*), the notion of prosody is swallowed up in the phonetician's study of the intonation of anyone's ordinary speech, narrative structure is assimilated to anthropological and psychoanalytic models that, by their very hypothetical nature, are reductive. All too often the purpose and experience of literary art are stretched on a scale not of aesthetic value but of utilitarian or ideological expediency.

I would adduce two chief reasons why the nature or status of the literary work of art seems peculiarly contested and embattled. First, over the past century there have been so many departures in great art from traditional norms, so many splendid and justly celebrated special or marginal cases, that the reader-spectator may be baffled or buffaloed into an acceptance of disorientation as normal or of obscurity as indispensable. He or she may perforce become an adept, an initiate, a hierophant, indeed a critic in some specious sense. Difficulty and novelty come to be prized for their own sake. The self-capitalizing Critics initiate or intimidate the reader and thereby aggrandize themselves. The second general reason for contesting or neglecting literary aesthetics is a common desire to pursue some sort of unified field theory in the humanities (*les sciences de l'homme, die Geisteswissenschaften*) that will, in academic jargon, bring about, by transnational and interdisciplinary means, a consummate cross-fertilization. Such an ambition has a serious history from Aristotle to Wilhelm Dilthey. Yet clearly it has, on lower levels, the danger of trivializing and homogenizing intricately different fields, modes of thinking, assumptions, and subject matter. On the one hand, literary texts may come in handy as documents for historians, psychologists, philosophers, and linguists. On the other hand, presumptive students of literature may eclectically and arbitrarily borrow from any number of other pursuits, laying out for themselves a whole cafeteria of "approaches" to literature. On both sides there may often be a confusion of motives, not necessarily the elucidation of a subject matter but rather its hoped-for justification from the outside (practicality in getting ahead, therapy in getting one's head straight, service to some modish ideology).

In its current exposed state, literature (along with the theory proper to it) has been buffeted by the winds of doctrine. Thirty years ago was the heyday of existentialism, Sartre's version or reinterpretation of Heidegger and Husserl, with roots more in Hegel the ideologue than in his master Kant the aesthetician. Indeed, the watchwords had a distinctive Marxian tone: absolute necessity or determinism of choice, political commitment (engagement), and social utility. It was a heady time for thousands of academic devotees. Where are they now? In the late 1960s there arose a vogue for "structuralism" that has since preoccupied many literary scholar-critics. Like existentialism, it required crash programs of homework. Only gradually was some knowledge acquired of the genealogy stretching from outmoded eighteenth-century speculation on language and Saussure's *Cours de linguistique générale* to the Prague Linguistic Circle, the phonol-ogy of Nikolai Trubetskoi and Roman Jakobson, the anthropology of Franz Boas and Ruth Benedict, and the popular latter-day works of Claude Lévi-Strauss (who in his fashion synthesized American anthropology and Jakobson's version of linguistic theory). This enterprise has led in so many directions that one can only summarize by naming neo-Freudian psycho-analysis, semiotics, and neorhetoricism. At least for a while the word *paradigm* (made current by Thomas Kuhn) seemed to sum it all up. If one adds the belatedly "discovered" Russian so-called formalists (along with the recently "recuperated" Bakhtin), one can account for the widespread preoccupation with linguistics and with "devices," to the extent that much of the attraction seems to lie in the elevation of linguistics to something like an exact science and in the succinct neatness of equating literary success with the employment of discrete devices (*priëmy*). Even more recently we witness the surprising success of a philosophical project to treat literary tests as objects of deconstruction (deconstrual? misconstrual?) in order to lay bare their pretensions to integralness and finality—in effect, to expose the inner workings of illusionism and the presumed slipperiness of language and therefore of any linguistic construct. Indeed, any text should do as object of deconstruction. The method is a kind of philosophical rhetoricism or rhetorical philosophy; it is close reading made closer than close, and it has about it the dissolving aura of Jacques Derrida's suprametaphysical attempt to overturn the whole of Western philosophy.

If one assumes that these widespread modes of thought or ideologies or methods are important and effective, one must also reflect that they leave the specifically literary text undefined or perhaps that they render it categorically nonexistent. Another way of putting the matter is to say that implicitly literary study becomes coextensive with philosophy. Yet philosophy here is most restricted indeed; it is a matter of words with no argued relation to reality. Thus, meanings can be produced from texts by fair means or foul, and any producible meanings whatsoever are somehow valid. The traditional endeavors of philosophy—logic, ontology, epistemology, theory of perception, metaphysics—may still be operative, but their levels and boundaries can be trespassed at will and their arguments and goals jumbled. Figures of rhetorics, for example, in *themselves* are taken to have large epistemological or even metaphysical meaning. A casual passage or word may suddenly be isolated and subjected to misplaced rigor. It is not easy for the amateur to know in what realm he is meant to be situated and what rules and controls can possibly govern the incessant flow of speculation.

IV

Beginning with Plato's, many aesthetics have subordinated art to other, apparently more momentous concerns. For Plato, art is either an unrational and divine gift (*Ion*) or a potentially dangerous stimulus to unruly emotions (*Republic*). Forms of Neoplatonism generally divinize beauty and trace its manifestations in art to a transcendental emanation. Aristotle's answer would recognize art as humanly crafted, shaped in various media available to the senses and to the mind, and related in some way to a concrete reality that is immanent and common in human experience. I would argue that Aristotle's concept of mimesis states in a word that mysterious, experimental, complex relationship between art and reality. With Lucretius and Horace begins the notion of art as instructing through pleasure, which has a long career stigmatized by Benedetto Croce as "art the meretrix" and "art the pedagogue." What Croce undertakes to do is to break from that view, to resolve antinomies of form and content, to dispense with classificatory systems like rhetoric and external histories in order radically to assert, as did Vico, the existence of a special and crucial human faculty, the imagination (*fantasia*). But once again the specificity of art gets lost in a general theory of intuition as expression. I sympathize with the motive of asserting the authentic existence of the aesthetic faculty and object. There are other attempts to salvage art by assimilating it to experience (John Dewey), to a general pleasure principle (George Santayana), or to symbol formation (Ernst Cassirer)—all considered essential aspects of human life and not merely leisure-time indulgences.

My own inexpert urge is to get back to a Kantian, ultimately Aristotelian view—at least to a recognition of the limits of human four-dimensional knowledge and of the need to argue consistently and systematically. Kant's attempts at formulating a concept of taste that is not mere whim or physiology, a concept of pleasure in art, and the relatively autonomous relation of art to practical and ethical pursuits are perhaps unstable attempts. I myself do not think so. That they are vulnerable is certainly true. That aesthetic pleasure is *interesseloses Wohlgefallen* or that art exhibits *Zweckmässigkeit ohne Zweck* may seem refutable or deconstructible or merely old-fashioned among the current counterclaims. Such formulations are hard won in Kant's context and, like any grand generalizations, require at least provisionally sympathetic consideration in a full awareness of the intrinsic and abiding difficulties they attempt to resolve.

Whatever the merits and interests of the various fashions of argument over the last thirty or so years—meaning those that are highly publicized and popular—they seem to lack concern for defining an aesthetic realm or acknowledging an aesthetic faculty. Yet the attraction and pleasure of a novel, a poem, a painting, a movie, a piece of music, a ballet remain central and essential for many of us. As with some of the more dithyrambic and hieratic notions of art among the Romantics, insufficient attention is paid to the *differentiae* or the *specifica* of literary art in particular, again because of its medium in words, which start so many hopping hares. Whole books are written on poetry with no attention to what makes it poetry. Novels are treated as social tracts or psychological case histories. Plays are discussed without regard to their existence in performance. Such complaints are not new, and their implied demands are difficult to fulfill. When is a rhyme successful? What are the norms of nonmetrical verse? How does a novel imaginatively "convince"? How do we know that an actor has not fully realized or perhaps has misunderstood a character? What kind of "justice" can a translation do?

Clearly, in my view, a critic of literature should have some elementary aesthetic views or convictions and should be able to state them even if defending them may be hard for a nonphilosopher. The critic is primarily a reader, in the sense that all good readers are critics. The critic is concerned with valuable and evaluable works, whose art is part of the indispensable life of the imagination.

V

By its very scope Comparative Literature as here discussed is a presumptuous study. It requires not only knowing many things but also knowing about many more. Obviously a deep knowledge of, say, four or five or more languages and their literatures would be a goal of the mature comparatist. Fundamental questions of literary theory and literary history have to be understood in their proper settings and arguments—not in pure abstraction but in circumstantial detail. One could continue. What is crucial is that all this must be happening, be present, in a single mind, in a single aesthetically aware sensibility. It is utterly illusory to think that by putting together a set of specialists one can create an enterprise or department of Comparative Literature. From the point of view of the study of literature in general such a grouping would in fact be less than the sum of its parts. It is also illusory to assume that the mere cultivation of literary theory makes one a comparatist or that Comparative Literature is the special repository of literary theory. That Comparative Literature has currently a certain adventitious modishness is as much an embarrassment as an advantage. Curiously, as theoretical activity has vastly expanded, the active canon of literary works seems to have narrowed. This is surely not a stable situation. One may quite easily surmise that few current theoreticians will have made a permanent mark, that gifted readers will continue to face the supposed perils and indeterminacy of polysemy and semiosis, that poets and fiction writers will continue at times to write masterpieces, and that the faculties of imagination, taste, and judgment will continue to be exercised by those who possess their gift in sufficient measure.

2

EXTREMES OF EXPRESSION

Language is of course not our only means of communication. We make things common, in the sense of mutually available or understood, by other systems of signs as well, from symbolic logic to traffic signs, from folk-rock to cathedral spires, from gestures to peasant costumes. The "signs" may be of all the sorts that can be received by our sensorium and set in some associative context. The general study of sign systems was named semiology by Ferdinand de Saussure and is now most often called semiotics. Great claims are made for it. In fact, it has been put forward as candidate for the title of universal science: the successor to ontology in the traditional philosophic sense or to Hegelianism or to all sorts of positivism.[1]

If it is indeed *the* basic science, critics and aestheticians should hasten to make distinctions, not simply to guard their own frontiers and preserve any old order, but to make sure that we are not witnessing a trivialization of knowledge or simply a rehashing in new and portentous vocabulary of things already explored and being explored in more familiar ways. Part of the rhetoric of our time is the vocabulary of the frontier, now really vanishing: to be on the frontiers of knowledge or to do trailblazing (sometimes rendered in the Germanism "pathbreaking" that may come from Karl May). But the frontiers of knowledge are already quite crowded. We have had lots of practice in frontiersmanship and we are quite used to the rhetoric of breakthroughs: an updated merging of Daniel Boone and Auguste Comte rendered plausible and emulable by the successes of the experimental sciences, particularly in this century. Now the program or "project" is more like oil-drilling than homesteading. First you make your model (a geometrical figure, a genealogical tree, an oratorical set of divisions and subdivisions), which you would now call your *heuristic device* and hope would lead to another form of the Greek verb—*Eureka*! Then you gather data, program them, make a run-through, and find the pattern or recurrence that may shadow forth a law. Finally you interrogate the science of interpretation, which we have learned to call *hermeneutics,* make all sorts of connections, and come up with a construct, a paradigm, a validation, or at the very least a structure or daunting aporia. All of this is attractive and even mind-blowing, for we all yearn somehow for the satisfying method that will produce the Answer. Such yearning is very human indeed; it expresses itself in the creation of scientific hypothesis and philosophical system, in theology and in literary production. What might get in the way of plausible results is the generalized yearning itself. Literary critics now set themselves up, not for the first time in history, as amateur philosophers, amateur linguists, amateur theologians, amateur anthropologists, often reducing intricate realms of discourse to their handiest handles or slogans[2] and inflating already pregnant utterances to cosmic explanations: the transvaluation of all values, *Je est un autre,* all acts are political (they used all to be sexual), consciousness is consciousness of something, class struggle, and so on. Each of these locutions is of course part of a system or mood of thought, but in our syncretic age many, instructed by the most general of general educations, become used to trying, and indeed expect to try, all doorknobs or to put all things in their mental hoppers.

By making random forays into others' territory we run the risk of losing our way or of getting caught, yet at the same time we see the prospect of booty—something more perhaps than a few beaver pelts, a bag of wampum, or the tribal gods whose names and rituals we do not know. Eventually, of course, peace sets in, boundaries are drawn and treaties signed, new things become familiar décor. Yet there is some danger of occupation under a ruling slogan, method, or dogma. Most conspicuous now are French savants and their followers, who seem to be occupying large tracts of territory (often ignoring the settlers already there) under various universal banners, and opening up second-story frontiers whose vistas certainly mesmerize the unhistoric young. While the late Jean-Paul Sartre—a name that used to be conjured with—fades as the ghost of a guru, slightly later celebrities such as Claude Lévi-Strauss, Roland Barthes, Jacques Lacan, Louis Althusser, and Julia Kristeva have busied themselves revamping the whole City of Man, which may look like Brasilia or Chandrigar, but still has the air of a peripheric Parisian arrondissement with an almost measurable half-life. More recently the heady practice of "deconstruction," with an ancestral line running from Hegel to Heidegger, has vaunted "rigor" in attempting to show the lability or dead-endedness of any use of language. As the indefatigable Jacques Derrida and his many followers cleverly or imitatively turn each branch of philosophy on its head (an old Socratic heuristic trickery that has lost all its humor among the humorless epigones), the literary work of art, indeed all works of art, stand as deconstructible frauds mired in aporias: so many old structures dynamited by implosion. Rather in self-defense, I have learned to say that I am not an anthropologist, I am not a philosopher, I am not a transformational or even a generative linguist, I am not a social scientist. I am proudly reduced to saying that I am a literary scholar and critic, though occasionally feeling quite exposed.

Criticism is a particularly vast concern in that it deals with a medium, language, that is used by everyone and in that even its traditional texts make reference to almost all of human experience. Its vastness has been exploited in the last two hundred years by poachers who make casual raids and by imperialists who attempt to establish portentous New Orders. The trick is to appropriate the prestige of literature without rendering service to it. I myself am more concerned with boundaries and even zoning laws than with creating empires.

My exordium is cautionary for several reasons: (1) in dealing with a language art I wish to suggest in Kantian and Crocean terms that it is somehow relatively autonomous as aesthetic realm; (2) my subject, perilously close to the vague and the portentous, is the problem of expressing what is somehow or other said to be inexpressible; and (3) I touch on matters we would all like to explore further in a yearning for true belief and for certainty in a life-and-death world in which one might well desire a privileged Epiphany, the Revelation of Apocalypse, the Explanation, or short of that, the Final Absolution.

My concern is not to vaticinate or to divine but quite simply to inquire into the ways we find in literature of saying that you cannot say something.

Logically, we cannot say what we cannot say, and any apparently rigorous attempt to express the unexpressible would be a mere put-on. Anyone with the early Wittgenstein's wit would fall silent. My aims are empirical and literary. I begin with a few commonplace instances from ordinary language or colloquial speech, then consider the *je ne sais quoi*, move on to mystical poetry, and end in fashionable silence.

In ordinary speech we use set phrases whose literal meaning we are scarcely aware of: How do you do (seldom spoken as a *question* anymore); Well, what do you know; Well, I never. Bronislaw Malinowski recorded speech sounds of tribesmen which they were unable after use in intense action to interpret; he called this *phatic speech* and suggested we all use it to establish feelings of social solidarity. Indeed, when such phatic speech, along with set phrases and clichés, is "foregrounded" as in Eugène Ionesco it produces comic and quasi-profound effects. Further along an improvised scale of complexity, we encounter expressions of this sort:

> I can't tell you how much I liked it.
>
> It was out of this world.

We soon get into the vast area of faddish expressions that can readily be divided into plus-words and minus-words, though perhaps there is always room for words like "quaint" or "kinky" or "kooky."[3] But that is something else. Indeed, the expression "You're something else" has itself, in recent years, taken on a derived nuance we all recognize, and that recognition makes us "with it." Speaking of "it," for those over fifty the loaded meaning of "it" still distantly evokes the publicity campaign for the film actress Clara Bow. There are those who have it and those who don't. Changing the emphasis, Clara Bow was said to have *it:* she became the It girl. The late Cyril Connolly willfully got it wrong in a parodistic piece he wrote about 1938, "Where Engels Fears to Tread":[4]

> "She's got what the Americans call 'that.'"
> "What?"
> "What the Americans call 'that.'"
> "What's that?"
> "'That'—that's what she's got."
> "But what the Americans call what? I don't even know that."
> "Oh, my dear Duchess!"

> For it was sometimes my privilege to give instruction to a very
> great lady.

Richer and older are the various expressions meaning "I know not what."
We may use phrases like "she has a certain something," meaning some
delicate quality or characteristic that is even enhanced by our reluctance or
inability to define it. The Roman expression *nescio quid* could be used
nominally or adverbially by way of deprecation or depreciation, as in Cicero:
nescio quid litterularum (*Letters to Atticus,* 15, 4, 1)—or by way of
enhancement as, again, in Cicero (*Pro Archia poeta,* 7): "Atque idem ego
contendo, cum ad naturam eximiam et illustrem accesserit ratio quaedam
conformatioque doctrinae, tum *illud nescio quid praeclarum ac singulare*
solere exsistere." (And I maintain this also, that when a certain training and
well-formed learning achieve an outstanding and illustrious character, then
that noble and unique something usually stands forth.) This more positive
sense of *nescio quid* was continued by the Latin theological tradition of the
Middle Ages in ways not yet fully documented. What is more to my purpose
is that the phrase was rendered into the vernacular languages and took on
a new life. An amusing instance occurs in the poetry of the Provensal
Trobador Raimbaut d'Aurenga who flourished in the mid-twelfth century.
"Listen, my lordings," he begins bravely, yet at once continues: "but I don't
know what it is I want to begin. It's not a lyric, an *estribot,* or a *sirventes,*
nor do I know any name to invent for it." The poem bumbles on with
seemingly interminable lines at the end of each stanza, to show how things
are continually getting out of hand. Finally at the end he says:

> Now I conclude my Whatyoumaycallit [Er fenisc mo no-say-que-
> s'es], for that's what I've wanted to baptize it [c'aisi l'ay volgut
> batejar]. Since I've never heard of anything like it, I must simply call
> it that. Whoever takes pleasure in it, let him recite it once he's
> learned it. / And if anyone asks him who made it, he can say: one
> who knows well how to do all things when he wants to.

In this poem, as well as in its subtext, "Farai un vers de dreyt nien," by the
earliest known vernacular poet, William (Guilhem), count of Poitou and
duke of Aquitaine, we have an instance of marvelous literary self-
reflexiveness expressed in this playful way as a *je ne sais quoi.*
    Skipping to the seventeenth century (to return shortly to the sixteenth
and Saint John of the Cross) we find, particularly in French, the phrase *je*

ne sais quoi widely and modishly used to signify that certain something that all gallant, elegant, polite, gentlemanly and ladylike people possess. Later in the seventeenth century the phrase is elevated in an almost technical term of aesthetic speculation in such writers as Vaugelas and Dominique (le Père) Bouhours; indeed the latter saw the *je ne sais quoi* as a sort of *grace* that he even divinized as our very hope of immortality. Perhaps the richest passage I could cite, except possibly for Baltasar Gracián in Spanish, is from an anonymous treatise *Entretiens galants* (Paris, 1681):

> La sympathie & le je ne sçay quoy ne sont plus difficiles à comprendre. Cette harmonie que vous établissez dans la nature explique bien des choses en peu de mots. Par les objets qui plaisent à nos sens nous jugeons bientost du raport qu'ils peuvent avoir avec nos ames. Ce raport mutuel est sans doute ce je ne sçay quoy, qui nous charme.

And elsewhere in the same work emerge rival expressions:

> Le bon goût va loin . . . Il va par tout . . . Je sçay qu'il a pris la place du bel air, du je ne sçay quoy, & du bel esprit, qui ont regné si long-tems en France. Le bon goût les a enfin détronnés.[5]

Here we raise an intricate and important issue in the history of aesthetics that leads to many consequences still with us today: how to define the indefinable or unanalyzable element of beauty, or the sublime or, if I may call it so, aesthetic competence. Even in an age of rules and precepts, the best aesthetic speculation was concerned with the inexpressible, the "grace beyond the reach of art," to cite Alexander Pope's phrase. ("Art" here surely means "craft," which can be taught by "rules" and practice.) Actually there were very few neoclassical theorists of art who did not recognize some sort of *je ne sais quoi* in art: the mindless reduction of neoclassical criticism to mere rule-serving parallels the current self-aggrandizing reduction of Anglo-American "New Criticism" to simple reading of poems outside their historical context. In general terms not bound by chronology, it may be said that the apparent obscurities, conundrums, oddities, devices, strategems, and aporias of poetry are precisely *not* mere examination topics or teasers for critics who have failed in philosophy. Those would-be critics who use such indeterminacies as launching pads for their flights take no risk, as they can also make their own verbal cushions and land wherever they please.

Reverting to the *nescio quid* and insisting on poetry in its context, I return to an earlier age and to the poetry of Saint John of the Cross (1542–91), who supremely uses the phrase in Spanish: *no sé qué*. Saint John's great poetry is almost all based upon a biblical text, the Song of Songs (Canticum canticorum), which entered the Hebrew canon quite late, toward the end of the second century B.C., and after long dispute was declared the holiest of holy books. (I leave aside entirely the anthropological pagan "origins," whatever they may turn out to be, and make my concern only the Vulgate version of the Christian canon of the Bible.) Christian theologians and exegetes took over the allegorical interpretation and in the course of the centuries have written at least a hundred full commentaries on the Song of Songs. The most famous such work is that of Saint Bernard of Clairvaux, in the form of eighty-six *sermones* on only the first third of that brief book. If one grants the theological and mystical assumptions of the method, Saint Bernard stands as a vigorous and tough-minded expounder, as in his distinctions among the various kinds of kisses or the significance of right and left breast. In general, there were three Christian allegorical interpretations of the Song of Songs: (1) as a dialogue between Christ and the Church; (2) as a dialogue between Christ and the Soul; and (3) as a dialogue between Christ and the Virgin Mary. It is the second with which Saint John of the Cross is concerned, as in his famous poem called (for convenience) "The Dark Night of the Soul."

The Song of Songs has two scenes in which the Bride goes looking in the night for the Beloved and during the day she sees him in a garden where they kiss and embrace in the midst of luxuriant nature within an enclosed garden (*hortus conclusus*). Their descriptions of each other are laden with rich exotic imagery. In fact, the detail is so vivid and sensuous that one may well ask how this peculiar biblical text can be so spiritualized as to be a prime vehicle for mystical or simply religious poetry and for technical exegesis. But that is precisely the point: the ineffable, inexpressible, infinite experience of divine presence or divine union can, in human language, be conveyed most directly by analogy to the direct pleasurable stimulation of sensory experience or of the sensuous imagination. It is of course only an analogy and carries with it a great danger: the confusion of sensual pleasure with supreme spiritual fulfillment. In brief, the great literary tradition of religious poetry inspired by the Vulgate version of the Song of Songs derives its strength and vitality from the biblically canonical sanction of the Song of Songs for expressing the spiritual in terms of the sensuous. Before looking directly at Saint John's *no sé qué*, it is proper to evoke in some detail the poem just mentioned, "The Dark Night of the Soul." The Soul leaves its house in utter quiet and goes in certain search of the Beloved, finds Him, joins Him. The last two stanzas read as follows:

> El aire del almena
> cuando yo sus cabellos esparcía,
> con su mano serena
> en mi cuello hería,
> y todos mis sentidos suspendía.
> Quedéme y olvidéme,
> el rostro recliné sobre el Amado,
> cesó todo y dejéme,
> dejando mi cuidado
> entre las azucenas olvidado.[6]

(The air from the battlement, as I was ruffling his hair, with its serene hand was wounding my neck and suspending all my senses. I stayed quiet and forgetful of myself, I rested my face on the Beloved; everything stopped and I left myself, leaving my care forgotten among the lilies.)

Here the simplest of language, evoking pleasurable sensations, leads almost imperceptibly to a spiritual transcendence beyond the senses: expressible not by negative particles or prefixes but by the analogizing reference to that familiar state of being forgetful or lost in thought.

In a longer and more elaborate poem by Saint John of the Cross, his *Cántico espiritual* (which is cast as a kind of dialogue or cantata), we first hear the Bride who cries:

> ¿Adónde te escondiste,
> Amado, y me dejaste con gemido?
> Como el ciervo huiste,
> habiéndome herido;
> salí tras ti clamando, y eras ido.

(Where have you hidden yourself, my Beloved, and left me moaning? You fled like the stag, having wounded me; I went out crying after you, and you had gone.)

She declares she will go looking for him; as she goes she sees the beauty he has left in the woods and meadows as he passed. But she yearns for his direct presence:

> ¡Ay!, ¿quién podrá sanarme?
> Acaba de entregarte ya de vero;
> no quieras enviarme
> de hoy más ya mensajero,
> que no saben decirme lo que quiero.
> Y todos cuantos vagan
> de ti me van mil gracias refiriendo.
> y todos más me llagan . . .

(Ah, who can cure me? End now by delivering yourself for real; please no longer send, from now on, any messenger, for they cannot tell me what I want. And those that wander tell me of a thousand graces of You, and they all wound me more . . .)

As before in the "Dark Night," the outwardly sensuous is linked with the inwardly painful ("quia amore langueo" in the Song of Songs): the whole sensorium is heightened in ways immediately intelligible to our limited human faculties and somehow expressible through ordinary language, though all the while signifying a reality beyond senses and language, indeed a reality prior to feeling and expression and unencompassable by either. The creatures of nature are messengers (= angels) but they are not the Beloved Himself. Their "eloquence" verges on the transcendentally unintelligible, on a transcendent *je ne sais quoi, un no sé qué*. The stanza ends:

> and it leaves me dying, [what?] an I-know-not-what that they [the messengers = angels = creatures] keep stuttering.

The full effect is conveyed of course only by the Spanish text, in which sense and sound corroborate each other in the simplest, most immediately eloquent way:

> y déjame muriendo
> un no sé qué que quedan balbuciendo.

The stuttering is there in the poetry: the inexpressible is somehow expressed.

This is only a sketch of an intricate tradition that requires much fuller understanding, both aesthetic and religious. Within that tradition we may now glimpse how Saint John of the Cross seems to express what is strictly inexpressible and to do so in the seemingly simplest way (see my "Note on the *Je ne sais quoi*," pp. 32–33).

Something of the same breathtaking reduction to the overwhelmingly simple takes place in Andrew Marvell's poem "The Garden." This poem has been perhaps too much written about in the recent past by critics, just as now we read reams of commentary on the "spots of time" in Wordsworth's *The Prelude*. These and many other currently favorite examples have one thing in common: they deal in artistic terms with the strain of expressing the ineffable. Some critics are teased into a misplaced sense of the profundity of their own comments. But then they may be existentially hoping for belief without commitment and responding outside the artistic realm to the expression of transcendence seemingly beyond words. There is a danger of willfully sacralizing secular texts and at the same time desacralizing the hermeneutic or exegetical method of theologians to arrive at a considerable confusion of belief and aesthetic experience. It is in the context of my secular ruminations that I presume to take a brief glance at Marvell's "The Garden."[7] The speaker of the poem has described the garden, its plenitude, luxuriance, and solitude or freedom from human entanglements. The real entanglements are with plants:

> Stumbling on Melons, as I pass,
> Insnar'd with Flow'rs, I fall on Grass.

Then in the sixth stanza the mind, replete with sensuous contentment, can withdraw into its *self*, described as an ocean where everything on land finds its transfigured correspondence. In its own inwardness, the mind can create other worlds and other seas, rendering all real creation nothing, but nothing with a difference: we are still in the realm of language where even nothing is somehow something. Marvell, with the wit and tact of his art, makes a fully metaphorical *je ne sais quoi*: "a green Thought in a green Shade."

> Mean while the Mind, from pleasure less,
> Withdraws into its happiness:

> The Mind, that Ocean where each kind
> Does streight its own resemblance find;
> Yet it creates, transcending these,
> Far other Worlds, and other Seas;
> Annihilating all that's made
> To a green Thought in a green Shade.

This is not, of course, mere fanciful wit. It has little philosophical or logical status, except perhaps to provoke urbane discussion of whether thoughts have color or whether color is a thought or a sensation or whether sensations are thoughts or vice versa. But if I may bracket philosophy and risk the poetically direct, I would simply state that a green thought is very appropriate to a poem about a garden. What is important here is that language is being used to point to the limits of language in its ability to express transcendent emotions (or emotion-thoughts): what may seem philosophically vague is poetically rich and also very witty. That the emotion-thought described as green is somehow transcendent is confirmed in the next stanza:

> Here at the Fountains sliding foot,
> Or at some Fruit-trees mossy root,
> Casting the Bodies Vest aside,
> My Soul into the boughs does glide:
> There like a Bird it sits, and sings,
> Then whets, and combs its silver Wings;
> And, till prepar'd for longer flight,
> Waves in its Plumes the various Light.

This is then indeed a privileged moment, quite beyond the exactitude of explanation: it is something of a mystical experience or as close to a mystical experience as possible in a secular, urbane, and deeply witty poem. Here commentators may overload us with lengthy notes on Neoplatonism, pseudoscientific lore of the time, or speculations rising from their own depths. But having read the poem with truly helpful guidance, we may possibly have become optimum readers of the poem, that is, people who through wide reading already know some traditional theology, Neo-platonism, and the biblical texts, and can allow their learning to be subtly evoked as part of the whole aesthetic experience.

I mean to strike a balance, not to be generally dismissive. It does happen that certain favorite and intriguing texts that venture toward expressing the inexpressible seem to invite the indelicate attentions of well-meaning critics who lavish every aid to help the bumbling author to *say what he means.* Yet what he means may not admit of more precise utterance. Or put another way, he may have said what he means and not be ready to thank, if that were possible, the "false wit" of a copious critic. In ordinary situations we do help out our friends who for a moment seem to be looking for the right word that occurs to us before it occurs to them. But we are not always right and are not always thanked. Often the very attempt at expression, however halting and awkward, can convey the meant emotion-thought better than a pondered copybook statement.

In ordinary life, language or expression can seem at times to get in the way of feeling. We often try on or try out expressions, discard them, and test others. Sometimes the expression we haphazardly use seems to express what we feel or perhaps even *changes* what we feel because we suddenly find it so apt. We are more caught up in the fiction and feedback of words than we sometimes think. (Here I leave aside the absorbing speculations of Freudian determinism.) This is especially true in the everyday realm of slogans and clichés, but all that is fairly obvious and I do not presume to scale the slopes of social psychology. In literature it is more interesting that modern fiction seems to begin with Don Quijote's taking words purporting to express the inexpressible rather too much to heart. He was an addict of the printed word and spent much money and time on books of chivalry that were composed with late-blooming elegance. Perhaps, to speculate idly, if he had read mystical theology he might have harkened to another calling than knight-errantry. But this is what he read in his very favorite of chivalric novelists, Feliciano de Silva:

> La razón de la sinrazón que a mi razón se haze, de tal manera mi razón enflaqueze, que con razón me quejo de la vuestra fermosura.
>
> (The reason of the unreason done to my reason in such a way enfeebles my reason that with reason I lament your beauteousness. [The original is in archaizing Spanish.])

"With these *reasons,*" says Cervantes, "the poor gentleman lost his judgment." He stayed up nights trying to understand and disentangle them when even Aristotle himself, resuscitated for that purpose, would have failed. Some readers may think Cervantes himself too addicted to words, and his novel too long and long-winded. But for the indispensably leisured reader, the "desocupado lector," the only possible optimum reader, some of the finest parts are seemingly the least necessary from the crude angle of the "story-line." Among the seemingly superfluous elements are, by way of example, the long meandering conversations between Don Quijote and Sancho Panza as they almost aimlessly reveal their characters and enrich their relationship in random or even phatic speech. Such abundance of discourse, typical of the abundance of the whole novel, is measured with great artistry. *Don Quijote*, though shorter than many a book of chivalry or *roman galant*, is by any reckoning a long work in its two linked parts. Its style (meaning mainly tone and syntax) is fluent and supple, open almost to the point of intimacy and yet able to maintain distance; it is a style that can accommodate any eventuality in its own world except perhaps the convoluted intricacy, however shallow, of the passage from Feliciano de Silva that ensured Don Quijote's madness. Cervantes's style is, in a word, realistic, quite obviously different from the poetic texts considered before. The contrast I am making is meant to be rough for the purpose of raising the question of the extraordinary copiousness of language in the modern novel—and, I should add, much modern poetry from Walt Whitman to Pablo Neruda. What then (to stay with the novel) is the function of such abundant expressivity, seemingly the contrary of intense lyric attempts at the inexpressible?

One point to be made—and, in actual practice, made again and again in many great novels of the last three centuries—is that seemingly superfluous or irrelevant detail can work artistically to give the reader the illusion of fullness, of reality, of what Henry James called "the solidity of specification."[8] (James of course did draw the line somewhere, and so must we, though perhaps differently.) Extraordinary elaboration of detail was almost a program of the so-called naturalistic novel of the later nineteenth century that aimed at something like "scientific" or "experimental" precision. For obvious reasons the matter and manner are hard to illustrate in brief, and so a number of aesthetic questions must go begging: How much superfluous or irrelevant detail can the reader accept before he loses focus or interest? At what point does meticulous description become self-indulgent and self-defeating? How do we account for the superabundance that can become plainly grotesque and therefore nonrealistic? Besides, there is an important related question: How is it that ordinary life may be presented in its drab or prolix or boring aspects without the novel itself becoming drab or prolix or boring?

There is a curious culmination in the nineteenth and early twentieth centuries of two apparent extremes of expression: on the one hand the great long novels of Dickens, Dostoevsky, and Hugo, to mention only those; and on the other hand the extraordinary compression, almost to the point of cryptic unintelligibility, of the poetry of Mallarmé, Hopkins, and Valéry. Since then much art, often proclaimed or acclaimed as advance-guard, has exploited the two extremes of fullness and compression. They are often not mutually exclusive, as in Joyce's two great novels and in Proust's final intricate *finding* of how it all *really* was, and in the *Personae* and *Cantos* of Ezra Pound. In Mallarmé's *Un coup de dés* we have in fairly brief compass, constellated typographically on double pages, a cryptic and also vast poem of human, indeed cosmic, destiny. Seldom before were such enormous energies used to expand or to concentrate. Indeed, perhaps never before were those energies so openly revealed as such and exploited as part of artistic expression and effect. In keeping with such general propositions I leave the notion of detail imprecise; getting down to cases would involve such matters as kinds of detail, rhetorical figures, syntactic patterns, the breadth and degree of familiarity of reference, the tone, the narrator's means of self-characterization, and much else. But if my macroscopic approach is provisionally indulged, two examples, one from Gogol and one from Mallarmé, may serve.

In the great seriocomic novel *Dead Souls* (1842) the hero-antihero Chichikov goes about the real-unreal Russia buying up serfs (serf-names) who are dead (but whose death has not been reported to St. Petersburg) in order to have that "property" for social standing and as collateral for loans. No wonder, then, that such "ambivalence" of real fantasy and fantastic reality, in all permutations, gives rise to heightened awareness of the ambivalence of language that is outwardly prosaic and rambling, concrete and gratuitously particular, but always atmospheric and always about to take on larger and even symbolic meaning. Chichikov goes to the house of a miser with the literally plushy name Plyushkin; he meets him and mistakes him for the housekeeper-serf. He is told to go into an inner room of the house and this is what he sees:

> Opening the door he at last found himself in the light and was struck by the disorder that appeared before his eyes. It seemed as if a general house-cleaning were going on and all the furniture had been piled up here for the time being. There was even a broken chair standing on one of the tables and, side by side with it, a clock whose

pendulum had stopped and to which a spider had already cunningly attached its web. Here, too, with one of its sides leaning against the wall, stood a dresser with antiquated silver, small carafes, and Chinese porcelain. Upon a bureau, with a marquetry of mother-of-pearl mosaic, which had already fallen out in places and left behind it only yellowish little grooves and depressions filled with crusted glue, was lying a great and bewildering omnium gatherum: a mound of scraps of paper, closely covered with writing, pressed down with a paper-weight of marble turned green and having an egg-shaped little knob; some sort of ancient tome in a leather binding and with red edges; a lemon, so dried up that it was no bigger than a walnut; a broken-off chair-arm; a wine-glass with some kind of liquid and three dead flies, covered over with a letter; a bit of sealing wax; a bit of rag picked up somewhere; two quills, dirty with ink that had dried upon them consumptively; a quill tooth-pick, perfectly yellowed, which its owner had probably been picking his teeth with even before Moscow had been invaded by the French.[9]

It all goes on at even greater length. One notes that the very minuteness of description, the fullness of linguistic expression that goes far beyond chaotic enumeration, creates a sense of something more than the objects or the character of their owner. It also serves the function of conveying drabness without boredom or disgust, of rendering the waiting experience of the implicitly very observant scalawag Chichikov, and, in a word, creating dramatic suspense. Alternatively, one could cite passages from the realist-grotesque Dostoevsky, whose psychological probing goes so much deeper, or passages from Tolstoy, James, Proust, or Faulkner (or, I suppose, the no longer *nouveau roman* and Thomas Pynchon), in which elaborate description, floods of language, lengthy nuancing dialogue or inner monologue, and minutely described humdrum acts all can give us the aesthetically authentic feeling of fullness of life, which is indeed so often absorbingly commonplace, and can suggest, even in that exhaustive fullness, something beyond. By such means the skillful novelist creates, by his very explicitness, successive hypotheses in the reader's mind or some degree of indeterminacy that the reader becomes engaged in hoping to fill as he reads along.

In great contrast we have the concentration of poetry such as Mallarmé's, which creates by far other means an involvement of the reader. To be appropriately paradoxical, the poems may be precisely *about* indeterminacies, the empty spaces or absences, the *un*said, for which we must as readers provisionally invent or imagine the context or even the things themselves. A poem should, Mallarmé states in an early letter (October 1864), "peindre, non la chose, mais l'effet qu'elle produit."[10] Later in his jottings called "Crise de vers" (c. 1874), he writes as part of a grandiose project to say *the* word and write *the* work (La Parole, L'Oeuvre):

> Le vers qui de plusieurs vocables refaît un mot total, neuf, étranger à la langue et comme incantatoire, achève cet isolement de la parole: niant, d'un trait souverain, le hasard demeuré aux termes malgré l'artifice de leur retrempe alternée en le sens et la sonorité, et vous cause cette surprise de n'avoir ouï jamais tel fragment ordinaire d'élocution, en même temps que la réminiscence de l'objet nommé baigne dans une neuve atmosphère.

> (The verse that out of several vocables remakes a word whole, fresh, strange to the tongue and as if incantatory, culminates in this isolation of the word [parole]: negating by a sovereign stroke the chance situated in terms despite the artfulness of their alternating reimmersion in sense and sonority, and it causes in you that surprise of never having heard such an ordinary fragment of elocution, at the same time that the remembrance of the object named bathes in a fresh new atmosphere.)

Or again, Mallarmé writes in another much-quoted jotting:

> Je dis: une fleur! et, hors de l'oubli où ma voix relègue aucun contour, en tant que quelque chose d'autre que les calices sus, musicalement se lève, idée même et suave, l'absente de tous bouquets.

> (I say: a flower! and outside the oblivion where my voice banishes every contour, in so far as something older than the known calyxes [chalices], musically arises—idea, itself and delicious—the absent [flower] from all bouquets.]

Finally continuing, at the risk of mystification, to the next aphorism:

> Au contraire d'une fonction de numéraire facile et représentatif, comme le traite d'abord la foule, le dire, avant tout, rêve et chant,

retrouve chez le Poëte, par nécessité constitutive d'un art consacré aux fictions, sa virtualité.

(Saying—the opposite of a function of facile and representative coinage as the mob readily treats it—saying, above all, dreams and sings, finds again in the Poet, by a necessity constitutive of an art devoted to fictions, its virtuality.)

If I may summarize for my own present purpose these programmatic notes, Mallarmé is making the claim that poetic use of words is not mere naming or iteration or realizing or representing; rather it is evocative, creative, allusive, phonic. Objects named or alluded to in poetry are *virtual* objects entirely dependent on the words, in their sound and meaning, with which the objects are expressed. Hence, to simplify, the Word becomes more important than its reference or, rather, its ordinary speech referent. The Word then becomes almost hieratic or magical and assumes an almost unbearable potency. And only the adept, the initiate, the *mystes*, can ever know and interpret the mystagogue and his mystery.

Here I draw back from the ultimate consequences, whatever they may be, that Mallarmé was willing with such a strain to try to discover and to face. From my distant perspective, high and superficial though it may be, the two extreme nineteenth-century tendencies of "superfluous" detail and the supreme Word alone can be instructive in pondering the expressivity of language (ways of attempting to say the seemingly unsayable) and in observing the reflected tendencies and attempts of art in our own time. One of the overt desires of the advance-guard artist (as well as those that bring up the rear) has traditionally been to *épater le bourgeois*—to flatten or flabbergast the man in the street. What could ultimately dumbfound if not silence?

In folk wisdom silence is golden as a respite from chatter. It can also be hostile, as when people cease to speak to each other or as when the Slavs encountered Germanic people who, since they spoke no Slavic, were dubbed the dumb ones [*nemtsy*]. One could even compile an anthology of silent poetry or poetry of silence, including such texts as these:

> When to the sessions of sweet silent thought
> I summon up remembrance of things past . . .
>
> Thou, silent form, dost tease us out of thought
> As doth eternity . . .

How can the heart express itself?
How can another ever understand you?
Will he understand the thing you live by?
A thought once uttered is a lie.
Roiling the springs, you only cloud them.
Just drink of them—and be silent.[11]

We could also note the carefully timed "performances" of silent music in the
manner of John Cage or the hanging of empty canvases in the manner of
Robert Rauschenberg or even Christo's sheathing of coasts and mountains
in polyethylene. We could abut on the transitory delights of concrete poetry
("eyeleveleye") or on the non-humdrum conundrums of nonsense and dada
("bevor dada da war war dada da"). But these are limited and limiting cases;
if they occur too frequently they begin to cloy and to collapse our interest
span, and, by the way, to make aesthetics and literary theory repositories
of mere oddments and oddities.

Much has been made recently of silence, drawing somewhat indiscriminately on various contexts and meanings of the word: sometimes vulgar-
ization of mystical doctrine and modes of expression; sometimes
complaints about the straitjacket or the fetters of language; sometimes
assertions that language has been perverted by bureaucrats, advertisers,
bad novelists, dishonest politicians, and death-camp wardens. Without
going into all the charges and the real misuses, we can hardly take any
comfort from indicting language-in-general, just as it would be unreasonable
to indict oxygen because it is essential in the production of smog and fire
storms. Silence is of course an alternative and at times a necessity (not only
for the Trappist monks but also for the laity): an alternative to saying
anything and also a necessity in regulating and marking and signifying
utterances. Some uses of silence are wittily shown in Heinrich Böll's story
"Dr. Murkes gesammeltes Schweigen." An informative book on Russian
formalism and French structuralism claims to take its alarming metaphorical
title from Nietzsche: I refer to Fredric Jameson's *The Prison-House of
Language* (1972). In Jameson's translation the passage, which he uses as
an epigraph, reads:

> We have to cease to think if we refuse to do it in the prison-house
> of language; for we cannot reach further than the doubt which asks
> whether the limit we see is really a limit.

Jameson gave no reference and thus piqued my curiosity. When I traced the aphoristic statement to Nietzsche's jottings (*Aus dem Nachlass der Achtzigerjahre,* ed. Karl Schlechta, vol. 3, 862), I found a passage that could fairly be translated:

> We stop thinking if we don't want to do it in linguistic constraint; we come right up to the uncertainty of seeing here a limit as a limit.

And Nietzsche continues:

> Rational thinking is interpreting according to a scheme that we can't throw away.

> (Wir hören auf zu denken, wenn wir es nicht in dem sprachlichen Zwange tun wollen, wir langen gerade noch bei dem Zweifel an, hier eine Grenze als Grenze zu sehen. Das vernünftige Denken ist ein Interpretieren nach einem Schema, welches wir nicht abwerfen können.)

Yes, we do do our rational thinking under the constraint or discipline of language. How else? But we also dream wordlessly, we also play with words, we irrationalize them, we also—at least, some of us—write poetry. Language in the abstract is neither the Answer nor is it the "prison-house."[12] Poetry is not Belief or Religion. Criticism is not creative sing-along or an ego-trip on the poet's ticket. We can find and entertain in art myriad meanings and write about them in myriad ways. If writers cannot ultimately or flatly express the inexpressible, they can still make wonderful near-misses and continue their business of trying. Such use of language—poetic, speculative, critical—has its value even if it may seem at times (to borrow Mallarmé's line) an "aboli bibelot d'inanité sonore." Only with silence can sounds—speech sounds—resound, in our minds as well as in the air. After the chorus of Apprentices come the Mastersingers. So that they may perform their masterful songs, we, their audience, are given the order "Silentium!" and I obey.

Notes

1. See my "Signs of the Times: Semiotics 1974," *Yale Review* 64 (1975), 296–320.
2. In his *Journaux intimes* Baudelaire shows exemplary scorn for the slogans of his day, many of them with us still. In "Mon coeur mis à nu" he cites phrases like "littérature militante," "les poëtes de combat," "les littérateurs d'avant-garde," and reflects that "ces habitudes de métaphores militaires dénotent des esprits non pas militants, mais faits pour la discipline, c'est-à-dire pour la conformité." In *Oeuvres complètes*, ed. Y.-G. Le Dantec, Bibliothèque de la Pléiade (Paris: Gallimard, 1954), 1218–19.
3. I try to resist generalizing about our American revulsion at putting things into exact words for fear of killing the emotion or sounding abrupt or hoity-toity. It may be a stamp of present-day "modernism" that literary language has recently, in many tongues, incorporated so many phatic, indeterminate, and superlative expressions. Such impressions are of course hard to measure and to generalize.
4. In Cyril Connolly, *The Condemned Playground* (London: Routledge, 1945), 136–53, and also in his *Enemies of Promise and Other Essays* (Garden City, N.Y.: Anchor Books, 1960), 307–24.
5. Both of these passages are cited at somewhat greater length in the informative article of Erich Hasse, "Zur Bedeutung von 'Je ne sais quoi' im 17. Jahrhundert," *Zeitschrift für französische Sprache und Literatur* 67 (1956), 47–68.
6. This and the other texts quoted here of Saint John are taken from the volume in the series Biblioteca de Autores Cristianos, *Vida y obras de San Juan de la Cruz*, containing a biography by Crisógono de Jesús (revised by Matías del Niño Jesús) and the complete works edited by Luciano Ruano, 7th ed. (Madrid, 1973).
7. The text of the poem is quoted from *The Poems and Letters of Andrew Marvell*, ed. H. M. Margoliouth, vol. 1 (Oxford: Clarendon Press, 1927), 48–50.
8. In James's "The Art of Fiction" (1884), aptly cited and discussed in a fine essay by Martin Price, "The Irrelevant Detail and the Emergence of Form," in *Aspects of Narrative: Selected Papers from the English Institute*, ed. J. Hillis Miller (New York: Columbia University Press, 1971), 69–91.
9. From chapter 6 of *Dead Souls*. I quote the translation of Bernard Guilbert Guerney in Rinehart Editions (New York: Rinehart, 1948), 129, which takes a few minor liberties.
10. Mallarmé is quoted from his *Oeuvres complètes*, ed. Henri Mondor and G. Jean-Aubry, 2d ed., Bibliothèque de la Pléiade (Paris: Gallimard, 1951).
11. This last is my literal rendering of the middle stanza of the famous lyric "Silentium" by Fyodor Tyutchev (1803–73). For a later filiation in Russian poetry, see John E. Malmstad, "Mandelshtam's 'Silentium': A Poet's Response to Ivanov," *Vyacheslav Ivanov: Poet, Critic and Philospher*, ed. Robert Louis Jackson and Lowry Nelson, Jr. (New Haven: Yale Center for International and Area Studies, 1986), 236–52. The first quotation is of course the beginning of Shakespeare's sonnet and the second is from Keats's "Ode on a Grecian Urn."
12. If one is looking for philosophers' apothegms on language, here is one of Wittgenstein, quoted in the collaborative volume by Allen Janik and Stephen Toulmin, *Wittgenstein's Vienna* (New York, 1973), 202 (no reference is provided other than the date): "Anrennen gegen die Grenze der Sprache? Die Sprache ist ja kein Käfig" (17 December 1930).

A Note on the *Je ne sais quoi*

The history of the subject virtually begins with the third chapter of Benedetto Croce's *Estetica* (the historical part, of which the first five chapters were published whole in 1902). Some attention had been paid by Joel E. Spingarn, *A History of Literary Criticism in the Renaissance* (New York: Columbia University Press, 1899; 2d ed., 1925). Still of great interest is the latterly seminal article of Samuel H. Monk, "'A Grace beyond the Reach of Art,'" *Journal of the History of Ideas* 5 (1944), 131–50, where, among many other references, attention is drawn to the last two chapters of the *Entretiens d'Ariste et d'Eugène* (1671) by le Père Bonhours. E. B. O. Borgerhoff, in his fine book *The Freedom of French Classicism* (Princeton: Princeton University Press, 1950), emphatically deals with the matter as part of his general design to limber up conventional notions of seventeenth-century classicism. In 1951 and 1958 Giulio Natali published historical notes on the subject, mainly concerning Italian literature, but making a good theoretical distinction between casual use and, as it were, doctrinal use of the *non so che*; these notes are collected in his *Fronde sparte* (Padova: CEDAM, 1960), 39–55. Three useful studies by Erich Köhler are: "No sai qui s'es—No sai que s'es (Wilhelm IX. von Poitiers und Raimbaut von Orange)" (1964); "'Je ne sais quoi': ein Kapitel aus der Begriffsgeschichte des Unbegreiflichen" (1953–54); and "Der Padre Feijóo und das 'no sé qué'"(1955–56)—all included in his collection *Esprit und arkadische Freiheit: Aufsätze aus der Welt der Romania* (Frankfurt am Main: Athenäum, 1966). Fritz Schalk, in *Romanische Forschungen* 69 (1957), 210–13, chides Köhler (unreasonably) for incompleteness and (rightly) for facile sociological generalizations. An article by Ernst Haase, which deals almost exclusively with French literature, has been most helpful: "Zur Bedeutung von 'Je ne sais quoi' im 17. Jahrhundert," *Zeitschrift für französische Sprache und Literatur* 67 (1956), 47–68. For Spanish literature of the seventeenth century (only passing mention is made of Saint John) there is a gleaning of quotations with modest results in Alberto Porqueras-Mayo, "El *no sé qué* en la Edad de Oro española," *Romanische Forschungen* 78 (1966), 314–37. Vladimir Jankélévitch's *Le je-ne-sais-quoi et le presque-rien* (Paris, 1957) is a dense and prolix philosophical treatise that has nothing to do with the present subject.

Clearly, the *je ne sais quoi* and related notions are, as Croce, Monk, and Borgerhoff show, important notions for the history of aesthetics and for intellectual history in general. These scholars, along with the others cited, have gathered many materials that still need a shaping historical hand. Still, I thought it might be helpful here to draw attention not only to the depth of the subject, but also to its length and breadth and to the labors of gleaning that have been so far accomplished.

Bibliographical Notes

A topic such as this is like a feather pillow that can be fluffed or squeezed. Just as great "encyclopedic" works like the *Divina commedia, The Faerie Queene,* or *Paradise Lost* can tempt the scholar to subsume vast quantities of human knowledge into his notes and commentary, so the inexpressible or silence can generate galaxies of discourse. I cite here a few works that seem pertinent. The short book of the great scholar Christine Mohrmann, *Liturgical Latin: Its Origins and Character* (Washington, D.C.: Catholic University of America Press, 1957), makes out a good case (before the rulings of the Second Vatican Council) for keeping the Mass in Latin; to the present purpose, her general case for the *expressive*, in counterdistinction to the communicative, use of language is well argued. Susan Sontag, in *Styles of Radical Will* (New York: Farrar, Straus and Giroux, 1969), has a chapter on "The Aesthetics of Silence" that is an interesting jumble of remarks and insights, often perceptive, quite commonsensical, and wide-ranging among present-day arts. She recognizes the exploitation of "silence" as a sort of metaphor to the point that "the art of our time is noisy with appeals for silence" (12). Hans Mayer's vigorous little book *Das Geschehen und das Schweigen: Aspekte der Literatur* (Frankfurt am Main: Suhrcamp, 1969) contains a notable chapter on "Sprechen und Verstummen der Dichter" that rapidly surveys numerous twentieth-century writers in their relation to language. He singles out three poetically exploited or "foregrounded" elements: the stammering struggle with words to express an ugly meaningless present; the attempt to render banal chitchat in poetry; the writing of fragmentary poetry directly based on integral poems of the past. There is a polemical disapproval here that does not obscure the interest and insights. In his book *Language and Silence: Essays on Language, Literature, and the Inhuman* (New York: Atheneum, 1967; 2d ed., 1970), which by the way contains a piece on the Marxist Hans Mayer on the occasion of his flight from East Germany (1964), George Steiner has two essays on "The Retreat from the Word" and "Silence and the Poet" that survey, urbanely and concretely, instances of extreme concentration and expansiveness and of debasement in the use of language. A portentously titled book by Jerzy Peterkiewicz must be mentioned: *The Other Side of Silence: The Poet at the Limits of Language* (London: Oxford University Press, 1970). It can charitably be viewed as the work of a practicing poet who has read widely without much judgment; its sense of connectedness is obsessive and makes a vapid and overblown impression. A plainer and more disciplined book by Volker Roloff is far more helpful and suggestive: *Reden und Schweigen: zur Tradition und Gestaltung eines mittelalterlichen Themas in der französischen Literatur* (Munich: Fink, 1973). It deals with folktales and romances (by Chrétien de Troyes and others) in which silence is significant in itself or gives significance to speech, and it conscientiously provides a great deal of information on all sorts of related matters, such as the monastic rule of silence. Roloff recognizes, in more places than the index indicates, the excellence of the study by Alan S. Trueblood, "El silencio en el Quijote," *Nueva revista de filología hispánica* 12 (1958), 160–80; collected in his *Letter and Spirit in Hispanic Writers* (London: Tamesis Books, 1986), 45–64.

Much has been made of the famous personal crises of poetic language undergone at the turn of the century by Paul Valéry and Hugo von Hofmannsthal (see *Ein Brief*, 1902; that is, the fictional letter from Lord Chandos to Bacon). The whole subject of the difficulty, both individual and national, of fashioning new and adequate language in literature would greatly profit from a broadly conceived and dispassionate aesthetic discussion, free of alarums and excursions and the clucking of tongues.

3

THE KIND
OF
EARLY LYRIC

To take unbridled liberty in discussing genre is to stand like Aristotle or Linnaeus before the chaos of nature in the hope of discerning patterns. One steps over the undergrowth, discerns the creeping things, and descries the winged creatures of the air. From Mount Pisgah the forest looks green, undulating, and impenetrable; alternatively, the desert looks parched, rocky, and barren. One choice is to get *down* and botanize on nature's cradle and her grave. Another is to look for ascents, for flights. With a pair of historical binoculars and an exercised historical imagination, one should be able to observe what vegetates, creeps, or flies, to note patterns above the surface, and, while remaining firmly superficial, to formulate some configurations and a few generalities. From their tribal origins the Romans knew the avian auguries; from the Etruscans they later borrowed visceral haruspicy. What I propose is to look at things first in obvious movement and then to sketch a down-to-earth generic taxonomy of how things might have got there.

The two ages in which poetic kinds were generated are eighth to fifth century B.C. in Greece and A.D. 1000–1400 in Western Europe. I speak only of the Occidental tradition. Both generic *geneses* are unforeseeable and unaccountable. To some, the "question of origins" or the nature of literary beginnings has seemed terribly profound, usually in an abstract way: if something is said to begin there must have been a beginning before the beginning, something to beget beginnings. Yet nothing in the fragile history of cultures, not to mention true civilizations, seems to warrant this notion. It is simply that some *one* had an idea, and others followed, modified, improved at times, and either succeeded or failed in whatever sense. The Homeric poems began somewhere, but nobody knows precisely where or how or when or by whom. True, the time can be set within limits, and of course, the general place or region. But no one can fully explain who or how or why. That they happened is fortunately beyond dispute; that they *had* to happen is not. What about the traditional notion of the epic, the lyric, and the dramatic as somehow central to genre? In a vague sense you could say that first came the one and then the other two, in good summary Greek-literary-historical fashion. That is all right if you manage somehow to scrunch in Hesiod and Theognis and make more of the "short" poets than the fragments allow and modernize the dramatists as just so many forerunners of Shakespeare and Ibsen. The point might then be that it is not so important what the Greeks were to themselves as what they were thought to be, and imitated as, by later civilizations. What we have of Greek literary production has passed through many sieves, not the least of which is that which winnows papyrus from sand. The texts written from the eighth to the fifth century were, of course, adapted to the pedagogical curriculum of an aristocratically literate society that still, in spite of all, retained a sense of memorization and performance. Our first great theorist is Aristotle, who predilected tragedy because it was the most astonishingly successful genre, one that had evolved in the preceding century and had reached an almost demonstrable *perfectio*. No reason not to think that other tragedians would write, but the important thing was that the genre had demonstrated itself wholly *in actu* on the analogy to organic genera. But of course the genus tragedy became extinct in the early Christian era, whether or not as a result of churchly opposition (see Tertullian, *De Spectaculis*, in which, in effect, Christian life and anagoge are presented as the real "spectacle"). As we know, a rebirth, or rather, birth again took place in the late Middle Ages: the lines, though somewhat disputed, are pretty clear.

But what of the lyric? First one must be reconciled to the fact that not much coherence survives from the "Archaic" Age: military-patriotic poetry of Archilochus, Tyrtaeus, Simonides; seemingly intimate love poetry of

Alcman and Sappho; the limited body of Pindar's and Bacchylides' public odes and other pieces. We are told by some that lyric poetry at that time somehow takes part in an evolutionary process of revealing the soul,[1] that is, discovering the spirit, the inward spirit of man, on the civilized march to the present. Others will tell us that in most cases, if not all, the first-person singular is a public and representative device. At all events, it should be clear that the personal aspect of the early Greek lyric and the confessional *Innigkeit* of the Romantic lyric are two matters that should not be confused or collapsed. What is striking to the outsider, the nonprofessional classicist, is that during the great *classical* age of Greek literature there was apparently very little lyric poetry produced. I hasten to add that the choruses in the tragedies and in Aristophanes more than fill any supposed gap in purely metrical complexity or inventiveness. They can be anthologized and made somehow to seem independent. Yet their *context* is still massive and unavoidable; they are undetachable parts of much larger structures. In the continuity of lyric poetry, much more important are the Alexandrian poets, considerably represented by Callimachus and Theocritus, and in scattered fashion by the poets of the so-called Greek Anthology. It is really quite a new age and in our scheme of things leads on to Catullus, the Latin elegists, not to mention Horace and Virgil. We may have some notion of how that *translatio* took place. With the Romans we have a full range of epigram (often *taedium in parvo*), the epyllion, the eclogue, the verse letter, etc. Our modern sensibility, however, leads many to fasten on Catullus's passionately autobiographical love-poetry and on Horace's and Martial's self-characterizations as men of the world and men in the world. There is nothing in the lyric previously quite like Roman messy, problematic passion and its simultaneous urbanity: love-passion as a consuming center of life's whole purpose and the metropolis (the one and only *urbs*) as *the* way of life. In a sense, then, Roman lyric poetry is not simply an imitation or adaptation of Greek modes from Alexandria and earlier, it is a serious, imaginative parody. I mean "parody" in the sense that Joyce's *Ulysses* is a parody of the *Odyssey* or that Eliot's *The Waste Land* is a parody of Pound's *Hugh Selwyn Mauberley*—not an imitation, takeoff, or travesty, but a sort of transposition into a different key. At any rate, the great Roman lyric was over by the death of Martial (c. A.D. 104) and at its best had flourished from about 70 B.C. to A.D. 20—less than a hundred years.

Thus far we may count three rather brief ages of lyric poetry: Archaic Greek, Alexandrian Greek, and early oligarchic-imperial Roman. The continuities are most often stressed, yet (or therefore) the discontinuities are perhaps more striking. Continuities are, for example, quantitative meter and set patterns of feet; stanzaic forms, rhetorical situations like addresses to gods or lovers, laments, invitations, farewells, and so on; awareness in poems of other poets, either contemporaries or predecessors, as part of a group or "tradition."[2] Discontinuities, by way of emphasis, might include the very different tones and assumptions; freedom in being allusively "literary," thus stressing distance in time or direct homage to the past; reorderings of the relationship among speaker, addressee in the poem, and reader. All these would need illustration at length to be persuasive. But the most obvious discontinuity is historical time: great collective lyric flights in antiquity seem remarkably discontinuous.

Still, after Martial, a voice might say, lyric poetry in a broad sense did not just die out. There are Annius Florus, Nemesianus, Lactantius, Ausonius, Claudianus, and of course Anonymus. The broad sense, though, is too broad: they were not really lyric poets and they constitute a *verloren hoop*. Let us be summary: apart from the mysterious and beautiful *Pervigilium Veneris*, the Latin Christian hymns of Prudentius, Ambrose, and Fortunatus, Anglo-Saxon poetry, and a stray poem here and there, the next great lyric flight occurs around 1100—a thousand years after the death of Martial. The great lyric poetry of that flight is in Latin and in Old Provensal. Nothing in French or Middle English approaches it closely; in Italian one must wait till Guinizzelli, Cavalcanti, and Dante. The only rival is the Middle High German *Minnesang*, which began to flourish slightly later than Latin and Provensal. In fact, because the matter of origins is so obscure and probably impossible to establish, perhaps in this lyric flight there should be all three linguistic groups: Medieval Latin, Provensal, and Middle High German. Their interrelations are intricate and historically momentous—far beyond the illusory or combative question of primacy in time. What do they have in common? Certain subject matter (celebration of spring, rural life, perplexities of love, politics, war, and poetry itself); a sudden passion of rime and stanzaic forms that bursts forth in astonishing variegation (in utter contrast to older Latin, Romance, and Germanic practice)[3]; a relative personalization of the speaker in quasi-confessional or autobiographical fashion; a relative communal sense of poets and society in a shared real world.

The fact that Old English or Anglo-Saxon poetry stands outside the wide net of these generalizations should again be noted.[4] With no derogation of the intrinsic value of such poems as the "Dream of the Rood" and "The Seafarer" (in, it should be stressed, *ancient* Germanic alliterating unrimed meter), we might seize on it to underscore the general difficulty of positing origins, let alone transitions, and to suggest that there may be folk traditions of folk song that are entirely lost to us. Their importance cannot be assessed, although they seem to be a different sort of thing from the literate or oral-literate poetry I am implicitly, and now explicitly, concerned with. In this connection I should mention the Arabic hypothesis and bracket it in the words of its best and most original scholar, the late Samuel Miklos Stern: "I am strongly inclined to think that the majority of the proofs adduced in order to demonstrate that Western poets and Western writers at the beginning of the Middle Ages had knowledge of Arabic poetry or other forms of Arabic literature, and that they made use of their knowledge in their works, are lacking in validity."[5] Because I am highlighting historical discontinuities and avoiding any general scheme of European lyrical *Entstehung* and "evolution," I shall simply assert without much fear of controversion that the Provensal lyric just began and that it began fully formed in the remaining poems of Guilhem, ninth duke of Aquitaine and seventh count of Poitou (or Poitiers), who lived from 1071 to 1127 and about whom much documentation survives.

In Guilhem's poems we find a strong *I*, which observes the world's particularity and gathers the world about it; an audience of fellows to break bread with (*companho*); references in the poems to their own making, both demystifying poetry and concomitantly boasting of the worth of poetry and its maker's skill; nature settings; addresses to the beloved; and renunciation on going on a Crusade. Here is quite a range, indeed a miscellany of subject matter (all without mentioning the obscene poem about Guilhem as the mute stud or the poem on choosing horses and women, both of which are rather narrative in manner). Presumably the ten or eleven poems extant are not the whole of his works. The metrical, riming, and stanzaic patterns are quite varied, not in respect perhaps to the myriad possibilities actualized in the whole body of Provensal poetry, but certainly varied in respect to any that was written before. Apart from subject matter and external technique, what is remarkable in some of the poems is that Guilhem proceeds neither by narration nor by catalogue, neither by *formulae* nor by *figurae*, not even by some sort of simple logic. He proceeds by the *semblance* of thematic and logical concatenation in a way that seems to reason (compare this to the technical term *ragionare* of the *stilnovisti*) and to set forth propositions, but which turns and veers and flashes (in an image or metaphor), giving the impression of someone trying both to understand and to master his emotions. In Guilhem's poetry, as in that of other great Provensal poets, we do not have to suppose a composite audience with, say, a stanza directed at each little group,[6] nor do we have to acquiesce in some ponderous argument of the influence of Scholastic logic and poetics.[7] The tension between freedom and restraint (in language, in rime, in logical "forms," etc.) is part of the inexplicable novelty of the Provensal poem, and cannot be simply resolved into causal or casual "influences," whether the Arabs, the Schoolmen, or folk poetry.

One extremely interesting process that quickly took hold among the Trobadors is what pompously might be called inter-referentiality. At least two later poems, by Raimbaut d'Aurenga and Aimeric de Peguilhan, take up Guilhem's poem about "nothing" ("Farai un vers de dreyt nien"), which is superficially a riddle and more deeply a poem about writing poems. But this unmistakable lineage is only a primal instance of much that follows. In Provensal poetry there developed a remarkable kind of poetry, not only poems that answer other poems, but also poems that alternate stanzas written by two different poets; and not only those sorts of debates, but also poems that are debates within a single mind (as Lanfranc Cigala's "Entre mon cor e me e mon saber" [mid-thirteenth century]; see in the Arundel Collection, "Vacillantis trutine" [twelfth century]). The various designations are the *tenso*, the *partimen*, the *joc partit* (French: *jeu parti*, hence English "jeopardy"), but this is not the place to try to untangle the terms. More familiar types of poem are, of course, the *canso* ("song"), the *alba* ("dawn poem"), the *sirventes* (politically or morally polemical poem), the *sestina* (invented by Arnaut Daniel), the *planh* ("lament"), the *enueg* (poem of pet peeves), the crusade poem, as well as other less common types. What is remarkable is that Provensal poetry should so quickly constitute itself a whole system of poetic types and attitudes—lyric arenas for poetic display and rivalry—and that the system should be so satisfyingly self-referential or, better, intra-referential. By this system we are practically assured that very little of importance is missing or has been lost. Besides, we ourselves have the means to judge what is good or better or best. If Provensal poems can be provisionally said to come within the genus lyric poetry, they constitute an extraordinary range of possibilities, based largely on subject matter, as there seems to be no real correlation between subject matter and the wonderful variety of meter, rime, or stanza.

Through the mediation or continuation of Old French and Italian poets, these types are taken up by the late Middle Ages and the early Renaissance, though not all in equal measure. Certainly the loosely structured *canso* in a sense persists in the *canzone* and the "ode"; the lament and the dawn poem persist practically as human constants, and the *sirventes* might be said to mingle with Medieval and Roman Latin satire. At this point I come, however, within an ace of developing a theory of the "évolution des genres" and shall desist almost on principle. A new lyric type was presumably invented in Sicily by Jacopo da Lentini, notary at the court of Frederick II in the early thirteenth century: the sonnet, perhaps the most famous and notorious lyric type—short, intricate, and tight enough to attract innumerable imitators, practitioners, and definers. Perhaps it, as they say, answered a felt need: a way of concentrating the enormous affective range of subject matter of the Provensals and a perhaps salutary reaction to their infinitely repeatable and inventable stanzaic forms. Both its traditional subject matter and the concision of its form have recommended it to this very day as a promise of "infinite riches in a little room" (= *stanza*), to misgloss Marlowe's phrase. In his book *The Icy Fire*,[8] Leonard Forster kindly and correctly points out that the rampant sonneteering in the Renaissance represents at the least a schooling for apprentice poets (corollary: the often mediocre results should be understood and pardoned). The *canzone*, in Italian hands, was also a kind of schooling: in the *dolce stil novo*, to use Dante's hallowed phrase, it was a capacious type, somehow sanctioned by freewheeling Provensal usage, in which *doctrina*, if not *disciplina*, could be worked out and displayed. At a certain angle, Cavalcanti's "Donna me prega" and Dante's *canzoni* of the *Convivio* may seem, from a Provensal perspective, like tortuous and even tortured exercises, although I realize that they are important stages on the way to ennobling and angelizing the mission and the object of so much poetry, to wit, the Lady, and thus to narrowing the breadth of subject matter present in the Provensal *canso*.

By this time, the easily summarized and categorized forms and contents of lyric poetry had been generated. I make a halt in my historical schematizing at the very doorstep of Petrarch who, in refinement and voluminous skill, becomes purveyor, by appointment to the world, of the fecundity of the late medieval lyric flight.

In theoretical matters our earliest authorities are, as usual, Plato and Aristotle. Let it be said at once, summarily, that Plato banished the poets only in his early or middle utopia, the *Republic*, and precisely for reasons of state: Homer had been made a Bible by the Sophists (great-book teachers and academic wowsers) and the goings-on of the gods did not consort well with the beautiful = true = good. The *Ion* is a different matter. There the rhapsode is made out, with finest irony, to be a better weaver-of-song than he is a plain weaver or other sort of artisan and "man of 'action.'" The upshot is that Plato, playing with jest and earnest most seriously, was taken seriously as playing down play. In fact, Plato unmistakably knew and respected the power of poetry. He was not ready or willing to deal with it in *kind*. Something of the divine (not simply "demonic") hung about poetry or, more precisely, the dithyramb; the poet, in this sense, was for Plato *really* possessed by a god.[9] In other words Plato did not banish poets as such, but poets who are false theologians (some modern poets and their dependent critics might be considered as analogues); he wanted the rhapsodes to acknowledge their irrationality as something different, *positively* different. The notion, then, that Plato once and for all "banished the poets" is quite wrong in its generality. Plato, whose concern was hardly poetry, however much we would want it to have been, can give us no real help in our wish for some genre definition of lyric poetry. (He equally fails us in the matter of tragedy.) We turn, then, to his pupil Aristotle, the primordial master of taxonomy. By him, in the *Poetics* and the *Rhetoric*, we are told much about the general status and function of what we would call imaginative literature and of the linguistic usage that heightens literary and forensic composition. But the main doctrine concerns tragedy and speech-making, and what applies to the lyric is not systematically presented. One may conjecture along Aristotelian lines; yet so many have done so in the past that it seems otiose to add another sketch. It remains, nonetheless, important for literary theory that Aristotle was the first to propose seriously the whole problem of literary kinds (almost apart from the eternal merit he earns for what he says about tragedy in particular).

In regard to early reflections on lyric poetry, we may also find wanting Horace, Longinus, John of Garland, Geoffrey of Vinsauf, and Matthew of Vendôme—all of whom are concerned more with practicalities and minutiae of poetic and rhetorical language than with any "generic" specificity. It is, indeed, an open secret that neither in antiquity nor in the Middle Ages do we find important or useful accounts of the lyric as genre. There is much that we can deduce (and of course induce); yet literary theory on a fairly high level is concerned, in Croce's harsh terms, with "arte-pedagogo" and "arte-etera,"[10] and not with lyric art for something like lyric art's sake. Invoking Croce should now be the occasion for breaking with chronological schemes and considerations and for giving some general account of the lyric. From our own vantage point it is difficult to escape the Romantic notion of the lyric as subjective experience somehow versified and somehow rendered not only communicable but "universal." On the Romantic, not to say pre-Romantic, model, the "origins" would lie with the folk: in *Volkslieder* (the original title of Johann Gottfried Herder's collection later known as *Stimmen der Völker in Liedern* [1778–79, 1807] and of course

based on Bishop Thomas Percy's *Reliques of Ancient English Poetry*
[1765]), it is the people who write poetry ("das Volk dichtet," in Jacob
Grimm's later phrase). The old nostalgia persists that somehow the simple
forms at least are basic in a dynamic and persistent sense,[11] that Sappho is
a cry from the heart, the "ballad" a dance form (*ballata* from *ballare*), the
Lucy poems an epitaph (after all, there are Wordsworth's jottings on the
epitaph), or, perhaps, the sonnet a little tinkle. This doesn't really hold up:
there are not enough indices to tell us the degree of Sappho's subjectivity;
"ballad" as dance designation is like "chorus" and "carol" and "rondeau" in
the real sense that the dance part is lost, as well as its relevance, quite
early on; epitaphs, from the Sumerians to Hallmark, have been an
inexhaustible stock-in-trade (as witness any day's newspaper); and the
sonnet, originally a vague and casual term, has undergone the most
extraordinary metamorphoses of all (from Milton to Rilke to John Berryman). Greek lyric poetry, one can agree, probably had accompaniment
from lyre or cithara or pipes; but for the Roman lyric the mention of
instruments and dance must have been a pious fraud or mere convention.
Again, perhaps it was a matter of nostalgia; in remotest times, from which
there was no continuous *traditio*, there had been singing and dancing and
instrumental accompaniment. In the Middle Ages obviously there was
dancing and singing, as well as the writing of lyric poetry. All this is part,
in Vico's terms, of a continuous process of "rebarbarization" of the poetic
language and forms of "literate" writers. It is useful to stress that the Trobador
lyrics seem to have had no instrumental accompaniment. On the convincing,
though for some, unwelcome authority of Hendrik van der Werf, there is in the
Provensal manuscripts no indication, even in the illuminations, of anything but
the human voice as musical and declamatory transmitter of the poems.[12] It
may be that, way back when, *in illo tempore*, the "people" sang and danced,
and that out of those exertions was born the literary lyric. Anyone can froth up
such a theory, including Rousseau and Theodor Frings, and depend, for its
convincingness, upon an assumption of gradualness, a step-by-step rise and
evolution. (In a reverse causal way Albin Lesky can account for the dearth of
lyric poetry in the great Greek century by viewing it as "overshadowed" by the
achievement of Attic tragedy.)[13]

   There still may be something to theories of origin and evolution of the
lyric. The many boring treatises and passages on the lyric that purvey only
meters, lexical items, and their own descriptive jargon may indicate
something interesting. Perhaps the very measuredness—the recurrences
through feet, rime, and stanza—can be considered basic to lyric poetry. It

is of course true that the Homeric and Virgilian hexameter and the Italian *endecasillabo* and the English pentameter—all chiefly epic or narrative— recur in predictable variation in each line.[14] But in lyric poetry there seems always something to stem mere repetition, to halt the eloquent flow: the relatively brief and complex meters and stanzas of the Greek and Roman lyricists and then the sudden glorious invention of *rimed* stanzas by the Provensal and Medieval Latin and German poets, which become institu- tionalized for the whole Western tradition. It must be argued that experiments later on by, say, Campion and Schiller in quantitative meter depend upon the felt contrast with common accentual practice. After the invention of rime, rimelessness is the exception and depends upon rime for its recognition. (I should emphasize again that my context is lyric poetry up to and including Petrarch. What happens later, including Hölderlin, Whit- man and *vers libre*, can, at some length, be accounted for.)[15]

Throughout our early tradition poetry is prized above prose. Despite the development of *Kunstprosa* among the ancients and medievals, the *differentia* that makes poetry discernible as such seems, at least tacitly, to have been recognized as recurrence. Though etymology is a treacherous way to get at "truth," it can be instructive. A *good* etymology of *prosa* derives it from *prorsus* (from *pro* + *vorsus* [= *versus*]), meaning "headlong," "on and on," "straightforward." *Versus*, in contrast, signifies turning and returning and refers not to something that simply goes on and on, but to something that keeps coming back. The contrast is not absolute for there are kinds of recurrence in prose. Besides, one may point up a contrast between the hexameter and lyric measures. The Homeric hexameter, of course, keeps coming back, but with little rhythmic distinctness or surprise from line to line. In the Greek, the Roman, and the Provensal lyric, however, there is more emphatic recurrence: not only linear but stanzaic recurrence, recurrence modulated through complex initial expectations and their successive varieties of fulfillment. Meters derive their "feet" appropriately from walking, even "syncopated" limping, but then they become more or less set conventions separate from bodily movement. The study of meter, prosody, can appear to be a complicated, abstruse, and rather dull specialty: longs and shorts, anacrusis and caesura, syllable counting, synalepha and dialepha, as well as abstract "feet," are part of the bloodless nomenclature. Yet the whole matter becomes interesting, even crucial, when one makes an essential distinction between meter and rhythm: meter is the ideal measure ("ideal" in the sense that the Euclidean point and line are ideal concepts, clear and definite but *materially* unrealizable), and rhythm is the designation for the effect of approaching and distancing in any given line of verse to and from the ideal measure. It is the poet's business to be "irregular" within "regularity."[16]

Lyric poems, in our historical span, are relatively brief in length. Their brevity could of course be part of a prescriptive definition. But why not acknowledge it as part of a simple description? Perhaps, like Aristotelian tragedy, they must be "of a certain magnitude," clearly shorter than epics and plays, but how short or how long? The question promises to be quite sterile.[17] Answers could be sought in some general principle of human psychology, such as attention span, or in some notion of differentiation in the sense that a very long lyric becomes a sort of epyllion or that a very short lyric does not allow the aesthetic pleasure of complex recurrence. Perhaps the matter could be approached by way of elimination. A lyric refuses the recourse to circumstantial narrative or telling of the doings of a cast of characters in the thick of life and its interrelations and interactions (as in epic and novel). It also refuses the parceling out of awareness among a cast of characters (as in drama). In one direction the brevity of the lyric *fails* to provide narrative or dramatic scope: this failure is of course a positive failure, and calling it such is a conventional misuse of language that serves the purpose of emphasis. In another direction, the lyric *concentrates*: it provides one center with all attention focused on it. In simple terms, to avoid the dispersal of detail is to concentrate.

It is hard to obviate the obvious: lyrics are relatively complex in their recurrent mensuration; lyrics are relatively brief and concentrated. These general qualities are often allowed, passed over, and taken for granted. I would emphasize that they should not be neglected. Just as important is that they are formal qualities and not yet implicated in some description or prescription of necessary and sufficient lyric *subject matter*. I am concerned not simply to restate the flat assertion that the lyric is a brief songlike poem of personal subjective emotion. I am concerned also not to close the seeming circle by going "beyond" *die Lyrik* to *das Lyrische* and by discoursing in pseudophilosophic terms on *das lyrische Ich*, as supposedly distinct from *das epische Er* and *das dramatische Wir*. One thing we can positively learn from the prolonged avant-gardism of the last hundred years or so is the provisionality of genres, of generic divisions and jurisdictions, of the decorum of content or subject matter. No general topics are by their nature excluded from lyric poetry. The upshot, then, is that any definition of the lyric as genre must be a balance-in-tension, a dynamic configuration of formal elements (meter, rime, stanza), manner or tone (relative intimacy and individualism of the "rhetorical situation"), and subject matter (almost anything, provided it can seem *multum in parvo*, a nondiscursive concentration). Hence the radiating subjectiveness of the lyric: the unsaid is a propellent force that incites the reader to fill in and exemplify, to test or attest the poem according to his own properly vast range of emotional and aesthetic responsiveness. That instilled experience is part of the reading of lyric poetry and is certainly not wrong as a ground; what may be quite wrong are the reader's particularized or capriciously personal applications and bents which, even among sophisticated commentators, can lead to unwarranted search and seizure, expropriation for biographical or autobiographical ends, and irrelevant and inappropriate fingerprints or contusions on the delicate body poetic. In other words, with lyric poetry as well as with other genres, the wholeness and differentness, the independent existence of the aesthetic object must be both observed and respected.

Moving to a higher level of generality in our generic concern, we may quickly conclude from modern discussions of genre that each genre must be seen as part of a whole genre system and that genres are empirical classifications subject to modification in the face of actuality and intolerable as reifications or static prescriptions. The most radical commentary on genre is that of Benedetto Croce, who denied that genres, or, for that matter, rhetorical categories like irony and metaphor, had any *aesthetic* (as distinct from ethical, practical, or logical) status at all. We must realize that his radicalism was all in a good cause: to assert the inseparability of form and content, to fulfill the understandable demands, in the tradition of Kant, of his quadripartite philosophical system, and, on a more immediate level, to combat the mindless and sterile academic prescriptivism of his own day. Croce, though excessively radical, is refreshing in these days of undiscriminating permissiveness and ponderous academic readings of poetic texts as philosophical argument.

A perfect comprehensive poetics has never existed; each has tendentious faults, whether inclusive or exclusive, showing traits of favoritism or obtuseness. In the spirit of both *Scherz* and *Ernst*, here is a near-perfect poetics of genre that runs no risk of spoiling its perfection by going into detail. Its canny author is Alexander Roda Roda (1872–1945), the Austrian humorist and contributor to *Simplicissimus*. I quote it in full.[18]

Poetik

Ein Mann allein	Lyrik
Zwei Männer	Ballade

Ein Mann und eine Frau	. . . . . .	Novelle
Zwei Frauen und ein Mann	. . . . .	Roman
Zwei Männer und eine Frau	. . . . .	Drama
Zwei Männer und zwei Frauen	. . . .	Lustspiel

Apart from the easily adjustable sexism, nothing much need be added or subtracted within the starkly witty scheme. Yet we must note that epic is missing (perhaps: "eine Frau und alle Männer"), that the scheme is Romantic or post-Romantic, and that the Austro-Hungarian Empire could, for a while, assimilate anything but an epic poem. Clearly there are better schemes than Roda Roda's, and they often have the simple advantage of being tripartite. Paul Hernadi is so far the best chronicler and critic of that prevailing threefold urge.[19] He is finely aware of the trinitarian notions from Aristotle to Staiger and also of the direct criticism from the angle of Friedrich Sengle's call for a more flexible *Formenlehre* of genre theory[20] and also from the angle of Northrop Frye's exfoliating fourfold schemes. Hernadi's own attempt at synthesis (with its polarities of "action" and "vision") makes a nice place for lyric as "enacted vision" as distinct from "vision," "action," and "envisioned action"—that is, as relatively private and relatively direct in relation to the perceiver.

We might go on to say that there is a rich tension of the lyric that seems to aim at the particular or private and to involve thereby the common and universal. Yet the common and universal are not to be considered "communal" or directly shared among the "audience." In epic and drama, to varying degrees, the experience is meant to be shared in the context of a public: each person is an individual experiencer but nonetheless an experiencer as collective member of a body of experiencers (I acknowledge the awkwardness of the term). In the lyric the relation of the experiencer to the text is more direct and his relation to other experiencers is more distant: indeed, he does not feel himself to be part of an audience or public; rather, he senses an exclusiveness that constitutes only himself and the text, precisely to the exclusion of any actual shared, communal, or public experience. I do not mean to suggest that poems are not performances in some sense. I have an almost evangelical conviction that lyric poems *should*, in this lettered age, be performed, recited, or simply mouthed in private. Among the ancient Greeks and Romans, and also the Trobadors, there were recitations in public to the degree that the recitation-performance was considered the fullest mode of existence of the poem. But one can well conjecture that each member of the audience was more engaged as a person, an individual, than as a social being. The Trobadors sought public performance, yet each cherished his individuality and that of his fellow poets; everywhere these poets give credit, in the most precise terms and details, to each other's work. Naturally, in writing and publishing a poem, a poet has to go public to some extent, even the most intimate Romantic poet such as Novalis, Leopardi, or Keats (shared or even public intimacy can retain the emotion of intimacy). Still, the lyrical contract of intimacy or privacy is not necessarily broken. In the *Vita nuova*, Dante is confessional, intimate, but also testimonial, at least to his small circle of fellow poets, including his "first friend" Guido Cavalcanti, and, especially in his commentaries on his own poems, didactic and indeed rather pedantic. This early we encounter an instructive example of how intimacy or familiarity can be *cultivated* as an aesthetic means. (Any Romantic claim for an identity of intimacy and aesthetic value comes much later.) There is perhaps something adolescent about the *Vita nuova* and something deriv- ative about Dante's "hermetic" poetry: it is, along with the *stilnovisti* for the most part, in uneasy rivalry with the great Provensal example. A degree of anxiety may be present, but more likely a driving and winning desire to excel—as with such truly successful poems as "Già maï non mi conforto" of Rinaldo d'Aquino and the *ballata* "Perch'i' no spero di tornar giammai" of Guido Cavalcanti. It may well have been Dante who first in the West tried a sort of connectedness with his lyrics. Unmistakably it was Petrarch who made of that trial a form and fashion.[21] His *Canzoniere* or *Rime sparse* gave successful license to create a large, quasi-narrative, form out of single poems: *Rerum vulgarium fragmenta*, in Petrarch's own almost dismissive Latin phrase. His "fragments of a great confession" are genuinely so and must be respected as a modern turning point. His described emotions are delicate, pastel, momentary, partial—not so much *asserted* descriptions as hypotheses or tentative trials. The archaic Greeks have faded in this Petrarchan perspective, perhaps because they were almost unknown. The same is true of Catullus. Horace was prized simply in his paraenetic aspect. A novelty appears with Petrarch, one that *in execution* arouses in me only mild esteem. Yet it was Petrarch who in the West importantly and influentially affirmed the nature of lyric poetry as a configuration of sound and meter and rhythm and rime and sense. It was he who provided the examples for emulation, for spiritualization, for parody, and for copybook learning. His *Canzoniere* was an extraordinary invention and treasure-trove whose effect is, however remotely, with us still. By its brilliant and all-sufficing modernity it may well have seemed to epitomize all previous poetry. In the process it helped to obscure the aboriginal and abiding greatness of Provensal poetry and, by the same momentum, to elevate the early Italian lyric poets (with the exception of Cavalcanti) above their true measure.

Herein lies, I think, the innovative importance of Petrarch. It is significant that in a general, generic discussion of lyric poetry I should end by naming a poet whose work I do not fittingly admire. Without him could lyric poetry have had its subsequent survival into greatness with Shakespeare, Donne, Herbert, and Marvell, with Keats and Baudelaire, with Goethe and Rilke, with Laforgue, Apollinaire, Yeats, and Eliot, with Pound, Stevens, and Montale? If one were to measure the "distance" from, say, Cavafi to Celan or Merrill one would find in the calculation a sum of tradition, a persistence or carryover, a continuity that historically both emphasizes and negates the otherwise undeniable discontinuities in Western lyric poetry and theory.

Imitation, emulation, and parody, if broadly and positively conceived, are the main means of continuity and renovation in the history of lyric poetry. It is through imitation, emulation, and parody that lyric poetry changes or expands in the course of time. By imitation I mean both the fictional representation of reality (not only what is *out* there but also what is *in* there, not only external description but also internal states of mind or, simply, feelings) and the attempted close presentation of perceivably successful lyrics with diversity of subject matter and of local or "technical" effects. Parody is more of a transposition, parallel to the musical sense: a rendering, with considerable variation of tone and rhythm (or mode or simply content or subject matter) of something familiar and established; but still a rendering that emphasizes difference and strangeness and novelty. My analogy to music is perilously synaesthetic. I think of the trivial theme of Diabelli and then of Beethoven's successive variations (sober or passionate or sublime; strict and technical or even almost out of touch with the original theme). In Beethoven's *Diabelli Variations*, one may at the end return (though the score does not, as it does in Bach's *Goldberg Variations*) to the original melody and measure in it an unbelievable potency *in posse* and its distance from the great parodic variations achieved through parody. [22] Earlier I mention other instances of serious parody in literature. This is not the place even to sketch a grand theory. On a general level, a poet's *experience* of the poetry of his predecessors, along with life as a whole, is obviously crucial. It is a diffuse, seemingly casual, and idiosyncratic matter that cannot be reduced to formula or to external explanation. I prefer the awkward phrase "experience of" to the misplaced concreteness of the various reifications of the common word "influence." Emulation is the urge of a poet to make and break a tradition for his own use, that is, to draw up a practical canon for complexly personal and emotional purposes. Dante revered Arnaut Daniel for his extreme technical brilliance, but the Provensal words he puts into his mouth at the end of canto 26 of *Purgatory* are smooth and plain.

An adequate view of lyric poetry as genre must stay immanently aware of the particularities both of form (such as sound, rime, versification, and grammar) and of content (such as the rhetorical situation, use of tropes, tone, and evolution of attitude) and grant their indissolubility. As aesthetic mode the lyric is the most subjective of conventional genres. By "subjective" I mean a high degree of intimacy and sincerity, but only in the sense that those concepts are recognized as legitimately fictive and aesthetic. Naïve biographism or polygraph testing are uncalled for, and to call for them is to fail in aesthetic responsibility as optimum fictive readers. At another extreme some have argued that the first-person singular "I" in a lyric is somehow empty or depersonalized and therefore generic or universal, a mere fiction of subjectivity or even a fraud. In bad lyric poems it may indeed be so. But just as the narrator within an epic or a novel is a constituent part of the whole fiction, so in the lyric is the "I." That the lyric "I" seems more "sincere" and more directly accountable or vulnerable than the narrator in epic or novel (or indeed the moving spirit in a drama) creates a higher degree in it of intersubjectivity between text and experiencer. Yet a fictive contract between textual voice and experiencer remains fictive: the experiencer is aesthetically obliged to lend more of his subjective self to the text than in some or maybe all other genres. It is part of the experiencer's role as it is there composed within the text: the optimum reader must always take up his role as he finds it, thus becoming appropriately fictive and thus part of the fiction. Because of its intensive brevity and its marked subjectivity (in the utterly fictive sense) lyric poetry is something of a test case among genres. In it sound and sense especially interpenetrate.

Notes

1. See Bruno Snell, *Die Entdeckung des Geistes*, (Hamburg, 1946; English trans. *The Discovery of the Mind* [Cambridge: Harvard University Press, 1953]); Hermann Fränkel, *Dichtung und*

Philosophie des frühen Griechentums (1962; English trans. *Early Greek Poetry and Philosophy* [New York and London: Harcourt Brace Jovanovich, 1975]); and Albin Lesky, *Geschichte der griechischen Literatur* (1st ed. 1957; English trans. from 2d ed., *A History of Greek Literature* [London: Methuen, 1966]). An excellent, vivid, and sometimes bumptious corrective to *Geistesgeschichte* and guide to the *peculiarities* (rather than the touted universalities) of Greek literature is Charles Rowen Beye, *Ancient Greek Literature and Society*, 2d. rev. ed. (Ithaca: Cornell University Press, 1987).

2. An interesting, technical book that demonstrates the persistence of Alexandrian genre conventions into Roman practice is Francis Cairns, *Generic Composition in Greek and Roman Poetry* (Edinburgh: Edinburgh University Press, 1972). On early Greek lyric genres, see the fourth section of Carlo Odo Pavese, *Tradizioni e generi poetici della Grecia arcaica* (Rome: Edizioni dell'Ateneo, 1972).

3. Rime in classical poetry is of minimal importance. The exhaustive study of Eva H. Guggenheimer, *Rhyme Effects and Rhyming Figures: A Comparative Study of Sound Repetitions in the Classics with Emphasis on Latin Poetry* (The Hague: Mouton, 1972), is unable to show that rime was a common principle and is most useful in showing certain sound configurations. In Medieval Latin poetry there is the early and odd "Psalm against the Donatists" of Saint Augustine, then the Hibernian poetry of Gildas and Saint Columba, the poetry of Gottschalk and others in the ninth century, until the true efflorescence of rime appears in the *Cambridge Songs* and the *Carmina Burana* where, in many poems, it is fully established as an expected pattern. The relation to vernacular poetry in this respect, as in others, is mysterious. It should be noted that there is regular use of rime in Otfrid's Old High German version of the Gospels and in the Old English "Rhyming Poem"; its use seems bookish and awkward and, with all its thudding, quite unlike the later vernacular skill and variety. This is perhaps a more interesting example than the scattered use of rime in some short poems and snatches from classical and earlier medieval Latinity. Yet rime in popular formulas, proverbs, incantations, etc., seems to have been fairly common. For a good account of all this, see Hennig Brinkmann, "Der Reim im frühen Mittelalter," in his *Studien zur Geschichte der deutschen Sprache und Literatur* (Düsseldorf: Schwann, 1966), vol. 2, 58–78, which considers not only Germanic but also Latin poetry before the great flowering.

4. My inexpert impression is that Scandinavian poetry of the Elder (poetic) Edda and of the Skalds is of interest, but not of the essence here. Old English lyric poetry, by its greatness, is another matter, and I simply "bracket" it till I have a scheme that might do it some justice. See, as a broad and perhaps unequaled survey, Andreas Heusler, *Die altgermanische Dichtung* (in *Handbuch der Literaturwissenschaft*, ed. Oskar Walzel [Wildpark-Potsdam: Athenaion, 1929]). For an authoritative and up-to-date edition of some of the greatest Old English poems (datable between 665 and 1000), see John C. Pope, ed., *Seven Old English Poems* (Indianapolis: Bobbs-Merrill, 1966).

5. S. M. Stern, "Literary Connections between the Islamic World and Western Europe in the Early Middle Ages: Did They Exist?" in *Hispano-Arabic Strophic Poetry: Studies by Samuel Miklos Stern*, ed. L. P. Harvey (Oxford: Clarendon Press, 1974), 204. (Essay originally published in Italian in 1965.) Compare this opinion with the similar views of Henri-Irénée Marrou in *Les Troubadours* (Paris: Editions du Seuil, 1971). Yet now there is the erudite plea and program of María Rosa Menocal in her book *The Arabic Role in Medieval Literary History* (Philadelphia: University of Pennsylvania Press, 1987).

6. See the commentaries in Frederick Goldin, *Lyrics of the Troubadours and Trouvères: An Anthology and a History* (Garden City, N.Y.: Anchor Books, 1973)—especially in regard to Guilhem and to Bernart de Ventadorn.

7. See Linda M. Paterson, *Troubadours and Eloquence* (Oxford: Clarendon Press, 1974).

8. Leonard Forster, *The Icy Fire: Five Studies in European Petrarchism* (Cambridge: Cambridge University Press, 1969), 33.

9. The best treatment of the whole subject is E. N. Tigerstedt, *Plato's Idea of Poetical Inspiration*, in the series Commentationes Humanarum Litterarum of the Societas Scientiarum Fennica, vol. 44, no. 2 (Helsinki, 1969). (This series is sometimes found in card catalogues under the Finnish name of the Society, Suomen Tiedeseura.)

10. Croce, *Estetica* (1901; repr., Bari: Laterza, 1950): "Etera [= *hetaira*] e pedagogo, ecco le figure che (simboleggiano le due concezioni dell'arte divulgate) nell' antichità, la seconda delle quali allignò sul tronco della prima" (chap. 1 of the history part, 175).

11. See André Jolles, *Einfache Formen* (Halle: Niemeyer, 1930); Theodor Frings, *Minnesinger und Troubadours*, no. 34 of Vorträge und Schriften published by the Deutsche Akademie der Wissenschaften (DDR) (Berlin, 1949); and Leo Spitzer, "The Mozarabic Lyric and Theodor Frings' Theories," *Comparative Literature* 4 (1952), 1–22. More recently, see the enterprising book of Andrew Welsh, *Roots of the Lyric: Primitive Poetry and Modern Poetics* (Princeton: Princeton University Press, 1978).

12. See his book *The Chansons of the Troubadours and Trouvères: A Study of the Melodies and Their Relation to the Poems* (Ultrecht, 1972).

13. Lesky, *Geschichte der griechischen Literatur*, 413 in the English edition.

14. See the very suggestive article of Roman Jakobson, "Studies in Comparative Slavic Metrics," *Oxford Slavonic Papers* 3 (1952), 21–66. For multilingual metrical matters, see the collaborative volume edited by W. K. Wimsatt, *Versification: Major Language Types: Sixteen Essays* (New York: New York University Press, 1972).

15. For relatively "free" verse in the Middle Ages the great exemplars are folk verse (most often a mere supposition), Saint Jerome's quasi-metrical renderings of Hebraic verse passages in the Bible, and "new" liturgy from, say, the "Te Deum laudamus" of Nicetus of Remesiana (c. 400) to the flowering of the *sequentia* (c. 900–1200). This is a particularly interesting and unencumbered subject. The Provensal *canso* and the Italian *canzone* have their relative freedom. In more modern times the crucial configuration of influences on, say, Cowley, Novalis, Hölderlin, Christopher Smart, and Blake, would be the Bible, the liturgy, and also and *centrally* Pindar (who may not have been all that "misconstrued"), not to mention Ossian for those who read Macpherson after the craze began (1760).

16. See Lowry Nelson, Jr., "Spanish," in Wimsatt, ed., *Versification*, especially 168–69.

17. Meditation on Aristotle's seemingly arbitrary phrase could bear fruit on rereading Edward Bullough's general essay " 'Psychical Distance' as a Factor in Art and an Aesthetic Principle," which (much anthologized) first appeared in the *British Journal of Psychology* 5 (1912), 87–88.

18. To be found currently in Roda Roda, *Heiteres und Schärferes* (Vienna: Paul Zsolnay, 1969), 40.

19. Paul Hernadi, *Beyond Genre: New Directions in Literary Classification* (Ithaca: Cornell University Press, 1972).

20. See Friedrich Sengle, *Die literarische Formenlehre: Vorschläge zu ihrer Reform* (Stuttgart: J. B. Metzler, 1967; published first as an inaugural lecture in 1966). It is a vigorous polemic against the classical and Romantic and Emil Staiger's canon—all within the realm of *Germanistik*.

21. Of lyric cycles, sequences, coronas there are of course accounts for the Renaissance. A general European survey (aesthetic, historical, theoretical) is still to be written. A scattering of later names would be Rückert, Heine, Tennyson, Meredith, Rilke, Pedro Salinas, Montale, and Berryman. Discriminations naturally need to be made, but the subject is rich.

22. Fundamental in the matter of parody in my sense are Bruce W. Wardropper, *Historia de la poesía lírica a lo divino en la Cristiandad occidental* (Madrid: Revista de Occidente, 1958); and G. David Kiremidjian, "The Aesthetics of Parody," *Journal of Aesthetics and Art Criticism* 28 (1969–70), 231–42. Again, this is a topic insufficiently explored.

4

TOWARD A DEFINITION OF MYSTICAL POETRY

Though much has been written on mysticism in general, the two central questions concerning mystical poetry, its nature and its literary history, remain open. Any attempt to define the position of mystical poetry in literature is bound to be difficult, chiefly because the criterion of sincerity so often intrudes, and because tradition makes no sharp division between devotional and strictly mystical poetry. The history of mystical poetry is also vexed because of its close relation to biography and to the great quantity of mystical doctrine in the form of spiritual exercises and methods of interpretation. There is room, then, for an independent literary view that does not rest on, say, the fourfold interpretation of Scripture or on the doctrinal statements of the mystics themselves. In other words, there is a claim to be made, in the name of literary history, for mystical poetry simply as poetry. Here, then, I leave out of account the many good works on mysticism in general and on the religious significance of mystical poetry.

Literary historians must face possible alternatives that would be impertinent or unnecessary for those concerned purely with religious matters. At the very worst, for example, some apparent mystics may have deceived us

with seemingly true but false accounts. The reverse, too, is possible. It
may be that some of those who actually made the ascent were unable to
handle words persuasively. To be rigorously critical toward mystical
poetry, we must completely detach intention from performance, leaving the
first to ecclesiastical authorities as their proper concern and reserving the
second for our lay purposes. Once literary critics have asserted their rights
over the artistic works of the mystical poets they can turn to the question
of how to deal with them. There are some who sincerely feel that the critic
must temper his judgment with a reverence for the holiness of the poet
and, by extension, of his poetry. Marcelino Menéndez Pelayo, for example,
felt very reluctant to criticize the poems of Saint John of the Cross. He
confessed that he underwent a kind of "religious fear" at the thought of
"touching" them. "Through them," he wrote, "has passed the Spirit of God,
adorning and sanctifying everything."[1] But such an attitude might easily
lead to unfortunate confusion. It is implied, ever so lightly, that Saint John's
poems are props of his sanctity. It happens that he was a great poet as well
as an illustrious saint. But what about saints of perhaps even greater luster
who were mediocre or bad poets? Consider Saint Teresa, for example.

We are left, then, asking the properly literary questions. Can the word
"mystical" be used as a purely literary term? Are saints' poems a special
problem for literary criticism? More specifically, what problems of poetic
expression are involved? Or, to put it another way, is there an actual
literary mode we can call mystical? When the matter is seen in literary
dimensions, a few answers may suggest themselves.

Observing that the words "mystic" and "mystical" have had an inconclu-
sive lexicographical history, we have no choice but to start from the
beginning. Perhaps the surest way to make "mystical" a useful literary term
is to keep it from meaning the same as "religious" or "devotional" or
"meditative." If we decided to use the word "religious" to describe all
poems that have to do with the supreme supernatural, we would probably
have to admit to this category a poem like Yeats's "Sailing to Byzantium."
But its terrestrially crafted immortality, though "out of nature," hardly jibes
with the usual meaning of "religious" as relating to established cults of the
supernatural. It might, all the same, be considered simply "supernatural,"
the odd private transmutation of pantheism that it is. This suggests making
"supernatural" a capacious class of poetry, to include pantheistic and
animistic poetry, with lesser modes in, for example, strictly religious
poetry concerned with established doctrines, in ghost poems, and in
mystical poetry.

As a working definition, then, we may say that mystical poetry is supernatural, not necessarily pantheistic, animistic, or, in any strict sense, religious; and, furthermore, that it concerns union in some way with the single and transcendent supernatural. In this way we can distinguish it from special creeds and yet insist that it deals in its particular way with the supernatural. Here it could be objected that that is what mystical has always meant—descriptive of union with the divine. Yet so often the word is used, as we may see in anthologies of supposedly mystical poetry, to mean religious or devotional or philosophical or meditative or whatnot, according to the inclination of the user; traditionally it has been directly associated with particular religious doctrines.[2]

Within the bounds of a reasonably clear definition, we can make a further distinction. Conceivably and actually, there is poetry *about* the idea of having a mystical experience and there is also poetry that tries to communicate the experience itself. It is, of course, the latter sort that is most difficult to compose and discuss. At the risk of not always being able to maintain the distinction, we may try to exclude poetry about indeterminates and narrow interest only to those poems concerned with expressing a particular experience of the single and transcendent supernatural. But are not such experiences of their very nature inexpressible? There are degrees of the ineffable, but surely that kind of experience is the most ineffable thing we can impossibly imagine. Nevertheless, mystical poems, to a much greater degree than other poems, are committed to expressing the inexpressible—not in attempting to express what is almost inexpressible or expressible only with great difficulty or some colloquial *je ne sais quoi*, but what will always be unyielding to expression. Is this not, then, merely a flat paradox? Without qualification it certainly is. Nevertheless, poetry (not to say language) has at its command powerful means for characterizing a great range of indeterminate experience. All those means might be put under the paradoxical but useful heading of the rhetoric of the ineffable.

Whenever the natural and supernatural meet, they are bound to generate paradox. Even the mystical poets cannot free themselves of the natural dimensions of time and space. When they attempt to express their ecstasies they are encumbered, like the rest of poets, with earthbound words. Any adequate account of their experiences would, of course, be impossible. Their only recourse is to describe what led up to the ineffable experience and what followed it, in an attempt to show in what degree or in what way it was ineffable. The whole range of possible expression teems with paradoxes, all of which might be succinctly stated as universal but poetically deflationary commonplaces. Yet flat paradox in a poem is worse. Merely to say, as does Saint Teresa, "Que muero porque no muero" (I die because I do not die), and to gloss the paradox with others of the same sort, accomplishes little poetically; in fact, one could say that it wastes a great deal because it throws away far too soon the poem's chances. In all poetry that uses paradox the poet's main skill consists in keeping the members of the paradox from collapsing together. Had Milton, for example, said at an early point in "Lycidas" that the hero rises *because* he sinks, or had he failed within the poem to keep in suspense his hero's ultimate fate, we would have reason to call the poem a failure. In particular, mystical poetry is fraught with a basic paradox—the impossibility of expression and, though doomed to fail, the attempt at it. One of the richest recourses of mystical poetry is the power generated by that paradox.

Before considering poems that seem to be mystical in a restrictive sense, we may profitably consider why familiar poems like "Lycidas" and *Paradise Lost* are not. "Lycidas" deals with a supernatural reality and turns upon a paradox resulting from the conjunction of the human and the divine. Yet it is not concerned with a direct experience of the divine vision. The ultimate goal of the poem, as it turns out, is the vision of Lycidas in a rather conventionally bucolic Heaven. For the most part, transcendence and ineffability are assumed in the allegorical frame. The same is largely true of *Paradise Lost*. In scattered places, especially just before the battle in Heaven, the reader is made aware that the actual events were unspeakably different from the descriptions in human language. Yet the poem as a whole deals with explicit relations between man and his anthropomorphized God; little is made of the ineffable divine vision. There is nothing new in saying that Milton did not write mystical poetry; nor is this anything to his discredit. His great work may here be taken simply as a familiar point of reference.

In a few poems of the Middle Ages and, of course, in Dante, to some degree, and certainly in Saint John of the Cross, one finds true examples of mystical poetry. It should be said at once that most if not all of the great medieval hymns are not unfairly characterized as doctrinal or meditative poems: for instance, Saint Thomas Aquinas's hymn "Pange, lingua."[3] It expounds the doctrine of transubstantiation without focusing on the actual mystical experience. We are simply told,

> Verbum caro panem verum
>   verbo carnem efficit,
> fitque sanguis Christi merum . . .

(The Word made flesh by a word makes of the flesh true bread and the blood of Christ becomes wine . . .)

Saint Thomas makes little attempt to capture *poetic* faith in the mystery of the Eucharist. His interest is confined to the religious dogma. If perception should falter, the good Christian can draw his full conviction from religious faith:

> . . . et, si sensus deficit,
> ad firmandum cor sincerum
> sola fides sufficit.

(. . . and, if understanding fails, faith alone suffices to strengthen the sincere heart.)

It is not, then, among the hymns, but rather, so it would seem, mostly among those poems based on the Song of Songs, that one finds examples approaching mystical poetry in a restrictive sense.

A good example of a mystical poem derived from the Song of Songs is the one formerly attributed to Saint Peter Damian, "Quis est hic qui pulsat ad ostium."[4] It can most accurately be described as a poem about the near failure of the mystical experience. In all respects it follows closely the account in the Song of Songs, of the Lover's night visit and His unexpected disappearance. The traditional interpretation of the Song of Songs as a dialogue between Christ and the Christian soul is, of course, assumed. Christ, the Lover, announces himself in unmistakable terms:

> Ego sum summi regis filius,
> primus et novissimus . . .

(I am the Son of the highest King, first and last . . .)

As in the Song of Songs, the Beloved is not quick enough in answering His summons to open the door, and finds Him gone. Yet here the poet's resolution is significantly different from his source. (In a sense the poem represents an intermediate stage between the Song of Songs and Saint John's "Noche oscura.") In the Bible we read that the Beloved is, at least for a time, unsuccessful in finding the Lover. While she is wandering about in search of Him, she encounters the city guard:

> Invenerunt me custodes qui circumeunt civitatem;
> percusserunt me, et vulneraverunt me.
> Tulerunt pallium meum mihi custodes murorum.[5]

Later she finds him again and they lovingly commune. But in the poem the city guards grant her the means of keeping faith even in the failure of full mystical union.

> Vigiles urbs invenerunt me,
> exspoliaverunt me,
> abstulerunt et dederunt pallium,
> cantaverunt mihi novum canticum
> quo in regis inducar palatium.

> (The city watchmen found me, they stripped me, they took away my cloak and gave me one, they sang me a new canticle wherewith I shall be let in to the King's palace.)

In effect, they have turned into angels or ministers of God; they are no longer despoilers but rather purifiers and bringers of glad tidings that tell of future bliss.

What one misses in this poem is any explicit concern for the ineffable. There was, of course, no lack of means to express transfinite experience. The tradition of sacred theology and also the common stock of indeterminate expressions in any language would have supplied the need. In fact, it is possible to gather from Medieval Latin poetry a great variety of such words and phrases.[6] As an example of a poem that makes full use of linguistic means available to mystic poets, we may look at the anonymous sequence, "Dulcis Jesu memoria."[7] To begin with, it makes striking use of superlative expressions, both compared,

> Amor Jesu dulcissimus
> et vere suavissimus,

and relatively incomparable,

> plus millies gratissimus
> quam dicere sufficimus.

(The love of Jesus is sweetest and truly pleasantest, and welcomest a thousandfold more than we are capable of saying.)

And at several other points the poem transcends the comparable and reaches the absolute nonpareil:

> [Jesus] excedit omne gaudium
> et omne desiderium.
>
> Nec lingua potest dicere,
> nec littera exprimere . . .

([Jesus] exceeds all joy and all desire. The tongue cannot say nor the letter express . . .)

Furthermore, we find ourselves, as readers, committed to paradoxes, as the poet strains to enhance his expression of God's love. Though he is unworthy to speak, yet he will not keep silence. Jesus' love fills though it does not sate, yet the desire for more cannot be satisfied:

> qui te gustant, esuriunt;
> qui bibunt, adhuc sitiunt . . .

(Those who taste You are hungry; those who drink You are still thirsty . . .)

Here we have a not unfamiliar paradox; its use, along with other means, serves the poet's elaborate attempt to give an inkling of the experience of God's infinite love. This paradox, however, is supplanted by an even greater one—the endless desire for God's love will be satisfied, at least as far as our earthly minds can imagine, in the fullest mystical experience or in Heaven.

> Quem tuus amor debriat
> novit quid Jesus sapiat;
> felix gustus quem satiat,
> non est quod ultra cupiat.

(The one whom Your love inebriates knows the taste of Jesus; for the one whom blessed taste satisfies there is nothing more that he might desire.)

In a number of ways, then, the poet makes his readers vividly aware of the "incomprehensa bonitas" of God and of that experience of God's peace "quae omnem sensum superat." By a careful and culminating use of enhancements leading to inexpressibility, he approaches the ineffable ecstasy where any sort of communication ceases to avail.

More than anywhere else in the Middle Ages, one finds supreme mystical passages in Dante's *Commedia*. Whether the poem is viewed as the journey of someone called Dante or of the human soul in general, the goal remains the same: the constant direction of the journey, at least cosmographically, is up toward the direct vision of God. That the way seems at first to lead *down* into Hell does not alter the case. It is possible to conceive that the low point, the point farthest from Paradise along the route that must be taken, is the "dark wood," and that the descent into Hell really moves, in terms of both the "actual" and the spiritual journey, upward to God. In saying so, of course, one must simplify, but it is not just a manner of speaking; in Dante's cosmography it can be seen to work out that way. In fact, the itinerary is so concrete in detail that we need to be reminded now and then that the description of it does not in any way exhaust whatever the reality is. Yet it is that very concreteness of detail that commands our belief or suspension of disbelief from the very beginning of the journey and leads us plausibly up the reaches of Paradise itself to confront the supreme vision.

When we arrive at the very moment Dante is to achieve the vision of God, the poet uses a further strategem which seems so natural that even perhaps in spite of ourselves we readily lend poetic credence:

> Bernardo m'accennava, e sorridea,
>   Perch'io guardassi suso; ma io era,
>   Già per me stesso tal qual ei volea . . .

What we might have thought would be the center of description, what is really the goal of the poem, namely, the moment of vision, is suddenly and serenely assumed. The crucial word is *già*: already the gazing soul is losing itself in the divine.

> Chè la mia vista, venendo sincera,
>   E più e più intrava per lo raggio
>   De l'alta Luce, che da sè è vera.[8]

(Bernard was motioning to me and smiling that I should look up; but I was, all by myself, already just as he wished: for my eyesight, becoming pure, penetrated more and more into the ray of lofty light that of itself is true.)

Once we learn that the soul has at last reached the mystic vision, we are prepared to lend our sympathies to the succession of psychologically acute similes that aim at describing the indescribable.

Before considering Dante's use of simile, let us look at another mystical poem of central importance, the "Noche oscura" of Saint John of the Cross. At the risk of comparing disparates, we should note the simple fact that both the *Commedia* and the "Noche oscura" are journeys; in effect, therefore, they are preparations for the ultimate arrival. On one level of meaning, namely, the imaginative fiction we acquiesce in as willing readers, they are spatial journeys of the narrator; on another level, of course, they are spiritual journeys of the particular soul; and, on still another, they are spiritual journeys of the human soul in general. All three levels must be kept in mind at the same time because, from the point of view of the reader, they depend upon each other. "Dark night" must not be taken merely as another way of saying "receptive condition of the soul"; it is certainly that, but it is also an ordinary dark night on which extraordinary things occur.

In fact, as I have suggested in regard to Dante, a powerful means of commanding the reader's belief is to prepare for the supernatural with the most natural-seeming detail. "On a dark night," to paraphrase the narrator of the poem, "I waited till my house was quiet. Then I went out unnoticed, leaving in disguise by the secret stairs." So far the first two stanzas. Their cryptic joy ("¡oh dichosa ventura!") already leads us to expect something unusual. Our expectations increase when we read of the light that was burning in the heart of the narrator, a light surer than the light of midday.

> Aquésta me guiaba
> Más cierto que la luz del mediodía
> a donde me esperaba
> quien yo bien me sabía,
> en parte donde nadie parecía. [9]

(That [light] was guiding me more surely than the light of midday to where he whom I well knew was awaiting me in a place where no one was present.)

The tense, properly imperfect, is quite important; for in the very next stanza the narrator pauses, so to speak, to apostrophize, in the preterite, the night which made possible the secret journey.

> ¡Oh noche que guiaste!
> ¡oh noche amable más que el alborada!,
> ¡oh noche que juntaste
> amado con amada,
> amada en el amado transformada!

(O night that led me! O night more lovable than the dawn! O night that joined the beloved with the loved, the loved transformed in the beloved!)

There was already a hint that the goal of the journey was some "person"; and now we discover that it was the Lover, whom we know from the tradition of the poem to be Christ. But we discover it almost by accident—it seems almost to slip out in the apostrophe. And when we return to the running narrative of the poem, the meeting, the unimaginable moment, is assumed and taken for granted.

> En mi pecho florido,
> que entero para él solo se guardaba,
> allí quedó dormido . . .

(On my flowered breast, that was kept intact for Him alone, He there remained sleeping . . .)

The effect of changing tenses is almost equivalent to Dante's *già*. Again it is a way of leading up to and beyond the supreme moment, without doing violence to the multiple levels on which the poem moves and without straining our credulity with useless detail. As we can readily see, the levels of meaning in the poem are self-consistent and mutually helpful. In most obvious terms, the simple level of the journey helps to ease us gradually into the supernatural; and the levels of the supernatural provide the simple narrative of a lovers' meeting with all its mystical significance.

Dante's *Commedia* and Saint John's "Noche oscura" illustrate a resource of mystical poetry: the use of natural or plausible situations leading directly, with as little abruptness as possible, into some expression of the ineffable experience itself. In both instances, the first moment of vision or ecstasy is passed over so easily that the reader finds himself, almost before he knows it, accepting the reality of the experience and committed to trying, through the poet's skill, to comprehend it in figured language. Once having got the reader to accept the fact of the mystical experience, the poet must give some account of what it was *like*.

Saint John, for instance, ends his poem with images, in climactic order, of repose, unconsciousness, and oblivion. First we are presented with the tranquil scene of the Lover asleep on the "flowered breast" of the beloved, and we are presented with it as an accomplished fact. Then, ever so gradually, in a progressive past tense, the wind from the rampart wounded the beloved's neck, suspending all sensation.

> El aire del almena,
> cuando yo sus cabellos esparcía,
> con su mano serena
> en mi cuello hería
> y todos mis sentidos suspendía.[10]

In passing one notes how delicately St. John etherializes the biblical text: "percusserunt me, et vulneraverunt me. / Tulerunt pallium meum mihi custodes murorum."[11] Now, finally, in the preterite, everything ceased and the beloved left all care forgotten among the lilies.

> Quedéme y olvidéme,
> el rostro recliné sobre el amado,
> cesó todo, y dejéme,
> dejando mi cuidado
> entre las azucenas olvidado.

(The air from the rampart, as I was ruffling his hair, with its serene hand was wounding my neck and suspending all my senses. I stayed quiet and forgetful of myself, I rested my face on the Beloved; everything stopped and I left myself, leaving my care forgotten among the lilies.)

All the while we are mounting from one familiar lapse of ordinary perception to another, until we reach indeterminacy. In the end the ineffable remains, of course, unsaid, though we have a much clearer idea than before of its actual place.

Dante, in his use of figures, struggles more with memory than Saint John, and is able to command perhaps even more poetic plausibility. Not only does language falter, but also memory, and Dante is movingly explicit. The Dante of the poem feels like someone recalling only the emotion of a dream and nothing of the events in it.

> Da quinci innanzi il mio veder fu maggio
> > Che 'l parlar nostro, cha'a tal vista cede;
> > E cede la memoria a tanto oltraggio.
> Qual è colui che somniando vede,
> > E dopo il sogno la passione impressa
> > Rimane, e l'altro a la mente non riede,
> Cotal son io . . .

(From then on, my seeing was greater than our speech that gives way to such sight; and memory gives way to such excess. Like him who sees while dreaming, and after the dream the emotion impressed remains and the rest does not return to mind, such am I . . .)

Figure upon figure stresses the failure of memory to which we are all bound. Even what we can remember remains inarticulate through the relative inadequacy of language. There is nothing radically new in Dante's using such means, but there is in the way he uses them. They are all, as it were, raised to the higher power by the physically precise way the final vision is described. Its actual shape is quite clear: it was a "living ray" of light. In a sense, then, it is not indeterminate. After all, Dante enumerates what he saw in it.

> Nel suo profondo vidi che s' interna
> > Legato con amore in un volume,
> > Ciò che per l'universo si squaderna:
> Sustanze e accidenti e lor costume,
> > Quasi conflati insieme per tal modo
> > Che ciò ch' i' dico è un semplice lume.
> La forma universal di questo nodo
> > Credo ch' i' vidi, perchè più di largo,
> > Dicendo questo, mi sento chi' i' godo

(In its depths I saw that what is scattered pages through the universe gathers bound in one volume: substances and accidents and their mode as conflated in such a way that what I mention is a mere gleam. I believe that I saw the universal form of this conjunction, since all the more, in saying this, do I feel that I rejoice.)

We are lured into accepting it; we find ourselves getting in deeper, and finally committed, along with the poet and his visionary, to the impossible task of expressing the inexpressible. That must remain the mystical poet's final success.

Such a poem as Keats's "Ode to a Nightingale" might, if seen from the Christian tradition, be considered an instance of "secular" mystical poetry. Yet with the definition set forth here there is no reason to attach a further qualifier; it can be shown to fit a conception of mystical poetry in general. What similarities are there between the poem of Keats, on the one hand, and those of Dante and Saint John, on the other? They can, of course, be seen best as they gradually evolve in Keats's poem. At the beginning, the speaker of the poem finds himself in a state receptive to whatever the bird may induce in him; it is a state that "aches" and "pains" and "sinks," and yet, he tells the bird,

> 'Tis not through envy of thy happy lot,
> But being too happy in thy happiness.

Pain, then, is as elsewhere in mystical poetry the consequence of an excess of pleasure or desire. Indeed, by reason of that very synaesthesia, union with the supernatural is craved all the more. Because divine grace can hardly be invoked, the speaker must look for other means of transport. At first "a draught of vintage," enhanced by all the evocative power of its origin, seems the readiest way: it would not be the well water of the Muses but rather "the *true*, the blushful Hippocrene." It should work, says the speaker, to the effect

> That I might drink, and leave the world unseen,
> And with thee fade away into the forest dim:
> Fade far away, dissolve, and quite forget
> What thou among the leaves hast never known . . .

Yet in the process of describing from what cares he would then be unburdened, the poet feels strong enough in his craft of the imagination to reject the transport of wine and turn almost peremptorily to poetry.

> Away! away! for I will fly to thee,
> Not charioted by Bacchus and his pards,
> But on the viewless wings of Poesy,
> Though the dull brain perplexes and retards.

That, at least for the moment, seems the true and direct means. Indeed, while the reader is reflecting on the "dull brain," the appearance of union has been achieved: "Already with thee!" is the sudden and cryptic way it is expressed; we recall Dante's and Saint John's means. Because the moment is reached through nature, it is appropriate that, to use Wordsworth's word, all her "Presences" should conspire to fulfill the experience:

> tender is the night,
> And haply the Queen-Moon is on her throne,
> Cluster'd around by all her starry Fays;
> But here there is no light,
> Save what from heaven is with the breezes blown
> Through verdurous glooms and winding mossy ways.

It is quite unnecessary that there be moonlight to know that the "Queen-Moon is on her throne"; it is, in fact, more fitting that the only light that illuminates this mystical experience is blown with the breezes from heaven. Here we have a new version of the "noche oscura." It is, of course, quite distinct from Saint John's—fundamentally because Keats, like other Romantics, has chosen to achieve the mystical vision not by a detachment from all created things but actually through nature. Yet, at the same time, the senses subject us to the flux of sublunary nature and thereby impede our ascent. This is the basic paradox in spite of which the attempt is made. The poet moves toward a resolution of the dilemma by eliminating all the senses except smell and hearing. In the moment of ecstasy, the poet says,

> I cannot see what flowers are at my feet,
> Nor what soft incense hangs upon the boughs,
> But, in embalmed darkness, guess each sweet . . .

From his height of ecstasy, the speaker of the poem is driven to the thought of eternal consummation, which seems now possible only by the dissolution of the senses, by death. He has been at other times "half in love with easeful Death," and

> Now more than ever seems it rich to die,
> To cease upon the midnight with no pain,
>> While thou art pouring forth thy soul abroad
>> In such an ecstasy!

Indeed, the Romantic paradox of perceiving the mystical vision sensuously in nature seems soluble only in death.

Yet even that desperate means defeats itself:

> Still wouldst thou sing, and I have ears in vain—
> To thy high requiem become a sod.

At this impasse the poet shifts ground; though eternal consummation is not possible for the speaker, at least the bird and its song are immortal. Not only did ruler and peasant, and perhaps Ruth, hear the "self-same song," but it is also

> The same that oft-times hath
> Charm'd magic casements, opening on the foam
> Of perilous seas, in faery lands forlorn.

So the speaker's wide-ranging attempts to prolong the ecstasy, having led to the final frustration of death, gradually focus on the permanence, independent of the speaker, of the immortal and ecstatic song of the bird, and that permanence is seen reflected in the continuity of human experience. Still, the speaker's efforts are, after all, directed toward something easily lost, which is, indeed, "forlorn." The word itself forces the realization, as the poet is suspended between two "realities," that it is the mystical experience which is being lost as the bird's song recedes.

> Forlorn! the very word is like a bell
> To toll me back from thee to my sole self!

There is no other course than for the poet to return from being "already with" the bird to his "sole self." "Fancy" cannot sustain the moment beyond the actuality of the bird's song. Still, we are not set down with a jolt. As the "plaintive anthem fades," we, along with the poet, are left in a state of suspension.

> Was it a vision, or a waking dream?
> Fled is that music:—Do I wake or sleep?

Now that it has just ceased, the poet is not sure what the true nature of his experience was. His uncertainty and his hesitation between two realities enhance the depth of the experience he has just had. Here Keats is able to reap the advantage of setting his poem in the momentaneous present. We follow the narrative as if it were happening now for the first time. After we, as readers, have experienced each emotion in succession, we must ask ourselves the same questions and find that they cast backward a further enhancement of what we have just undergone in reading the poem. These final questions, then, stress the ineffability of the experience. Was it exactly as we thought the speaker described it? Or was it finally beyond description?

By such means Keats, like Dante and Saint John, is able to present a mystical experience, while at the same time demonstrating the final impossibility of expressing it. Keats's practice bears still other resemblances to Dante and Saint John. We have noticed his concern with connection between pleasure and pain (in the broadest psychological sense of those words), and especially with emotional states in which both sensations are intermingled. Even in Dante the aura of pain around human pleasure is not absent.

> Io credo, per l' acume ch' io soffersi
> Del vivo raggio, ch' i' sarei smarrito,
> Se li occhi miei da lui fossero aversi.

(Because of the sharpness of the living ray that I endured, I believe I would have been lost if my eyes had turned away from it.)

Here the range of meaning, with its Latinate basis, goes from "because of the sting I suffered" to "because of the keenness I sustained," and there is no reason why we should not encompass it all. Again, Dante says that at the moment of vision "la mia mente fu percossa / Da un fulgore . . ." (My mind was struck by a bolt . . .). This we may take as another such utterance whose force draws on both literal and metaphorical meaning. As for Saint John, we have already seen to what use he, following biblical precedent, has put the association of pleasure and pain. We find it not only in the "Noche oscura" but also in numerous other places in his poetry. In the "Cántico espiritual" the "bride" is wounded by the "Bridegroom" ("Como el ciervo huiste, / habiéndome herido"). Even the Bridegroom is Himself wounded ("Vuélvete, paloma, / que el ciervo vulnerado . . ."). In the "Llama de amor viva," love, mystical love, is actually called a wound: "¡oh regalada llaga!"

Thus, although Keats's association of pleasure and pain has its own peculiarities of time and place, it can be seen as conforming in its use to the practice of earlier mystical poets. Perhaps one reason it has greater importance in Keats's poetry than in the other poems discussed is that he cannot allow himself, as enhancements, Saint John's suspension of sensation or Dante's struggle with memory. In the first instance it is because he tries to achieve mystical union through the senses; in the second it is because his poem is a momentaneous present-tense record in which gradual perception, rather than memory, is the prime faculty.

No one would readily question that Dante and Saint John are mystical poets. It may seem as if we had ended up where we started. Yet along the way allegiance to special creeds has been abandoned; furthermore, some of the purely literary problems the mystical poet and the critic of his poetry face have been explored. Keats has stood as the instance of completely nonreligious mystical poetry. In a full survey of a duly secularized mystical poetry, then, one would have to consider such disparate poets as Henry Vaughan, Andreas Gryphius, William Wordsworth, T. S. Eliot, and Rainer Maria Rilke. There would be many marginal cases, and, in the end, probably few poems might be allowed. We can, nevertheless, rely on the centrally mystical poems, several of which have been discussed, to keep our attention on essentials. It is from them that one would draw matter for a rhetoric of the ineffable. In that rhetoric the first and most elementary paragraph should be devoted, as here, to such familiar enhancement as "I can't possibly do it justice." The next step would lead to the kind of explicit statement that affirms the impossibility of speaking about the supernatural in human terms—variations on Dante's phrase, "Transumanar significar *per verba* / Non si poria . . ." (to signify through words transcending the human would not be possible . . .). One might then consider straightforward attempts to deal with the ineffable by means of allegory. Beyond that there are such means as locating the inexpressible by a series of "near misses," and unexpectedly assuming the unimaginable. Finally there are the images and symbols and allusions. The deeper one goes, of course, the more first notions need revision. We would remind ourselves that the many mysteries (in the technical theological sense), however familiar they become, will in the end remain mysterious. We would always run the risk of confusing our sympathies with our literary judgment. Certainly we would remember that in literary terms the marvel is not that poets should have mystical experiences but that they should choose to try to give them metrical expression. I presume to share the skepticism of Federico García Lorca. "I do not believe," he wrote, "that any great artist works in a state of fever. Even the mystics work when the ineffable dove of the Holy Spirit is already leaving their cells and losing itself among the clouds."[12]

Notes

1. "La poesía mística en España," *Estudios y discursos de crítica histórica y literaria,* vol. 1 (Santander: Consejo Superior de Investigaciones Científicas, 1941), 97. Menéndez Pelayo does go on to consider Saint John's poetry in general, but always at a distance and with the conviction that "no es lícito dudar que el Espíritu Santo regía y gobernaba la pluma del escritor" (99).

2. See, for example, D. H. S. Nicholson and A. H. E. Lee, *The Oxford Book of English Mystical Verse* (Oxford: Clarendon Press, 1917), and *Poetas místicos españoles,* ed. Juan Gil-Albert (Mexico City: Mensaje, 1942).

3. *The Oxford Book of Medieval Latin Verse,* ed. F. J. E. Raby (Oxford: Clarendon Press, 1959), 401–2.

4. I use the graphic arrangement of Stephen Gaselee in his still sound anthology, also entitled *The Oxford Book of Medieval Latin Verse* (Oxford: Clarendon Press, 1928); see also the metrical arrangement in F. J. E. Raby, *A History of Christian-Latin Poetry,* 2d ed. (Oxford: Clarendon Press, 1953), 254–55, and in his version of *The Oxford Book of Medieval Latin Verse* (Oxford: Clarendon Press, 1959), 158.

5. Canticum canticorum, 5:7; see 3:3. The Biblia Complutensis does not differ in any significant way from this, the current text of the Vulgate.

6. It would be instructive to follow the history of such post-Augustan or postclassical formations as *ineffabilis, inenuntiabilis, inenarrabilis,* etc.; see Alexander Souter, *A Glossary of Later Latin to 600 A.D.* (Oxford: Clarendon Press, 1949).

7. Text in Gaselee, *Oxford Book of Medieval Latin Verse,* 111–17; see also his note on the text, 228–29. The same text with minor spelling variations is in Raby, *The Oxford Book of Medieval Latin Verse,* 347–53. Complexities of the textual history are discussed in André Wilmart, *Le "Jubilus" dit de Saint Bernard* (Rome: Edizioni di Storia e Letteratura, 1944).

8. All citations of Dante are taken from the text of C. H. Grandgent, rev. ed. (Boston: Heath, 1933). They are all from canto 33, *Paradiso.*

9. All citations are from the text of Dámaso Alonso, *La poesía de San Juan de la Cruz* (Madrid: Aguilar, 1946), 296–97.

10. In some manuscripts one finds *ya* instead of *yo* in the second line of this stanza; see *Obras de San Juan de la Cruz*, ed. P. Silverio de Santa Teresa (Burgos, 1929), vol. 2, 5n.

11. We have already seen how in the pseudo-Damian poem this cryptic and violent detail is turned to account. Saint John seems to combine the violence here with a suggestion from another passage of the Song of Songs, 4:9 ("Vulnerasti cor meum, soror mea, sponsa; / vulnerasti cor meum in uno oculorum, / et in uno crine colli tui"), and attribute the action to the Lover. At all events, the image becomes an objective correlative of mystical ecstasy.

12. "La imagen poética en Don Luis de Góngora," *Obras completas*, ed. Arturo del Hoyo (Madrid, 1954), 80–81. "No creo que ningún gran artista trabaje en estado de fiebre. Aun los místicos, trabajan cuando ya la inefable paloma del Espíritu Santo abandona sus celdas y se va perdiendo por las nubes."

5

CONDITIONS
OF
EARLY PROVENSAL
POETRY

Some common, mostly erroneous, notions of Old Provensal poetry and of the Middle Ages in general may preemptively be strung together by way of straightfaced parody.

Medieval European society was structured rigidly in a system we call feudal. Great lords of various ranks received their status and their possessions from the king, swore allegiance to him, and did him homage; they were obliged to do military service at his command and they transmitted their rights, possessions, and obligations to their eldest sons according to primogeniture. In turn lesser nobles were likewise bound to their lords. At the bottom, serfs or *vilains* were bound to the soil and treated as chattels *ad glaebam adjecti*. Feudalism permeated all aspects of life. Meanwhile the bourgeoisie not only was forming but had begun to *rise*. Clerics were the custodians of culture, such as it was, and wrote in Latin not only religious tracts but also hymns and, scandalously, secular poems with an amorous or satiric bent. Quite early and suddenly, so it would seem, Trobadors in the southern part of France around Provence began to write lyric poems about love that had a tremendous vogue and that were so unexpected that they must have come from somewhere else—from Latin hymn-writing, from Arabic poetry as practiced in Moslem Spain under the influence of Sufi mysticism, or from folk-singing in proto-Romance. These Trobadors or joglars roamed from castle to castle performing their songs in great royal or seigneurial halls hung with tapestries and warmed by blazing fireplaces, accompanied of course by consorts of ancient instruments and backup singers. Somehow they invented for the first time romantic love whose rules were conveniently codified in the later twelfth century by Andreas Capellanus at the court of Marie of Champagne, daughter of Eleanor of Aquitaine, granddaughter of the supposed first Trobador, William of Poitiers. This love was sexual, preferably adulterous, and secret—carried on between great ladies and landless younger sons of the nobility. It was also feudal in concept with the lady as lord and the lover as vassal. Conflicts between lovers were settled by courts of love originated by Marie at Troyes, the capital of the county of Champagne, and by Queen Eleanor, her mother, who though married (after the annulment with Louis VII) to Henry II of England, held court in Poitiers. Actually, romantic love took shape in the tale concerning Lancelot and Guinevere (*Le conte de la charrette*) written by Chrétien de Troyes, Marie's court poet, who got it from the Celtic bards. The joyous celebration of the natural world and the flesh, the ennobling ideals of courtesy and secular human worth and freedom—which constitute a whole civilization—were brought to an end by the religious bigotry and persecution manifested in the Albigensian Crusades and the Inquisition.

I could go on in this vein, but I pause to say that nothing I have said so far is wholly true. What I have done is simply string together some of the clichés that, despite canny modification and revision here and there, continue to haunt accounts of early Provensal poetry. These clichés are unsound answers to such questions as these: How did the vernacular lyric arise? What were its relations to contemporary society? Why did it deal as it did with romantic love or sexual passion? If its first idiom was in fact the Provensal language, why should it have come about in southern France?

It is useful to rehearse some basic matters. Old Provensal is a fairly homogenous language which was probably intelligible to alert speakers of Old French and Early Italian. Its closest relative, however, is Catalonian. There is good reason to call the language Occitanian, referring to the word for "yes"—*oc*. It was Dante in the *De vulgari eloquentia* (c. 1304) who first distinguished the major branches of what we call the Romance languages according to their words for "yes"—*si, oïl,* and *oc.* That he called the

"Occitanians" *Hispani* shows in a way the limits of his knowledge but also the shrewd recognition of Provensal as a distinct and illustrious language. Indeed for Dante and his contemporaries—as later for Petrarch and the whole subsequent European lyric—Provensal was, both directly and indirectly, the great original, the model, the treasure-trove for their own poetic practice. As Dante well knew, the geographic extent of Provensal as a literary language reached from Poitiers to Pamplona and from Bordeaux to Genoa, a region of perhaps 70,000 square miles—larger than all of England and Wales combined. In time the writing of successful poetry in Old Provensal extended from the end of the eleventh century to the end of the thirteenth, some two hundred years. And Dante himself, in piety and homage, wrote eight lines of Provensal *terza rima* as Arnaut Daniel's moving speech in canto 26 of the *Purgatorio* (c. 1315). In bulk, what survive are 2,542 compositions by some 350 poets known by name as well as others accidentally anonymous. The poems observed various line-lengths according to syllabic count and most often were organized into stanzas according to various patterns of rime—producing by permutation and combination almost 1000 extant strophic forms. Besides, 256 melodies have survived and it is assumed that all the poems were, in performance, sung. Finally, biographies (sometimes a sentence or two, often much longer) survive of 101 Trobadors (in one or more versions), not to mention about 60 summaries of poems called *razos*. Quite apart from the many considerations of quality, attribution, historical accuracy of the *vidas*, and other matters, this is an impressive body of poetry and poetic tradition. If one considers its inventiveness and its numerous works of genius, one may rightly acknowledge it as a very high achievement in the history of the Western lyric. There are in fact just three other rather short and discontinuous epochs of great lyric in the West before Provensal: Archaic Greece, Alexandria, and Rome. The subsequent great epochs—Old French, Middle High German and Early Italian, the Renaissance, the Baroque, Romanticism, symbolism, and modernism—form a more contin-uous sequence that is dependent in myriad varying ways on those four great originals. (In this scheme I leave out of account Old English, Old Norse, and Celtic poetry, partly for lack of competence but mostly because they lie outside the mainstream of European lyric.)

Having taken a measure of the gross dimensions of the phenomenon of Provensal lyric we can hardly avoid the question, Where did it come from? Because it so suddenly springs to knowledge with the skilled and seemingly unexampled work of Guilhem (William), seventh count of Poitiers and ninth

duke of Aquitaine (1071-1126), we may rephrase the question: Where did
he get it from? Answers are ready to hand, and the answerers many and
insistent: it comes from the Arabs by way of Spain; it derives from Latin
hymn and chant; it bubbles into literacy from immemorial folk tradition; it
was invented by someone earlier or perhaps by a guild or a committee. Or,
to take another tack, it came about because of feudalism or urbanization or
courtliness or the bourgeoisie. But all these questions and the mode of their
asking seem to suppose a cause as explanation and also to imply the
possibility of indefinite regress (what is the cause of that cause?). In this
sort of discourse, the word "origin" is practically synonymous with "cause,"
though not so much in fashion now, perhaps because of the association with
a naïve positivistic evolutionism that long dominated historiography. Doubtless there are sufficient and even necessary causes adducible in some
aspects of history, but literary history is an especially difficult arena in
which to vindicate such a notion. Rather than seek causes or origins, I think
it more useful to try to determine conditions or circumstances, indeed to
adduce a *set* of conditions whose assembly may plausibly account for or
partially yet significantly explain or at least somehow illuminate the
existence, from around 1100, of Old Provensal poetry. I shall list and
characterize some such conditions, but first I must earnestly question here
the "Arabic explanation" and invoke the words of the late S. M. Stern who
did so much to discover and analyze the Arabic and Hebrew *muwaššahat*
with proto-Hispanic refrains—which some hailed as the missing link
without asking where the Arabs got it (distant mysterious Baghdad
perhaps). He wrote in 1965: "I am strongly inclined to think that the
majority of the proofs adduced in order to demonstrate that Western poets
and Western writers at the beginning [*sic*] of the Middle Ages had
knowledge of Arabic poetry or other forms of Arabic literature, and that
they made use of their knowledge in their works, are lacking in validity."[1]

   At the same time those refrains would seem to indicate the presence,
among the Christian Romance-speaking inhabitants of Spain, of informal
folk poetry, and the bilingual poems themselves demonstrate once again
Américo Castro's argument that seven hundred years of Moslem and
Jewish presence in Spain constitute not so much a *reconquista* as a
convivencia.[2] There are elsewhere indications that unrecorded folk poetry
existed in Romance and Germanic lands, though it is precisely my intent to
avoid discussing once again Caedmon's hymn and the bilingual *alba*. Even
the scattered lyrics in Latin over the several centuries before the twelfth
might be seen as suggestive tokens of a persistent habit. The prestige of

poetry over prose certainly prevailed among the literate clerics. Here then is one condition: the presence, whether literate or oral, of the habit and potential of measured language, of poetic numbers.

I would see another condition in the way society in the South of what is now France (the region called Proensa by its inhabitants) was in the process of constituting itself. My impression is that outside the undergraduate classroom so-called feudalism is becoming less and less an explanatory label and less and less the designation of a rigid code and social structure. One must ever more carefully differentiate not only among epochs but also among regions. This is no news to currently informed historians: what I would strongly stress is that in Proensa of the eleventh and twelfth centuries political and social organization was far less rigid, conventionalized, and centralized than in the North. To begin with, the "majority of the knights [*milites*] were free, but they were not noble," and they were not generally considered noble till the late twelfth and the early thirteenth century.[3] On the other hand there were the true nobles, the counts and viscounts and dukes who constituted a class but who did not necessarily pass on their holdings and titles to their eldest sons. Only gradually and differentially did the two classes, knights and nobles, come later into conjunction, interdependency, and intermingling. Particularly in the South, dependent relations were loose, complex, and relatively unrestricted. Until Philip Augustus (reigned 1180–1223) the Frankish monarchy was weak, and even then his main challenges were from the great lords of the North, including King John of England whose army, in league with Otto IV, Philip finally defeated at Bouvines in 1214. In the South the older looseness prevailed: there was no rule of primogeniture as in the North. Only toward the beginning of the twelfth century can one see in the South a fairly generalized "caste" of nobles who could transmit with some security their nobility to the next generation.[4]

At all events, what I am by implication claiming is that in the vast "Gallo-Roman" South, the beginnings of feudalism were much weaker than in the Germanic North, that the lords of the South were barely confined by their officially subordinate relation to the distant king, that their own interrelationships up and down the ladder were quite loose, and that in general—with a decent level of commerce, a relative scarcity of conflict (wars or invasions), and a fair number of long-established cities and towns—the inhabitants of Proensa could lead a stable life in quite prosperous circumstances with the benefits of a mobile society only gradually taking on something of a feudal character. Thus, stability and mobility and liberty were all in some sort of dynamic balance that may have aided a remarkable cultural, especially literary, activity that in turn seems to reflect freely chosen associations and community of interest. The first Trobador was indeed a great lord of unusually old lineage, yet he was hardly remote or invested with austere and transcendent authority. His jaunty, witty, sensual, irreverent, even matey character appears not only in his poetry (or even fully there) but also in accounts by the severe and serious historians William of Malmesbury (c. 1080–c. 1143) and Ordericus Vitalis (1075–c. 1142).[5] The next surviving Trobador, Jaufre Rudel, called "princes de Blaia" in the *vida* and viscount elsewhere, has his own remarkable theme of far-off love ("amor de lonh") for a lady beyond the sea. But in some of his poems one may well see a conscious successor to Guilhem, a fellow noble as well as skillful poet, composing lyrics already in the lifetime of the first Trobador. Indeed Jaufre may have been in some very loose feudal way a noble dependent of Guilhem. The almost exact contemporary (in *floruit*) of Jaufre, known as Marcabru, seems to have been of an entirely different status and region: a lowborn Gascon who perhaps started out as a mere entertainer. He is only the first of many humbly born Trobadors, and soon the social scale will be filled out with more nobles (even a king, Alfonso II of Aragon), with clerics, with merchants (one who became bishop of Toulouse, Folquet of Marseille), with knights and with burgesses. Certainly among the early Trobadors there were true professionals but none, it would seem, who depended on a single patron or court.[6]

The conditions of relative stability, mobility, and liberty seem especially clear in the highly individual and varied corpus of forty-four poems that bear Marcabru's name. His obvious individuality can be perceived in his vigorous, often earthy and colloquial, sometimes highflown and obscure language. Variety is evident in the wide range of his stanzaic forms and in the large number of poetic kinds he composed in: debates, invectives, pastourelles, crusader songs, satires, and so on. He has his ideals of pure love, of virtue, of valor, but rarely if ever does he sing of them alone or celebrate them as blissfully realized. It is here that he strikingly differs from Guilhem and Jaufre in their supposedly most typical poems. He is clearly a moralist, though neither a bigot nor a prude, and nonetheless a true and devoted artist. In his work a whole world begins to open up: a world of broad expanses and issues (from Spain to Rome to Palestine, from ethical conduct to holy Crusade to practical politics); and also a world of poetry and fellow poets. He trades insults with a poet N'Audric; he debates with the poet Uc Catola on the nature of love, sustaining a polemically sardonic view; and elsewhere, in defending true love against false, he dissociates himself from the love-poet N'Ebles de Ventadorn whose works are attested though not now extant. Here, then, is a community of poets and poetry, a whole intercommunicating institution of literature, a self-generating and self-corroborating tradition. There is nothing like it since the Romans, and in this matter it far surpasses them; for the next hundred years or so after Marcabru, the incidence of what are now fashionably called intertextuality, self-referentiality, *citationalité*, and an homage-rendering openness (rather than angst) of "influence," is multiple and continuous.

Was the earlier twelfth century an age of opulence and grandeur, of patriotic and chivalrous wars, of refined pleasures and ease of life? Hardly: not the sort of glamour as at the fourteenth-century Angevin court of Naples described by Boccaccio in his early poems or the sort of airy luxury in the villas near Florence where the lovely company of young gentle folk tell each other the tales of the *Decameron*. Before Boccaccio it is difficult to amass detailed information about daily living conditions in southern Europe or specifically in Proensa. Any generalizations such as mine are intended as plausible. Castles and palaces in early twelfth-century Proensa were hardly luxurious, not even very comfortable by later assumption. Castles were after all fortifications and were still in their early stage of development. Townhouses even of lords or gentry had to squeeze within narrow, walled precincts. The difference between North and South is again marked: in the North fortified castles were scattered generally in the countryside, whereas in the South the ancient towns, with their walls and towers, were not only fortresses but also the seat of the military nobility. *Aventure*, in the manner of Chrétien's knights-errant (from *itinerantes*), was thus apparently less likely in the South. In dwellings of whatever sort furniture was sparse; windows were seldom glazed but rather covered by green or black cloth; wall-hangings were heavy cloth against the chill stone or wooden walls, not fancy tapestries, which began to be used only about 1200. But clothes were comfortable and also brightly colored; and there were some fine artifacts, tools, and conveniences, though *the* "convenience" was as crude as imaginable. Sumptuary extravagance and waste were not yet on haughty display. In castles and great houses there were generally two stories, the second of which was taken up by the main hall, where practically everything went on. Alcoves off to the side or possibly a third story were sleeping or private quarters. But often, apparently, people, even the lord and lady, simply retired to sleep behind a curtain at one end of the hall. In this regard

it is interesting to note that "court," "curtain," "courtesy" all derive from
the homely Latin word *cohors* meaning "a courtyard" or "body of people
contained in an enclosure."[7] Without attempting any further atmospherics,
I would say that here is another condition: an incipient amplitude of space
and comfort and an incipient privacy in a protected enclosure, whether
castle, house, or walled town. Privacy and convenience, privacy and
company—these are oftentimes dilemmas that a degree of civilization and
ease can reconcile. Much of this seems to me emblematized in the family
of Provensal words deriving from the Classical Latin participle *adjacens*
("adjacent," "contiguous"). It gives *aizin* = "dwelling," "family"; *aizinar* =
"to approach," "to reside"; *aizir* = "to enjoy," "to accommodate," "to be at
ease"; *aitz* = "ease," "permission," "opportunity." Through Old French it is
of course the origin of English "ease" and "easy" (and also the legal term
easement). A rich verbal emblem, then, of comfort, property, society, and
privacy, all in their place within reach, "adjacent."

Cortezia concerns behavior within, social manners in an enclosure, or
more to the point, an ideal of life at a court. Both the physical place and the
mode of behavior were *in statu nascendi* during the twelfth century. The
parallel notion of chivalry (*cavalaria* in Old Provensal) had to do with
horsemanship, the knight's way of life, eventually an ideal of conduct. It is
perhaps significant that some sort of concept of chivalry developed earliest
in the more warlike and unstable North. Yet it is not clear to me when, in
the North, "chivalry" came to designate an ideal of conduct rather than
simply horsemanship or being an able knight.[8] Neither *cortezia* nor chivalry
occurs very early as a single abstract concept. To stick with the example
of *cortezia*, we first encounter it as an adjective and verb in Guilhem to
describe the power of *joi* (= love-fulfillment): it can heal the sick (as *ira*
[sadness or gloom] can kill the healthy), craze the wise, disfigure the
handsome.

> E·l plus cortes vilanejar
> E totz vilas encortezir.

(And make base the most courtly and make courtly all the base.)

This is a lover's enhancement of his beloved. Jaufre Rudel makes something
of the same point (III, iv), as does Marcabru (xxx, 32) who also uses the
noun for the first time (xv); and he does so in a poem appropriately
dedicated to the tender and gentle Jaufre. While Jaufre exemplifies *cortezia*

in his few poems though he himself hardly ever uses abstractions, Marcabru in his moral fervor writes of *cortezia* as an ideal in danger always in company of other values like *pretz, donar, valor,* and *deport.*

It is we who prospectively single out *cortezia* or *cavalaria* as the most general category, and it does serve a purpose; still, we must remind ourselves that it is one of a number of terms whose congeries is a value system, though one without a generic name and one whose components are not precisely distinguishable. That is as it should be; poets are not theoreticians or sociologists and fortunately leave something for literary historians to do.

So far I have discussed a number of "conditions" that seem to me propitious for the appearance of Provensal poetry. They have in common what might be called a secure yet dynamic incipience: the relative and persuasive character of stability, mobility and liberty. Nonetheless this is an attempt at *ex post facto* explanation of a phenomenon that is not a life-or-death matter, not an economic or social or geographic imperative, not a survival response to disaster, but rather a superfluous and dispensable activity. While poetry in some form or other seems to exist in all societies, in so-called civilized societies its great ages of originality or renovation are not frequent and not predictable. Even if my "conditions" do seem propitious or at least adequate, I must finally acknowledge that the Provensal lyric does after all simply burst into being. No one coerced Guilhem into writing his poems; no single social force or circumstance guaranteed that great numbers of other poets would be born or made; no special class or institution took charge of the means of production. Still, it was not merely a fad or a fashion. This first great body of vernacular poetry perhaps simply happened and was an authentic beginning. These matters of origin or of propitious conditions also involve questions regarding the most famous subject of Old Provensal poetry: love—courtly love, romantic love, or, to use the common Provensal phrase, *fin'amor.*

Before settling on love, one should view the whole panorama of subject matter in early Provensal poetry. Just taking Guilhem and his eleven poems, we find a whole gamut. Two are high-spiritedly gross (I and V). In the first he asks his mates to help him decide which of two horses he should keep: one is a fine runner and wild; the other is incomparably beautiful. But they can't abide one another. "Knights," he says, "a word of advice in my quandary. I was never so stumped by a choice. I hardly know which to keep: Lady Agnes or Lady Arsen." Suddenly it's women. Can't he have two of everything? He had two castles after all. The other poem also has two ladies in it whom he wants so much he pretends to be a mute and mutely suffers their torture of making a cat claw his back. When he doesn't cry out they allow him to make furious love with them both. In one manuscript there is an envoi:

> Monet, tu m'iras al mati,
> Mo vers portarai el borssi,
> Dreg a la molher d'en Guari
> 　　E d'en Bernat,
> E diguas lor que per m'amor
> 　　Aucizo·l cat.

(In the morning, Monet, you'll go on my behalf and you'll take my poem in your purse straight to the wives of Lord Guari and Lord Bernat; and tell them out of love for me to kill the cat.)

In other poems he writes about a woman protesting to him that she is kept under guard (II), about unexercised pudenda (III), about his prowess as lover and dicer (VI); one gives high-minded advice on love (VII), and one is precisely about downright nothing (IV). Only three of Guilhem's poems are earnest and charming love poems, poised between devotion and fear, between memory and exultant consummation.

> La nostr' amor vai enaissi
> Com la branca de l'albespi
> Qu'esta sobre l'arbre tremblan,
> La nuoit, a la ploja ez al gel,
> Tro l'endeman, que·l sols s'espan
> Per las fueillas verz e·l ramel.

> Enquer me membra d'un mati
> Que nos fezem de guerra fi,
> E que·m donet un don tan gran,
> Sa drudari' e son anel:
> Enquer me lais Dieus viure tan
> C'aja mas manz soz so mantel!

(The way our love goes is like the hawthorn branch that trembles on the tree at night in rain and frost till the morning when the sun sheds its light over the green leaves on the branch. I still recall a morning when we made peace of war and she gave me so great a gift, her full love and her ring. May God let me live long enough to have my hands again under her cloak!)

Finally, we possess a great lament of Guilhem written apparently when he was wounded in a local war (1111 or 1112) and had mortal thoughts. It is a poem of contrition and also regret: not grandiose or sweeping penitence for an ill-spent life so much as resignation in the memory of pleasure and in the face of death. Having commended himself to God, he writes:

> Toz mos amics prec a la mort
> que·i vengan tut e m'onren fort;
> qu'ieu ai agut joi e deport
> loing e pres et e mon aizi.
>
> Aissi guerpisc joi e deport,
> e vair e gris e sembeli.

(I ask all my friends that at my death they all come and do me a great honor, since far and near and in my dwelling I have had joy and amusement. Thus I renounce joy and amusement, and vair and grey and sable.)

The furs he mentions at the end are of course symbolic of comfort and affluence and status; they were all to become fixed in the later codification of heraldry but already had their noble resonance. That he ends with them in their material particularity is moving in the mysterious way of great poetry.

In his few poems Guilhem shows extraordinary variety, and his successors widen the range far more. Though love is the famous subject, it is but one among many, as with Marcabru. With that point firmly stressed I would briefly reflect on two other Trobadors of the early age whose works are all about love and who, more than any others, have affixed the love label to the common notion of Old Provensal lyric poetry: Jaufre Rudel and Bernart de Ventadorn.

Jaufre's *vida* (some performer's capsule "biography") is perhaps the most "romantic" of all. It tells how he fell in love simply by hearsay with the countess of Tripoli (in the Levant) and wrote poems about her. But out of a desire to see her, he became a crusader and went to sea. On board he fell ill and when the ship landed in Tripoli he was carried to a dwelling and thought dead, till the countess herself came and he regained his senses, but only to die in her arms. Out of sorrow the countess became a nun. This is touching or sentimental, perhaps, depending on one's mood. Yet there is some substance there: Jaufre apparently did go on a Crusade and may have died abroad. There are certainly real-life instances of love by hearsay. Besides, all of his six surviving poems deal with a sort of sweet or bittersweet pining for love, and two of them are explicitly about love at a distance or far-off love (ii and v). The most famous, "Lanquan li jorn son lonc en may," could be seen as the actual source of the *vida*, though some have argued that the two are independent and corroborative. That poem expresses a desire to take up pilgrimage to reach the beloved for "the love of God." They will talk and dally and everything will be solacing conversation and eternal devotion. Yet there is also the strong suggestion that the present state of desire and imagination is something desirable in itself and might suffer from reality.

> Iratz e gauzens m'en partray,
> S'ieu ja la vey, l'amor de lonh:
> Mas non sai quoras la veyrai,
> Car trop son nostras terras lonh;
> Assatz hi a pas e camis,
> E per aisso no·n suy devis . . .
> Mas tot sia cum a Dieu platz!

(Sad and joyful I'll take leave of her, if ever I do see her, [my] love from afar; but I don't know when I *shall* see her, since our lands are very far apart. There are plenty of paths and roads, and in this matter I'm not predicting anything. . . . But let it all be as God pleases!)

At the end he laments his ill fate that his godfather should have bewitched him with loving and never being loved in return.

Moods of longing and of fear seem iridescent in Jaufre's meditations on love. Such complex states of mind are barely exampled in previous love-poetry, except perhaps in single poems or fragments of Sappho and Catullus. With Bernart de Ventadorn we reach a poet whose forty-five poems all deal with aspects of love—mostly the state of active, fearful desire that is often thwarted by the perhaps unattainable lady who is indeed often a lordly sort of mistress (he sometimes addresses her with the masculine *midons*). The unusual narrowness of Bernart's compass and his high degree of verbal skill clearly made a deep impression on his contemporaries and on much subsequent poetry. If one reads all his poems together in a short time, one may well have a sense of repetitiveness and even lack of individuality. But that impression is certainly not to his discredit. One should first of all acknowledge his primacy as a lyric psychologist of the love situation he defines. Its elements are the devotion of the lover who will sacrifice all in service to his lady; the lady who has the power to withhold and to hurt and who is beautiful and desirable in spite of all; the beauty of nature and its creatures in a world apparently conducive to love. The poet may boast of his love and his skill as a poet; yet in the same poem he may turn humble and beseeching. The lady may be beautiful, kind and loving, yet cause him pain; or she may be distant and haughty, yet he will forgive her and just hope she bestows on him at least a glance. Besides, at the end of a passionate poem urging on the lady a very private communion, the poet may reflect on what a good poem he has written or send it off to a friend ("Chantars no pot gaire valer"). For those who demand "sincerity" at all costs or who demand to know whether or not the lovers might commit adultery or at least fornication, these poems will not be satisfactory. For those less demanding or less naïve—and also more knowledgeable in the modes of art—quite a number of Bernart's poems are fine lyric delineations of moods and situations of love. At their best his poems can contain, with artistic success, conflicting or warring or even oxymoronic emotions. His most famous poem is also one of his best.

> Can vei la lauzeta mover
> de joi sas alas contra·l rai,
> que s'oblid' e·s laissa chazer
> per la doussor c'al cor li vai,
> ai! tan grans enveya m'en ve
> de cui qu'eu veya jauzion,
> meravilhas ai, car desse
> lo cor de dezirer no·m fon.

(When I see the lark beating from joy its wings toward the [sun's] ray, and swoons and lets itself fall for the sweetness that enters its heart, oh such great envy comes over me of anyone I might see rejoicing that I marvel my heart does not then and there melt with desire.)

He thought he knew about love but now knows only how little he knew. She let him look in her eyes as in a mirror and now in that mirror, with deep killing sighs, he is lost like Narcissus. But all women are alike, he cries, yet he has behaved like a fool and perhaps aimed too high. His saving grace is gone and he no longer even deserves it. All that is left is to go into exile, to give up making songs, and to hide far from joy and love. Such a quick summary at least shows an evolving continuity of feeling. More exactly it outlines a vertiginous evolution of attitude from the lark's and poet's ecstasy to the renunciation of song and love. As the first poet of both the heights and the depths of love, Bernart de Ventadorn was not surpassed by Dante or Guido Cavalcanti, nor in my view by Petrarch. Perhaps we must look 450 years ahead to some of Shakespeare's sonnets.

Love now has come to the fore and I should take some account of it. What may have conditioned, if not caused, its appearance at a high level of complexity in vernacular poetry? There is every indication that simple love-poems existed among the Romance folk, and indeed they were imitated in Arabic and Hebrew poems as we now know. But I shall here make an invidious distinction between low and high art, and leave those simple refrains and the simple folk out of account.

In dealing with love in the twelfth century one must begin properly with the Latin vocabulary of the Church. Saint Jerome in the Vulgate and the early Fathers in general avoided the word *amor* and rendered the corresponding Hebrew and Greek words as *caritas* (from *carus* and no relation to the Greek *cháris*) and *dilectio* (from *diligere*). As Isidore of Seville wrote in his *Differentiae*: "Inter *amorem* et *dilectionem* sive charitatem hoc differt, quod amor et dilectio media sunt, et ad utrumque parata, modo in bonum, modo in malum vertuntur. Charitas autem non nisi in bonum" (*Patrologia Latina* 83, 92; between *amor* and *dilectio* or *caritas* there is this difference, that *amor* and *dilectio* lie in the middle, ready to turn either way, now to good, now to bad. *Caritas*, though, only turns toward good.) The prime word to express holy love was *caritas*, and not for nothing did Saint Augustine, the most influential Father in the West, come to be known as Doctor Caritatis; yet he himself in the *Civitas Dei* (XIV, 7) defends the use of *amor* and *amare* in a good sense as equivalent to *dilectio* and *caritas*. With the rise of the vernacular (in our case Old Provensal and Old French) unholy or secular connotations gathered around *diligere* and *carus* and their substantive derivations. With *diligere* came perhaps a confusion with *delectare* (to enjoy), so that "delight" or "pleasure" were and are the immediate associations; at all events, there is no spoken Romance derivative of *diligere*. With *carus* and *caritas* came associations of "valuable," "expensive," "scarce," "begging for alms," and "caress"—all meanings attested in the tenth to twelfth centuries.[9] In the surviving Old Provensal translation (c. 1130 or earlier) of chapters 13 to 17 of the Gospel according to John, the frequent words *diligere* and *dilectio* in the Vulgate are universally rendered *amar* and *amor*.[10] Thus the vernacular has abolished the ancient distinctions of the Vulgate and the Fathers, and has posed again the general notion of love as *amor*, whether *in bonum* or *in malum*. It is curious to note in this connection that *amor* in the Latin New Testament occurs only three times, and then only to render, in the compound form *amor fraternitatis*, the Greek *philadelphía*.[11]

At the same time that a new theology of love comes into prominence with Saint Bernard of Clairvaux, William of Saint Thierry, and others, we have suddenly a poetry of secular love, both carnal and idealized, making use of the word *amor*, which has the same form in Latin as in Old Provensal. It may well be more than a philological curiosity that a newly prominent *amor* in both Latin theology and Old Provensal poetry seems plausibly to have impeded the normal sound-change in Old French to **ameur* instead of actual *amour*. By way of fair exchange, the Provensals apparently borrowed *joi* from Old French to signify something like love-fulfillment. Yet, for its part, love-poetry may also be making distinctions and precisions with other concomitant terms such as *deport, gaug* (from *gaudium*), *druderia* (from Gaulish-Celtic *drutus*, "strong," "fertile"), and the strongly evocative *joi* (apparently from Old French *joie*, derived from Latin *gaudia*). Thus the old distinctions of kinds of love or delight with their elaborate philosophical and then Christian theological vocabulary (from Plato to Cicero and Seneca to the Church Fathers and beyond) are collapsed again, in the perennial mouth of the folk, to a single *amor* and its congeners.

What is cause and what is consequence in this matter of love, divine and mundane, in the twelfth century is too large a matter to deal with summarily: it even risks being so vague and capacious as to be a nonsubject. It is certainly a fertile field for superficial and grandiose speculation, and *Kulturphilosophen* such as Denis de Rougemont and Robert Briffault have not been backward in their tillage. I myself would suggest that what we have is not the invention or discovery of a new human activity or attitude, but rather the fairly common phenomenon of an important aspect of life and experience coming into prominence, becoming an open, explicit, problematical issue. Presumably there are psychological or emotional constants through the ages, such as family affection, friendship, falling in love, love affairs, and conjugal love. Their prominence in life, conversation, or literature varies in time, just as does the prominence of art and natural beauty (= landscape) and the relative value of pleasure and asceticism or luxury and frugality. In the matter of physical love the current wisdom of recent times is that what is perceived as repression and secrecy should be dispelled in favor of a high-minded openness and indulgence according to enlightened handbooks of performance and therapeutic purgation. It is not too much to suppose, however, that even in the Dark Ages people managed to fall in love and felt some uplifting experience in love without writing documents about it. To take something for granted is not necessarily to esteem it lightly. Besides, we well know that love-poetry can become conventional and trite (as it perhaps is now) and that great sentiments of other ages, such as patriotism (*amor patriae*), are embarrassing to many now or even despicable.

The danger here is to make everything continuous and to declare that there is indeed nothing new under the sun. If there is, despite the bicameral brain, a continuity in human nature, nonetheless there are those prominences and dips in history that are of the essence in our understanding of the past. Nothing can gainsay or explain away the sudden emergence of great lyric poetry in Proensa around the year 1100. That is a fact of art and its survival. That its particular and peculiar conventions persist still through change reflects not only art but also human nature.

Notes

1. Samuel Miklos Stern, "Literary Connections between the Islamic World and Western Europe in the Early Middle Ages: Did They Exist?" in *Hispano-Arabic Strophic Poetry: Studies by Samuel Miklos Stern*, ed. L. P. Harvey (Oxford: Clarendon Press, 1974), 204. Originally published in Italian in 1965.

2. See Américo Castro, *España en su historia* (Buenos Aires: Losada, 1948); final rev. ed. *La realidad histórica de España*, 3d ed. (Mexico: Porrúa, 1966), which is often more tendentious than I would accept.

3. Joseph R. Strayer, "The Two Levels of Feudalism," in *Life and Thought in the Early Middle Ages*, ed. Robert S. Hoyt (Minneapolis: University of Minnesota Press, 1967), 51–65; quotation is

from 56. Reprinted in Joseph R. Strayer, *Medieval Statecraft and the Perspectives of History* (Princeton: Princeton University Press, 1971), 63–76, along with another important essay, "The Development of Feudal Institutions," 77–89.

4. In general, see Archibald R. Lewis, *The Development of Southern French and Catalan Society, 718–1050* (Austin: University of Texas Press, 1965). See also Charles Higounet, "Le Groupe aristocratique en Aquitaine et en Gascogne (fin X^e–début XIIe siècle)," *Les Structures sociales de l'Aquitaine, du Languedoc et de l'Espagne au premier âge féodale*, Colloques Internationaux du Centre National de la Recherche Scientifique (Paris, 1969), 221–29; Philippe Wolff, "La Noblesse toulousaine: Essai sur son histoire médiévale," *La Noblesse au Moyen Age, XIe–XVe siècles* (Mélanges Robert Boutrouche), ed. Philippe Contamine (Paris: Presses Universitaires de France, 1976), 153–74.

5. Willelmus Malmesbiriensis, *De gestis regum anglorum libri quinque*, ed. William Stubbs (London: Rolls Series, 1889), vol. 2, 510–11 (Liber v, para. 439). *Ecclesiastical History of Ordericus Vitalis*, ed. Marjorie Chibnall (Oxford: Clarendon Press, 1975), vol. 5, 324 and 342. See also the historical documents in *The Poetry of William, VII Count of Poitiers, IX Duke of Aquitaine*, ed. Gerald A. Bond (New York: Garland Publishing, 1982), 92–141.

6. Biographical, social, and historical aspects of the Trobadors and their poetry are well presented and authoritatively sifted in the magnificent and magisterial work of Martín de Riquer, *Los trovadores: historia literaria y textos*, 3 vols. (Barcelona: Editorial Planeta, 1975).

7. For some details and speculations on early medieval life see the account based on Alexander Neckham's *De naturis rerum* by Urban T. Holmes, Jr., *Daily Living in the Twelfth Century* (Madison: University of Wisconsin Press, 1952); the popular work by Joseph and Frances Gies, *Life in a Medieval Castle* (New York: Crowell, 1974); and appropriate entries in *Dictionary of the Middle Ages*, ed. Joseph R. Strayer (New York: Scribner, 1982–89).

8. In the *Chanson de Roland* the adjective occurs twice in the repeated phrase: "E Oliver, li proz e li curteis," line 576 and line 3755. See Jean Frappier, *Amour courtois et Table ronde* (Geneva: Droz, 1973), p. 3, in the useful essay, "Vues sur les conceptions courtoises dans les littératures d'oc et d'oïl au XIIe siècle," 1–31, which cites numerous later instances. Here and elsewhere in the volume Frappier insists on distinguishing between courtesy and courtly love. As for *cavalaria* in Old Provensal, the noun occurs first in Duke Guilhem's poem "Pos de chantar m'es pres talenz." A useful general book is Glynnis M. Cropp, *Le Vocabulaire courtois des troubadours de l'époque classique* (Geneva: Droz, 1975).

9. See *Dictionnaire de l'ancien français*, ed. A. J. Greimas, s.v. *cher* I and II; and *Petit dictionnaire Provençal-Français*, ed. Emile Levy, 5th ed., s.v. *car* and *caritat*.

10. It is interesting to make a census of the biblical words for "love" in the Vulgate. One should bear in mind of course that they render a number of words in Hebrew, Aramaic, and Greek, and that Saint Jerome was choosing Latin words for the sake of accuracy and precision. Moreover, like all the early Church Fathers, he was avoiding words with scandalous pagan associations. See the many articles by Christine Mohrmann collected in *Etudes sur le latin des chrétiens*, 4 vols. (Rome: Storia e Letteratura, 1958–77), though she has none specifically on *amor*. On the early vocabulary of love in the patristic age only, there is Hélène Pétré, *Caritas: Etude sur le vocabulaire latin de la charité chrétienne* (Louvain: Spicilegium Sacrum Lovaniense, 1948). The Provensal chapters of St. John are fully edited by Peter Wunderli, *La Plus ancienne traduction provençale (XIIe s.) des chapitres XIII à XVII de L'Evangile de Saint Jean (British Museum* MS. *Harley 2928)* (Paris: Klincksieck, 1969). In those five chapters the Vulgate has *dilectio* four times always rendered *amor* in Provensal and twenty forms of the verb *diligere* always rendered by the corresponding forms of the Provensal verb *amar*. In addition the Vulgate has two forms of the Latin verb *amare* rendered by the corresponding forms of Provensal *amar*. One can conjecture that *caritas* would also, had it occurred, have been rendered by Provensal *amor*.

11. In 1 Peter 1:22 and 2 Peter 1:6 and 7—all three times in the phrase *amor fraternitatis*

rendering the Greek *philadelphía*. The seventeen occurrences in the Old Testament all refer to family relationships. The phrase *amor Dei* does not occur anywhere in the Vulgate; the biblical phrases are either *dilectio Dei* or *caritas Dei*. The extraordinary result of reducing many forms in Latin to a single Romance verb and noun directly derived from *amor* and *amare* (not to mention Germanic forms such as *lufu*, *Minne*, and *Liebe*) can be deduced from the following tabulation of key Latin terms in the Vulgate according to *Novae Concordantiae bibliorum sacrarum iuxta vulgatam versionem critice editam*, ed. Bonifatius Fischer, 5 vols. (Stuttgart: Frommann-Holzboog, 1977).

	OT	NT
amor	17	3
amare (and inflected forms)	31	23
amans (as noun)	7	0
dilectio	28	20
diligere (and inflected forms)	249	135
caritas	11	95
amicitia	41	0

It will be noted, though it is not essential to the main point, that the Old Testament is roughly four times the length of the New Testament. A fuller tabulation would of course take into account the *Vetus Itala* and the Semitic and Hellenic texts.

Bibliographical Notes

I cite here a few generally helpful works and certain studies that seem to me especially important for a consideration of the historical matters raised in this essay.

There is a fine commented bibliography of Provensal literature: Robert A. Taylor, *La Littérature Occitane du moyen âge: Bibliographie selective et critique* (Toronto: University of Toronto Press, 1977). Among current anthologies with pedagogical apparatus and commentary are those edited by Thomas G. Bergin et al., *Anthology of the Provençal Troubadours*, 2 vols. (New Haven: Yale University Press, 1973), by Pierre Bec, *Nouvelle Anthologie de la lyrique occitane du moyen âge* (Avignon: Aubanel, 1970; with French translations), and by Frank Hamlin, P. T. Ricketts, and John Hathaway, *Introduction à l'étude de l'ancien provençal* (Geneva: Droz, 1967). Frederick Goldin's *Lyrics of the Troubadours and Trouvères: An Anthology and a History* (Garden City, N.Y.: Anchor Books, 1973) has texts with English translations and interpretative introductions. A much fuller anthology is that in Spanish by Martín de Riquer, *Los trovadores: historia literaria y textos*, 3 vols. (Barcelona: Editorial Planeta, 1975), which offers translations, discussions, and surveys of the scholarship of 122 poets and some anonymous lyrics. With these aides, and with editions of individual poets, students and scholars are well served.

A full and yet compendious survey is that by Henri-Irénée Marrou, *Les troubadours* (Paris: Editions du Seuil, 1971). Two selective works in English are James J. Wilhelm, *Seven Troubadors: The Creators of Modern Verse* (University Park: The Pennsylvania State University Press, 1970), and L. T. Topsfield, *Troubadours and Love* (Cambridge: Cambridge University Press, 1975). A highly suggestive essay is that of Pierre Bec, "Quelques réflexions sur la poésie lyrique médiévale: problèmes et essai de caractérisation," *Mélanges Rita Lejeune* (Gembloux: J. Duculot, 1969), vol. 2, 1309–29.

In several articles beginning with "Observations historiques et sociologiques sur la poésie des troubadours" (*Cahiers de civilisation médiévale* 7 [1964], 27–51) and continuing with "Sens et fonction du terme 'jeunesse' dans la poésie des troubadours" (*Mélanges René Crozet* [Poitiers], vol. 1, 569–83), Erich Köhler has argued that the class referred to as *iuvenes*—unattached or dispossessed "aristocrats"—provided a milieu for Provensal poetry. This sociological "explanation" makes use of Georges Duby's data from *northwest* France and fails to take into account the absence in the South of a rule of primogeniture and the positive fluidity of "feudalism" and of rank almost everywhere, but especially in the South, during the eleventh and twelfth centuries. More recent studies of local conditions and specific periods have called into question many of the textbook generalizations about European "feudalism." A useful selection in English translation of ten German and French studies, along with an extensive bibliography, is Timothy Reuter, ed., *The Medieval Nobility: Studies on the Ruling Classes of France and Germany from the Sixth to the Twelfth Century* (Amsterdam: North-Holland Publishing, 1978). For France some of the best studies have been published by Georges Duby; most useful for present purposes is his *Guerriers et Paysans* (Paris: Gallimard, 1973; English trans., *The Early Growth of the European Economy* [London: Weidenfield and Nicolson, 1974]). More particularly concerned with the South are those works cited in note 4; to them may be added the work of Jean-Pierre Poly, *La Provence et la société féodale (879–1166): Contribution à l'étude des structures dites féodales dans le Midi* (Paris: Bordas, 1976), which, though geographically restricted and highly technical, gives a good sense of the differentness of the South and of the pioneering state of "feudal" studies.

At present it is still difficult or impossible to form a secure notion of what a city or a castle in southern France was like. Documents are most often not very exact in their descriptions and details, and archeology of medieval sites in urban centers has not progressed far enough to allow very precise regional accounts. Understandably most books on houses and castles deal with those that have survived and that are late and impressive. A survey of the "morphology" of medieval towns, *L'Urbanisme au moyen âge* by Pierre Lavedan and Jeanne Hugueney (Paris: Arts et Métiers Graphiques, 1974), is schematic and solid. Donald A. Bullough presents a survey in "Social and Economic Structure and Topography in the Early Medieval City," *Topografia urbana e vita cittadina nell'alto medioevo in occidente* (Spoleto: Settimane di Studi del Centro Italiano di Studi sull'Alto Medioevo, 1974), vol. 1, 351–99. These two austere studies give some firm basis, in what they tell about the south of France, for conjecture as to how towns looked and functioned in the eleventh and twelfth centuries. A succinct and cautious survey of dwellings in the eleventh to thirteenth centuries is given by Dominique Barthélemy in *A History of Private Life*, ed. Georges Duby (Cambridge: Harvard University Press, 1988), vol. 2, 398–423; the evidence is suggestive though inevitably sparse in detail and geographically scattered.

A few other matters. On Eleanor of Aquitaine and Marie de Champagne, the reliable works are not the overblown biographies of the former, but John F. Benton, "The Court of Champagne as a Literary Center," *Speculum* 36 (1961), 551–91, and Elizabeth A. R. Brown, "Eleanor of Aquitaine: Parent, Queen, and Duchess," in *Eleanor of Aquitaine: Patron and Politician*, ed. William W. Kibler (Austin: University of Texas Press, 1976), 9–34. Two good books on love are John C. Moore, *Love in Twelfth-Century France* (University Park: The Pennsylvania State University Press, 1972), and Leslie T. Topsfield, *Troubadours and Love* (Cambridge: Cambridge University Press, 1975). On the Cathars the best balanced account is Joseph R. Strayer, *The Albigensian Crusades* (New York: Dial Press, 1971). Andreas Capellanus is outside the chronological scope of concern here, yet it may be useful to cite a penetrating essay that sees the *De Amore* as a muddled attempt to exalt secular love in incompetent emulation of Cicero or Seneca: Gustavo Vinay, "Il 'De Amore' di Andrea Capellano nel quadro della letteratura amorosa e della rinascita del secolo XII," *Studi medievali*, n.s. 17 (1951), 203–76. For those who see Andreas as the sovereign authority on twelfth-century love a fine corrective is John F. Benton, "The Evidence for Andreas Capellanus Re-examined Again," *Studies in Philology* 59 (1962), 471–78.

6

CAVALCANTI'S CENTRALITY
IN EARLY
VERNACULAR POETRY

I

When Cavalcanti began to write lyric poetry, presumably around 1280, a great vernacular tradition had already been long established by the poets of Provence. The first generation of Guilhem (William) VII of Poitiers, Marcabru, Jaufre Rudel, and Cercamon had created a whole poetic community of poets, styles, and forms expressing a great variety of subject matter, all before 1150. Old Provensal lyric poetry, then, comes first and constitutes a system that will persist in Europe through the Italian connection, well into the seventeenth century. Its example spread first, however, north to Germanic lands (though the manner remains mysterious) and to northern France (where the *trouveres* hardly achieved greatness), and it was continuously replenished by successive generations of poets who wrote in Old Provensal, some of whom in latter years were of Hispanic or Italian origin. But the most crucial juncture was with Sicily and the Sicilian court of Frederick II Hohenstaufen. There, during the earlier thirteenth century, a number of educated and fairly accomplished poets adapted to their own language mostly the amorous vein of the Provensal Trobadors and showed that an Italian "dialect" was capable of some grace and skill. This is the Sicilian School, so-called by historians of literature, which comprises such diverse authors as Rinaldo d'Aquino, Guido delle Colonne, Pier della Vigna, and Jacopo da Lentini. The last is the most famous and perhaps the best and the one who seems to have invented the sonnet. What the Sicilians accomplished was to fashion a poetic language which, while remaining Sicilian, freely borrowed Provensal words, formations, and idioms (and occasionally French ones): here was a prototype of Dante's later notion of the "volgare illustre." The example of Sicilian lyric practice was fairly soon taken up in northern Italy, most notably for our purpose by Guittone of Arezzo in Tuscany and Guido Guinizzelli of Bologna in Emilia. In some ways it is surprising that the northerners did not draw their example directly from the Provensals (precious codices of Provensal poetry were copied there and at least two notable early thirteenth-century Provensal poets were Sordello of Goito near Mantua and Lanfranco Cigala of Genoa), but rather borrowed it from the Sicilians along with some Sicilianisms and even Sicilian rimes that would be impossible in Tuscan.

It is useful, then, to look more closely at this process within the Italic domain, with the hope that Cavalcanti's achievement can be more carefully pondered in its proximate context. If we put together the plausible poetic periods of flourishing of the chief *lyrical* poets, we get this chronological configuration: Jacopo da Lentini, 1230–40; Guittone d'Arezzo, 1256–94; Guido Guinizzelli, 1260–76; Guido Cavalcanti, 1280–1300; Dante Alighieri, 1285–1310. While much here is uncertain and variable, nonetheless some fairly stable results emerge. (1) The whole period of lyric activity at its widest lasts from 1230 to 1300, a mere seventy years during which Italian vernacular poetry was founded and vastly elaborated by a large number of poets of whom those mentioned here are simply the major ones. (2) The central formation of the "dolce stil novo" (sweet new style) can perhaps be narrowed to the conjectural and approximate dates 1260–90 (between Guinizzelli starting out and Cavalcanti having composed a body of poetry) or even 1270–85 (between Guinizzelli having hit his stride and Cavalcanti having hit his). (3) Many things were developing perhaps at the same time almost independently of chronological age or a historian's neat notion of how matters should evolve. Though such speculation is quite hazardous, it does stress that the great tradition of Italian lyric poetry—Guinizzelli, Cavalcanti, Dante, and on to Petrarch—came about rather quickly and without much time for a sedimented past or a set of discrete stages to take form.

Looking at that "contemporary" tradition from the imaginary vantage point of Guido Cavalcanti in, say, 1280, I shall make some empirical observations concerning his "contemporary" predecessors, Jacopo, Guittone, and Guinizzelli (known conveniently as "the first Guido"). Dante's later retrospective judgments and schemata will be postponed.

The standard critical edition of Jacopo da Lentini (known as the Notary) presents as authentic sixteen *canzoni,* one *descort,* and thirty-eight sonnets. Whether or not he is the earliest or the most original of the Sicilians, Jacopo may be considered the best and most accomplished of them. We owe him, by common consent, the invention of the sonnet (in effect a single stanza) and possibly the canonical Italian version of the *canzone.* The Provensals had invented the systems of the stanza with almost infinite combinations and permutations of rime-pattern, line-length, and substructures, and they had exemplified it on a vast scale. But Jacopo and his fellows seem to have codified the *canzone* as consisting essentially of two sections: one called the *fronte* (with two or more *piedi*) and the other called the *sirma* or *sirima* (with usually two parts called *volte*). Also, to be used at will, there was the *congedo* (tornada, commiato, envoi) as a send-off. Besides, the Sicilians seem to have introduced occasional use of extra riming hemistichs to the last lines of each *volta* of the *sirma* and also elaborate schemes of internal rime. Finally, they made more prominent use than the Provensals of repeating in a new stanza a word or phrase from the last line of the previous stanza. These formal properties, dull to us perhaps in their seemingly mechanical prescriptiveness, were obviously exciting to earlier poets all the way from the true innovators, the Provensals, to Petrarch and far beyond. Indeed, they should be looked upon not simply as patterns to be filled in but more significantly as generative principles of inspiration. Thus the *canzone* was well under way as the most elevated of verse forms. Implicit in this momentous development is an ever greater distancing from music or song in the literal sense that the word *canzone* (from *cantio* and *canso*) etymologically possessed. With the sonnet and the new conception of the *canzone* the Sicilians made fresh and fundamental contributions to the native vernacular poetic tradition. In the process the lines of fixed syllable-count and the rules of synaeresis and synalepha, diaeresis and dialepha, became more or less standardized. Other forms, such as the *ballata,* so central to Cavalcanti, had different origins and fates.

In point of subject matter Jacopo is representative of the Sicilians in narrowing the great scope of the Provensal lyric to the love situation, the amatory or erotic drama. It may have been this very narrowing that inspired the whole enterprise of *theorizing* about the love-process, an enterprise that begins on a broad Provensal basis with Jacopo and the Sicilians, gains intensity with Guittone and Guinizzelli, and reaches a climax in Cavalcanti and in Dante. This stress on theoretical content seems to parallel the elaboration of the "formal" aspects which, without it, might begin to seem empty technical virtuosity practiced on trite themes. In Jacopo the theory aspect is not much pursued in his *canzoni*, though a "canzonetta novella" (as he calls it) shows awareness of the "phenomenology" of love. Having confessed that he looks secretly at his lady without showing love, he acknowledges that he looks at the image of her he has painted in his heart. A grief burns in his heart like fire he tries to keep hidden. If he does look, he does not turn around to look a second time.

> S'eo guardo, quando passo,
> inver' voi, no mi giro,
> bella, per risguardare.

(If I look, as I pass by, toward you, I don't turn around, my pretty one, to look again.)

Because she is aloof he wants her to know that he has sung her praises, if not by hearing his tongue, then by "signs," meaning his verses, including the present poem whose message is autographed:

> Lo vostro amor, ch'è caro,
> donatelo al Notaro
> che'è nato da Lentini.

(Your love, which is dear, do give it to the Notary, who was born in Lentini.)

More to the point are some of his sonnets, both as single compositions and as parts of "debates" or *tenzoni* with "the Abbot of Tivoli" and with Jacopo Mostacci and Pier della Vigna. In one he asks how a big lady can enter through his little eyes and rest in his heart: it is of course not the person but her figure ("no [*sic*] la persona, ma la sua figura"). Elsewhere he evokes the figure Love that cures the wounded lover by wounding, giving life that is death. Most theoretically, he replies to the pair of poets: "Love is a desire that comes from the heart through the fullness of being greatly pleased; and the eyes first generate love, and the heart gives it nourishment." He allows that sometimes a lover may love without seeing the lady, but love "con furore," presumably the real kind of love, is born of eyesight and conceived by the heart, which cherishes the desire it has fixed in image. And this love dwells in the world ("e questo amore regna fra la gente"). As the best of the Sicilians (whose total production is quite substantial in bulk), Jacopo thus left a distinctive mark on formal technique and on the subject matter for later vernacular poets; though he hardly goes beyond the more complex Provensal example in theory, he nonetheless carries it over in practice to a new tongue and an incipient tradition.

Guittone d'Arezzo and Guido Guinizzelli can only be considered contemporaries, as we do not know when either one matured as a poet. For the poets grouped by Dante and later historians as the *stilnovisti* (practitioners of the "dolce stil novo") these two older poets represented a polemical choice: Guittone, for reasons not immediately obvious, must be rejected, and Guinizzelli must be embraced as forerunner and model. Yet surely the well-known and prolific Guittone was part of a neophyte poet's experience, even if he did not become one of his numerous followers, and surely his example was part of the excitement of forming one's own canon and banding together. His verse, both amatory and moral-religious, is amply preserved, consisting, in Francesco Egidi's edition, of 50 *canzoni* and 251 sonnets. Reading Guittone now without partisan prejudgment can be quite exhilarating. He is a fluent discourser and rhymer, a snapper-up of unconsidered words from the Provensals, the French, and the Sicilians, a displayer of rhetorical tricks, and a teaser in wordplay. He often elicits a cluck of the tongue or a good-natured groan, but also a perhaps grudging wonderment. At the end of an outrageously rimed *canzone* he sets two envois, of which this is one:

> Scuro saccio che par lo
> mio detto, ma' che parlo
> a chi s'entend' ed ame:
> ché·lo 'ngegno mio dàme
> ch'i' me pur provi d'onne
> mainera, e talento ònne.

(I know that my poem seems obscure, but that I speak to whoever dotes and loves: for my imagination suggests to me that I go on proving myself in every manner, and for that I have the will.)

Quite a few poems are in this vein of the learned man's play, corresponding to the unbuttoned popular poetry that was beginning to be written down copiously. Even at this level Cavalcanti and Dante had something to learn. In other "formal" matters Guittone was no great inventor. Yet in subject matter he displays a great range: a poem in defense of women, laments for a dead friend and for those who died at Benevento, *canzoni* to Saint Francis, Saint Dominic, and the Virgin Mary, and an invitation to dance for Christ (perhaps the first *lauda*), not to mention the amatory *canzoni*. His most interesting poem may be the one that some take to be an autobiographical account of giving up secular life to become a *frate godente* in the newly established order: "Ora parrà s'eo saverò cantare." In it he reevaluates love, honor, praise, valor, and other familiar words of amatory poetry, for the purpose of exalting their religious meaning in conjunction with rectitude and reason. The closeness of the two sets of vocabulary is instructive and suggestive. While granting that interchange between secular and sacred modes of expression occurs often in the Middle Ages (as with parodies and contrafacta), one may speculate that few poets, among them Marcabru and Guittone, ventured to make the discrepant likeness a subject of discourse. The *stilnovisti* seem in particular to avoid any direct confrontation: that may even be a reason for their disparagement of Guittone. Certainly direct reference to religious doctrine would endanger the exalting and divinizing enhancements of the lady and of erotic passion. Indeed Dante's whole poetic career could be seen as a process of handling such a collision of values and allegiances. Guido Cavalcanti, in his doctrinal poem "Donna me prega," darkly explores the matter, and does so in an elaborate scheme of riming of which Guittone's *canzone* is a forerunner. At the beginning Guittone declares his rejection of *Amore*: "for I hear a man considered wise say that no one not pierced by Love can know how to compose poetry or succeed; and yet he seems to me far from the truth if he fits his thinking to his speaking, since everywhere that Love holds sway folly is king in place of wisdom . . ."

> ch'a om tenuto saggio audo contare
> che trovare non sa né valer punto
> omo d'Amor non punto;
> ma' che digiunto da vertà mio pare,
> se lo pensare—a lo parlare sembra,
> ché 'n tutte parte ove distringe Amore
> regge Follore in loco di savere . . .

Guittone's subject matter may well have seemed perilous or cautionary to Cavalcanti if he knew this poem, but, if he did, the formal properties of it could only have intrigued him.

A greater poet than Guittone was Guinizzelli, "the first Guido" and the first complete master in the Tuscan vernacular. Of him we know little more than that he was of Bologna and wrote the five *canzoni* and the fifteen sonnets that survive (along with two brief fragments). He exchanged sonnets with Guittone and the Guittonian Bonagiunta, and in the first instance made a fine pastiche of Guittone's style while calling him "caro padre meo" and "mastro." Or perhaps as a tyro he went through a Guittonian period, as one could speculate from other texts, especially "Lo fin pregi' avanzato," with its tortured punning rimes. In his sonnets, which evince the earliest full mastery of that form, Guinizzelli presents a few recurrent thematic images which, though not strictly original, had a direct impact on Cavalcanti and his fellow *stilnovisti*. For instance, there is imagery of battle, as when Love casts a dart that cleaves his heart; within him there is a "battle of sighs." The figure, glance, and salutation of the lady can be generous and thaumaturgic. But then he can be forlorn, with "death written on his face," or like a desiccated leaf, or he can remain unrequited and yet can pathetically or stoically cling to hope. Besides, there are two good sonnets of ethical reflection and two jocose and racy sonnets on eccentric women who may well be prototypes of Cavalcanti's grotesque "scrignutuzza."

But Guinizzelli's best and most potent poem is the *canzone* "Al cor gentil rempaira sempre Amore." In form it is moderately intricate and occasionally, in minor matters, inconsistent and obscure, though in such ways as to suggest preference of sense over device. Its argument is properly poetic in that it proceeds by a gentle concatenation of ingenious analogies from the natural world to the human microcosm, as at the very beginning: "Love always homes to the noble heart as the bird in the woods does to the greenery." That is the first proposition, illustrated roughly thus: the noble heart and love are co-eternal like the sun and its light; love in the heart is like fire on a torch, but wicked nature is like water to fire, and so on. The next main point is that the noble heart is not noble merely by legal or social inheritance. The lady is said to shine in effect like a heavenly body and the lover to receive like water the shining ray. Analogies here become either tortuous or obscure; the upshot is that, as God shines his will upon the "intelligence" of each heavenly sphere, so the lady shines in the eyes of her noble man ("suo gentil") who desires ever to obey her. The third point, by implication, is that the lady is indeed exalted (indeed "ad imaginem Dei") and powerful. The analogy of the lady to God is daring for the lover to indulge in. The final stanza begins: "Lady, God will say to me 'What is your presumption?' as my soul is there before Him. 'You have passed through the heavens and have come up to Me and you have given Me as a term of comparison to vain love: for to Me the praises are proper and to the Queen of the worthy realm through which all sinfulness ceases.' I'll be able to say to Him: 'She had the semblance of an angel who was of your realm; it was no fault of mine if I placed love in her.'" The dramatized self-justification leaves the lady still enhanced and angel-like and at the same time allows a distant analogy to the Virgin. Thus Guinizzelli by his mode of argument puts the love-situation on an inward ethical basis, connects it with the macro-cosmic process of God's universe, and gives it a Christian justification. By such imaginative and mellifluous means the "first" Guido, drawing on past tradition since the Provensals, presents in this *canzone* a poetically shaped manifest, indeed a manifesto, of motifs for the rapt contemplation of the "second" Guido and his brothers in poetry.

II

Guido's predecessors and contemporaries for the most part wrote poetry about love (*amore*) as an attraction and affection between a man and a woman. Pagan Roman poetry had of course used *amor* in the same way; in contrast, the Vulgate eschewed the word *amor* as tainted for any sense of "love" that referred to man's relation to God. Nonetheless, Latin *amor* had, in theological discourse, begun to be used in a sacred sense, and when the vernaculars, beginning with Provensal, came to be used for biblical translation and sacred disquisition the various forms, *amor, amore, amour, liebe,* also came to be used for both sexual and sacred senses. This can be said to have facilitated Dante's extraordinary enhancement of his angel-like lady, Beatrice, and his exaltation of her and his love for her. Beginning with the *Vita nuovà* and culminating in the *Commedia*, Beatrice gradually becomes a bearer not only of health and of salutation (*salute, saluto*) but of salvation (*salute*). Dante's overwhelming experience of love (*amore*) for Beatrice becomes transformed into a sacred spiritual force (again *amore*) that is consonant with God's fictional dispensation through love (*amore*) that allows Dante (by Beatrice's mediation, her sacred love now requiting, after the fact, his agonized passion for her) to journey while still alive into the afterlife, including his largely invented Purgatory. When Dante refers to Guido in his colloquy with the father Cavalcante de' Cavalcanti (*Inferno,* canto 10, 61–63) he mentions his "disdain" in a particularly famous and superabundantly commented passage:

> "Da me stesso non vegno:
> colui ch'attende là, per qui mi mena
> forse cui Guido vostro ebbe a disdegno."

Leaving aside the father's anguish at hearing the definitive preterite "ebbe," and acknowledging that "colui" can refer only to Virgil, the sense may plausibly, or even best, be interpreted as alluding to Guido's refusal long ago to accept the special exaltation of Dante's Beatrice (*Guido's* Beatrice, Farinata's daughter, had become his fiancée when Guido was perhaps as young as twelve). The words of the fictive Dante in the poem are delicately couched with a tentative "forse" and a periphrastic "ebbe a disdegno" (for *disdegnò*). What gives trouble in this formal and compressed language is the "cui" which serves two functions: locative and dative. To paraphrase: "I do not come by my own effort: the person (Virgil) who is waiting there leads me through these parts, perhaps to her whom your Guido rejected." Dante the poet writes the statement according to his own interpretation and he is, in this, the only witness. There is no reason not to suppose that the two poets had at one time a fundamental disagreement about the salvific power of love between man and woman. Certainly no one else went so far as Dante in the supernalizing of his lady love. That Dante made a huge poetic or fictional success of it should not make us caricature Guido as an eternally disdainful wet blanket or *guastafeste.* Likewise, if we accept Dante's various groupings of an in-group of *stilnovisti,* we need not rigidify and homogenize them into a band of doctrinaire true believers and exclusively gifted poets.

Because of prestige and written record it is all too easy to take the various pronouncements of Dante as canonical and binding. The usual reduction is to conflate references in his *Purgatorio* and *De vulgari eloquentia* and assume that, putting everything together, there was a conscious group of refined poets (Guido, Dante, Cino da Pistoia, Lapo Gianni, Dino Frescobaldi, and Gianni Alfani) who took as their master Guinizzelli and wrote elevated poetry on love. That leaves as summarily excluded and inferior a great number of poets of the immediate past and of the present, and it leaves out of account a great range of themes other than love. A more liberal interpretation of Dante's intentions is also possible, one that would ascribe worth to other, perhaps lesser, poets and validity to a wider repertory of subject matter. We may do a disservice to Dante in attributing to him an exclusivity or clubbishness when he was simply commending orthopoetic models and defending lyric poetry by showing it capable of the most serious and ennobling content. It is striking, for instance, that there is in general almost an avoidance of religious matters. Dante, of course, with possible trepidation reaches up in his *Convivio* to philosophic or quasi-religious themes, but the course that leads on to the *Commedia* is Dante's own unique trajectory, no less hazardous because it was so successful and so nearly obliterated other trajectories. In his prose as well as in his poetry Dante often expounds "doctrines" at various levels for those who would learn or who are already in the know: true lovers of women, true connoisseurs of philosophy, true believers in religious teachings according to Dante the expositor. Indeed, Dante's case is so consistent, so bold, so imaginatively convincing, and so documented that it may perilously overshadow and determine for us the cases of his contemporaries. Especially Guinizzelli and Cavalcanti, his predecessors of true genius, who were far less consistent and doctrinal, stand in danger of being dragooned into the Dante pageant. Cavalcanti should be allowed to stand, on his own premises with the selective help of Dante as one witness but not as final judge of the state of Italian poetry.

In that spirit we may recall Dante's early praise of Guido in the *Vita nuova* and consider it an acknowledgment of his "first friend's" preeminence in Italian lyric poetry up to that time (c. 1293). It seems licit to go further and declare that the *Vita nuova* was built upon the poetic lessons of Cavalcanti, selectively culled. Naturally the older generation of Guinizzelli and Guittone was for both a foundation. Dante's innovations were in creating a narrative and at the same time providing an immanent poetics. The narrative would continue into the far broader context of the *Commedia,* and the poetics would find further elaboration in the unfinished and prescriptive *De vulgari eloquentia* and *Convivio.* (Beyond both Guido and Dante lay the completely lyric witness in the *Canzoniere* of Petrarch uneasily set in his whole protohumanist and religious lifework.) More to the point than Dante's treatises in assessing his view of the "sweet new style" is the occasion of his naming of it in his encounter with Bonagiunta da Lucca in *Purgatorio,* canto 24. Bonagiunta cites as "nove rime" the poem in the *Vita nuova* that begins "Donne ch'avete intelletto d'amore" in what, for the present Dante,

is a retrospective evocation of his poetic apprenticeship. His answer I take
to be gently ironic:

> I' mi son un che, quando
> Amor mi spira, noto, e a quel modo
> ch'e' ditta dentro vo significando.

(I am one who, when Love breathes into me, takes note, and
according to that way he dictates inwardly I signify [in writing; that
is, by alphabetic *signs*].)

The ingenuous Bonagiunta exclaims: O brother, now I see . . . the
hindrance that kept Jacopo da Lentini, Guittone, and me from the sweet
new style that I can hear. I see clearly how your pens follow exactly the
dictates of love, as ours certainly did not. Such, in paraphrase, is the
sense of:

> "O frate, issa vegg'io," diss' elli, "il nodo
> che 'l Notaro e Guittone e me ritenne
> di qua dal dolce stil novo ch'i odo!
> Io veggio ben come le vostre penne
> di retro al dittator sen vanno strette,
> che delle nostre certo non avvenne . . ."

Bonagiunta is thus made to characterize as both "sweet" and "new" a sort
of lyrical breakthrough of which Dante is the immediate and recognizable
representative. Here Dante is revisiting his past, as also in his encounter
with Guido Guinizzelli two cantos later (26). Guinizzelli he calls "my father,"
perhaps evoking Guinizzelli's like address to Guittone—of all people. At all
events, Dante can be generous when he calls Guinizzelli "my father" and
father "of the others better than I who ever made use of sweet and graceful
rimes of love":

> il padre
> mio e de li altri miei miglior che mai
> rime d'amor usar dolci e leggiadre . . .

Here the Dante of the *Commedia* is giving to his reader generous tribute
to the master of himself and his "betters" who long ago wrote love poetry.

After looking with fixed admiration on Guinizzelli, Dante replies to polite inquiry by explicit direct address, explaining the cause of his wonderment:

"Li dolci detti vostri,
che, quanto durerà l'uso moderno,
faranno cari ancora i loro incostri."

(Your sweet poems which, so long as modern usage lasts, will make ever precious their written texts.)

And Guinizzelli responds with like generosity in turning aside Dante's praise and pointing out Arnaut Daniel as the best or better fashioner of his mother tongue ("fu miglior fabbro del parlar materno").

The point in revisiting these grandly familiar passages is to put them in context. We may, I think, conclude that Dante in the *Commedia* is selectively looking back on his youth as a poet of love in mature retrospect. He may be slighting the great friend and exemplar of his early years, Guido Cavalcanti, but only in the sense that Guido chose not to go along on the greater enterprise of Dante's conceiving and also died just before the fictive date of the action of the *Commedia*. Still, the encounter with Bonagiunta allows Dante with fine irony to toss off a version of his experience of poetic inspiration; and when Bonagiunta contrasts the practice of Jacopo, Guittone, and himself with the "sweet new style," Dante has him use the plural *your* (they speak to each other with *tu*), thus acknowledging, without naming others, a group of *stilnovisti*. Apart from the didactic and speculative treatises of Dante, that is all we have to go on. We proceed further only by conflating the early Dante with the later, so different in purpose and accomplishment, and by then ordering forever an arbitrarily fixed group and doctrine according to Dante's supposed authority. Thus the *dolce stil novo* becomes in the hands of much later historians a solidified entity, conveniently excluding a multitude of poets on factitious grounds, enhanced by the master's prestige, and providing the critic with ready-made judgments and boundaries. It is preferable to return unprejudiced to the texts of the early Italian poets, in order to appreciate the essential patrimony from the Provensals to the Sicilians to Guittone and Guinizzelli, and thus to be able to contemplate the younger group of Cavalcanti, Dante, and their friends in their own spirited comradeship.

Without going deeply into a complex and speculative matter, let it suffice to contend that Guido was the contemporary moving force who set the themes, showed the technical possibilities and prowess, and gave the example of high genius within his somewhat narrow compass. Among the happy company, Lapo Gianni and Dino Frescobaldi are accomplished minor versifiers who elegantly show mastery of Cavalcantian modes. Cino da Pistoia, much more prolific with his 186 surviving poems, and also a famous legal scholar of long career, was especially favored by Dante in the *De vulgari eloquentia* as the exemplary poet of love; yet many recently have, in spite of Dante's blessing, found him somewhat insipid and monotonous. But Dante was being preceptorial and was of course right to commend Cino's skill. The fact of the matter is that Cavalcanti's direct influence is to be found in all those poets, including Dante, and Dante's most accurate account of the mainstay of the happy fraternity is to be found in the generous acknowledgment in the early *Vita nuova* and the jaunty sonnet addressed to Cavalcanti in those days, "Guido, io vorrei che tu e Lapo ed io." Guido, "il primo amico," was indeed supreme in his compass and was outshone only when the mature Dante transcended the rules and categories he fussed with and wrote the *Divine Comedy*. It is in this retrospective context that one may read the passage in *Purgatorio,* canto 11 (especially lines 96–99), in which Dante reflects on fame and vainglory and remarks that "Thus the one Guido [Cavalcanti] has taken from the other [Guinizzelli] the glory of the language; and perhaps there is one born who will chase both from the nest." Who?

Several factors have determined the fortune of Cavalcanti: the various assemblages of Dante's miscellaneous pronouncements; Dante's own eclipse for long centuries that implicated all early Italian poetry; and the supervenience of the vast success and reputation of Petrarch's poetry. It may well be that the fame and potency of Cavalcanti's poetry faded faster than his folklore notoriety as a "philosopher" and haughty aristocrat: witness the tales in Boccaccio's *Decameron* (v, 9) and in Franco Sacchetti's *Trecentonovelle* (LXVII), both of which have the air of archetypal anecdotes hung on a famous name and neither of which can be taken seriously as historical evidence. Meanwhile, in the thirteenth and fourteenth centuries there was much copying of manuscripts and compilation of anthologies, thus blessedly preserving the texts of all the early poets we know, from the Provensals to Dante. The vast and haphazard history of the manuscript transmission of Cavalcanti's own poetry shows at least antiquarian zeal and also, surely, genuine appreciation. His name was also kept alive by commentators on Dante, such as Boccaccio, Buti, Della Lana, l'Ottimo, and others, as well as by some who directly commented on his own poems (especially "Donna me prega"), such as Dino del Garbo, pseudo-Egidio Romano, Il Verino, and Girolamo Frachetta. Rhetoricians and "poeticians" could latterly cite, however sparingly, from the 13 sonnets, 11 ballate, and "Donna me prega" (as the only *canzone*) in the volume *Sonetti e canzoni di diversi antichi autori toscani in dieci libri raccolte,* published by Bernardo di Giunta in 1527. But more and more the glory of Petrarch as prime lyric poet overshadowed the *stilnovisti* and even the Dante of the *Commedia*. Not till the later eighteenth century did Dante as poet of the afterlife begin a comeback that gained momentum through the nineteenth century and into the twentieth. Only with the Romantic historians of literature did the true nature of early Italian poetry begin to be appreciated. All that is part of the story of modern erudition in the recovery and dissemination of texts, the development of a reliable sense of history, and in general a huge pan-Western enterprise to order and evaluate past accomplishments and vicissitudes, often, though certainly not always, in a spirit of patrimonial nationalism.

III

The glory of Dante after long eclipse was again ensured, and it remained to make known and to appreciate his setting as lyric poet. Guido therewith returns to some prominence. An enterprising serious edition by Antonio Cicciaporci appeared in Florence in 1813, superseded by a somewhat better one, also in Florence, in 1881 by Nicola Arnone. Besides, anthologies and commentaries setting forth early Italian poetry were published, to the effect of making Cavalcanti a staple. Though Ugo Foscolo animadverted rather casually and condescendingly to Guido, surely the first to get matters authoritatively and decisively right was Francesco De Sanctis who, in his *Storia della letteratura italiana* (1870–71), reviewed, with capable and characteristic independence, the poets and poetasters before Petrarch, found merit in some, praised the pre-Petrarchan grace and tenderness of Cino da Pistoia, and saw in the Florence of those times the birth of "a new sense, the sense of form." The highest fulfillment was Dante. But next to him stood Guido, who apart from his pretensions to "philosophy" or "science," could reveal himself a true poet when his inspiration came as solace or expressive outburst. "Guido is the first Italian poet worthy of the name, because he is the first to have a sense and feeling of the real. . . . Poetry, which formerly thought and described, now narrates and presents, not in the simple rough manner of the older poets, but with that grace and finish at which the language had now arrived, handled by Guido with perfect mastery." De Sanctis goes on, quite properly, to devote a massive part of his history to the achievements of Dante. Since then, of course, uncountable works have been published in Italy on individual poets and on the now-hallowed notion of a band of privileged *stilnovisti*, sanctioned and sustained by Dante's inundating fame and achievement.

Yet a decade before De Sanctis, a far less erudite though just as potent an example was set by Dante Gabriel Rossetti in his volume *The Early Italian Poets from Ciullo d'Alcamo to Dante Alighieri (1100–1200–1300) in the Original Metres, Together with Dante's Vita Nuova*, first published in 1861, which in its 450 pages of translations from 58 poets, along with helpful introductions, made a great and lasting impression on English and American poets, painters, and literati. The first half is devoted to "Poets chiefly before Dante" and the second to "Dante and his Circle," yet even the latter part is by no means committed to a canon of *stilnovisti*. After the whole of Dante's *Vita nuova* and 14 poems, come all of 29 poems of Cavalcanti, including three no longer thought canonical—a clear sign of emphatic recognition, as is the space given to an account of Guido's life, which is fully informed for the time. The translations are quite good in the conventions and constraints they observe, though occasionally paraphrastic and faulty. Just as important is Rossetti's rounded judgment: "As a poet, he has more individual life of his own than belongs to any of his predecessors; by far the best of his pieces being those which relate to himself, his loves and hates." Here justice is resoundingly done. Rossetti goes on, in iron duty bound, to comment on "Donna me prega" which he eruditely knew to be the subject of much learned fuss. "A love-song," he writes, "which acts as such a fly-catcher for priests and pedants looks very suspicious; and accordingly, on examination, it proves to be a poem beside the purpose of poetry, filled with metaphysical jargon, and perhaps the very worst of Guido's productions. Its having been written by a man whose life and works include so much that is impulsive and real, is easily accounted for by scholastic pride in those early days of learning." Needless to say, he does not translate it. But his high and reasoned praise for most of Cavalcanti's poetry anticipates and chimes with that of De Sanctis.

The cult of Dante in England and America (Rossetti and the Pre-Raphaelites, Charles Eliot Norton and Longfellow, as well as the general scholarship and proliferating translations in many countries) reaches to greater practicing poets in a long line from Robert Browning to Ezra Pound and T. S. Eliot, and to the institutionalization of societies and cultural styles. The most effective proponent of Cavalcanti in this wave of Dantimania turned out to be Ezra Pound who, alongside his lifelong *Cantos*, celebrated Dante's first friend in essays and translations beginning in 1910 and continuing to 1966. Besides these works, often revised, Pound produced in 1931 an edition of Guido's poems with the despairing title: *Le Rime, edizione rappezzata fra le rovine* ("patched together amid the ruins"). He had slaved over the manuscripts, which he sought out in various Italian libraries, had perused with impatience the scholarship, and, understandably bewildered, had indeed patched together an edition with passionate devotion but unfortunately without disciplined method and knowledge. It is better not to dwell on his stubborn and often fruitless attempts at erudition and understanding (particularly of "Donna me prega"), but it is right to recognize that his advocacy and translation of Guido worked powerfully to give him a place in twentieth-century poetic awareness. For many readers of English the name of Guido Cavalcanti has been rendered talismanic by Pound.

Meanwhile, owing to the immense efforts of Guido Favati and the supervisionally refining judgment of Gianfranco Contini, we now have as good a basic text as we could ever expect. The example of careful sensitive commentary set by Contini (1960 and 1966) and Mario Marti (1969) has now ensured that manuals, anthologies, and subsequent full editions have to be substantially informed and aware. Through the learned polemics and resources of such scholars as J. E. Shaw, Mario Casella, Bruno Nardi, Otto Bird, Paul Oskar Kristeller, and Maria Corti, we have a clearer, though still speculative, knowledge of Cavalcanti's possible intellectual milieu.

IV

On its own terms the major poetry of Guido Cavalcanti is mainly about love—its mysterious inception, its exaltation, its many moods, and its common legacy of pain and regret. As such, it reflects not only a widespread interest and obsession of the thirteenth century, but also the narrowing of the originally great range of subject matter in Provensal poetry. If thirteenth-century Italian lyric poetry is taken as a whole, including that of Guittone and dozens of Guido's contemporaries, the general range remains broad. Yet if quality and a continuous tradition are the ruling criteria, Guido's narrowing prevailed through the *stilnovisti* and on to Petrarch and his numberless successors. What remains to us of Guido's poetic work (perhaps the bulk of it, though we have no way of knowing precisely) also contains occasional poems, such as the sonnet on the image of Our Lady (xlviiia), the one on the hunchback woman (li), the *mottetto* to Gianni Alfani (xliii), and one to Nerone Cavalcanti (lii), together with "correspondence" poems that may be on the subject of love but are slanted to the correspondent. These occasional poems give hints of firmly held views that could be incorporated into a speculative biographical sketch. The poems on love, though, are the main concern: in their mass and their achievement they challenge the critic to say something useful about their procedure and value as works of art. In doing so, it is fairer to compare Guido to his predecessors, to the tradition he refashioned, than to the lessons that Dante and Petrarch may have learned from him. Since Petrarch put his indelible stamp on the long tradition that continued for centuries, we are now, retrospectively, in duty bound to strive to read Guido's poetry with an effort of the historical imagination that would find it fresh and novel and even extraordinary—all meanings in Guido's use of the word *novo*. I shall assume, as good hypotheses, that Guido wrote his love-poems around 1275–95 and that the order, established plausibly by Favati, is roughly chronological.

The first four poems express unalloyed wonderment and exaltation in edenic or quasi-mystical glory at the appearance of a beautiful woman who can thus evoke in the male beholder a serenely exultant joy. Yet after epiphany comes contemplation; after experience come speculation, doubt, replayed emotion, and self-torment. Guido explores a wider range than any of his predecessors in dramatizing the phenomenology of love, wider than that of Bernart de Ventadorn and Guinizzelli, and, for that matter, of Petrarch. Dante, in this regard, takes up his unique stand of eventual theologian, rather than phenomenologist, of love. It is thus the moods of love that mostly concern Guido: hope for requital, supplication, sense of unworthiness, suffering, self-torture, hopelessness, cynicism, and almost clinical detachment. These moods are not necessarily progressive, from exaltation to abasement, in a simple biographical line; they may well fluctuate according to the craftsman's artistic wishes at any stage of his experience. Here again one may honor Dante's achievement in creating the autobiographical *prosimetrum* of the *Vita nuova* and Petrarch's in creating a purely poetic, sequential, amorous autobiography, and yet find it more fitting to avoid imposing such schemes on Guido's disparate and unmarshaled poems. In Guido's case, if one provisionally accepts the now customary order as roughly chronological, one also accepts, again provisionally, something of a lowering of mood, buoyed up on occasion by the encounters with the young lady of Toulouse (xxix and xxx), with the two little country girls (the "foresette" of xxx and xxxi), and with the shepherdess (xlvi). Such fluctuations may of course occur over a longer or a shorter period or may respond simply to poetic imagination. We have no real way of knowing in Guido's case beyond an intuition of poetic maturity and of thematic continuity and change. It seems clear, nonetheless, that Guido in his "maturity" explored the lower depths of love and, for that, has often incurred the rigidified characterization of a pessimist, a cynic, or an embittered man. Yet one presumes too much in boiling down a poet to a peculiar essence.

In a decoction of that sort the lighter and brighter elements would be the first to volatilize: the gift of untroubled love, the precious sensibility of the apt lover, the happy chance, the aesthetic satisfaction of beauty, and so on. These are also notably present in Guido's poetry and he is resourceful in depicting them. While being in real life an aristocrat, he is willing to adopt Guinizzelli's crucial establishment, following the early Trobadors, of the noble heart as an attribute of gifted personal sensibility rather than merely a prerogative of inherited rank or blood. Still, that sensibility, for all its enviable rewards, is vulnerable. The beloved may not respond or she may show indifference and disdain. For whatever reason, some interaction ensues that constitutes drama or engagement, describable poetically at some length or briefly as in a sonnet. It is fairly common human experience that love can be uncertain and painful, and literature may also be called to testify in the words of Shakespeare's Lysander:

> Ay me! for aught that I could ever read,
> Could ever hear by tale or history,
> The course of true love never did run smooth . . .

These ingenuous words are fitting for a comedy, yet they can be made to suggest a starker etiology of love as it may be depicted in tragedy. When love is thwarted its course may be traced as a pathology, though none the less common for that. What I am suggesting is that the phenomenology of love must include its pathology and that Guido, in writing numerous poems on the torments or disillusionments of love, does not exclude for ever and a day its possible joys and fulfillments. In Guido's putative background there was the medical lore of Galen and the Arabs, the classical myths and characters, and the practical prescriptions of Andreas Capellanus. In "Donna me prega," too often taken as summative or "doctrinal" and somehow superseding all his other poems, he quite uniquely attempts a philosophical or "scientific" delineation of the processes of love with considerable solemnity, elegantly undercut by the casual pose at the beginning and the apparent irony at the end. Personified Love quite often lords it over the lover and occasionally appears almost like nemesis or fortune; in this prosopopeia we may see the commonplace of the urbanely capricious Cupid in Ovid, but I think it more accurate to see Guido's Amore as personifying the fearfully gratuitous, fateful, and uncontrollable consequences of involuntary enamorment. For all his contemplating and ordering of erotic phenomena, Guido does not settle for some medical prophylaxis and catharsis or for the didactic behaviorism of Andreas Capellanus. He seems artistically far more interested in an expansive range of erotic moods as dramatic situations.

Once we accept to read the poems as little dramas we must grant that the "I" is an actor along with the lady or the addressee or Amore or whatever else interacts or is made to interact. Guido's impulse to dramatize is so strong that even when the poem is inwardly self-contemplative he often enhances what may conveniently be called the endogenous processes of both thought and physiology with an aura of personification. The most common are the heart and the various faculties of thinking and feeling (*mente, pensero, anima*), which at times function in their conventional places and associations and at times seem to take on independence from their customary subordination and go their willful ways as the "I" looks helplessly on. The same is largely true of the *spiriti* or *spiritelli*, which Guido took over from Aristotelian and current medieval medical physiology that was concerned, in effect, to explain how mind and body interact and how perceptions of the external world are internalized. In both categories Guido enterprisingly found matter he could set in motion. The effect is often to enhance the pathos of the helpless lover and to concretize his diffuse emotions. Besides, the movement of thoughts and the motion of faculties describe experience as process and as continuum. Rather than a striking evolution of attitude within the individual poem or a static description, the result is a dramatized process. Even when most abject, the "I" is an actor if only as the necessary first-person narrator of what is happening. At one extreme the "I" disappears and is spoken of in the third person by his writing instruments (XVIII): the pathos is gentle but deep; the "dramaticality" is extraordinarily original. At another extreme the "I" does not simply send the freshly composed text in an envoi to its intended recipient, but actually addresses the ballad directly from the very beginning and personifies it as "he" is writing "it"; then he directly addresses "his" voice and tells it to go off with soul and ballad; finally he addresses them all three together and also one by one, telling them what to do when they reach the lady (XXXV).

More usual forms of dramaticality are present, the norm being discourse directed unswervingly to the lady. At times there is imaginary or hypothetical quotation and at times there is direct speech issuing forcefully from Love or the Lady. In the pastourelle (XLVI) there are direct quotations from the shepherdess that vivify the narrative of the raconteur. But in the first of the two "foresette" poems (XXX) not only are the two girls both quoted but also the narrator quotes himself. A further means of enlivenment is to address a plural audience or to evoke people as witnesses to something. Thus, though the poems are fairly few in number, the range is great: from internal solipsism to single and multiple addressees to a general audience of competent beholders. The intensity and the breadth of these means are far greater in Guido than in his predecessors. Guido's example of such dramaticality was not lost on the dramaturgic Dante. While Guido explored his artistry within smaller lyric compass, Dante sought a grander form till in the *Commedia* he invented a vast genre of only one member. Perhaps "Donna me prega" showed Dante not only that learned discourse could "ennoble" a *canzone* but also that a personal voice, a speaking "I," could assert itself in it.

Intrinsically connected with the intensity of Cavalcantian love and lyric drama is his vivid visuality. For the kind of love that is Guido's prime subject the essential organs are the heart and the eye. He seems more than other poets before him to register the sharpness and immediacy of visual images: first comes the direct striking of the image on the eye, then the psychophysiological process of receiving and contemplating it; there is also the character and significance of his glance and her glance, in the sense that a glance or a look is both receptive and also expressive. It is as if Guido were suspending the whole experiential process at that enigmatic instant of what we glibly call infatuation for the purpose of exploring its momentous essence. After that there is the further enigma of how the process goes on inevitably to engage body and soul, how the physical object seen can become a mental image, how a creature becomes a desire. The later

Petrarchan mode will speed and simplify transmission by having the beautiful image go straight through the eyes and end up in the ready repository of the heart. In contrast, Guido's elaborate and slow-motion concern with each stage in the process is perhaps remotely similar to that of an experimental psychologist. At all events there is something new here that can be called, in its intensity, peculiar to Guido. The whole framework of perception in process gives deeper meaning and resonance to words like *sembianza, figura, colore, sembrare, parere, imaginare,* and others.

Rhetorically Guido's poetry exemplifies a range of high, middle, and low, and generally a presiding sense of traditional decorum. The occasional Gallicisms and Provensalisms and "Sicilian" rimes may be viewed as bows to the tradition and the inherited poetic language. Apart from a few difficult expressions and some occasionally imprecise syntax, Guido's command of his language is firm and yet ductile. He ranges from simplicity and terseness to syntactical sweep and emphasis. Even at a time when all sorts of poets were writing with various tinges of local speech and attempting various levels of style, Guido stands out as able, within his restricted compass, to contain and modulate the flow of direct conversational speech through the exigencies of rime and stanzaic form. His starts or *attacchi* are famously arresting, whether beginning a proposition ("Perch'i non spero di tornar giammai"), directly addressing witnesses ("Vedete ch'i son un che vo piangendo"), asking a question ("Chi è questa che vèn, ch'ogn'om la mira"), or merely direct statement ("Veggio negli occhi della donna mia"). Though the lines are metered and rhythmical, and thus different because of that recurrence from ordinary speech and prose, they can nonetheless convey the force or the casualness of colloquial language. Perhaps his prominent use of diminutives is also part of that stylistic impulse. One may suppose that, in all this, he indirectly gave instruction to his contemporaries and to his heirs. Certainly he was carrying on a great Provensal tradition and certainly he showed he could keep decorum. Yet it may have been also that for younger poets who experienced his poetic achievement he stood as the fullest modern exemplar of the art, broader and richer and sharper than the venerable Guinizzelli and more complex and controlled than the facilely inventive Guittone.

It is plausible to surmise that Dante's judgment of his friend's work evolved from disciplehood to divergence, whatever their personal relationship may have been at any given stage. The evidence is slender and filtered through Dante's highly conscious retrospection. We may suppose that there indeed was a friendly band of Florentine poets, led by Guido, whose adopted poetic father was Guinizzelli. That Dante later has Bonagiunta fictively call their style *sweet* and *new* has induced many to make vast semantic excursions and extrapolations. If those words are an augury of truth, they may perhaps be summarily made to signify that Guido, who predilected the word "novo," made the style new and that Cino, faithful to Guinizzelli, kept it sweet. At all events, our judgment need not be mesmerized by Dante's pronouncements nor will any certain truth come from their further haruspication. Guido can be read independently for his own sake. Categories of his art can be adduced and comparisons made with other poets of his epoch. Here, in summary fashion, I have delineated some main characteristics of his poetic achievement which, to be properly effective, would require much longer and more evaluative argument. De Sanctis was probably right to call Guido the first Italian poet entirely worthy of the name. The reason, in De Sanctis's terms, is that he had "a sense of the real," that is, of the concrete and the actual and of poetry as a concrete universal. I would concur and conclude that Guido Cavalcanti was the first *great* Italian poet, that he outshone in the lyric his Italian predecessors and contemporaries, and that his originality and skill were and remain exemplary.

Note

1. Both here and in my edition, *The Poetry of Guido Cavalcanti* (New York: Garland Publishing, 1986), I follow the numbering of Cavalcanti's poems as established by Guido Favati and adopted by such standard collections as those edited by Gianfranco Contini (*Poeti del Duecento*, 2 vols. [Milan: Riccardo Ricciardi, 1960]) and Mario Marti (*Poeti del Dolce stil novo* [Florence: Le Monnier, 1969]).

7

CLOSE READING
OF
LYRIC POETRY

So far as I know there exists no history of methods of literary interpretation in the Western tradition. There are, of course, histories of philosophy, of aesthetics and taste, of literature according to nation, epoch, and genre, of literary criticism, and of general "humanistic" scholarship. Some of them are indeed excellent and indispensable. But what I desiderate is a history of ways of reading and explaining literary texts that would be based on the notion that those texts are imaginative (that is, aesthetic objects) and also integral (that is, neither random nor mere fragments of universal discourse). For many modern works of literature it is fairly easy, however laborious, to reconstruct a *Rezeptionsgeschichte* or a *Wirkungsgeschichte* based on reviews, diaries, opinions, and formal essays. We would thus reconstruct the *fortune* and the *influence* of a literary work according to canons and perceptions of past times. (The traditional terms I use here—fortune and influence—seem to me just as useful as *Rezeption* and *Wirkung*, currently much discussed in Germany and elsewhere.) For older works the evidence would be much scantier and the range of conjecture much broader. What I propose would be a vast simplification of the histories of aesthetics, literature, and criticism to which I allude. All extraneous matter—biography, aesthetic generalities, aspects of personal taste and development, random remarks, *non*literary works, the vicissitudes of texts and textual scholarship, and much else—would be excluded, and in the process, admittedly, much of great interest would in this context be left out. At the same time a clarity might well shine forth that could illuminate the history of purely aesthetic response to literature and could set in perspective our own practice of reading and methods of criticism. I would include in such a survey an account, so far as retrievable, of modes of performance: formal recitation, dramatic staging, silent or audible reading, types of readers and audiences. Granted, such a project would exclude much essential cultural enterprise, such as collecting, preserving, emending, and copying of texts, defenses of the worth of literary creation and appreciation, many of the issues of critical controversy or partisanship, and finally the relation of literature to other pursuits and activities of the mind. In practical terms, the evidence, especially in earlier times, would be hard to come by and hard to evaluate. Much would be internal and therefore inferential. Besides, it would deal with works that are sometimes condescendingly called "privileged" and it would be what is sometimes scornfully called "*ergo*centric" by highly *ego*centric discoursers who are prone to "privilege" their own critical discourse. But literature is not all things, and not all things can or should be done to literature.

Yet it would be falsifying to pretend that there is not a vast body of general discourse about literature or "letters" that provides some continuity and setting from antiquity down to the present. Plato's views in the early *Ion* and the middle *Republic* are notoriously reductive. Aristotle, in reply, defends literature as aesthetic artifact. More momentous for continuity than Aristotle's *Poetics* was his *Rhetoric*, which laid the foundation for a millennial confusion between forensic oratory and imaginative literature. The Alexandrians and the Romans, for the most part, found that confusion handy and fashioned a mode of talking about literature that ranged from the simple gloss to moral or historical exemplariness and argumentative persuasiveness. Besides, the Romans had to justify both their appropriation of Greek modes and also the worthiness or *dignitas* of Latin in comparison with Greek. Thus a pattern was set for the Middle Ages: the pervasiveness of the rhetorical prescription (the *Rhetorica ad Herennium* was known but not the *Poetics* of Aristotle); the elegance of local effect without much concern for the whole, as in Horace's characteristic *Epistula ad Pisones,* known as his *Ars poetica;* and eventually the defense and illustration of the vernacular. Often in the Middle Ages we encounter didactic or purely pedagogical works such as Bede's treatise on metrics (a rather arcane subject, as Latin had by then lost any native vowel quantity it may have had) or the treatises and handbooks of Geoffrey of Vinsauf, Matthew of Vendôme, and John of Garland. Here and there one finds interesting opinions concerning particular works: some flashes in scholia, in introductions to manuscripts (*accessūs*), and in manuscript marginalia, as well as in the letters and treatises of a few great "proto-Humanists" like Lupus Servatus and John of Salisbury. Such *testimonia* are rare enough to be precious and worthy of painstaking study.

Concomitantly, there are various traditions of interpretation. Perhaps the oldest was the pre-Socratic and then Neoplatonic allegorizing of Homer the Theologian. Certain Jewish modes of interpreting Scripture were taken over by Christians and then Jewish and Christian methods went their separate ways—necessarily so, as what came to be the distinctively Christian method, figural interpretation, was based on the notion that the New Testament is a historical fulfillment of the Old, *gratia* supervening on *lex*. When the line between sacred and secular became blurred, as with Dante, the result was a tantalizingly sporadic reading of secular works in their integrity and also their particularity. I do not wish to dispute the grand theme of Ernst Robert Curtius, that there is a continuous *rhetorical* tradition through the Middle Ages and Renaissance that was a major civilizing and preserving force—an authoritative force that governed not only Latin but also the vernaculars of Romania and Germania and gave those great medieval realms a kind of wholeness and cultural unity. Civilization and literature were somehow preserved, but the intrinsic aesthetic nature of literature went unexplored and even uncomprehended except by writers in their practice and readers or audiences in their rarely attested enjoyment.

Here I imply a discrepancy between theory and practice. Such, I think, did exist. To put it another way: theory was not adequate to practice. Imaginative writers wrote better than critics could say and created much without the help of fully argued criticism. Some progress in devising ways to talk about literature has been made since the Middle Ages, and properly one would trace it along the flow of time. What I propose here, however, is to heighten my argument by proceeding in retrograde motion from the nineteenth and then the twentieth centuries on back into our Renaissance legacy. My concern is not literature as a whole or literature in its canonically grander forms such as tragedy and epic—so often discussed and debated in the Renaissance—but with lyric poetry and its interpretation.

Nowadays we are so familiar with the notion of analyzing and interpreting lyric poems, often to a surfeit, that we may not have any clear idea as to when and how it all began. Certainly in the nineteenth century there are reviews, critiques, and occasional essays that center upon the texts of poems and that go from simple praise or blame and singling out of passages or lines as Arnoldian touchstones to a general characterization of the whole production of a lyric poet. And there are some brilliant formulations that seem particularly illuminating though not fully satisfying. At best we have some excellent accounts of poetic "personalities," sharply or sympathetically characterized, roundly focused to give us a global notion of the poet's whole work. One could cite, in particular, Coleridge on Shakespeare's poetry, Matthew Arnold on Wordsworth, De Sanctis on Leopardi, or Sainte-Beuve on certain rare occasions. I stress again that I am not talking about poetics or theory of literature in general, but about interpretation (and also not about theory of interpretation or hermeneutics in the abstract), and that I am talking about the interpretation of lyric poetry.

Treading for a moment backwards into the eighteenth century, we may think of Thomas Warton and Samuel Johnson (in so many ways ahead of their Continental counterparts), who often characterize shorter poems, though briefly and rather piecemeal. Indeed, it comes as no surprise that there is little to my special purpose in the eighteenth century. The larger genres would naturally afford much richer substance for an "evolutionary" account of interpretation or indeed of literary theory in general. And I freely admit that much concerning the lyric can be gleaned, for example, from Vico, Thomas Warton, Bishop Percy, Dr. Johnson, and Herder.

If, suddenly, we jump ahead to the late nineteenth and earlier twentieth centuries, what we find, I think, are very much closer and more thoroughgoing interpretations of lyric poetry. We seem to be in a totally new age of interpretation, one that is very familiar to us of course, but which I am trying by historical perspective to make strange in its newness. What brought this about I can only suggest here. First there was the Romantic stress on symbol and upon the organic analogy: symbols should be pervasive and consistent; poems are more like plants in their wholeness than like machines in their detachable parts. Next, and just as important, is the example of philology (in the somewhat narrow sense), both classical and vernacular. In order to discuss poems in their textual wholeness simply for the purpose of grammatical elucidation or scholarly emendation, the good scholar had to have a firm grasp on the way the poem worked in all its aspects. I am aware that there was in practice a pervasive discontinuity between the rigors of emending classical texts and the belletristic and high-flown "appreciation" of ancient writers. Yet the example of necessarily close reading was there. Finally, I would suggest that our familiar twentieth-century systematic interpretation of lyric poems derives in part from a reaction to the Romantic strain of poetry now gone to seed in this period. One could facetiously characterize it, instead of being of the earth earthy, as being of the moon moony. Primacy in this matter of salutary reaction goes probably to Ezra Pound, T. S. Eliot, I. A. Richards, and to the American New Critics; though French *explication de texte,* the Russian so-called Formalists, and Leo Spitzer and literary stylistics are original, parallel, and fairly convergent phenomena. This great age of close systematic interpretation may now have run its course, but its lessons are, I hope, permanent in the longer run. What we have now in some literary quarters (I leave aside modish ideologies) is a reaction against "close reading" or "formalism," and also such a hankering for theory that masses of serious students of literature on every level have got into the *act* of theory and into the *business* of theorizing about theory. Not a deplorable situation perhaps, but one that often exhibits much pretension, historical shallowness, competitive confusion in terminology, overpopulation of theorists and journals, and that can also induce a sense of surfeit or boredom. So-called deconstruction, for example, goes beyond close reading to a repetitive "closer than close" demonstration, by whatever means, of the radical unreliability of language itself.

Pulling another switch on my time-machine, I go back to the Renaissance where we find some of the things I have just been complaining of in our present situation: a sudden excessive and repetitive proliferation of theoretical treatises, a shaky historical sense (understandable then), and, among the best, a presumptuous and prescriptive cockiness. Often, of course, fine things were written, not only about epic and tragedy, but also about the *Divina Commedia* and the *romanzi* of Ariosto and Tasso. The lyric, however, was slighted, and at best, in the systematic treatises, we get the old Alexandrian parceling-out and cataloging of iambus, elegy, epigram, etc., along with descriptions of vernacular verse-length, stanza, and forms like the sonnet and the *canzone.* The treatises of, say, Girolamo Ruscelli (*Del modo di comporre in versi nella lingua italiana,* 1558) and Antonio Sebastiani, known as Minturno (*L'Arte poetica [thoscana],* 1564), are intelligent and interesting, particularly for the examples given, for their catholicity and practicality, and, not least, for their ennobling of vernacular poetics. Moreover, there are brief discourses or "lessons" concerned with poems by Cavalcanti, Petrarch, and others, that do concentrate on the poems, though, one may firmly say, almost wholly as vehicles for para-Platonic philosophizing. The most original and interesting of such *lezioni* are those of the young Torquato Tasso, especially one he devoted to explicating a sonnet of Giovanni della Casa. Here the Platonic mode and Tasso's scruples of orthodoxy are set aside in favor of a clear and learned account of levels of style and some fine minute observations on the liaison of vowels, on metaphor, and on the use of contrasting adjectives. The arguments for the worth of poetry as useful and philosophic are explicitly subordinated to pleasure ("diletto") and general intelligibility. After quoting from several poems of Petrarch, he asserts that the "divinità di questi versi, non dalle profondità de' sensi filosofici, ma dalla vivacità degli spiriti, e dall'ornamento dell' elocuzione deriva" ("the divine quality of these lines derives not from profundities of philosophic meanings but from liveliness of spirits and from the adornment of their expression"). Such methods and views are not, however, typical of Tasso's critical work nor of his age.

In the Renaissance proper this brief *lezione* of Tasso bears the nearest resemblance I have found to a close reading of a single, integral text. Some of the most famous names of Renaissance literary criticism are absent from my account—Castelvetro, Mazzoni, Bembo, Sidney, Puttenham, Jonson, Du Bellay, and Etienne—either because they did not treat lyric poetry or because they only quoted from it to illustrate rhetorical and prosodic terms. So often on the one hand there is the ringing defense of literature and on the other a rather dry compilatory handbook. That state of affairs generally continued into the seventeenth century, into what I am used to calling the Baroque, in which the most famous treatises are those of the Spaniard Baltasar Gracián (1601–58) and the Italian Emanuele Tesauro (1592–1675). To take the latter first, Tesauro's hefty Aristotelian spyglass, *Cannocchiale aristotelico*, was first published in Turin in 1654 and reached a fifth edition by 1670—deservedly because it is intelligent and lively, full of anecdotes and terminology, and because it stresses wit, cleverness, ingenuity, inventiveness, and other kinds of mental pleasure. But, for all its vivacity, it is mostly a candied rhetoric quite solidly based on Aristotle's *Rhetoric* and quite lacking in deep and thorough analysis of specifically literary works. One of Tesauro's key terms is *argutezza*, referring to the quality of being finely and sharply *argued* and *proven* (from Latin *arguere*). The usual thing here is to say that that was typically of Baroque style and to look upon

Tesauro as simply a codifier of current practice. But he was less that than a continuer of a Renaissance tradition of rhetoric that goes back eventually to Aristotle.

More original and more to the point was Baltasar Gracián, Jesuit, author of works of worldly wisdom, one considerable novel *El Criticón*, and the remarkable treatise *Agudeza y arte de ingenio* (first edition, 1642; much enlarged in 1648). Here *agudeza* is sharpness or acuteness, not quite the cleverly argued or rhetorically proven point of Tesauro's *argutezza*. The words are different in origin and perhaps I exaggerate their difference; Gracián's treatise is also rhetorically based; but it is also more original and almost wholly devoted to poetic practice. Gracián's great insistence is that poetry is more than adornments and devices; it is also continuous concepts or concatenations of thought-images. His central notions of *agudeza* and *arte de ingenio* need not be explained in modern terms to free them from the deadening schematism of literary histories. *Agudeza* is indeed acuteness, but it is also freshness and not mere cleverness. *Arte de ingenio* might be taken to mean the art of exercise of the imagination. What is involved here is something like Aristotle's notion of metaphor as stated in his *Poetics* (not his *Rhetoric*): "But the greatest thing by far is to have a command of metaphor. This alone cannot be imparted by another; it is the mark of genius, for to make good metaphor implies an eye for resemblances" (trans. S. H. Butcher, xxii). Gracián's distinctions and varieties of poetic means are quite clearly delineated, but unlike his predecessors and successors he produces apt and copious illustrations and comments on them. His illustrative texts are drawn from ancient poets of course (Virgil, Horace, and Martial for the most part), from some Italian and Portuguese poets, and with overwhelming abundance from estimable Spanish poets from the sixteenth century to his own near contemporaries in the seventeenth. What we have here in Gracián's treatise is not the pedantic or pedagogical handbook of rhetoric for all sorts of discourse and not the high-flown and high-minded general "defense" of letters, but a deliberative and original inquiry into poetic structure and poetic utterance that mediates particularly well between the particular and the general. True, most of his illustrations of whole poems are sonnets, but surely that is as much for convenience as for a taste for the pithy. Gracián should not be reduced to being a mere participant in the dull and confused debate dear to literary historians between, supposedly, the *conceptistas* and the *culteranos*.

Perhaps I exaggerate somewhat Gracián's modernity. I should acknowledge that he remains in the rhetorical tradition so much concerned with defining and cataloguing figures of speech or *colores rhetorici*. What in sober terms is most original in him and superior to his Renaissance predecessors and his Baroque contemporaries is this: he does not put the rhetorical categories first and then perfunctorily illustrate them with poetic quotations; instead he puts the poetry first and tries to help the reader grasp its great variety and artistry.

Up to this point I have, in my search for critical interpretation of whole poems, gone from the nineteenth and twentieth centuries back to antiquity and the Middle Ages, landed in the Renaissance, and proceeded to Baroque. Now I return to the late Middle Ages and the Renaissance for the purpose of considering two special instances of thoroughgoing holistic interpretation of poems: the *Vita nuova* and especially the *Convivio* of Dante and the *Noche oscura*, the *Cántico espiritual*, and the *Llama de amor viva* of Saint John of the Cross. Each is an individual case, and none do I claim as a forerunner of modern or contemporary codes of interpretation. Yet they seem to me outstanding and unusual.

Dante in the *Vita nuova* adapted immaturely the Boethian model to his own quasi-autobiographical purpose. In Boethius the poems are, as it were, continuous with the prose and are not explicitly commented on. In Dante the prose is the setting and explication of the poems. Not that Dante here does much more than mark out, rather perfunctorily, the divisions and general structure of his poems. The *Convivio*, incomplete as it is, has a much grander scheme: the poetic texts, in the elevated form of the *canzone*, come at the beginnings of books 2, 3, and 4, and are then most elaborately interpreted according to their literal and their allegorical sense. Surely the *Convivio* is the first elaborate commentary made by a poet upon himself, that is, upon his own work. More important, it is also the first elaborate exegetical or interpretative work on secular poems. In the latter regard, one must at once ask two questions: Are the poems indeed secular? and: Is the method of interpretation likewise secular? What, indeed, about the allegory of poets versus the allegory of theologians? The matter, of course, leads on to the Epistle to Can Grande, usually attributed to Dante, and the whole question of the exegesis of the *Divina Commedia* and the notion, in particular, of figural interpretation reserved traditionally for Scripture and providentially conceived history. But I make bold to say that even the *Divina Commedia* is largely an invention (drawn of course from the Bible and *traditio*, but also from Virgil, Boethius, and elsewhere)—an invention so grand and so poetically imaginative and successful that many critics nowadays proceed as if it *were* Scripture and can only take for granted and approve Dante's own application to it of the method of sacred interpretation. The *Commedia* is a wonderful imaginative achievement on Dante's part and one in which he must, somehow, have believed. What I would call Dante's unexampled arrogance is, at least in my own secular terms, aesthetically justified as no other work I know.

But to return to the *Convivio*, we have here a work midway between the *Vita nuova* and the *Divina Commedia*. In the *Vita nuova* Dante first saw himself as almost unique in a providential scheme of things that made it possible for him to see his own love-poetry (derived from the *donna angelicata* enhancements of the Siculo-Tuscan followers of the Provensals) as susceptible to a quasi-sacred interpretation. In the *Convivio* distinctions are blurred even more: the *canzoni*, at a further stage of "angelization" than in the *Vita nuova*, now seem to strive for the dignity of philosophy. Because philosophy can easily be taken as Boethius's personified *Philosophia* and because Boethius was thought to be a Christian (as he was in other tracts), we reach, with Dante, a remarkable state of affairs in which the poems are ambiguously secular (however autobiographically "providential") and the interpretations are at times brilliantly and thoroughly secular (a thing new in history)—yet the combination is extremely uneasy and extremely rich in its novelty. This whole matter could be swiftly resolved by those who would sacralize every medieval work that has come down to us. I do not accept that, just as I do not propose any grand scheme of secularization as the true march of modern civilization. What I wish to stress is the uneasy, ambiguous, original achievement of Dante in giving us something approaching close secular readings of whole poems that not by accident happen to be of his own writing.

In a sense more complicated, and yet much less self-consciously literary, are three works of Saint John of the Cross: the interpretations of his own poems contained in *Noche oscura, Cántico espiritual*, and *Llama de amor viva*. Though Saint John's poems are, of course, his own, they are woven of threads drawn mainly from the Song of Songs—that most sacred of Old Testament books because, perhaps, it was so clearly susceptible to direct secular and erotic interpretation. I would guess, counting both texts printed and texts still in manuscript, that there are almost a hundred exegetical interpretations of the Song of Songs, the most famous of which are the eighty-six *sermones* on the first third of that short book by Saint Bernard of Clairvaux. What Saint John does, in effect, is to write poems based on the sacred scriptural text of the Song of Songs and then provide his own interpretations, in biblical exegetical fashion, on his own poems.

Perhaps, instead of more complicated, this could be called simpler than Dante's procedure, in that we remain within the realm of biblically sanctioned sanctity, or at least of personal mystical experience. Certainly in Saint John there are fewer obvious tensions or contradictions at work than in Dante. But that greater simplicity is perhaps deceptive. For in Saint John the poems almost imperceptibly take on scriptural status since they are so deeply grounded in Scripture, and the interpretation of them is so direct and, in somewhat anachronistic terms, so aesthetic, that we have something unexpectedly close to modern close reading. The prime text of the Bible itself (mainly the Song of Songs) is taken as an almost infinite web of associations, from the most concrete to the entirely ungraspable. It is not simply that everything can have a literal, allegorical, moral, or anagogical meaning (according to the desire of the interpreter); it is that the chain of connection from the most concrete to the most universal is continuous and unbroken and can be traversed at will from one link to another. Saint John performs, in poems and interpretation, a remarkable and moving balancing act, as he treads or leaps along the chain. It is undeniable that many or most of his local interpretations are traditionally figural (allegorical, moral, or anagogical) and that he often jumps from the poetic concrete to the spiritual general. Nevertheless, there is no hesitation in that his *poetry* is always splendidly concrete and free of didactic or explanatory padding and in that his self-*interpretation* often securely mediates between that concreteness and the larger realm of traditional signification hallowed in the code of codes.

At the end I may confess to a certain degree of disingenuousness. It can be objected that I have not fully taken into account the manifest intentions of Dante and Saint John: their preoccupation with varieties of religious truth. In spite of that, I would insist that they are our first good, close, systematic readers of lyric poetry and that from their ages to our own there is a great gap of time. Can it be called an irony that hermeneutics (the science of interpretation), which is now so fashionable, has its roots in traditional theological practice? At all events, the fairly recent reestablishment, in the earlier part of this century, of "close reading" or systematic interpretation and its full secularization for purely literary purposes are great achievements.

In reaction to so-called formalism it will simply not do to replace theology with some current pseudophilosophical ideology or with any other ulterior purpose that would attempt to expropriate or to trivialize the autonomous art of the lyric and the freedom of its properly humble, even reverent, aesthetic enjoyment and interpretation.

Bibliographical Notes

In making a survey of this sort one begins with the sturdy old treatise of Ciro Trabalza, *La critica letteraria: dai primordi dell' umanesimo all'età nostra* (Milan: Vallardi, 1915), and then plunges into the large assemblage of Bernard Weinberg, *A History of Literary Criticism in the Italian Renaissance*, 2 vols. (Chicago: University of Chicago Press, 1961). Before and after there are the good briefer accounts by Joel E. Spingarn, *A History of Literary Criticism in the Renaissance* (New York: Columbia University Press, 1899; 2d ed., 1925), and by Baxter Hathaway, *The Age of Criticism: The Late Renaissance in Italy* (Ithaca: Cornell University Press, 1962) and his shorter but broader *Marvels and Commonplaces: Renaissance Literary Criticism* (New York: Random House, 1968). Weinberg's four-volume collection of *Trattati di poetica retorica del Cinquecento* (Bari: Laterza, 1970–74) contains a great number of works, often undistinguished yet interesting to peruse when pursuing some specific question. Treatises—whether in Italian, Latin, French, or English—that seemed promising for my present inquiry almost always divided themselves into the following loose categories: general treatises concerned with doctrine and some practice (e.g., Gian Giorgio Trissino, *Poetica*, 1529; Girolamo Ruscelli, *Del modo di comporre in versi nella lingua italiana*, 1558; Minturno, *Arte poetica*, 1564); manuals of poetic composition (e.g., Mario Equicola, *Instituzioni al comporre in ogni sorta di rima della lingua volgare*, 1541; Lodovico Dolce, *Osservazioni nella volgar lingua*, 1550); and treatises on poems by Cavalcanti, Petrarch, and other poets (e.g., Alessandro Vellutello, Franco Nicolò, Giovanni Andrea Gesualdo, Lucio Oradini, Francesco Patrizi, Sebastiano Erizzo, and others, including of course Torquato Tasso). I should note that Tasso's "Lezione" has not to my knowledge been recently reprinted. It can be found as "Lezione di Torquato Tasso recitata da lui nell'Accademia Ferrarese sopra il sonetto *Questa vita mortal ec.* di Monsignor Della Casa" in *Opere di Torquato Tasso*, 33 vols., ed. Giorgio Rosini, vol. 11 (Pisa: Capurro, 1823), 42–60. It is followed by "D'Incerto al seguente sonetto di Torquato Tasso" and Tasso's own "Risposta," 61–81. The categories are by no means neat; I simply wish to indicate the range of texts that often do not yield what one might hope to find; such is true of this last category that at first glance seems so promising.

While my concern here is with the pre-history of close reading of the lyric in the familiar modern sense, the scope of inquiry could be considerably enlarged to include other forms of literature. With proper categories of what constitutes systematic or holistic critical reading, one should consider whole treatments of single novels and plays along with the tentative treatments of whole poems in Eliot and Richards. Then one would go on to delineate the development with such landmarks in view as William Empson's *Seven Types of Ambiguity* (1930), *Understanding Poetry* (1938) by Cleanth Brooks and Robert Penn Warren, Warren's essay "Pure and Impure Poetry" (1942), and Brooks's *Modern Poetry and the Tradition* (1939) and *The Well Wrought Urn: Studies in the Structure of Poetry* (1947). At a certain point the value of holistic reading became widely accepted and even taken for granted. It must be stressed that poems were not simply read in isolation by the best critics of this new stripe; they were generally well trained in the skills of historiography and were fully aware of the vast terrain that lay about the plots they cultivated. Recently the so-called New Critics and their followers have come in for censure by those who caricature them in the name of a kind of pseudophilosophical expansionism or a bloodless semiotic typology.

8

THE
MATTER OF RIME

Sonnets of Sidney, Daniel, and Shakespeare

*To rhyme or not to rhyme
is not the question—
The perfect poem
is a perfect crime.
—Aleksis Rannit*

Poets may be born but poems are made. As even poetasters know, the ring of a word, the aptness of a phrase, the interlacement of motifs, the shaping of a form, are achieved at some expense of labor and feeling. Writing in meter and rime is a subjection to discipline and also an exploitation of constraints. In crude terms, the sonnet may well have been such a common form since the late Middle Ages for the very reason that the rimes suggest collocations and continuities and endings that throw up a challenge to ingenuity which may seem very much like inspiration. A sonnet or any other rimed lyric form is a pattern that requires fulfillment in words rhythmically set in grammatical idiom and words that rime at appropriate places. Often if the pattern is adequately fulfilled it is simply taken for granted and neglected. In English a breach of pattern or form often goes unrecognized or more often is tolerated as a peccadillo, perhaps, or as a puzzle for the workaday prosodist. One should now be more precise and say *poetic* prosodist, as linguists have taken to using the word "prosody" to refer to suprasegmental features (such as intonation, juncture, and stress) in *any* use of language. The poetic prosodist, then, will describe the passage or line in terms of a vocabulary that includes words like feet, caesura, hypermetrical, stress, trochee, and all the rest. Let us assume he has a proper notion of what he is about. For one thing, he must distinguish between meter and rhythm. He must recognize that "regular" and "irregular" are neutral terms and that it is the poet's business to vary and to avoid monotony. In describing rime, he must be aware of historically changing pronunciation and of regional variation. He must have some criteria of exactness and approximation. Above all, any poetic effect depends on some kind of performance, from silent reading to recitation, that evokes the text as an aesthetic entity in sounds and meanings.

Performance in the sense of reading that is aesthetic or artistically aware, whether silent or aloud, was assumed by Renaissance poets and should— though it often is not—be assumed by us. Not much is known, beyond the poetic texts themselves, and their occasional musical settings, of the manner or manners of performance. Yet it seems within reason to posit modalities of success and go beyond description to arrive at some judgment of quality. I confine myself to rime, an obvious phonic feature of much poetry and one that often either goes unheard or unremarked. My sampling is from three English poets over a period of about thirty years. The normative poetics I assume is, I think, congenial to their own. Rime is most closely associated with rhythm, but not without reason.

In the Western world rime fairly exploded into vernacular being with the first Trobadors around 1100. It does have a prehistory, but that is not my concern here. From the Trobadors the vogue of rime spread quickly to France, England, and the Germanic lands. But for the English Renaissance (not to mention the high English Middle Ages) the line of rime went by way of Sicily to Emilia and Tuscany, and, with Boccaccio and, most clearly, with Petrarch and his followers in Europe, it came to England along with many other conventions that went native. Until this century normal verse was rimed, and perhaps only now can one say that rime is no longer the normal expectation in poetry, and that "unrimed verse" may, at least for a time, be as obsolete an expression in English as "the talkies." Of course in previous centuries unrimed Latin poetry was written, experiments were made in quantitative vernacular poetry, and in England blank verse since Surrey has had great vogue and great success almost always in larger compositions than the lyric.

My brief account of the riming practice of three outstanding poets does not set out to prove anything definitive or establish rules of thumb or examine all instances. Nor can it rely on a compilation of statistics whose upshot could well be depressingly fractional and characterless. What remains is to attempt some characterization of riming practice based upon the range of possibilities. It will be assumed that variety, contrast, and novelty, as well as evenness, likeness, and familiarity, are essential to the modulations of art. The main criteria I have in mind are: (1) rime between monosyllables; (2) rime between a monosyllable and a polysyllable; (3) rime between polysyllables (withal/befall); (4) rime between two-word phrases (to all/through all); (5) rime between the same or different grammatical categories and forms; (6) masculine or feminine rime; (7) eye-rime; (8) slant rime; and (9) archaic or historical rime. Then there is of course botched or even absent rime. But no issue should hinge upon dogmatic declarations of how a word was then pronounced or should now be pronounced: it is reasonable to suppose that "love" and "move" rimed for many English ears then; but it is improbable that "eye" and "enmity" ever did about 1500, though both final vowels may have been more rounded than now. Conventional eye-rimes or slant-rimes are often "explained" otiosely as conventional. My notion, however, is that a poet would prefer a true rime and has, for whatever reason, settled for less. A poet must, of course, settle for the rimes existent in his language. English is not notably rich in rimes, and often striking rimes can simply manufacture the subject matter: heart, dart, smart, part (not to mention amore, cuore, dolore, furore or amour, jour, tour, séjour). Nearly "obligatory" or at least very common words such as the forms of the verb "to be" or the pronouns or words with marked endings like "-ness" or "-ly" can be used in rime. Even in English, as well as in highly inflected languages, such obligatory words and endings can quickly become blemishes if overused. Yet when singling out rime to observe one must naturally be mindful that the whole line, indeed poem, gives space to prepare the fleeting though essential effect. Roughly speaking, two stratagems are special emphasis and special deemphasis, with a whole gamut in between.

I briefly consider, as prolegomena to an intrinsic and aesthetic study of rime in the English Renaissance, Sir Philip Sidney's *Astrophel and Stella*, Samuel Daniel's *Delia*, and William Shakespeare's *Sonnets*.

Sidney was the first modern English virtuoso of letters. His poetry shows far more of a schooling in Italian and French practice than his most noteworthy, though halting, forerunners, Wyatt and Surrey. He can be quite free in his variations on the Petrarchan sonnet form, though for the most part in *Astrophel and Stella* he conforms to it. As with later English poetry, his staple of rime-words is monosyllabic and disyllabic nouns and verbs: show/pain/know/obtain/woe/entertain/flow/brain/stay/ blows/way/throws/spite/write (Sonnet 1). To fit in "entertaine" he is put on his mettle. Two syntactical inversions in the line cast the rhythm first adrift and then press toward the final stress: "Studying inventions fine, her wits to entertaine," where the "expanded" trochee (or more pedantically, substitute dactyl) is compensated for by the unusual stress on "fine" and on the final syllable of "entertaine" (itself an unusual word in this meaning for the time). Elsewhere in this sonnet the rhythm is varied most skillfully to keep the twelve-syllable line from plodding or breaking. In general the rimes in this sonnet are what might be uninvidiously called conventional. Their placement shows skill: in particular the one runover line ("to see if thence would flow / Some fresh and fruitful showers") keeps its shape and the rime-word "braine" is neatly set off by the striking epithet "sunne-burn'd."

One of Sidney's great virtues in his sonnets is his ability to convey a sense of the sweep and wholeness of a colloquial utterance. He takes risks. In Sonnet 55 he renounces the muses' eloquence in favor of simply crying Stella's name, and at the end the eloquence collapses (perhaps by design?):

> For let me but name her whom I do love,
>> So sweete sounds straight mine eare and heart do hit,
>> That I well find no eloquence like it.

His hope to find something better than "eloquence" seems belied by the rather awkward rhythm of the first line quoted, by the monotonous monosyllables, and by the graceless use of "hit" (sweet sounds *hit?*) and the riming combination hit/it. Oddly, only the word "eloquence" mitigates the failure. The sonnet had begun fairly well. In contrast, to my ear, the next sonnet (56) is quite generally strained and inferior:

> Fy, schoole of Patience, Fy, your lesson is
>> Far far too long to learne it without booke:
>> What, a whole weeke without one peece of looke,
> And thinke I should not your large precepts misse?
> When I might reade those letters faire of blisse,
>> Which in her face teach vertue, I could brooke
>> Somewhat thy lead'n counsels, which I tooke
> As of a friend that meant not much amisse:
> But now that I, alas, do want her sight,

> What, dost thou thinke that I can ever take
> In thy cold stuffe a flegmatike delight?
> No Patience, if thou wilt my good, then make
>> Her come, and heare with patience my desire,
>> And then with patience bid me beare my fire.

The spoken flair and the wholeness of utterance found elsewhere in *Astrophel and Stella* are here compromised by uncertain rhythm and by rimes which, though in themselves unexceptionable, are ill-used. Patience's book too long to memorize is a good conceit undetermined by the willful phrase "peece of looke" (which others may defend as a schoolboy colloquialism). "Is" riming with "misse," "blisse," and "amisse," we may accept as either a common conventional off-rime or as an authentic pronunciation. Yet the strained sense of "misse" in line 4 is simply compounded by the awkward sound, rhythm, and inversion of the line—surely one of the ungainliest. By this time the reader's own patience is tried and he may not indulge "letters faire of blisse" or the uninteresting use of the remaining conventional rimes. In a better setting the eighth line could have shown, in its rhythmical looseness, an effective colloquial litotes: in this sonnet it seems merely lame and ill-fashioned simply for the rime-word. Others may disagree and cite, point for point, some occurrence registered in the *OED,* but it seems to me that Sidney is bending idiom to the breaking point for the sake of rime, which then becomes egregiously prominent and loses its subtle structural value.

   It would be easy to catalogue at length Sidney's fine use of ordinary rime (as in Sonnets 39 or 94 or in "Leave me ô Love, which reachest but to dust"): some of his best poems make no more than skillful unobtrusive use of rime. There are instances, though, of unusual inventiveness in finding rimes and in setting them off. In Sonnet 13 we encounter a good conclusive use of monosyllable riming with polysyllable: "then / . . . Gentlemen"; and in 29 an especially effective use is made of noun ending in "-ity" and pronoun:

> So *Stella's* heart, finding what power *Love* brings,
>> To keepe it selfe in life and liberty,
>> Doth willing graunt, that in the frontiers he
> Use all to help his other conquerings.

The word "he" requires pause and emphasis, but also fulfilment in the next line. Both this heightening and also the very sense of the passage deliver great stress on the word "all" and, contrastively, some emphasis on "other." One good result is that the weak rime brings/conquerings seems more natural as part of colloquial intonation. A similar example occurs in the striking sonnet on two negatives making a positive (63). Stella has "twise said, No, No," and the poet exults:

> Sing then my Muse, now *Io Paen* sing,
> Heav'ns envy not at my high triumphing . . .

Modern readers at least must often pause to consider how the lines are to be read. According to Latin grammar one would describe "envy not" as optative subjunctive. But the rime sing/triumphing may seem awkward till one determines to lay the otherwise wavering stress fully upon the syllable "tri." As if to prepare for that and to solemnize the phrase, thus drawing out all the syllables of "triumphing," including the final riming one, this word is preceded by the same diphthong [ai] in "my" and "high." For full effect the line also requires that the word "not" receive careful emphasis. The finish of the sonnet is indeed a fine triumphing flourish:

> But Grammer's force with sweet successe confirme,
> For Grammar says (ô this deare *Stella* weighe,)
> For Grammar sayes (to Grammer who sayes nay)
> That in one speech two Negatives affirme.

The concluding rimes have a stable and measured authority that proclaims *quod erat demonstrandum.*

More unstable in rhythm and rime is Sonnet 31 ("With how sad steps, ô Moone, thou climb'st the skies"). The rimes are commonplace (wit/yet was not then substandard), though the word "descries" in the sense of "cries out" or "proclaimes" needs a modern gloss. But they are freshened in several ways. In the first three lines the ambiguous distribution of stress holds movement back noticeably and thus does not make prominent the commonness of the rimes. Then the movement begins to surge forward as we find that even the first proposition is a question and will soon know that the whole poem is pitched interrogatively. The audacious epithet in line 5 propels us to its end and into the following lines:

> Sure, if that long with *love* acquainted eyes
> Can judge of *Love,* thou feel'st a Lover's case;

> I read it in thy lookes[;] thy languisht grace,
> To me that felt the like, thy state descries.

Even the rime-word so weakly intonable in "Then ev'n of fellowship, ô Moone, tell me" is justified or naturalized rhythmically as the line spills over into the next. And the final rime-word of the poem, polysyllabic and commonplace in its substantive suffix, gains, by the forward sweep, a potential force that nonetheless requires a sudden, careful, and questioning articulation:

> Do they above love to be lov'd, and yet
> Those Lovers scorne whom that *Love* doth possesse?
> Do they call *Vertue* there ungratefulnesse?

Indeed that forward rush almost compels us to take "possesse" in the sense of being possessed by a god. "Love," italicized in the text, comes into full personification. The internal monorime of "love-" is also, of course, part of the phonic echoing (as in "above"), along with end-rime and, for that matter, the notable alliteration and assonance. Besides, "love-," in its various occurrences here, takes varying stress and so partakes of the hesitant interrogative mode.

Sidney's master was Petrarch, whom he clearly read with far more comprehension of language and understanding of technique than did any of his English predecessors. It was Petrarch who gave the universal example of rime in vernacular poetry. That there should be some attempt to imitate quantitative unrimed Latin poetry in English is not surprising. Practically everyone learned Latin and read not only classical poetry but also the vastly cultivated Neo-Latin verse written by Pontanus, Politian, Buchanan, and a host of others, including many poets in English who wrote in Latin as well, from More to Milton and Marvell. Perhaps rime did need a defense, which Samuel Daniel elegantly supplied on provocation by Thomas Campion's lightweight challenge, in order to repel the threat "to overthrow the whole state of Ryme in this Kingdom." Rime, for Daniel, gives "both to the Eare an Eccho of a delightfull report & to the Memorie a deeper impression of what is delivered therein." It provides a "knowne frame" for "those due staies for the minde, those incounters of touch as makes the motion certaine, though the varietie be infinite." In general, Daniel's principles and strictures are sensible, and his committed earnestness is at times even moving. One feels almost invited into the poet's workroom to hear him talk of his indispensable tools. We might presume, then, to inspect the jointure of his artifacts.

Most of Daniel's sonnets are in fact workmanlike, fashioned well, conventional in conceit, and smooth. Rather too insistently the poet plays the theme of the "cruel fair" who opposes her immobile disdain to his modulating praise and complaint. Only occasionally does Daniel succeed in working out an original or skillful conceit as Sidney could: it would seem that he tried, as with the notion of "reining in" in Sonnet 25. He attempts a whole sonnet in correlative verses in Sonnet 11, but the crucial last lines are poorly rimed:

> Yet will I weepe, vowe, pray to cruell Shee;
> Flint, front, Disdaine, weares, melts, and yeelds we see.

The potentially striking ungrammatical "Shee" entirely misses being clinched and thus "justified" by a powerful rime-pair. In Sonnet 15 he again tries for effect and fails to join his fine phrases:

> And if a brow with cares caracters painted,
> Bewraies my loue, with broken words halfe spoken,
> To her that sits in my thoughts Temple sainted,
> And layes to view my Vultur-gnawne hart open . . .

The "caracters" or broken words traced on his brow are strikingly half-spoken, but the brow lays bare his heart in a phrase that ends in the daring off-rime "open" spoiled by odd idiom, lame rhythm, and the ineffective sound of the ambitious phrase "vultur-gnawne."

Not to say that some of his rimes are not enterprising. Apart from possible dialectal exact rimes (thoughts/notes in Sonnet 9 and thoughts/dotes in 20), there are such unusual rimes as: horror/for her (20), Lady/made I (26), merit/were it (26), speedy/need I (27), fire/nye her (28), honor/uppon her (31), t'inwoman/assomon (37), and theaters/waters (48). Though they are not too ingeniously muted into place and though they require extraordinary tact in performance, nonetheless they deserve a sort of experimental honor. They show the earnestness, even doggedness, of Daniel's artisanry; though he tinkered with his poetry from edition to edition, he did not change them. His use of feminine rimes in such sonnets as 16 (sestet), 17 (throughout), and 27 (all but the last two lines), is clearly another mode of experiment. Some fine effects are achieved in Sonnet 34:

When Winter snowes vpon thy golden heares,
And frost of age hath nipt thy flowers neere:
When darke shall seeme thy day that neuer cleares,
And all lyes withred that was held so deere.
   Then take this picture which I heere present thee,
Limned with a Pensill not all vnworthy:
Heere see the giftes that God and nature lent thee;
Heere read thy selfe, and what I suffred for thee.
   This may remaine thy lasting monument,
Which happily posteritie may cherish:
These collours with thy fading are not spent;
These may remaine, when thou and I shall perish.
   If they remaine, then thou shalt liue thereby;
   They will remaine, and so thou canst not dye.

The rimes in the first quatrain are commonplace, but in their end-stopped similarity they help convey a tone of solemn sobriety. Line 3 interestingly holds back from merely saying "thy day shall be thy night," yet the delicacy is marred by the echoing relative clause in the next line, which has the flatness of filler unredeemed by its rime: "that was held so deere." Interest is enhanced in the second quatrain by a freshening of the conceit of the lady's portrait done in words. The portrait is indeed to be read, as the poem says with admirable succinctness: "Heere read thy selfe." Rime helps greatly in conveying meaning and nuance. "Which I heere present thee" has, in its feminine ending, a pathetic formality. Its rime-pair, "that God and nature lent thee," economically heightens the pathos in expressing the transitoriness of her beauty in the word "lent." It is also a *good* instance of this sort of relative clause, which can often seem mere filler to plaster in the rime, as happens, I think, in line 4 of this sonnet. The other set of rimes is even more unusual phonically and successful conceptually. "Not all vnworthy" is an appropriately muted, rather latinate boast which enhances the almost casual but moving "and what I suffred for thee." The "picture" will convey not only her youthful beauty but also his suffering or the reason for his suffering. In the sestet the poem gains force from the polysyllabic rime-word "monument," which raises expectations that are then fulfilled in its riming line: "These collours with thy fading are not spent." She fades, but the colors of her picture, his art, do not. And those colors, we need not be told, are also the colors of rhetoric: the poet's pen-pencil is "not all vnworthy" because it expresses communal and universal language. With mingled boast and humility the poet, after including himself in mortality ("when thou and I shall perish"), gradually rises from "These may remaine" to "If they remaine" (propositional) to "They will remaine"—all in an impressive echoing iteration. The final couplet has a quiet and simple definitiveness that makes this sonnet an outstanding example of the plain Petrarchan mode in which Daniel took such pains to do well.

His two most famous sonnets, "Care-charmer sleepe, sonne of the Sable night" (45) and "Let others sing of Knights and Palladines" (46), should of course be acknowledged in any account of his work. In this context of rime they do not, despite their almost Sidnean virtues, contain striking novelties. A proper discussion would have to go into the textual problems for which there is no time. I should, however, like to express my preference for the earlier version of the last lines of Sonnet 46. Daniel's preference seems to have differed; in the last printings (1601–11) during his lifetime the lines read:

> Though th'error of my youth in them appeare,
> Suffice they shew I liv'd and lov'd thee deare.

("Them" refers to his verses as "the Arkes, the Tropheis I erect.") Their smooth triteness is unexceptionable: they are straight from the supply house of sonneteering. For nearly the whole previous decade (1591–98), they were printed thus:

> Though th'error of my youth they shall discouer,
> Suffice they shew I liu'd and was thy louer.

It is not so much the use of the word "lover" as a general term that surprises; it is the direct and particular first-person assertion "I . . . was thy louer" that, in its conclusiveness and singular outspokenness, startles as it rimes in final place.

The perils of the sonnet lie not so much in its high technical demands as in its challenge to proliferation. It is like an addicting puzzle with confines, rules, and infinite fulfillment by hook or crook: many a collection in the Petrarchan vein may deserve the collective "a surfeit of sonnets." But the practicing sonneteer may have a special affection even for his least successful "solutions," an affection that may not attach to freer forms that can be amended or improved or shaped by discursive addition. Among the many things we do not and shall not know about *Shakes-speares/ Sonnets/ Neuer before Imprinted* (1609) is whether Shakespeare would have published them all as they now stand. Apart from matters of order, many of the 154 sonnets seem poor or mediocre or merely tolerable. Apart from matters of psychobiography (a good use here for that parlous word), the printed order seems to indicate that Shakespeare took up a theme and elaborated it in a run of sonnets and then went on to another theme. That the vague scheme is so unpredictable and so resistant to our making a full story out of it invites the conjecture that in reading the sonnets we are in Shakespeare's workshop. Surely all the poets of short poems work differently, but they are all makers as well as self-expressers and what they make is a technical feat, an artifact. Whatever Shakespeare's project may have been—whether to publish a set of sonnets with a title and perhaps a plot or whether not to publish any sonnets at all—we are free to imagine that someone purloined a sheaf of working papers which then George Eld printed for the publisher Thomas Thorpe. For some reason we do not know, they were not reprinted until 1640. Short of wishing to write yet another scenario for the *Sonnets,* I advance the supposition that what we have is a sheaf of poems from a poet's workshop.

Like any sonneteer, Shakespeare had to choose his rimes and take artistic chances with the rhythm and the sense. Indeed, an intimation of rime is an intimation of possible meaning, and with several sets of rimes (and provisional alternatives) the range of meaning becomes more defined and at the same time more complex. Accommodating rime to its place in the poem entails, then, the dynamic triad of rime, rhythm, and sense. For the most part Shakespeare's rimes are not unusual, but rather part of the stock familiar from reading such of his immediate predecessors as Sidney and Daniel. In Sonnet 76 he concludes, for the nonce, "So all my best is dressing old words new, / Spending again what is already spent," on the grounds that his theme and "addressee" also remain the same. On more general grounds there is truth in this. Most often he rimes familiar English monosyllables, at times based on now-archaic pronunciation but occasionally forced, and perhaps too often [ai] and [i] as in die/memory (1) and eye/majesty (7). All told, this "eye-rime" occurs thirteen times, though trisyllabic nouns ending in "-y" are sometimes loosely but interestingly rimed as in flattery/alchemy (114), memory/eternity (122), or husbandry/ posterity (3). In Sonnet 55 there is a finer use that is even flaunted by the two contrasting pairs, masonry/memory and enmity/posterity, which have the *force* of riming in two syllables. On rare occasions Shakespeare rimes inexactly, as in field/held (2), fleet'st/sweets (19), o'erread/dead (81), and open/broken (61). But almost always, even in the poor sonnets (of which there are too many for a great poet), the rimes are good and serviceable, as rime in the main ought to be.

As a conscientious poet Shakespeare had the conviction of his rimes, and in some clear cases was put to shifts to make the sense and rhythm come out at least acceptably. A common fault in rimed poetry—which Shakespeare in his best sonnets worked to avoid—is, as I have noted, the lame relative clause or descriptive phrase that could better have been a single word. It is, of course, difficult to distinguish padding from convincing colloquial prolixity; besides, extreme compression can well be a fault, as it is in quite a few of Shakespeare's sonnets that have to many seemed obscure. In this regard it is interesting to compare Sonnets 55 and 116, the first in the *exegi monumentum* vein, the second on the constancy of love. In 55 we read, as the poem exaltedly and rather verbosely flows,

> . . . your praise shall still find room
> Even in the eyes of all posterity
> That wear this world out to the ending doom.

The rime and the notion are accommodated. Yet the last line given here seems rhythmically weak and too long as an enjambed descriptive clause, lamely and otiosely modifying "doom" with "ending." In 116, which perhaps begins less strikingly, we find "doom" (which I take to be a true rime here in Shakespeare's pronunciation) again in the same position at the end of the twelfth line:

> Love's not Time's fool, though rosy lips and cheeks
> Within his bending sickle's compass come;
> Love alters not with his brief hours and weeks,
> But bears it out even to the edge of doom.

Here, to begin with, the clause is independent and the verb-phrase "bears it out" is not weakened by a long object ("it" versus "this world"). The trochaic stress on "even" tilts the line toward a strong conclusion with two climactic stresses on "edge" and "doom." Thus the word "doom," resonant in both sound and sense, can express its full and elemental import. Incidentally the rhythmic force, to my ear, shortens, "even" to "evn."

These two passages are clearly related, not so much in subject matter or sense as in sound and technique. We are in Shakespeare's ear.

Such experiments in sound, and more particularly in the potency of rime-words in different contexts, are naturally part of a poet's activity. Other instances could be adduced—for example, the rime hope/scope in Sonnets 52 and 29: in the first it is used in the concluding couplet with the then-ordinary meaning of "scope" as "purpose" or "means"; in the second ("Desiring this man's art and that man's scope") these forceful words are tensionally separated in the second quatrain, and "scope" takes on what was then a new meaning of "range." There are numerous other instances in which it could be argued that Shakespeare might have been thinking in rime-pairs and testing them out. One must, however, be wary and aware that some of his best sonnets show no remarkable inventiveness in rime and that some of his virtuoso rimes (as well as wordplay and conceits) occur in faulty and lightweight poems.

In larger terms of technique it is fascinating to observe the sequences, however brief, of poems on more or less the same theme, such as love-servitude, time, flattery, praise, demise, and poetry, not to mention procreation, beauty, blackness, and triangular passion. Some sonnets seem closely matched in theme, though different in quality, to the point that, fancifully, one may imagine a poor sonnet to be an acknowledged botch and a good one to be a more finely achieved response to the "same" challenge of expression. Thus I think of Sonnets 50 and 51, both dealing with a journey on horseback away from the beloved; of 80, 85, 86, all three concerning the poet's failing craft and the notorious Rival Poet; and 64 and 65, which, along with 63, are most interesting to compare. It would be foolhardy to claim that, in irrecoverable reality, Sonnet 65 was a rewriting of 64: whichever one was written first, my claim is only that they are intimately related and that 65 is far better. Sonnet 63 may less plausibly be considered the botched start of the series.

A glance shows that they share no rime-words or even rime-sounds except decay/decays:

64

When I have seen by Time's fell hand defaced
The rich proud cost of outworn buried age,
When sometime lofty towers I see down-rased
And brass eternal slave to mortal rage;

When I have seen the hungry ocean gain
Advantage on the kingdom of the shore,
And the firm soil win of the wat'ry main,
Increasing store with loss and loss with store;
When I have seen such interchange of state,
Or state itself confounded to decay,
Ruin hath taught me thus to ruminate,
That Time will come and take my love away.
    This thought is as a death, which cannot choose
    But weep to have that which it fears to lose.

65

Since brass, nor stone, nor earth, nor boundless sea,
But sad mortality o'ersways their power,
How with this rage shall beauty hold a plea,
Whose action is no stronger than a flower?
O, how shall summer's honey breath hold out
Against the wrackful siege of batt'ring days,
When rocks impregnable are not so stout,
Nor gates of steel so strong but Time decays?
O fearful meditation: where, alack,
Shall Time's best jewel from Time's chest lie hid?
Or what strong hand can hold his swift foot back,
Or who his spoil of beauty can forbid?
    O, none, unless this miracle have might,
    That in black ink my love may still shine bright.

Both poems are meditations on the theme of time's destructiveness. The rimes of 64 seem appropriate and pregnant with suggestion, especially age/rage, shore/store (in Shakespeare's favorite sense of abundance in reserve), and decay/away. "Kingdom of the shore" prepares for "state" in the sense of high or assured position. "State" makes a good rime for "meditate," and that word certainly would have fitted. But instead we find the less usual word "ruminate," not itself very elevated but making an obvious local effect in alliteration with the strong and emphatic "Ruin." But a rime for "decay" may have suggested the next disappointingly trite line,

"That Time will come and take my love away," which would have been all right in a different context, but not as a climax to a somber and even violent thought. Now Time "comes" and "takes away" rather weakly, though at the beginning "Time's fell hand" more powerfully "defaced." Choose/lose is certainly as effective a couplet-rime as any, but the conceit of the thought as "a death" that cannot help weeping over future loss seems ordinary. The remaining rimes, defaced/down-rased and gain/main, would in this context seem fertile in suggestiveness to the practicing sonneteer. Defaced/rased may have been an off-rime for Shakespeare; at any rate, he has to insure the less common meaning of "rased" by adding "down." That is in keeping with the other redundancies of the poem, as is also the riming phrasal pair: the hungry ocean gain/of the wat'ry main. Over such rimes a supersensitive poet might weep in his watery beer.

Sonnet 65 makes use of the same words (brass, rage, hand, love) and more or less specific notions, but it proceeds and culminates far more impressively. The first magnificent line ends in the emphatic word "sea," which, when defined by so rhythmically and phonically effective an epithet as "boundless," is surely richer than "ocean" (especially "hungry ocean"). "Mortality" is stronger when not rivaling Time for space and when not tied up in a phrase like "mortal rage" (meaning "ravages of mortality") which is, however, characteristically Shakespearean, one must grant, and concise. If there is some loss in not using "rage" as rime-word, it gains in Sonnet 65 by being directed lawlessly against beauty's lawful innocence: the simple legal terminology humanizes the geodetic landscape. Summer also will succumb. The interrogative mode is a skillful way of avoiding platitudinous assertion. Besides, there is a climax of mortality's destructiveness when even "gates of steel" are not "so strong but Time decays." Indeed it is, finally, inhuman Time that destroys; the verb "decays" used transitively has the convincing force of "destroy," while as a noun in 64 it comes as anticlimactic filler in the line "Or state itself confounded to decay." With the exclamation "O fearful meditation" the poem takes itself seriously, indeed desperately so in the questions that follow. It also takes itself seriously in answering the questions in an honest conditional. By a miracle, mere ink may survive what seemingly solid substance could not. Again, the rime-words of this final couplet could serve as well as any other: might/bright is certainly a common rime. Yet the emphatic, trisyllabic and necessary word "miracle" alliterates with "might" and the whole line rushes in rhythm to the last word. Thereby the following, final line becomes, in its consistent, mostly closed monosyllables, solemn and deliberate: "black ink" is truly climactic; "my love," only now mentioned, may have some chance of permanence both somber and bright.

It can be as useful to discuss rime in poetry as to discuss any other constituent of art: one may talk statistically or mensurally of the incidence of patterning of rime just as in painting one may note the angle and curvature of a line or the saturation of colors. But rimes and lines and colors are found in contexts that possess value and somehow confer value on all their constitutive parts. So it is that in discussing a relatively nonconceptual element in the language-art of poetry like rime, one may easily falter in trying plausibly to encompass rime-in-the-abstract, a particular set or use of rime, and a single value-laden context—a particular poem. One reason I confine myself to the sonnet is that it reduces the variables of comparison. My three authors are convenient temporally and aesthetically in that they are the great English masters of the sonnet before Donne and Milton. I know of only a few attempts to discuss the use of rime in this period (or any other in English literature) as both a technical and an aesthetic means of poetry. The subject to some may seem pat, to others unimportant or antiquarian. As to its place in English poetry, we cannot help recalling what Milton said on rejecting rime for the "Heroic Verse" of *Paradise Lost:* rime was the "Invention of a barbarous age, to set off wretched matter with lame Meter; grac't indeed since by the use of some famous modern Poets, carried away by Custom, but much to their own vexation, hindrance, and constraint to express many things otherwise, and for the most part worse than else they would have exprest them." The whole prefatory paragraph is a fine spate of special pleading, a veritable "example set . . . of ancient liberty recover'd to Heroic Poem from the troublesome and modern bondage of Riming." Even under Charles's son Charles, the aged Areopagite proclaims yet another "ancient liberty." Of course pugnacity is understandable in a great and masterly poet, but we can be grateful that Milton did not carry his reverence for free unriming Homer so far as to turn quantitative.

No revolutions in literature are permanent. We are now in a time when the most prestigious poetry is rimeless and often meterless, however rhythmical it may be. At the same time the loudest criticism currently mocks what it calls formalism (using, perhaps unwittingly, Leon Trotsky's opprobrious term) or New Criticism (caricaturing a supposedly unified doctrine of form in isolation), and instead often reduces poetry to language in general or to "discourse" subject to further but equal discourse in a tropological and ideological vein or to simply the flow and froth of words in their capricious suggestiveness. The technicality, the formality, the art of poetry are at best taken for granted. Indeed most critics, of whatever persuasion, write about poetry as if it could just as well have been prose. But even in an unrimed age, aesthetically successful rime can hold its own. As modernism and its eddies continue to recede and stagnate in repetition, perhaps we can look for a renewed cultivation of craft and for a renewed formal mastery, not to mention fresh transformations of reality in art. Historically, rime since the Trobadors has been a potent poetic resource and remains so still potentially. In rimed poetry, rime, as part of the matter, matters.

Bibliographical Notes

The standard editions I have used are Sir Philip Sidney, *The Poems,* ed. William A. Ringler, Jr. (Oxford: Oxford University Press, Clarendon Press, 1962); Samuel Daniel, *Poems and A Defence of Ryme,* ed. Arthur Colby Sprague (Chicago: University of Chicago Press, 1965; corrected from the first edition of 1930); and William Shakespeare, *The Sonnets,* ed. Douglas Bush and Alfred Harbage (New York: Penguin, 1970). The first two are properly old-spelling editions, the Shakespeare follows the convention of modernization and I have checked it against the facsimile reproduction of the 1609 edition published by the Scolar Press (Menston, England, 1968).

The best account of rime is Viktor Zhirmunskij, *Rifma, eë istorija i teorija* (Petrograd: Voprosy Poètiki, 1923), reprinted now definitively in his *Teorija stikha* (Leningrad: Sovetskij Pisatel', 1975). Of equal importance are the many studies of Roman Jakobson, as collected in volume 5 of his *Selected Writings: On Verse, its Masters and Explorers,* ed. Stephen Rudy and Martha Taylor (The Hague: Mouton, 1979). Other important studies, including collaborative exegeses, are conveniently collected in *Questions de poétique* (Paris: Editions du Seuil, 1973). The later *Shakespeare's Verbal Art in Th'expence of Spirit* by Roman Jakobson and Lawrence G. Jones (The Hague: Mouton, 1970) is a particularly apposite instance of Jakobson's method of practical criticism.

George Saintsbury's *A History of English Prosody from the Twelfth Century to the Present Day* in 3 vols. (London: Macmillan, 1906–10) is leisurely, chatty, and not very helpful. Much more trustworthy is the linguistically informed treatise of John Thompson, *The Founding of English Metre* (New York: Columbia University Press, 1961), which culminates in celebrating Sidney as the first poet in modern English to reach metrical "perfection"; but almost nothing is said of rime. The best essay in English on rime is William K. Wimsatt, "One Relation of Rhyme to Reason," in *The Verbal Icon: Studies in the Meaning of Poetry* (Lexington: University of Kentucky Press, 1954), 153–66; originally published in 1944. For reliable discussions of the relation between rhythm and meter the most useful volume of reference is W. K. Wimsatt, ed., *Versification: Major Language Types* (New York: Modern Language Association/New York University Press, 1972); in my contribution, "Spanish Versification" (169–70), I state my own general views. Currently the best historically minded and aesthetically perceptive analyst of the relation between sound and sense, including rime, is John Hollander, *Vision and Resonance: Two Senses of Poetic Form* (New York: Oxford University Press, 1975).

It is not to my immediate purpose to cite any of the stylistic analyses of Sidney, Daniel, and Shakespeare. I am not aware of any direct indebtedness to such studies in questions of rime.

9

CIVIC POETRY

There is, fortunately, no end to classifying poetry. We are told that there are short poems and long poems, or more cautiously, shorter and longer ones. We note that some poems are rimed and others are not. Some establish patterns we call stanzas and then proceed to repeat the pattern a varying number of times. Others take the pattern of a single line, as in blank verse, and simply stamp out any number of subsequent lines. Already enough formal factors have been mentioned to create by permutation a fairly elaborate system of poetic species. If we add categories of subject matter we can derive many species of the type "shorter riming pentameter poem on love." Classification according to formal properties has a long tradition and is the staple of handbooks. With the Greeks, and, to a lesser extent, the Romans, it was common to associate certain subjects with certain verse forms. But in a broad sweep of Western poetry it often happens that a given subject may be treated in verse of almost any form. My concern here is with the subject matter as a means of classification. It interests me to inquire what the subjects or topics of poetry are that conventionally and usefully are employed to sort out poems. Thinking of standard and recent anthologies, I would list: love-poetry, religious poetry, meditative poetry, narrative (that is, storytelling) poetry, pastoral poetry, visionary poetry, satirical poetry, and even "useful" poetry. Scholars are given to positing further categories, such as topographical, panegyrical, celebrational, and funereal poetry. How they all fit together— whether as simply a list or as a hierarchy or as a set of sets and subsets—and how illuminating they are for our appreciation of poetic art, remain open questions. Usually, I think, one is presented with a group of poems under a certain subject heading and one simply assents to the rightness or the convenience of having them so headed. Another slightly different reason for accepting ad hoc someone's subject heading is that often familiar poems are seen in a new light, not necessarily revelatory but possibly refreshing. As with any good work of art, so with a good poem: the last classificatory word will never be said about it.

One possible category of poetry that, for what it's worth, intrigues me is what I choose to call civic poetry. I have never seen that designation in English but have noted that the resourceful librarians who compile subject catalogues in English do recognize these related headings: political poetry, social poetry, revolutionary poetry, patriotic poetry, and poetry of protest. They inevitably suggest crisis, urgency, propaganda, and nonartistic "relevance." We may think of the use of ballad and folksong modes, complete with music, which from the Spanish Civil War to the Indochinese War have been made to express attitudes of solidarity or opposition. Those headings also suggest patriotic songs and poems such as "Columbia, the Gem of the Ocean," "Rule Britannia," "America the Beautiful," "Old Ironsides," and "In Flanders Fields"—a familiar though not poetically distinguished list. An obvious category are the official national anthems, some of which are even internationally famous at least for the music. They may be typed as entreaties to the Deity, as assertions, as exhortations, or as narratives. In monarchical countries, for instance, God will be asked in the imperative to "preserve the sovereign," as in: "God save Our Gracious Queen," "Gott erhalte Franz den Kaiser," or "Bozhe, Tsarya khrani." Under assertions we might put "My country, 'tis of thee . . . of thee I sing," or "Deutschland, Deutschland über alles, über alles in der Welt." Under exhortations would fit the "Marseillaise" ("Allons, enfants de la Patrie") and the Mexican "Himno Nacional" ("Mexicanos, al grito de guerra, El acero aprestad y el bridón"). Narrative anthems may be less common, but narration enters into many, including the "Star-Spangled Banner," whose grammar and syntax remain for most Americans an unprobed mystery for life. In fact, though we can all perform our perfunctory duty on ceremonial occasions in singing that anthem, it nonetheless costs us effort to recite and parse the words without the music. When we do, we may create for ourselves a shock of recognition mingled perhaps with some embarrassment.

That tinge of embarrassment may have its validity. And yet when we cast an eye over the sweep of Western poetry we are constrained to acknowledge much poetry that has to do with, in a word, patriotism: the father/motherland, the crises of national life, the exploits of leadership and citizenly virtue. We grant the Greeks and Romans their civic pride as expressed in poetry; we look admiringly on the line of Italian poetry that for long centuries envisaged a finally united Italy; we lend our aesthetic sympathy to Russian poems of affection for Mother Russia. I say "we," using that shifty pronoun precisely to suggest that many Americans and Britishers nowadays often seem wary of any civic sentiment overtly expressed about their own countries. It is curious that, in contrast to many other countries, Americans (and may I add the British?) do not use the expressions "fatherland" and "motherland," nor have they much in the past. Perhaps it is some long-lasting revulsion consequent upon the First World War, or the Second, or Vietnam, or perhaps it comes of a diverse or divided society with fairly safe frontiers. Certainly there is a fear, in the name of propriety, of incurring jingoism or chauvinism and simply an embarrassment in uttering platitudes or glorying in complacent power. It is indeed difficult to describe the present situation because all the words seem loaded or trite and, though pretending otherwise, many of us are alert to any breach of decorum that might expose "us" or "them" to peer-group disapproval as flag-waving bigots and superpatriots. Dr. Johnson once uttered a sudden apothegm: that "patriotism is the last refuge of a scoundrel." It is clearly symptomatic that that phrase is commonly taken as denigrating patriotism, whereas for Dr. Johnson, as anyone should know who has read in his works and in Boswell's life, the most heinous thing a scoundrel can do is claim to be a patriot, to wrap himself in the flag.

Granted that patriotism, like all *isms*, should be scrutinized and granted also that ideas and feelings generally associated with patriotism vary from age to age, it is only a single aspect of what I shall try to characterize as civic poetry. One may speak of amorous or erotic behavior, religious or contemplative behavior, and also "observational" behavior in the sense of simply contemplating nature or the passing scene. I would say that there is also civic or perhaps communal behavior, arising in the family and homestead and expanding to neighborhood, town, city, country, and perhaps even to the whole sociable world. Significant social relations and exchanges take place that are the subject matter of a species of poetry and of literature in general. Social poetry might do as a designation, but the word "social" is vague and ambiguous: it is too contaminated with the strong connotations of the word "society," which so oddly may refer either to the upper crust or to the middle and lower orders and which suggests a marked sociological approach that I do not intend. So I hold to the epithet "civic."

By civic poetry I mean poetry that has as its subject matter the behavior of those within a true community who as members go about their daily business, who govern and are governed, who are conscious of their national and historical setting, and who can respond communally to threat and crisis. Thus civic poetry is *not* about private introspection, meditation, or prayer, nor is it about private individual love or self-fulfillment, nor yet is it about the remote, the uncanny, and the mythical. Its range of tone does not include love-passion, religious effusion, satiric force, or individual tragedy. Positively and succinctly, civic poetry is concerned with community, that is, with cohesion, duty, honor, honesty, belongingness, and communal survival. I mean all these terms to be descriptive and defining, not just a list of namby-pamby virtues. Besides, since I am ranging broadly, I should emphasize that civic behavior and civic assumptions vary greatly from age to age and country to country. Against the vulgar habit of recognizing only plus and minus (what is not a virtue is a vice, or praising virtue can only be vapid), one must at least historically grant that cohesion, for example, does not necessarily connote xenophobia or that doing one's duty does not necessarily make one a prig or a chauvinist. To read civic poetry from the past requires an understanding of the past and of old imperatives.

We lend our historical understanding more readily perhaps to narrative or epic poems than to terser lyrics, for the circumstantiality of narrative powerfully affects our aesthetic credence. The poems of Homer should at least be touched on here. We rightly read them as a kind of historical fiction that focuses attention on characters and events as shaped in a plot. The *Iliad* we designate as an epic or heroic poem so as to classify it. But it has elements in it of civic poetry, perhaps most strikingly in the characterization of Nestor and in the description of the shield of Achilles. Hephaistos, forging the shield, represents on it communal scenes: two cities in diverse activities and a variegated countryside. In one city there are marriages and festivals and also a public quarrel that goes to court. But the other city is bravely holding out as it is besieged by two rival armies; the two armies clash and one wins in the passionate battle. The country scenes are wholesome, industrious, and festive. No judgment is implied. What we have is not a utopia, but a panorama of normal human activity. In the *Odyssey* the central character of Odysseus is far more developed and circumstantial than even Achilles, and the central concern is not friendship between buddies and the spoils of war but rather the return home to wife and family and kingdom of a man who is defined by his uniquely individual genius *and* by his communal skills and virtues. The people and societies Odysseus and Telemachus encounter are often instructively civic, and are enhanced by contrast to the prepotent lovers Circe, Calypso, and Polyphemus. If I come close to an excessively ethical reading of the Homeric poems, I am content to draw back and simply reflect in wonderment on how Homer mitigates the extremes of battle pieces and adventure tales on the one hand and ethical example or allegory on the other. In his representation of communities he occasionally strikes a markedly civic note.

Homer's successor poets in Greece show great variety in subject matter, and indeed founded perdurable themes that continue still as historically canonical. Hesiod in his *Works and Days* mingled the practical and the ethical and in his *Theogony* gave us raw genealogy of the early Greek gods. Sappho, Alcman, Alcaeus, and others wrote, of course, of love, drinking, the gods, natural beauty, and so on. But Alcaeus was perhaps the first to liken the state or community to a ship in peril. And before him the Spartan poet Tyrtaeus urged young warriors to fight bravely and die gloriously for their fatherland (*patris*). Somewhat later Simonides of Ceos (556–467 B.C.) wrote lines in praise of the bravery of the Spartans at Thermopylae, most famously: "Stranger, take this message to the Spartans: that here we lie, obedient to their orders." One could argue that the most civic of all the early Greek poets was Pindar, who in his elaborate odes celebrated athletic victories, weaving together strands of the victor's family, the example of gods and heroes, and local patriotic pride. The great athletic contests that gave Pindar his subject matter were communal, civic, and also international. Much later, Renaissance poets took up not the themes but rather what they perceived to be the free-wheeling metrical and stanzaic forms.

Within my purview the prime heir to this mostly fragmentary Greek witness was the Roman Horace, who, in his *carmina* or odes especially, created an image of civic behavior that put the best construction on the new comity created by Caesar Augustus. One must recall the succession of civil wars that wrecked the Republic in order to appreciate Horace's fervency, for all his gracefully discursive casualness. Many of the odes are concerned with his friendships, with dining and drinking, with his little Sabine farm, with casual adventures and mishaps, and with the diversions of nonchalant love affairs. Sometimes there is an overt moral or admonition, but usually the tone reflects a tolerant, mildly skeptical, enjoyable Stoicism. These have the air of occasional poems depicting moods and attitudes elaborated by fairly free association, by contiguity, and by examples. I would hazard to say that about fifteen of the odes could be called strongly civic. Several are cast in religious terms(ɪ:12, ɪ:21, and the *Carmen saeculare*), but it is the old communal religion as sturdy way of life: Jupiter and the other gods, heroes like Tarquin and Camillus are invoked to keep watch over Augustus who rules the empire justly; boys and girls are exhorted to praise the gods, especially Diana and Apollo, and to ask their aid. We are reminded that the Roman gods in their multiple aspects were still close to ordinary matters of daily life; this suited Horace who was far from theological and more than a little superstitious. An ode to Fortune (ɪ:35) cautiously invokes her, as do the poor farmer and the mariner and even the savage, in the knowledge that true hope and loyalty will not incur her presence in its baleful aspect: only the faithless rabble and the false courtesan, like perfidious friends, decamp when the wine runs out. The goddess is asked to preserve Augustus on a military expedition and also his new swarm of young warriors, as they strike fear into distant enemies. The fratricide and criminality of recent times, including profanation of altars, provoke the urgent hope that Fortune will forge anew the blunted arms for use against the Massagetes and the Arabs. This is a poem of deep civic concern, earnestly yet ambiguously addressed to the solemn and unpredictable Lady Luck.

A number of odes concern the corruptions of the commonweal, contrasting the communal past with the too luxurious present (ɪɪ:15), the life of productive leisure with greed and aggrandizement (ɪɪ:16), farm life with covetous wealth (ɪɪ:18, ɪɪɪ:16), or simply lamenting the decline into decadent living (ɪɪɪ:6, ɪɪɪ:24). The state of affairs is presented soberly in each case and without the strident tones of satire or ridicule. They concern communal quotidian life and general social situations. On the other hand there are some odes that are strikingly historical, that is, particular in their historical reference, and that largely deal with Augustus as victor (ɪ:37), ruler (ɪv:2), and even demigod (ɪv:5). In them there is a sense of national purpose and importance as the state is ruled and protected and as the people celebrate victories. The earliest is about the news of Antony's defeat at Actium. Opprobrium falls heavily on Cleopatra with nearly savage glee. "Nunc est bibendum, nunc pede libero / pulsanda tellus," for the queen who madly prepared ruin for Rome has suffered disaster along with her degenerate court of eunuchs. This, then, is a day of national salvation. Yet what makes the poem remarkable is the image of Cleopatra, the "fatale monstrum," choosing a noble death: not to flee or to be paraded in a triumph as a captive, but to take her own life by snakebite. A Roman way to die: by her mode of death Cleopatra enhances the victory of Augustus in showing herself a worthy foe. In its convivial social setting this ode traces a surprising trajectory from relief at the danger past, to loathing of the fierce enemy, to an acknowledgment of her high worth. The poet accomplishes this in his own private yet also civic voice and ruminations.

In fact, Horace characterizes himself as a poet along a whole range of tonalities. In these civic poems of his the poet is naturally part of the body politic as well as its observer. In his most famous assertion of himself as poet, "Exegi monumentum aere perennius" (III:30), Horace boldly proclaims his work as eternal as Rome. Why? He says: "I shall be spoken of . . . as the first to have brought back Aeolian [Greek] song to Italic measures." That is a conquest of sorts. He uses the word "deducere," which has many meanings, one of which he used in the Cleopatra ode: Cleopatra was unwilling to be brought back (*deduci*) for a proud triumph. At least his poetry can be conceived as a civic accomplishment. A far more self-depreciating version of the poet appears in a late ode (IV:9) in which the poet, speaking to a friend, urges him not to undervalue the durability of humble lyric meters. Besides, many worthy folk have gone unremembered and unmourned because no "vates sacer" was at hand. The sacred bard, the priestly poet, the national laureate are to be found among the Greeks and, with Horace and Virgil, among the Romans. It is true of course that Virgil, that tender melancholy poet, addressed himself to writing a national epic of ethnic origins; the patriotic fervor is there but it is muted by a pervasive sense of the hardness of fate and the great cost of enterprise ("tantae molis erat Romanam condere gentem"). A pattern is set by Horace in his odes and by Virgil, not only in the *Aeneid* but also in the *Eclogues* and *Georgics*, which later ages were so often to emulate. One need only mention the complex patriotic flair of Dante, the national hero Vasco da Gama in Camões's *Os Lusíadas*, and the civic poems in Spenser's *The Shepheardes Calender* and prominent civic elements in his *Faerie Queene*. The civic bard comes again into his own in many countries during the Romantic period. If

Virgil is the more obvious pattern of grandiloquent national poetry, Horace, in the odes I have mentioned, was a durable instance, especially in the ode of, so to say, civic self-praise (IV:9). Here he begins by granting Homer's preeminence, though not without first proclaiming his own originality in exploiting lyric measure in Latin. Brave men lived before Agamemnon, but they are all unwept and unknown for lack of a "sacred bard." And he turns to address his friend Lollius (consul, 21 B.C.), a "new man" like himself, who serves the cause of civil justice. He is an example of the hardy patriot for whom Horace provides the model of a man "who has acquired the art of using the gifts of the gods wisely and of bearing harsh poverty, and who fears disgrace more than death: he is not fearful of dying for dear friends or for the fatherland" (non ille pro caris amicis / aut patria timidus perire). Horace's too is the phrase "dulce et decorum est pro patria mori," which can be rendered, "it is comforting and glorious to die for one's country" (III, 2). But, as often in Horace, this is not mindless jingoism addressed to young Romans. The next lines run: "and death pursues the fleeing warrior, nor does it spare youth's unwarlike knees or fearful back." Horace is sensible without being stuffy; Virgil is sensitive without being irresolute. Their civic legacy is thus all the more remarkable.

In the Middle Ages, during much of which Virgil and Horace (though not his *Odes*) were school texts, civic concerns were often identified with Rome and Christianity and with loyalty to prince and emperor. The annals of poetry are filled with satire, complaint, and mockery directed at churchmen and secular rulers, as well as lesser culprits. But outside Dante and Petrarch one would be hard put to find the sort of civic poetry I am dealing with. It was Petrarch who, in his *Canzoniere* of 366 poems, has at least one that is noteworthy as civic, his *canzone* "Italia mia" (no. 128). It may have been written during a siege of Parma (1344–45), but there are innumerable other such events that for centuries lacerated the country. After invoking the Ruler of Heaven, Petrarch addresses himself, in a singularly personal voice, to the many rulers of Italy, the local strongmen and *condottieri* who hold the reins of "lovely regions" (*belle contrade*) stretching from the Po River to the Arno and the Tiber. Who will rescue us, he asks, from the human deluge invading from lawless barbaric lands? Nature has provided the Alps as a defense; the ancient examples of Marius and Caesar show what "our steel" could do; but "your divided wills are spoiling the loveliest part of the world." "It now seems," he continues, "that (by whatever malignant stars) heaven holds us in detestation, thanks to you, to whom so much was entrusted." He asks the quarreling rulers what cause they have for harassing poor neighbors, persecuting the unfortunate, and hiring foreign mercenaries. He is constrained simply to tell the truth: instead of being guided by alien treachery, they should rally native valor, for it is not dead in Italian hearts (*ne l' italici cor*). With some sense of the history of those times, one may well wonder to what ideals or principles Petrarch can appeal. The popes were to continue residing in Avignon, exiled by the unruly Romans and held captive by the French; they were impotent and politicized. Merely appealing to standard morality could avail little, although Petrarch beseeches them to turn from violence to worthier pursuits of hand or intellect, to graceful praise, to some virtuous study. "Thus down here [in Italy] one may enjoy oneself, and find open the way to heaven." All that would seem unlikely to persuade competing tyrants in their fierce bellicosity.

There is something both pathetic and innovative in Petrarch's poem. The very word "Italy" must have sounded strange to contemporary ears. Even among the ancient Romans there was not much of a feeling of Italy as a separate national entity; indeed Italy was no more than a sort of home province of varying frontiers. And Petrarch's age was a time of only incipient and embryonic nationhood. Not really until 1871 would Italy be flimsily united. But at the same time this *canzone* can be considered as the beginning of a long tradition of an Italian *patria* or fatherland kept alive not by any political reality but by poets in their civic poetry. As is proper in a *canzone*, the poem ends with a send-off, an *envoi*. It is, after all, a message addressed to the native rulers and warlords. Petrarch tells his poem that its mission will be hazardous in confronting vicious and inveterate custom. Yet there are the magnanimous few to whom the words should be: "Who will preserve me? I go crying: 'Peace, peace, peace!'" (di' lor: "Chi m'assicura? / I' vo gridando: 'Pace, pace, pace!'"). Thus by writing a poem the poet has committed a patriotic act, but for a *patria* that exists only as an imaginative conception. And it is he alone, in his private, personal, yet civic voice, who addresses the magnates and earthshakers in the name of some future comity among the "belle contrade."

In subsequent history the question arises, how effective *politically* have such poems been as this of Petrarch, the Romantic poems of Foscolo ("I Sepolcri") and Leopardi ("All'Italia"), and indeed "La Marseillaise" and "The Battle Hymn of the Republic"? That may be mostly a matter of history and sociology, yet it undeniably concerns the life and function of literature as institution and tradition. But that is not my emphasis here. I am most interested in civic poems that are good as poems, not simply noteworthy for their practical effect. It is not surprising that very many civic poems are mediocre or bad, however effective as part of a national tradition. What is striking is that sometimes some of them are good and should be especially respected and cherished. The emotions to be evoked are surprisingly there. In British literature many people can be moved by the Old English poem known as "The Wanderer" or by Sir Walter Scott's "Lay of the Last Minstrel," which has the famous lines:

> Breathes there the man, with soul so dead,
> Who never to himself hath said,
>   This is my own, my native land!
> Whose heart hath ne'er within him burn'd,
> As home his footsteps he hath turn'd,
>   From wandering on a foreign strand!
> If such there breathe, go, mark him well;
> For him no Minstrel raptures swell;
> High though his titles, proud his name,
> Boundless his wealth as wish can claim;
> Despite those titles, power, and pelf,
> The wretch, concentred all in self,
> Living, shall forfeit fair renown,
> And, doubly dying, shall go down
> To the vile dust, from whence he sprung,
> Unwept, unhonor'd, and unsung.
>
> O Caledonia! stern and wild,
> Meet nurse for a poetic child!
> Land of brown heath and shaggy wood,
> Land of the mountain and the flood.

Here we have a whole nexus of motifs: the wanderer in danger of losing native roots, nostalgia for mother country, the prospect of death among strangers, the national sacramental role of the poet, and so on. There is an ample literature of such motifs, not so well represented in English and American literature on a high level, but common in, say, Russia and Spain and in numerous smaller and not insignificant countries. Yet the names of Wordsworth and Whitman come to mind, or Whittier and Frost, certainly Yeats, and of course Shakespeare.

A reader of English Renaissance poetry readily accepts the cult of Britain and its monarchy. Despite the bloody wars and strident enmity among the English, Welsh, Scots, and Irish, we remember that the Tudors were Welsh and that the Stuarts were Scottish. The ancient Roman appellation Britannia is supremely operative, especially in Spenser's *Faerie Queene*. But in Shakespeare, Drayton, and Herrick the usual term is England, though sometimes as *pars pro toto*. And in Marvell and Dryden the ever-present ambiguities of nationhood are more in tension. Shakespeare in the famous passages is quite Anglocentric. John of Gaunt's melancholy ruminations on the plight of England under Richard II occur in a play whose ruling image is a garden gone wild under the hand of a regal gardener. It is a magnificent series of anaphora: "This throne of kings, this scept'red isle, / This earth of majesty, this seat of Mars, / This other Eden, demi-paradise,"—with a total of fifteen iterations of "this," all varied and modulated memorably. By this stirring rhetorical flight the dying John rouses the civic passions of the dramatic audience. Green, fertile England protected by the encircling sea has now been indentured by criminal self-conquest. Eloquence, as often in such poetry, is fired by crisis. That is true also of the king's exhortation in *Henry V* before the battle at Agincourt. The English forces are reported outnumbered, but Henry turns that to a positive: "I would not lose so great an honor / As one man more me thinks would share from me / For the best hope I have." It is the eve of Saint Crispin's day and on the morrow great deeds will be done whose scars will endure as marks of honor. The individual strain of patriotic and civic honor is at issue:

> And Crispin Crispian shall ne'er go by,
> From this day to the ending of the world,
> But we in it shall be remembered—
> We few, we happy few, we band of brothers.

All the more glorious is the battle for the common good waged by the exemplary few: quite different—though Crispinus and Crispian were cobblers—from the rabble in massed ranks as invincible host. Here, in general terms, is a dilemma of civic poetry that can be expressed in the assertion that the individual and spontaneous participant does make, if multipled in kind, a difference. The "Star-Spangled Banner," for instance, begins, in paraphrase, "O *tell* whether you can see . . . that which . . ." Those who were there are the fortunate minority, the happy few. Shakespeare the civic poet needs no further illustration. What needs pondering in perspective are our own audience reactions to his dramatist's appeals to patriotism, citizenship, and duty. Why do we not dismiss them, especially out of their dramatic context, as sanctimonious?

Even Americans, who fought two wars with England, seem able to leap immediately from the particular (historically vague data) to the general (propulsion for the right cause). Poetry about unusual virtue seems often, owing to our fallen state, doomed from the start. Are emotions nowadays aroused more by the grand malefactor than by the humble saint? Virtue, so long as it is modest, rural, and knows its place, can be unanimously praised; the "brave, bad man" may be more interesting. Monotonous virtue pales beside polyphonous vice. To be a hero means to be singled out, to be perhaps egregious but also exemplary. The fate of the word "egregius" (out of the flock; in English, "egregious") might caution would-be heroes. But when passions rise the human tendency to dichotomize increases also: either/or, both/and, on the one hand/on the other. Such straitening binary opposition invades civic poetry, because the assumption is that there is a community *and* that there are always threats to its cohesion. Yet the obverse may occur when the community is so broadly based and so fervent that it may even tolerate outsiders and opponents. Or, beyond that, it can rise to a historically aware state in which winners, victims, and losers are all part of a dynamic, complex, communal process.

A major poem in English that exhibits this most generous perspective is Andrew Marvell's "An Horatian Ode upon Cromwell's Return from Ireland." By the time Marvell composed his poem, Oliver Cromwell had become the preeminent leader of the victorious parliamentary and Protestant forces. Charles I had been beheaded in 1649. In 1650, the probable year Marvell composed his poem, the future could bode only the powerful thrust of Cromwell, battling first in Ireland and then in Scotland to preserve the traditional realm of Great Britain. Wherever Marvell's sympathies lay, his prescience could hardly have envisaged with assurance the Restoration ten years later. He grew up, at home and abroad, at a time of national disruption. In 1650 he was 29; later in the decade he would be, presumptively, implicated in the efforts to restore the Stuarts, that is, Charles II. So little the evidence and so young the author, we have no choice but to reserve a tentative judgment on Marvell's allegiance and its propriety. Horace, too, was living through great events; that he became an "Augustan" is perhaps less remarkable than that Marvell survived to become a monarchical supporter of Charles II: the stakes were higher and more permanent in Horace's Rome. It is still a historical conundrum to decide, in *our* terms, who was on the "right" side, yet Marvell's manifest desire to write in the line of Horace at that juncture in his nation's history must have given his contemporaries and must give us similar historical breadth. Ambivalence or resignation are not the right words; rather, a complex awestruck acceptance of great turns in events.

It is disconcerting perhaps for the modern reader to find juxtaposed the descriptions of Cromwell's triumphs and the affecting scene of Charles's beheading. How, we may ask, can we readers countenance the enhancement of Cromwell alongside Charles's noble martyrdom? If we do, under what circumstances and by what belief? Perhaps for Marvell the circumstances were close enough. Augustus Caesar had settled a long succession of bids for power and civil wars and was consolidating his regime by moving against the Britons (1:35) and other far-flung dependencies. Where would it all stop? How are we to know? Here we must be alert to the all-important, historical "shifter," the "we." Who is living through what? It is not only the perception one might have of a trajectory of historical process during a time of communal crisis, it is also the time at which a poet, during that unstable period, might think to write a poem. Francis Scott Key wrote his much lesser text, as we know, during a single night. Marvell had, perhaps, a more provisional resolve. When, at the end, he exhorts Cromwell, may it not be with resignation? After all, Cromwell seems to be heaven's mysteriously anointed:

> But thou the Wars and Fortunes Son
> March indefatigably on;
> > And for the last effect
> > Still keep thy Sword erect:
>
> Besides the force it has to fright
> The Spirits of the shady Night,
> > The same *Arts* that did *gain*
> > A *Pow'r* must it *maintain.*

We are in the realm here of Horatian ambiguous but deep irony. The word "Pow'r" has its universal meaning perhaps, but also that of an army—one that requires command, loyalty, and success. Will it last, we are asked almost to question. The whole propulsion of the poem carries us in its onrushing violence to a point where we, as historically immersed readers, must feel some need to answer yes, but then to realize that we do not know, nor did the poet, and, if for the time being we must bow to force, in the end some peace may providentially come. For both Marvell and Horace there is a presiding providence or fate in history; for both of them survival of the nation, that is, the people and the state, is uppermost. But the parallels can be forced. After all, Horace became even a panegyrist of Augustus, but Marvell maintained an ambiguity that responds to the insecurity of the continuing militancy of the moment. What Horace provided were models in lyric poetry of critical communal concern. What Marvell found were classical models (with all their prestige) for a grave, deeply ironic and personal meditation on the factional politics and violence of his day without the fanaticism of the factions. Marvell's "Horatian Ode" was published only three years after his death in the *Miscellaneous Poems* printed by his fictional widow. Just two copies of that volume survive with the poem unexcised. The factions almost prevailed.

Marvell's best known poems are pastoral and amatory. He can wittily praise solitude to the point of solipsism ("Two Paradises 'twere in one / To live in Paradise alone"). Or he can urge his beloved to join him in mastery over time ("Let us roll all our Strength, and all / Our sweetness up into one Ball"). "The Garden" and "To His Coy Mistress" are clearly not civic poems. "Upon Appleton House," on the other hand, clearly is in its brilliant celebration of teeming nature and a vigorous family whose garden and house had supplanted a cloistered nunnery.

In the violent divisive times in which Marvell wrote such a range of poetry, there were other fine poets in England writing abundantly on love, on religion, on nature, and on country life with no necessary hint that battles and polemics were taking lives and fouling the air. One such was Robert Herrick who, at the mature age of 57, published his first volume *Hesperides* in 1648. A notable civic poem of his concerns the bringing home of the last cart of the fruits of summer: "The Hock-Cart, or Harvest Home: To the Right Honourable Mildmay, Earle of Westmorland," which addresses his noble friend, the poet Mildmay Fane, and also the tenant farmers. For nostalgic devotees of Merrie Olde England it is a *locus classicus* in more than one sense, having as its subtext Tibullus's evocation of a pagan Roman country festival ("rura cano, rurisque deos": II, i) in honor not only of Bacchus and Ceres, but also of Cupid and Venus. Both poems exhort all present with liberal imperatives to join in, whatever their station may be. For Tibullus the festival is religious in that, to us, diffuse Roman sense. For Herrick the occasion is a folk festival of which the significance in communal cohesion should be celebrated.

> Come Sons of Summer, by whose toile,
> We are the Lords of Wine and Oile:
> By whose tough labours, and rough hands,
> We rip up first, then reap our lands.

Mildmay is urged to come and see the cart crowned by the "harvest swains and wenches" who have decked both it and the animals in clean linen. The country folk, shouting, laughing, and coddling their harvest, are gently exhorted to come to the great feast at their "lord's hearth" where the abundance will be savored.

> And for to make the merry cheere,
> If smirking Wine be wanting here,
> There's that, which drowns all care, stout Beere.

Drink freely, they are urged, to the agricultural implements and to the girls, but also

> to your Lord's health
> Then to the Plough, (the Common-wealth).

How, one may ask, is the plough the commonwealth? There is the age-old image of the plough that needs a hand, a firm hand, to make it turn up a straight furrow. There is the saying of the transfigured Jesus in Luke 9:62: "No man having put his hand to the plough, and looking back, is fit for the Kingdom of God." Besides, turning up the soil is the means of making it hold the seed that sprouts and produces everyone's abundance, the common wealth. Time will soon return when the agricultural season must be gone through once more with toil and pain.

> And, you must know, your Lords word's true,
> Feed him ye must, whose food fills you.
> And that this pleasure is like raine,
> Not sent for ye for to drowne your paine,
> But for to make it spring againe.

So the poem ends with an ostensible plea to the country folk not to drink too much and not to brew and swallow all the harvest grain. There has been frolicking and feasting, celebration of the fruits of labor, due reverence to rank and place. Yet odd things happen in this poem. Who are the "we" in "We are the Lords of Wine and Oile"? Are they the "Rurall Younglings"? Wine and oil are more appropriate to Tibullus's Latin landscape. Perhaps those lords are Mildmay and Herrick who, like their fellow gentry, were accustomed to import the grape and the olive from abroad. The next uses of "Lord" clearly refer to the Earl of Westmoreland ("my Lord," "your Lords Hearth," "to your Lord's health"). At the end of the poem "your Lords word's true" might seem to suggest a truly supernal Lord, the one who stands at the pinnacle of the whole hierarchy of earth and heaven. The humble beer is the "Lord's" bounty but it is also like God's rain, not sent to drown (after the covenant with Noah of the rainbow) but to revive the spirit of natural toil on the now unflooded earth. There is something a tinge pagan and also unself-consciously elitist in all this. Summarily, I would characterize it as a finely evocative rural poem about universal divinely sanctioned communal subservience for the common good in a world of man rewarded for his appointed toil by God in nature.

The societies celebrated or deplored by such intimately civic poets as Horace, Petrarch, Marvell, and Herrick have all gone into the history books and require a learned play of the historical imagination. Moments of crisis since have brought forth fine civic poems and serviceable anthems. Meditative, thoughtful poets like Carducci, Nekrasov, Whitman, Esenin, Yeats, Eliot, Frost, Lowell, and Auden have given us civic poems that we may habitually read but do not recently see emulated. We still of course sing the American national anthem, written in 1814 but made official only in 1932, though few can con the words. It is remarkable that the most widespread anthem ever written still is sung in many parts of the world almost daily. It is "L'Internationale" by Eugène Pottier (1816–87) and Pierre Degeyter (1849–1932); Pottier wrote the words at the time of the Paris Commune in 1871 and Degeyter set them to music in 1886. In the original text the rhetorical flourishes lie well within the exhortatory decorum of French poetic practice. To cite the refrain (which reappears at the end) and the first stanza:

> C'est la lutte finale:
> Groupons-nous, et demain,
> L'Internationale
> Sera le genre humain.

Debout! les damnés de la terre!
Debout! les forçats de la faim!
La raison tonne en son cratère,
C'est l'irruption de la fin.
Du passé faisons table rase,
Foule esclave, debout! debout!
Le monde va changer de base:
Nous ne sommes rien, soyons tout!

The Russian translator, Arkadii Iakovlevich Kots (1872–1943), whose text was sung as the Soviet national anthem till 1944, gives his version of Pottier's first, second, and sixth stanzas, strikingly adding his own heavy measure of violence. The Russian text of the first stanza, which puts the refrain after, may be rendered thus:

Arise, branded with a curse,
All the world of the hungry and the slaves!
Our mind seethes with indignation
And is ready to lead to deadly battle.
We will uproot the whole world of violence
Down to its foundation, and then
We will build ours, a new world.
He who was nobody will be everybody.

This will be the last
And the decisive battle.
With the International
The human race will spring up.

Such a crudely expressed program as this—the total destruction of the old world and the establishment of a universal, egalitarian, materialist, earthly paradise—would have horrified the poets I have mentioned and many more. These words about the whole human race leaping up to make a radically reconstituted world negate in their absolutist and confrontational directness much of what I call civic poetry.

10

VICO AND GOZZI
AS
INNOVATORS
IN
POETIC CRITICISM

In extraordinary contrast to the great and continuous fame of Petrarch, who was translated, imitated, and revered by countless poets and exalted by countless critics in the major countries of Western Europe for four centuries, Dante's fortune seems exiguous indeed. Even in his own native land that prime poetic pilgrim of eternity had surprisingly little echo among fellow practitioners of poetry. After the pieties of biographers, editors, copyists, and printers in the fourteenth and fifteenth centuries, the *Divina Commedia* seems to have been relegated to a few theorists and antiquaries who kept the poem in print and in the awareness of the learned. It is as if the vanguards of later ages simply did not know what to make of the poem and, despite the efforts of Jacopo Mazzoni and a few others, were unable to grasp it whole. Try as they might, no effort was sufficient to make it a "regular" epic or to render its subject matter even interesting for a postmedieval age. That state of affairs continued, by and large, till the final overthrow of Neoclassicism in the Romantic revolution.

As we know, the eighteenth century was less an apogee of strict Neoclassicism than a sort of battleground for richly rivalrous forces. In theory the prestigious genres continued to be epic, tragedy, and the elevated lyric; in practice, the successful genres were the novel, comedy and satire, all shot through with a strong vein of parody or parodic inspiration. In this regard Voltaire is a most complicated figure. We now most honor him as a great writer of satiric fiction, yet he most honored himself as a writer of epic and tragedy and a defender of the Neoclassical canons of decorum. It is not surprising that so learned and witty a man should rather casually in the course of his vast output have things to say about Dante that seem to us provocative and wrongheaded. It is surprising, however, that he should give rise indirectly to the best favorable account of Dante published before Foscolo: I refer to the odd treatise customarily titled *Difesa di Dante* (1758), published by the quintessential Venetian Gasparo Gozzi (1713–86). It is useful, I think, once again to evaluate that treatise, its immediate provocateur Saverio Bettinelli (1718–1808), and the lighthearted instigator Voltaire—all in the context of eighteenth-century Dante criticism (which must of course include Giambattista Vico, whose brief reflections on Dante could be put in some perspective only much later). It seems appropriate first to deal with Gozzi and his adversaries, then, doing minor violence to strict chronology, to expound briefly Vico's view of Dante.

The vast and profuse mind of Voltaire keeps reasserting its principles: decorum, rationality, tolerance, deism, and belief in an essentially good, though often perverted, human nature. The past was to be understood and also judged according to those principles; national oddities can simply be looked on as provincial and inessential. In his late *Lettres chinoises* (1776) Voltaire says that, as in the case of Dante, one should be cautious in "reproducing" (refurbishing?) the antique works of one's country: "c'est un travail aussi ingrat que bizarre de rechercher curieusement des cailloux dans de vieilles ruines, quand on a des palais modernes."[1] Fifty years earlier he had been at work on his *Essai sur la poésie épique*, an advertisement and defense of his own epic *La Ligue*, later called *La Henriade*. In the essay he merely mentions Dante in connection with Petrarch as living in an age when there was no tolerable work of prose: of the Italians, Tasso receives the highest marks (though one should mention that outside serious epic Ariosto was Voltaire's abiding favorite). Voltaire's true comments on Dante are sparsely scattered along his career, in the *Essai sur les moeurs* (1756), a letter to Saverio Bettinelli (1759), the *Dictionnaire philosophique* (1764–65), and the late *Lettres chinoises, indi- ennes, et tartares* (1776) just quoted. Perhaps nowadays Voltaire's entry on

"Dante (Le)" in the *Dictionnaire* is the best known and therefore the most notorious text. In jaunty Voltairean fashion we get a sketch of the life and work that ends with a mock translation in irregularly rimed pentameters of the Guido da Montefeltro episode in *Inferno*, canto 27. Some praise is bestowed on "des vers si heureux et si naïfs qu'ils n'ont point vieilli depuis quatre cents ans, et qu'ils ne vieilliront jamais."[2] But it should surprise no one that the taste exhibited by the *Commedia* is described as "bizarre." Any Italian then or now who felt this judgment a sort of *lèse-patrie* might console himself by reflecting that Voltaire had far less interest and competence in Dante than he had in swatting reactionary Catholicism and in enhancing Neoclassical polish.

It is in the grand and sweeping context of the *Essai sur les moeurs* (1756) that Voltaire gives his most measured and serious view of Dante in part of a brief paragraph in the context of the rise of Italian letters from barbarism. The *Commedia* is a "poëme bizarre, mais brilliant de beautés naturelles," a work in which the author rose above the bad taste of his age and subject matter, at least in its details, and filled with passages as purely written as if they belonged to the age of Ariosto and Tasso.[3] One may well suspect that Voltaire was expressing the majority opinion of his age. The provincially polished Jesuit Saverio Bettinelli did not have to be a toady or a cultural traitor to concur generally in this view. As a worldly priest and literatus of suave cultivation, Bettinelli might well have felt serenely in the swim on receiving a dictated letter from Voltaire (18 December 1759) that acknowledges some acquaintance with Bettinelli's *Lettere virgiliane* (1757) and commends him for having the courage to say that Dante was a fool and his work a monster. But then Voltaire immediately adds, "j'aime encor mieux pourtant ce monstre que tous les vermisseaux appellés Sonetti qui naissent et qui meurent par milliers dans L'Italie, de Milan jusqu'à Ottrente."[4] Clearly Voltaire—who seems to have read Italian fairly well and in his affair with his niece Mme. Denis used it as a written code to foil the servants—was aware of the continuing Dante controversy in Italy but took only polite and minor interest in it.

With no trouble at all one can absolve Voltaire of malice or obscurantism. On balance his appreciation of Dante was fair and consistent for his age and taste. Bettinelli is far more thoroughgoing and blinkered. Had he been pungent and magnanimous one could complain less of the *Lettere virgiliane*, with or without the passages on Dante.[5] But in our age all that apparatus of news of colloquies from the Elysian Fields is rather arch and tedious stuff that exhales the musty charm and self-congratulation of the arcadian academies. Bettinelli strains too hard for urbanity and wit, and his Virgil comes through as not only a snob but also a prig. Besides, the devaluation of Dante entails a failure to understand Virgil as a passionate and melancholy poet. Dante himself of course understood Virgil far better. Leaving aside Bettinelli's misfired sophistication in the still-popular mode of Lucian and the Montesquieu of the *Lettres persanes,* we can easily find his revisionist view of Italian poetry summarized in the ninth of these letters. All the old poets and contemporaries of Dante are to be consigned to the Accademia della Crusca (which stands for pedantry) or to the fire. Dante is to be shelved with books of learning like a codex or ancient monument, with the exception of the passages sanctioned in the third letter by the Elysian poets, amounting to about five cantos. Petrarch is to reign above the others, but not tyrannically and certainly not without censure and purgation of a third of his output (indeed, in the fourth letter he is treated quite condescendingly). Ariosto gets off rather lightly; Tasso less so, except for his *Aminta.* Least to be purged are Annibale Caro's translation of Virgil and Tassoni's *La secchia rapita.* And so it goes: the ideal is a kind of universal smoothness in style and safe sophistication in subject matter. The critic's role is to snipe and snip. Dante could hardly have been invited to such a tea party.

It is in the second and third *Lettere virgiliane* that Dante is discussed. A ridiculous Neapolitan poetaster is made to sing the praises of Dante at the beginning of the second letter, most likely to indicate some danger that imitation of Dante among living Italian poets might be the coming thing. Indeed, Bettinelli may well have sensed in midcentury the quaking of the new sensibility: if he had had the prophetic gift he could have foreseen the Dantimania that would spread abroad from Foscolo to Browning and Rossetti to Ezra Pound and beyond. At all events there seems to be in his mind the notion that an ounce of prevention is worth a pound of cure. So Dante comes in for it. Bettinelli's Virgil had done his polished best to engage the shade of Dante in Elysian conversation, but he found him taciturn and unintelligible. Out of curiosity this Bettinellian Virgil takes up the tome of Dante and remarks on the odd title and the division into three parts like a scientific treatise. He is perhaps flattered by Dante's praise of him, but cannot recognize his own poem, the *Aeneid,* as the object of Dante's imitation. Dante's hell, for example, has such a clutter of ill-sorted people in it and the myriad grotesque postures and bizarre torments hardly do credit either to hell or to the poet's imagination. Yet Dante was remarkable for his time "in mezzo a tanta ignoranza e barbarie," and after all did carry over into his poetry the science of those days. But then so many better poets have arisen since.

What about his style? The allegory, the antiquated vocabulary, the curious and abstruse references encumber the poem. Thus he is a poor example for the young. Still, his poem does have strong memorable passages and fine lines that perhaps insidiously make one forget his faults. In sum, "Dante lacked nothing other than good taste and discernment in art. But he had a great soul and a sublime one, acute and fertile inventiveness, vivid and picturesque imagination, such that from his pen fall wonderful lines and passages.' But then there are those awful rimes like "Austericch/Tabernicch/fatto cricch." The only thing to do is make an anthology, "un piccol volume di tre o quattro canti veramente poetici."

What is left out of this account is the grand conception of the whole poem, the worldview encompassed in it, the concrete historical matter that is dismissed as forgotten lore or gossip, the second and third *cantiche* for the most part, and much else. Praised are a few passages of nature description, a simile or two, and the Ugolino episode. This latter, along with the episode of Paolo and Francesca as a poor second, somehow struck practically all readers of Dante most deeply from about 1750 through the Romantic age. Bettinelli's revisionist history of Italian poetry professes to ward off possibly malign influences emanating from Dante. It is true that Dante had a few imitators at the time, particularly Alfonso Varano (1705–88) whose earnest *Visioni* were later appreciatively anthologized by Giacomo Leopardi. But in retrospect we can see that Bettinelli was doomed to lose. What makes his *Lettere virgiliane* more interesting than otherwise is that they are part of the continuing skirmishes between the Classicists (followers of the *philosophes*) and the "Romanticists" (melancholics, Ossianics, and sensibilists). A vast new synthesis was in process. What is most immediately my concern here is that Bettinelli sparked a quick response in defense of Dante on the part of that genial and melancholy man of his age, Gasparo Gozzi (1713–86).

Bettinelli was a deliberate reformer, prospecting a future that never came about. Gozzi, in contrast, could be called a conservative, defending older literature in which he was well read and responding with journalistic alacrity to a momentary call. Gozzi too was an arcadian "academic," belonging to the Accademia dei Granelleschi, but he would also become, however briefly, the most literary and contemporary journalist in the Italy of his time. It was in the line of writing for hire that Gozzi composed his treatise entitled formally *Giudizio degli antichi poeti sopra la moderna censura di Dante attribuita ingiustamente a Virgilio,* better known as his *Difesa di Dante.*[6] The Venetian publisher Antonio Zatta had commissioned the young poet Filippo Rosa Morando (1732–57) to prepare a grand edition of the *Divina Commedia* with summary headings for each canto in *terzine* by Gozzi; on the appearance of Bettinelli's *Lettere virgiliane* Zatta also invited Gozzi to write a defense, doubtless in the hope of spirited publicity. The result is far from a periwigged set of letters. Gozzi assembles a whole medley of Lucianic modes: letters, dialogues, set speeches, and a fable.

But he begins with a rather straight preface that shows considerable learning. The important questions here concern the title of Dante's poem, his rimes, and his language. Indeed the title hardly matters, according to Gozzi. Dante not only called it *Commedia* out of humility, but also within the poem showed some uncertainty by referring to it as tragedy (here Gozzi is wrong), poem, or sacred poem, reflecting by that very uncertainty its "novelty and extraordinary originality." Gozzi conjectures that it must often have occurred to Dante to call his poem the *Danteide,* as he himself is the chief character, but out of fear of being taken to compare himself with the heroes of antiquity he did not do so. It was Bettinelli who brought up the matter of the title, just as he deplored some queer rimes and vocabulary. In reply Gozzi argues with balanced common sense and historical accuracy that in Dante's day Austria was called Ostericch and that Dante's language *was* understood and prized even by the people as well as the literati: in sum, Dante wrote "netto e chiaro a' giorni suoi" (29). Here *historical* arguments are ably adduced, not by way of excuse, but of understanding sympathetically past usage. Next, Gozzi creates his own man in Elysium in the figure of Anton Francesco Doni (1513–74), who in real life was a somewhat disreputable miscellaneous writer in racy Tuscan—an amusing foil to the supercilious Bettinelli's supercilious Virgil. Doni writes, according to the fiction, three letters and sends on, as well, a dialogue, a set speech, some annotations, and a fable supposedly narrated by Aristophanes. The letters from Elysium are to the publisher Zatta. The grand line of poetic descent from Homer to Virgil to Dante is stressed in such a way as to answer some of Bettinelli's petty cavils concerning the division of the *Commedia* into three parts, the allegorical beasts, and the Veltro prophecy. The arguments go on rather too long, but several interesting observations are made on the sanction to be derived from Plato's *Ion* and from Longinus, the example of Virgil's sixth book, and the defense of allegory especially in relation to prophetic texts of the Bible. In polemical imitation of Bettinelli's method, Gozzi has his correspondent Doni report a dialogue with Virgil in which other classical poets then engage. Virgil here eloquently defends the virtues of Dante's poem and in an amusing passage (52) shows how a censorious critic could reduce even the *Iliad* to a silly tangle (this is of course a witty trick of Voltaire). What emerges is a commonsensical view of imitation: you follow models till you can take flight on your own if you have the talent; otherwise by imitating you are at least saved from breaking your neck. What you create need not conform; indeed Virgil is made to commend Dante's inventiveness as "new and original," such that he went beyond all human thought and in reading him "ti pare ogni genere di poesia, ed è la poesia di Dante" (61). So much for the niceties of genre: the poetry of Dante is *sui generis*.

Part of the charm and even the force of Gozzi's *Difesa* is its variety. As if by polemical design it conforms wholly to no genre, let alone the mere epistle. Though contained in a letter of Doni there remain to be discussed two set-pieces that assert their own generic form: a discourse and a fable. The discourse is set in the mouth of a certain Trifone Gabriello (corresponding historically to a Venetian humanist whose surname is usually given as Gabriele and who lived from c. 1470 to 1549 and among other things wrote a brief set of annotations on Dante) and is nicely couched in an orotund cinquecento style that gets much racier as his passion rises. With admirable assertion of the glories of the "egotistical sublime" (to use Keats's phrase applied to Wordsworth), Gabriello proclaims that Dante possessed a great and honorable love of himself that fired him to glory and made him magnanimous. By this inner strength ("intrinseca forza") he was transported to the sublime (65). Here we are in the critical ambience of Longinus. Dante's ambition and forcefulness are considered entirely positive qualities that informed the political theorist and activist and also allowed him to achieve poetic glory. By lengthy quotation from the *Monarchia* Gabriello shows Dante to be philosophically serious and skilled. It is even more of a challenge to rise from philosophical reflections to *furor poeticus* and to contemplate all vices and virtues in poetic terms: "ed eccolo da quella sua immaginazione, sempre . . . riscaldata dalla grandezza e sublimità delle cose" (70). The whole realm of marvels opened up by Dante is passionately summarized with a disdainful indirect reference to Bettinelli's doubt that Dante possessed discernment in art. What is stressed in Gabriello's long exposition of the sweep of the *Commedia* is its grandeur and religious purport—a version of *utile dulci*—as well as Dante's pictorial and dramatic force. Of the comments of Gozzi's Elysians that follow, the most telling are those of Virgil who insists in effect that one must read a work *whole* in order to judge it. The implication, not at all unjustified, is that Bettinelli, like many others, read at most the *Inferno* and skipped around elsewhere.

Remembering his role in the *Symposium*, Gozzi puts in the mouth of Aristophanes a fable that tells the story of Orpheus in terms that indirectly draw the parallels Orpheus/Dante and Eurydice/Beatrice. At a certain point Orpheus, aware of his poetic gifts, sets himself to thinking how he can instil in his depraved and brutish fellow countrymen the good and the beautiful, indeed good taste. That is how it must have been, editorializes Aristophanes, in a time of such barbarousness ("in un tempore così intenebrato dalla barbarie e da' vizi degli uomini" [87]). Orpheus retreats to the woods and invents a fine fable of descending to the underworld to retrieve Eurydice—and when he returns to his people what does he recite but the beginning of the *Divina Commedia*! Then Orpheus, in reply to the insistent curiosity of his Thracian countrymen, tells, "under the veil of his fiction," of what and whom he encountered on his supernatural journey. The fable is of course quite elementary and transparent. Yet it contains an argument of taste and historical appreciation that is stressed toward the end "under the veil of this fable." Dante, declares Aristophanes in a fine rhetorical flourish, created by himself alone, through his inner vigor, the idea of the good and the beautiful that had been lost in this world for over a thousand years. Even though born in the darkness of barbarism, he was capable of "imitating" most variously and regularly the nature of all emotions ("la natura di tutte le passioni"). Can such a poet be called lacking in good taste? Dante modulates his style, as he should, according to the subject matter. Knowing how to use style properly comprehends all good tastes, that is, *universal* good taste ("contiene in sé tutt'i buoni gusti dello stile, cioè il buon gusto universale" [90]). Thus Dante is a special case; he is both unique and universal, he observes and he transcends the canons of art. The safe urbanity counseled by Voltaire and Bettinelli is thus overruled.

This whole debate is obviously contained well within the bounds of the eighteenth century, indeed within the years between 1728 and 1758. From our perspective Gozzi, however eccentric, is by far the most sensible participant. He was not entirely alone in Italy but this is not the place to summarize the whole story of Dante's fortune in the eighteenth century. Suffice it to call him the most penetrating critic and defender of Dante in his day, with the exception of Giambattista Vico (1668–1744), who was practically unknown and remained so for almost a century. Even if the definitive and posthumously published edition of the *Scienza nuova* (1744) had been properly noticed, the consequences for Dante's place in the poetic universe would have been slow to be drawn. In that work Dante's name is mentioned a number of times; still, the whole third book on "The Discovery of the True Homer," with its argument that the *Iliad* and *Odyssey* are repositories of the pre-rational (that is, "poetic") wisdom of the Hellenes, could have inspired a full reappraisal of the position and "dignity" of Dante as monumental and encyclopedic master of *fantasia*. Indeed it would be possible even at this date to attempt such a thorough placement of Dante in the grand Vichian system. Fortunately, though, we can content ourselves with less, for Vico left two brief documents that are finely suggestive on a more modest scale. They are a systematic sketch entitled "Discovery of the True Dante, or New Principles of Dante Criticism" (dated between 1728 and 1730) and a letter to a pupil of Vico named Gherardo degli Angioli (26 December 1725), who was barely twenty at the time.[7] These brief works, together with some brief mention elsewhere, constitute our texts. Vico's views are remarkable for themselves, but all the more remarkable in that they came into being in an age of the supremacy of reason. Their independence and contemporary neglect sanction treating them out of strict chronological order in this present context.

Vico's letter to his favored pupil Gherardo degli Angioli was written to acknowledge receipt of some sonnets and a *capitolo* (a didactic or satiric composition in *terzine*) written by the then 19-year-old poet and sent from his native town of Eboli. Vico is impressed by their independence of prevailing, presumably arcadian, modes and is all primed, having completed the first *Scienza nuova* (1725), to comment in his new terms. He himself applies his views of "the true Homer" to the somewhat similar case of Dante. Lamenting that the young poet lives in an age in which the faculties of the spirit, especially the imagination, are benumbed and rigidified by excessively analytic and austere philosophy, Vico praises Gherardo both for his inner sensibility and for his powers of observation. Inventiveness can be destroyed by abstract reason; indeed it was in barbarous times that great discoveries were made, such as the compass, the sailing ship, the circulation of the blood, gunpowder and musket, paper and the printing press, the architectural dome, and, at the very end of barbarism, the telescope. (All of this will go into the second edition of the *Scienze nuova*.) All the more favorably, then, may one appreciate the greatness of Dante and understand the circumstances of his greatness: Dante was born "in seno alla fiera e feroce barbarie d'Italia" that had lasted for four centuries and had become even more cruel. Civil conditions were savage and the vernaculars undisciplined. Like Homer in Greece, Dante fashioned a language enriched by borrowings from "all the peoples of Italy." "Così Dante, fornito di poetici favellari, impiegò il colerico ingegno nella sua *Comedia.*" Here the word "poetico" carries a sense of almost primitive unreflective force, and "colerico" is positive in suggesting a mighty overflow of properly heroic passion. We are in the precincts, as Vico makes plain, of the *Iliad* and Achilles's wrath with which Dante's *Inferno* is to be compared; it is there that Dante "spread all the greatness" of his *fantasia*. Vico is not repelled by the pitiless torments and ferocity, but rather even glories in their historical appropriateness as with Homer and with Greek and also English tragedy; just as Dante, with less immediate historical appropriateness in the *Purgatorio* and *Paradiso*, wonderfully presents heroic patience and supreme spiritual peace, in parallel to the *Odyssey*. In these historically conditioned, but strikingly positive terms, Vico praises Gherardo for his direct and unreflective poetry (what Schiller seventy years later would call "naïve") whose subject matter is taken not from philosophy but from unmediated observation. Clearly Vico was full of his freshly discovered principles, which yielded a new historical and aesthetically positive evaluation of Homer and Dante, and he enthusiastically saw some recrudescence (something of a *ricorso*) in his pupil. Gherardo, however, four years later became a friar and devoted himself to sacred matters and duties till the end of his long life.

Plainer and more systematic is Vico's short account of Dante on the occasion of a commentary on the *Divina Commedia*—the "Discoverta del vero Dante," composed between 1728 and 1730. At the beginning he simply declares that the *Commedia* is to be read under three aspects: "as history of the barbarous times of Italy, as fount of the most beautiful spoken tongues of Tuscany, and as example of sublime poetry." Under the first aspect Vico comes right out and asserts that Dante, like Homer and Ennius in their times, was a true-speaking historian of his own barbarism. It is just at the beginning of the civilizing process ("sul cominciare ad ingentilirsi la lor barbarie") that by *nature* and without reflection poets can speak openly and truthfully. The truth of Dante is of course the Christian truth; if in his use of allegory he mixes in fiction, it is simply in the nature of reading history that one must reflect to some extent and draw profit from the examples given of others. The second aspect, concerning language, is a bit obscure. Vico denies that Dante literally gathered his language from all the people of Italy, first because Florentine speech had much in common with that of

other places and, second, that one lifetime would not have been sufficient for such linguistic gathering. The terms themselves are ambiguous: *parlari*, a substantive plural, seems to refer to levels of style or local quirks of vocabulary. Finally, Vico recommends that the Accademia della Crusca take a census and compile a catalogue of the modes of speech of the lower orders all over Italy. The clouded upshot here seems to be that Dante did mold a convincing and expressive language for himself that differed from the Tuscan of the cinquecento in some respects and was erroneously thought to have derived its differences from outside Tuscany. At all events, Vico seems well on the way to denying, rightly, that Dante wrote no proper language or formed an artificial composite. Rather, he would seem to argue that Dante's language sprang from deep sources of popular speech and was authentically and positively "barbarous," implying that Dante created it as an artistic system in his great work.

As the most aesthetic aspect, Vico discusses Dante as "a rare example of a sublime poet." Sublimity is a faculty and a quality not attained by any skill or art. Homer, the most sublime poet of all, certainly did not need the precepts of Longinus, who himself declared that the two prime faculties were granted by heaven. These are in Vico's version (1) an elevated spirit that thirsts only for glory and immortality, spurning those things coveted by greedy, ambitious, and soft men; and (2) a spirit compounded of great public virtues, above all magnanimity and justice. What was most intrinsic in Dante's sublimity was being born a great genius ("grande ingegno") in a time of dying barbarism ("spirante barbarie"), and Vico makes the analogy to long-fallow fields that, at first cultivation, yield superabundantly, but then, he adds, being more and more *cultivated* they yield less and less. Not only Dante in sublime poetry, but also Petrarch in "delicate" or elegant poetry and Boccaccio in pleasing graceful prose are incomparable and cannot be equaled; in cultivated modern times, on the other hand, fine works are produced that others can hope not only to equal but also to surpass.

Thus Vico's historical theory and aesthetic conviction, as fully expounded in the *Scienza nuova*, allow him to set the highest value on *fantasia* as it exists in that transition from a divine barbarous age to an age of heroes or heroic age. While he can, as he shows elsewhere, appreciate the great works produced in an age of men, he in no way could agree with, say, Voltaire and Bettinelli (the majority opinion of the time) that cultivation, polish, and refinement had far outstripped the products of barbarism. Vico uses the same word they use ("barbarie" in Italian) but has completely reevaluated the meaning. Not that he is patronizing toward poetry, nor that he merely records the inevitable in the manner of a strict historicist. With a complex view of man's destiny and a religious view of God's providence, he describes in his theory of man's own creations—his history—the excellence as well as the depravity of every age. In regard to poetry the comparison with Schiller's treatment of *naïve* and *sentimentalische* poetry (Erich Heller translates "spontaneous" and "reflective") is highly suggestive. Vico's contribution to philology in the proper enlightened sense is very great, as Erich Auerbach has stressed.[8] His near-contemporary Gasparo Gozzi, in his charming earnest way, went quite far in the same general direction. Their achievements in regard to Dante criticism in the eighteenth century are of major importance, as is Voltaire's in far other fields than poetry and its criticism. The next age, in whose making they participated, would finally, after centuries, be able to vindicate the genius and the sublimity of Dante's poem.

Notes

1. Voltaire, *Lettres chinoises, indiennes, et tartares à M. Pauw par un bénédictin* (1776), in Louis Moland, ed., *Oeuvres complètes* (Paris: Garnier, 1877–83), vol. 29, 497.

2. Voltaire, *Dictionnaire philosophique*, in *Oeuvres complètes*, vol. 18, 313.

3. Voltaire, *Essai sur les moeurs et l'esprit des nations et sur des principaux faits de l'histoire depuis Charlemagne jusqu'à Louis XIII*, in *Oeuvres complètes*, vol. 12, 58.

4. Voltaire, *Correspondence and Related Documents* in *The Complete Works of Voltaire*, ed. Theodore Besterman (Banbury: Besterman, 1971), vol. 21, 48–49.

5. Saverio Bettinelli, *Lettere virgiliane e inglesi, e altri scritti critici*, ed. Vittorio Enzo Alfieri (Bari: Laterza, 1930).

6. I cite from the Riccardo Ricciardi volume *Letterati, memorialisti, e viaggiatori del settecento*, ed. Ettore Bonora (Milan, 1951); *La difesa di Dante* is on pages 22–91.

7. I cite from the most authoritative and convenient edition of the major works of Vico, that of his *Opere* in the Riccardo Ricciardi series, ed. Fausto Nicolini (Milan, 1953). The letter to Gherardo degli Angioli is on pages 121–26 and the "Discoverta del vero Dante" is on pages 950–53. For the sake of completeness Nicolini cites in a note on 953 the other mentions of Dante in Vico, except for the definitive edition of the *Scienza nuova*, which is here printed in full. There is an index of names to the whole volume, which allows one to look up all passing references to Dante.

8. See his essays on Vico in *Gesammelte Aufsätze zur romanischen Philologie* (Bern: Francke, 1967), 222–74: "Vico und Herder," "Giambattista Vico und die Idee der Philologie," "Vico und der Volksgeist," "Sprachliche Beiträge zur Erklärung der *Scienza nuova* von G. B. Vico," "Vico's Contribution to Literary Criticism," and "Vico and Aesthetic Historism." In 1924 Auerbach published his abbreviated German translation of the 1744 *Scienza nuova*.

Bibliographical Notes

The most comprehensive accounts of Dante's fortune through the ages are that of Mario Apollonio, *Dante: Storia della Commedia* (in the collaborative and multivolume Storia letteraria d'Italia), vol. 2 (3d ed., Milan: Vallardi, 1965), chaps. 92 to 109, and that of Werner P. Friederich, *Dante's Fame Abroad, 1350–1850* (Chapel Hill: 1950). An *ex parte* sketch is to be found in Benedetto Croce, *La poesia di Dante*, 2d rev. ed. (Bari: Laterza, 1921), 173–205. On Dante in the eighteenth century, see especially Aldo Vallone, *La critica dantesca nel settecento ed altri saggi danteschi* (Florence: Olschki, 1961) and Alfred Noyer-Weidner, "Das Danteverständnis im Zeitalter der Aufklärung," *Deutsches Dante-Jahrbuch* 37 (1960), 112–34. Two works of Mario Fubini are excellent: *Dal Muratori al Baretti* (Bari: Laterza, 1946) particularly for an account of Bettinelli and *Stile e umanità di Giambattista Vico* (Bari: Laterza, 1946), especially "Il mito della poesia primitiva e la critica dantesca di G. B. Vico," 173–205.

On Vico in general there is of course a vast amount of commentary and exposition; on Gasparo Gozzi there is very little. I refrain from elaborate citation in the conviction that nowhere else are there the emphases and juxtapositions I make in this essay.

11

BOTTOMLESS SOUNDINGS

Poems by Lomonosov, Wordsworth, and Leopardi

Methodological Reflections

In literary history one tries to account for the great evolutionary process from one sensibility to another. The matter can be approached ideologically with regard to philosophical, psychological, and aesthetic conceptions: a history of ideas in a fairly restricted sense. Or it can be approached in terms of lesser, common, informal, even bad literature on the grounds that the "atmosphere" or "background" is somehow richer and more directly illuminating or representative there, though a clear objection could be advanced that the "popular mind" is relatively slow, conservative, and receptive rather than creative. It can also be approached by dealing with peculiar figures, such as Chatterton, Blake, Hölderlin, or Novalis, whose private worlds may arguably be taken as representing the true spirit of the age or possibly the age to come even though they were not fully recognized by their contemporaries. Or it may deal with the innovators who quickly became, after initial controversy, the important or canonical authors. Finally, of course, one may simply eschew any historical argument and proceed with literary texts considered *per se* or set in a conventional and unargued historical framework.

If one chooses a number of literary texts distributed over a manageable time segment, one may be saying useful things about them and yet, for any historical argument, be stacking the evidence. The hypotheses implied necessarily reach down to the ground of aesthetics, literary theory, and historiography: what is good, what is significant, what is comparable, what comparative terms are relatively free of question-begging? Caught in a tangle of first principles, we may nonetheless argue, for small purposes, a fairly sophisticated consensus—meaning, in effect, a gifted and knowledge-able reader—and proceed to add nuances, highlights, slight changes of force in a system of vectors, corroborations, modified perspectives, to the point of making some conjectures, some arresting or interesting combina-tion of the familiar and the new, even some titillating hypothesis not immediately capable of proof but still a usable focus of thought. Any historical or aesthetic generalization is of course a hypothesis to be proved according to the nature of proof desired or accepted in a common effort to historicize the past. Are we still heirs in direct succession to the Romantics or to the Romantic revolution in sensibility? Or was Romanticism, to use that relatively recent term, over and done with when it came to be historicized? If so, then how after the Romantic age, and by what way in the labyrinth, did our sensibilities come to be what they are now? Are we now post-Romantic, post-Christian, post-Modernist? Or perhaps neo-Some-thing? But then we must inevitably ask, what led up to Romanticism? Naturally, it was pre-Romanticism. All these notions beg to be defined in a context of argument and according to a responsive theory—which, after all, we can always postpone in order to go on neologizing in our own fashion about the past and our present in relation to it, thus relinquishing the tasks of perspective to those who are even now standing on our shoulders.

Misgivings always arise when generalizations are based on just a few texts chosen for a great many reasons. Not everything can be handled at once: there should be a Heisenberg's law for literary historiography. What I think crucial in this inevitable tangle is the level of generalization to which one may rise without breaking the cable between evidence and speculation, between the mooring and the balloon. What I propose here is to examine three poems written during the time span 1740–1820 by three European poets. In minimal terms, the poems are chosen because they are good, relatively short, meditative in mood, distributed in time, and comparable in technique and subject matter. In maximal terms, the poems are exemplary of a coherent new sensibility, of a communicable subjectivity, of turning points along an important route that is in the process of discovery: in other words, a set of important European signposts in literary history.

"Thought" and Poetry

There is a certain wisdom in naming our species *homo sapiens* and not *homo sciens*: the kind of knowing implied in the Latin verb *sapere* includes feeling and response to feeling, subjective as well as objective capability, memory and mnemonic colorations, responsiveness to the new and responsible preservation of the old; in complementary contrast *scire* includes factual knowledge, relative perfection of learned skills, objective or generally accepted schemes and classifications, and matters of public record. Such a contrast might well put the reader on guard as to what lies in prospect. A theory of knowledge or a history of sensibility or a semantic study of key terms or even a psychology of human awareness? I undertake none of these things here. My only proposals are that three otherwise unrelated poems are successful poetic expressions of thinking and feeling the limits of thought and emotion in terms of the illimitable and that in the face of traditional Christianity and what we now call "scientific thought" they variously assume or claim a wholeness of experience that could in English be called wisdom or sensibility or simply mind. Part of the difficulty lies in the terms available in English and other tongues. The ideal word is "ideology," but it has been captured by political discourse. Though these three poems are not "ideological" in that sense, they do touch upon grandly familiar ideas about being in the world; yet it would be unprofitable to reduce them to their "ideas" or their "historical representativeness" or to hitch to them a theory of general intellectual history between 1743 and 1819, the dates of the first and last poems. All poetry of the past that deals in some way with abstractions and immeasurables cannot but suggest to the latter-day reader philosophies, theories of history, climates of opinion, systems of knowledge, and all the other paraphernalia of ratiocination whether diachronic or synchronic. Hence the vast number of studies of poets and poems explicated and explained according to dominant ideas, influences, outmoded lore, reconstructed systems of thought and belief, volatile spirits of the age—often to the point that masses of miscellaneous learning and portentous significance are assembled repetitively or irrelevantly to encumber the texts and obliterate individuality. We need perhaps a historical encyclopedia of *topoi* to which we all may conveniently refer as taken for granted in the learned community; we also need a dictionary of ideas ("unit ideas," idées-maîtresses, idées-forces) for the same communal purpose. Misapplied learning and "false wit" can clog the organs of learning. Not only do abstractions in poetry tempt the fillers-in of "background" and the footnoters with no clear conception of their intended reader, but also what I call "immeasurables" suggest to enthusiastic interpreters a pullulation of profundities and paradoxes quite beyond the texts, which precisely by their nature should be the controlling and limiting authority. Whenever notions of the infinite and the uncanny are expressed in poetry the interpreter may be stimulated beyond the bounds of the texts to become himself philosopher, hierophant, or mystagogue. And whenever the temporal and the eternal, the finite and the infinite, the sacred and the secular, the human and the divine intersect, the controlled flashes of paradox, wit, and profundity may too easily become the critic's own uncontrolled *feux d'artifice* or the *feux follets* of a self-appointed demiurge. To put it plainly, three factors—the integrity of a text, its historical position, and the proper, though never-ending, preparation of what I call not the "ideal" but the optimum reader—should somehow collaborate in true literary history.

No fully argued historiographical claims rest on the three poems chosen here. Yet even mere juxtaposition begets correspondences, and the spans of time and place suggest provisional continuities and discontinuities. All I would care to claim at this point is the integralness of the texts, their delicate and complex relation to the world outside them, and their concern with thought-feeling. The hyphenation is uncomfortable. It is meant to call attention to the existence of a seemingly single mode of perception and self-awareness and meditation for which vocabulary changes both historically and from language to language. *Mysl'* in Lomonosov, *thought* in Wordsworth, and *pensiero* in Leopardi have more in common with each other than they have with the formal present-day acceptations in their respective languages. This would call ideally for an essay in comparative historical semantics. Suffice it here simply to indicate that contemporary informal English seems to allow some apposite interpenetration or interchangeability of meaning between the two words (e.g., "What are your thoughts [feelings] on the matter?"; "It was just a momentary feeling [thought]"; "I was lost in thought"). In parallel to contemporary usage, the earlier breadth of meaning of the word "thought" condones what in formal discourse might be improper looseness. The word "thought," as well as *mysl'* and *pensiero*, has a richer function, as we shall see.

It is again tempting to speculate why Linnaeus, in his *Systema Naturae* (10th ed., 1758), chose *sapiens* to modify *homo* for our species instead of some Latin participle connected with thinking in the broad sense I am discussing. He would have been hard put among the alternatives: *cogitans, sentiens, cernens, aestimans, meditans*, etc. Perhaps *sentiens*, along with its rich cognates *sensus* and *sententia*, might have served in a classical Latin context to express the human quality of self-reflexiveness, but even it was not general enough: the Romans perhaps did not have a sufficiently general word and the words in their vernacular evolutions became even more particular. As a good example of the unfathomable oddity of evolutionary semantic choice, the word that eventually gave the Romance vernaculars the general meaning of "think" and related forms, was *pensare*, frequentative of *pendere*, both with the root meaning of "weigh." Short of drawing the consequences here, we may wonder how Pascal might have translated into Latin his designation of man as "un roseau pensant" or his assertion that "toute notre dignité consiste . . . en la pensée" (*Pensée* no. 347).

However that may be, it is with this general meaning of "thought" that I begin. More particularly it is with the notion of "thought" in the face of the uncanny or illimitable. If the words "thought" in Wordsworth and "pensiero" in Leopardi take over some of the field of meaning of "imagination," it should be stressed that this last word is not the *only* designation of a faculty of the mind so often studied as if it were somehow expressed in that word alone. This is a complicated problem in historical semantics. The problem exists also in Russian where simple *mysl'* also reappears radically in *razmyshlenie*, meaning "meditation," as well as in other similarly related words. If our subject were "imagination" (word and concept) we would have to deal with the apposite German texts and rehearse the complicated matter of Schelling's and Coleridge's formulations and also deal with Russian *voobrazhenie* which, with its root *obraz* = image, is originally a calque on *imaginatio* or *Einbildung* and which then takes on the general European Romantic resonance. But that matter has been much discussed in its theoretical aspects and the words "imagination" and "fancy" or "fantasy" (and their cognates and calques in other languages) have been collected like specimens and made even notorious as *termini technici*. It is undeniable that during the expanse of time encompassed here a faculty of mind or sensibility was exalted as aesthetic and empowered with privileged depths: a faculty not of *Verstand* or *Vernunft* but of *Zweckmässigkeit ohne*

Zweck or *sinnliche Anschauung.* It is the phenomenon itself that is important and not necessarily the term or label. Here, though in the same general context as those more famous designations, I discuss the humbler notions of "thought" and the "immeasurable" as they arise from reading three poems: "Evening Meditation" (1743) of Mikhail Vasil'evich Lomonosov, "Lines Written a Few Miles above Tintern Abbey" (1798) of William Wordsworth, and "L'Infinito" (1819) of Giacomo Leopardi.

A Boreal Meditation

Lomonosov, the great Russian polymath and poet of the earlier eighteenth century (1711–65), has no need of the Soviets to exaggerate his scientific genius or of the late nineteenth-century Russian poets and critics to belittle his pompous public odes in the high style that he invented for modern Russian. He achieved a sufficiency in both science and poetry to command our interest. As for poetry, it was he who not only effectively and argumentatively laid down the stress principle of modern Russian poetry but also at its very beginnings wrote several fine poems of historical importance and aesthetic interest. His best poem is worthy of discussion in and of itself and also as reflecting a historical sensibility of general European dimensions and as an imaginative and aesthetic formulation still meaningful to us. In its full title we find the circumstances that suffice for quick description: "Evening Meditation on God's Majesty on the Occasion of the Great Northern Lights." It is of interest to us that Lomonosov grew up in a peasant family in the far north of European Russia, near Archangel, and that all his life he took great scientific interest in the phenomenon of the northern lights, which he related to contemporary notions of electricity and "ether." It is also of interest that his origins as a serf forced him to be devious about obtaining status and an education: in the Russia of his day he was almost miraculously a self-made man. In contrast to his two other noteworthy poems, the companion "Morning Meditation on God's Majesty" and the "Ode, Selected from Job," Lomonosov does not rely here on conventional biblical eulogy and enhancement or psalmic and Jobian imagery. Rather, he evokes observed natural phenomena according to contemporary science and finds them a wondrous corroboration of the Creator's creativity, the intricacy and profundity of Creation, and the limits not of man's ability to think and feel but of his ability to explain.

In the first stanza the early nighttime setting is established in simple terms with slight conventional personification:

> Лице свое скрывает день;
> Поля покрыла мрачна ночь;
> Взошла на горы черна тень;
> Лучи от нас склонились прочь;
> Открылась бездна звезд полна;
> Звездам числа нет, бездне дна.

(Day hides its face, dark night has covered the fields, a black shadow has gone up the mountains, the rays have slanted far from us. The bottomless has revealed itself full of stars; there is no number to the stars, no bottom to the bottomless.)

To render *bezdna* as "the bottomless" is not only to stress the simple meaning of its components, but also to avoid the word "abyss," which in English is less simple, being somewhat learned and learnedly conventional. It also permits the serious pun, *bezdne dna* [*net*]. We are, then, prepared for the meditation of the speaker, who in the second stanza characterizes himself by comparisons to tiny objects or particles that are insignificant or lost. According to the physics that the young Lomonosov learned from the Leibnizian philosopher-scientist Christian von Wolff at Marburg, the universe was composed of motes or atoms, which had certain properties of combination to be investigated and which were interpenetrated by "ether." The particles here evoked are the conventional ones of ordinary experience, but they take on greater than usual symbolic value within the scientific context of the poem.

> Песчинка как в морских волнах,
> Как мала искра в вечном льде,
> Как в сильном вихре тонкий прах,
> В свирепом как перо огне,
> Так я, в сей бездне углублен,
> Теряюсь, мысльми утомлен!

(Like a grain of sand in the waves of the sea, like a little spark in eternal ice, like a fine speck in a powerful whirlwind, like a feather in a raging fire, so I become lost, sunk in this bottomlessness, exhausted by thoughts!)

Again there is only the simple expression of common experience: the feeling of being lost in thought or thoughts in the presence of the vast and unknowable. Yet the speaker is exhausted by his thoughts and is sunk deeply in what lies above. We know that in such situations height and depth may be substitutes for each other in general abstract feeling. Poetically, however, as well as practically, it is important to distinguish between the movements of sinking and rising: one can be good and the other bad; the poet may choose to react to strong emotion in the midst of nature by "soaring" in the manner of Shelley or "sinking" in the manner of Wordsworth; the reader may gravitationally resist the extreme pulls of *hupsos* or *bathos*, unless the poem carefully succeeds. Lomonosov takes a more complex view: he becomes lost in the outer upward abyss into which he goes deeply or sinks, then is inwardly overcome by the thoughts such experience evokes.

Those thoughts are given expression in the rest of the poem and they concern the boldness and success of *premudrye*, contemporary "sages" or "scientists" (our English vocabulary hardly gives us a historically appropriate single word for the Russian), in coping with the phenomenal universe and also the incomprehensible and inexplicable that remain and may always remain to attest not only the skill of the Creator but also the ultimate incomprehensibility of Creation. The wisest of men may tell us, to the universal glory of divinity, that other worlds exist, but what about this extraordinary, even counternatural, phenomenon observable right here on earth, the northern lights?

> Уста премудрых нам гласят:
> Там разных множество светов;
> Несчетны солнца там горят,
> Народы там и круг веков:
> Для общей славы божества
> Там равна сила естества.

(The lips of sages declare to us: there are a great many different worlds there, countless suns burn there, there are peoples there and a cycle of ages: for the universal glory of the divinity the force of nature is there the same.)

In the phrase "the lips of sages declare to us" we find a certain heightened or Slavonically archaizing diction: presumably men who are "enlightened" in both science and religion are invoked to express this new and untraditional view that, as hypothesis, may indeed be valid. But in the fourth stanza,

Nature, in her Latin name, is invoked to explain what has become of her customary law (presumably accepted as such by the sages) if dawn can arise from midnight regions, that is, from the north:

> Но где ж, натура, твой закон?
> С полночных стран встает заря!
> Не солнце ль ставит там свой трон?
> Не льдисты ль мещут огнь моря?
> Се хладный пламень нас покрыл!
> Се в ночь на землю день вступил!

(But where then, Nature, is your law? Dawn comes up from midnight regions! Is not the sun setting up its throne there? Do not the ice-bound seas throw forth fire? Behold, a cold flame has covered us! Behold, day has entered upon the earth at night!)

These seeming paradoxes of nature need no facile enhancement. Their mystery is proclaimed in these simple terms of questioning and exclamation. In no way does their expression resemble bombastic flattery of the beloved's eyes as sudden suns or the exaggerations of occasional poems on martial glory or on mere fireworks. Lomonosov turns again to the sages, not in deprecation of their knowledge or in obscurantist dismissal, but in the spirit of true wonder.

> О вы, которых быстрый зрак
> Пронзает в книгу вечных прав,
> Которым малый вещи знак
> Являет естества устав,
> Вам путь известен всех планет, —
> Скажите, что нас так мятет?
>
> Что зыблет ясный ночью луч?
> Что тонкий пламень в твердь разит?
> Как молния без грозных туч
> Стремится от земли в зенит?
> Как может быть, чтоб мерзлый пар
> Среди зимы рождал пожар?

(O you whose swift glance pierces into the book of eternal laws, to whom a little sign in a thing reveals a statute of nature, to you the path of all planets is known—tell what it is that troubles us so.)

(What ruffles the bright ray in the night? Why does the thin flame strike the firmament? How does lightning without thunderclouds race from earth to zenith? How can it be that frozen steam in the midst of winter engenders a great fire?)

These are questions of wonderment and also inquiry: the sages or scientists can observe and ask such questions, and indeed the speaker, or Lomonosov, is one of them. There is no limit to their answer or answers, but only proof can be acceptable to science and only truth can be acceptable to religion. Yet, for this poem, to put the issue thus would be to put it falsely. Restrictive notions of science and religion are not present in the poem; by strong implication proof and truth are the same for both and neither need fear the other. For whatever reason, the familiar debates of the eighteenth and nineteenth centuries are not present here—nor are they present in the poems of Wordsworth and Leopardi to be considered later. A whole and integral sensibility is expressed in the poem.

What then is the answer to the question posed by the uncanny northern lights? The answers are several and indeed they are not answers but hypotheses actually put forward in Lomonosov's day: darkness struggling with water; the sun's rays refracted through dense air; the volcanoes of Iceland reflected on ice; the tension (electrical in nature, as Lomonosov was later to argue) between unruffled waves and the pervasive element of "ether."

> Там спорит жирна мгла с водой;
> Иль солнечны лучи блестят,
> Склонясь сквозь воздух к нам густой;
> Иль тучных гор верьхи горят;
> Иль в море дуть престал зефир,
> И гладки волны бьют в эфир.

(There thick darkness struggles with water; or the sun's rays glimmer as they are bent through the dense air toward us; or the peaks of fertile mountains are on fire; or on the sea the zephyr has stopped blowing, and the smooth waves beat against ether.)

Arguable hypotheses, but none that carries proof or conviction. Their variety is even bizarre and, at least when mentioned in this fashion, poetic. We are fortunately spared scientific exposition of the sort that can soon date and seem ridiculous. This poem escapes the science versus poetry controversy so boringly familiar and still maintained by the neophytes and philistines of both parties. It also escapes the meshes of the cruder sort of history of scientific ideas in poetry. Most important, of course, it is a successful poem that gives expression to experience at the farther limits of thought.

The "answer" of the sages is not clear and categorical, it is "full of doubts." That is not to their discredit; they are not being denounced or dismissed by a riming parson. Yet it is consonant with "scientific" inquiry to ask ulterior and even ultimate questions which, answerless, help in some way to express the limits of human knowledge.

> Сомнений полон ваш ответ
> О том, что о́крест ближних мест.
> Скажите ж, коль пространен свет?
> И что малейших дале звезд?
> Несведом тварей вам конец?
> Скажите ж, коль велик творец?

(Your answer is full of doubts concerning what lies around nearby regions. Say then, how vast is the universe? And what is beyond the smallest stars? Is the limit of creation unknown to you? Say then: how great is the Creator?)

They are not asked to give up their questioning as if it were irreverent. They are not reprimanded for presuming to scan the universe. They are not given "the religious answer." Instead, they are encouraged to continue boldly with their questions and not stop until they have posed, in Lomonosov's terms, the final one. It is thus appropriate in this fine poem to end on a question, to keep the issues in complex balance, and not resolve them into the trivial truths of man's puniness and the unknowableness of creation or "whatever is is right" when "right" is not the right word.

Alexander Pope could brilliantly sustain an argumentative poetic essay on man but it is questionable whether he could have managed a lyric poem such as Lomonosov's. "The Universal Prayer" (1738), with its emphasis on faith and moral action and its nice balance between orthodoxy and deism, must stand as his effort. It falls short of Lomonosov's poem because it remains so generally pious and includes so little of questionable experience: there is nothing that lingers to trouble us; it is all very neat. Still less impressive in comparison to "Evening Meditation" is Joseph Addison's familiar "Ode" (1712), which begins:

> The spacious firmament on high,
> With all the blue ethereal sky,
> And spangl'd heav'ns, a shining frame,
> Their great original proclaim.

We are told that the celestial bodies in their unvarying movements day and night give evidence of "the work of an Almighty Hand." No matter if we "find" no real voice or sound, we hear in "Reason's ear" the singing stars and planets:

> What though, in solemn silence, all
> Move round the dark terrestrial ball?
> What though nor real voice nor sound
> Amid their radiant orbs be found?
> In Reason's ear, they all rejoice,
> And utter forth a glorious voice,
> Forever singing, as they shine,
> "The hand that made us is divine."

Apart from serious philosophies of optimism or deism, and apart, especially, from their vulgar debasements or misrepresentations, we are concerned with good poetry. When all allowances are made, Pope's and Addison's poems are quite mediocre in comparison to Lomonosov's. I know of nothing of the same general sort in French or Italian of the eighteenth century that is any better. Doubters may do penance by rereading James Thomson's *The Seasons* (1726–30) or, more to the point, "A Poem Sacred to the Memory of Sir Isaac Newton" (1729); or alternatively, *Les saisons* (1769) by Jean-François de Saint-Lambert or the encyclopaedic *Invito a Lesbia Cidonia* (1793) of Lorenzo Mascheroni, chiefly the section entitled "Museo di storia naturale e gabinetto di anatomia comparata"; or again, in Germanic lands, Albrecht von Haller's *Die Alpen* (1729) or Klopstock's "An Gott" (1745–51).

For this essay let it suffice to consider some of the consequences of Lomonosov's achievement as they will relate poetically, in the fullest sense of the word, to the poems of Wordsworth and Leopardi. "Evening Meditation" is a poem of solitary reflection in the midst of nature on things beyond human grasp. The same description would apply to "Lines" and to "L'Infinito." Lomonosov remains of his time in that the natural setting, apart from the northern lights, is quite spare and simple and at the same time in that the focus is on a startling natural spectacle. Only in the first two stanzas does the observer refer directly to himself and his subjective feelings. For the most part he addresses the "sages" in a way that includes himself and other men as sharing a common troubled wonderment. And of course at the end he directly refers to the presence of the "Creator." To this extent his poem is hardly eccentric for its time. Yet the deviations or nuances emerge as highly significant and allow our use of the poem as a kind of prelude to the later poems of Wordsworth and Leopardi: he is lost, sunk, and "forthought"; the "laws" of nature are not simple, scientific, and all-satisfying; there is a certain exultation in the mysteries of the universe; he is somehow alone among men who are also somehow alone and perhaps do not know it. Even the Creator evoked at the end is immeasurably "great" and hardly the "personal" God of orthodoxy.

Religio naturae in Early Wordsworth

In Wordsworth's "Lines" we find a poem of meditation very much more personal, circumstantial, and searching. Its "doctrine" lies outside orthodox religion, outside deism, outside Lomonosov's feeling of indwelling mystery in an explorable universe, and poetically expounds a very peculiar, in the most familial sense Wordsworthian, kind of *religio naturae* rather than pantheism. That the poem is a great poem is generally acknowledged and that it contains the prime elements of the early Wordsworth's "doctrine" is usually accepted, though often indiscriminately. Yet some complain of its vagueness or inconsistency; others like to explain it according to Hartley's psychology of vibrations, vibratiuncles, and association, or to account for it in biographical circumstance both before and after its composition. Before looking closely at this openly autobiographical poem it would be prudent to sketch briefly the personal and intellectual circumstances, not to raise extraneous questions but to lay them.

Five years before, Wordsworth had returned from Republican France, where he had joined in the libertarian enthusiasm, fallen in love, and begotten a child. He returned for lack of money and then could not go back because England had entered the war against France. In July 1793 on his way secretly to rendezvous with Dorothy, he parted from his traveling companion on Salisbury Plain and by himself walked to Bath and Bristol, crossed the Severn and headed up the river Wye toward the north of Wales. The ruins of Tintern Abbey, along his route, served him later as a convenient landmark; he passed up the chance then and later to write a mighty pile or gloomy ruin poem on it: he kept his distance from that earlier common habit. It was during his first walking tour up the secluded valley of the Wye that his mind was in great turmoil, apparently the greatest of his life, and also, according to his biographer Mary Moorman, the most obscure. Everything was at stake: his notions of politics and society inherited from the English Republicans, including Milton, and the Enlightenment through William Godwin; his vocation as a poet; the fate of his love and his child—in general, the emotional and intellectual turbulence of a highly sensitive young man barely twenty-three and in solitary crisis. Soon his father's death would leave him an orphan; he would soon reside with his sister, twelve months his junior; and four years later, in June 1797, he would begin the close friendship with Coleridge. At some point then he read Hartley's *Observations on Man* (1749) and, with Coleridge, for a time became a convert to the associationist theory of psychology, in the process abandoning Godwinian notions of nature and reason derived from Rousseau. By the end of those five years, he and Coleridge had compiled their *Lyrical Ballads* and arranged for their printing and publication at Bristol. During their stay near Bristol in July 1798, as the book was being set, Wordsworth and Dorothy together crossed the Severn and headed up the Wye as far as Goodrich, past Tintern Abbey, and then returned to Bristol where Wordsworth wrote down the poem he had composed in his mind, gave it to the printer, and immediately set about preparing for the journey in September to Germany with Dorothy and Coleridge.

In rehearsing these circumstances I simply mean to stress the following: the poem is that of a young man of just twenty-eight who had spent five years of turbulent immersion in love and politics and in achieving a gradual calm; his younger sister accompanied him to that, for him, momentous river valley as a neophyte to share his experience of reexperiencing and to become, in his eyes, an initiate; remembered notions of Milton, Godwin, and now Hartley were not simply philosophical positions but emotionally charged and held convictions; something like a conversion had taken place and was being affirmed. This biographical excursus is meant mainly to counter any misconception that the poem argues a mature philosophical position, that it was composed in direct consultation with Hartley's views, that it was written by an ageless sage.

In the first verse paragraph of the poem the setting is clearly drawn: the speaker is immediately present on the banks of the river Wye in the midst of a natural landscape; the external objects that matter to him are all mentioned except for his sister whose inclusion later on is a dramatic stroke. A long five years have passed through all their seasons and the waters have flowed but, like the speaker, they both remain the same and are different. The coordinates in time and space are determined now with a second visit to the strange-familiar place and with another momentous experience at another stage of time.

> Once again
> Do I behold these steep and lofty cliffs,
> Which on a wild secluded scene impress
> Thoughts of more deep seclusion. . . .

Sublimity, seclusion, and implied solitude are all there, but they are soon to be modified. In the first instance, though the cliffs suggest a conventional "pre-Romantic" sublimity, the conclusion of the sentence sets them more docilely in nature:

> . . . and connect
> The landscape with the quiet of the sky.

Their energy is thus contained within the general scene: indeed the words "scene" and "landscape" have compositional force greater than they do in current English, for the artistic meanings still resounded in them. At the same time they do not merely signal conventional pictorial or topographical poetry of long-standing tradition. Moreover, it is not an uninhabited unhuman setting: there are "plots of cottage-ground," "orchard-tufts" (clumps of fruit-bearing trees), hedgerows, and "pastoral farms / Green to the very door." But they are carefully and brilliantly made one with the natural landscape. Even the smoke that rises is sent up in silent "wreathes" as if indicating "vagrant dwellers in the houseless woods" or a lone hermit by his fire. The speaker, by his familiarity and by his invocation also belongs to what is, by convincing oxymoron, a solitary company; yet he receives the impress of "Thoughts of more deep seclusion," suggesting that nature is hallowed in him and in him has revealed herself. Indeed those "forms of beauty" from his first visit have, as he tells us in the second paragraph, evoked feelings so deep they have become a saving part of him.

> But oft, in lonely rooms, and mid the din
> Of towns and cities, I have owed to them,
> In hours of weariness, sensations sweet,
> Felt in the blood, and felt along the heart,
> And passing even into my purer mind
> With tranquil restoration:—feelings too
> Of unremembered pleasure; such, perhaps,
> As may have had no trivial influence
> On that good portion of a good man's life;
> His little, nameless, unremembered acts
> Of kindness and of love.

Here he is not merely expounding Hartleian doctrine, with tinges of Rousseau and Godwin, and perhaps getting it wrong. Rather, he is setting forth poetically the unbroken chain from sense-impression to unconscious moral behavior. It is not so much a general psychological theory as an attempted description of his actual experience: in the process of taking into account the beneficent experience of nature and the "unremembered pleasures" that somehow are connected with it, Wordsworth invents or discovers the unconscious for himself. Any charge of inaccurate or unproductive vagueness must be dropped in the light of this momentous fact. The words used, as for example "feelings too / Of unremembered pleasure," are no vaguer than a contemporary psychological notion of "euphoria" as a state of well-being safely between "depression" and "elation" (in modern psychological usage). Indeed if read in context and without prejudice they are impressive rhetorical means of expressing the nearly inexpressible.

The chain of sensation, feeling, well-being, and love, which may well have been created by "those forms of beauty," may also have bestowed "another gift, / Of aspect more sublime," a gift or faculty capable of attaining

> that blessed mood,
> In which the burthen of the mystery,
> In which the heavy and the weary weight
> Of all this unintelligible world

Is lighten'd:—that serene and blessed mood,
In which the affections gently lead us on,
Until, the breath of this corporeal frame
And even the motion of our human blood
Almost suspended, we are laid asleep
In body, and become a living soul:
While with an eye made quiet by the power
Of harmony, and the deep power of joy,
We see into the life of things.

It lies within his capability to induce in himself a mood of freedom from the perplexity of everyday reality—people and things and existence itself—and from the unanswerable questions that might pose themselves, a mood that is blessed (that is, comforting, pleasurable, privileged) and also serene (that is, not feverish or turbulent). Indeed, anxieties must all be in abeyance for the body to be utterly relaxed—to put it in blunter modern terms. That mood in which subjectively the body seems suspended and the totality of our subjective being becomes "a living soul" is a mood of ecstasy, not in the old medical sense of extreme agitation or mad fit, but rather in the mystical though not strictly religious sense of serene liberation from the subjective body and absorption into the transcendent or the whole or whatever one may call it: here any choice of word will seem inappropriately tendentious. The utter "harmony" and "joy" depend upon utter serenity. In this state of balance or transcendence the "eye made quiet"—no longer a Hartleian eye but the eye of the soul contemplating spirit—"sees," as in the orthodox mystics, "into the life of things." Again, in paraphrase, one would be tempted to suggest the words "ultimate reality." Such paraphrastic temptations, not to mention doctrinal irrelevancies, should not obscure the simpler and more eloquent obscurities poetically necessary and successful in Wordsworth's mode of expression, which is here more "revolutionary" for his time than the "rustic speech" he had so much trouble explaining to his readers and they so much trouble in understanding and accepting. It is noteworthy that almost imperceptibly in this passage Wordsworth generalizes his apparently deepest and most personal experience by encompassing his readers in the persuasive plural "we." Not merely adepts or hierophants, but all *human* nature is capable of such experience. Besides, the metaphorical means of expression is visual or, more portentously, epiphanic: both the outer and the inner eyes see "what is there." Eye, thought, imagination, memory are aspects of the total ability to experience what Wordsworth in *The Prelude* called "spots of time" or what we may, with Joyce, call epiphanies in all the etymological and experiential senses. Not, however, in the traditionally religious sense: a god whether personal or abstract is not mentioned; nature has not yet been evoked, and when she is fleetingly personified much later it is in the context of a "prayer" for his sister. What we are given so far is very tentatively, however searchingly, given. "If this / Be but a vain belief," nonetheless in the midst of anxiety,

> when the fretful stir
> Unprofitable, and all the fever of the world,
> Have hung upon the beatings of my heart,

his spirit has often recalled the "sylvan Wye":

> thou wanderer through the woods,
> How often has my spirit turned to thee!

No claims are made here for systematic psychology or religion. There is nothing here but a grappling with profound experience and a simple yet dramatically searching aesthetic attempt to express it in the face of near-impossibility.

After the brief third paragraph we are led back to the present scene and its principal element, the river. In the fourth paragraph the complex of experience and memory is enlivened in its strange familiarity or familiar strangeness.

> And now, with gleams of half-extinguish'd thought,
> With many recognitions dim and faint,
> And somewhat of a sad perplexity,
> The picture of the mind revives again.

That "picture of the mind," that pictorial image laden with emotion, reforms again and the effect is one of renewal, change, and pleasure in the process—but now a pleasure that will endure and be "life and food / For future years." Here again any comfortable complacency is dispelled by the hesitant phrase "And so I dared to hope, / Though changed, no doubt, from what I was." Indeed, it is a falsification of the poem as a whole to treat the delicate hesitancies as if they were bumbling or stagy and to reduce searching expression of the process of thinking to some imposed abstract doctrine: thought or spirit or mind are not used with philosophical rigor here. Comparisons with the "Intimations" ode (written 1802–4; published 1807) or with *The Prelude* (1805–50) are not only premature but largely irrelevant. In this fourth long paragraph, then, we are vouchsafed a tentative account of how a whole state of mind came to be now, in the present of the poem. On first journeying to the Wye valley alone, five years before, he experienced a turbulent sense of freedom,

> when like a roe
> I bounded o'er the mountains, by the sides
> Of the deep rivers, and the lonely streams,
> Wherever nature led; more like a man
> Flying from something that he dreads, than one
> Who sought the thing he loved. For nature then
> (The coarser of my boyish days,
> And their glad animal movements all gone by,)
> To me was all in all.

There was something compulsive about it, some giddy energy of escape. The things of nature haunted him; they were a pressing need, "an appetite." Indeed, they allowed him no respite or reflection as they seemed to impel and to agitate him unreflectively with their presence and his turbulent response.

> Their colours and their forms, were then to me
> An appetite: a feeling and a love,
> That had no need of a remoter charm,
> By thought supplied, nor any interest
> Unborrowed from the eye.

His relation to natural objects was then purely sensuous or sensory: the "remoter charm" of reflection had not formed in his thought (or imagination) nor did he feel any involvement or commitment (the proper meaning of the word "interest" in Wordsworth's day) beyond immediate visual apprehension. Now it is otherwise:

> —That time is past,
> And all its aching joys are now no more,
> And all its dizzy raptures.

Those were gifts of passionate feeling for which the almost oxymoronic descriptions, "aching joys" and "dizzy raptures," should be taken not as clichés but at their full youthful force. Yet

>   other gifts
>   Have followed, for such loss, I would believe,
>   Abundant recompense.

Those are the gifts of reflective memory, concern for others, and a feeling of profound meaningfulness that binds all together. Instead of lamenting past unreflective youth in a conventional way, the speaker hesitantly and without smug certitude, indeed with understatement, believes he has found some wisdom or insight that is ample requital for the loss.

>   For I have learned
>   To look on nature, not as in the hour
>   Of thoughtless youth, but hearing oftentimes
>   The still, sad music of humanity.

Now his mind is whole, he has learned something, and that is to look on nature not with the sensuous eye of youth without memory or imagination or, simply, "thought," but actually hearing in the midst of nature also the presence of *humanity,* which in the context must therefore be read as an emphatic word. "Humanity" has somehow become for Wordsworth a part of nature, and solitude is no longer a necessary and sufficient condition. Even more important, his youthful passion is transformed into a serene feeling that "disturbs" him but does so "with the joy / Of elevated thoughts," a feeling that is difficult or impossible to describe, but which may partly be described in strong comparison with that earlier "appetite" of "thoughtless youth": "a sense sublime / Of something far more deeply interfused." This phrase of comparison, too easily dismissed with a derisive question "than *what?*" must be taken to refer to the earlier state, difficult enough in itself to describe. The word "something" again is vague, but here precision of a reductive sort is out of place, and the almost colloquial breathlessness of it finds release in the satisfyingly compound, learned word "interfused," release that then flows freely in a loose syntax of enumeration and repetition that serves to enhance:

Whose dwelling is the light of setting suns,
And the round ocean, and the living air,
And the blue sky, and in the mind of man,
A motion and a spirit, that impels
All thinking things, all objects of all thought,
And rolls through all things.

The "vagueness" is functional; it expresses the effort of trying to express essentially inexpressible thought and feeling. That release of vast emotional thought has a dramatic force in the poem; it spills out in a controlled setting, not as high-pitched pantheistic incantation but as serenely joyous celebration within a modest, hesitant, meditative poem. "Thinking" and "thought" are far more than the merely discursive faculty: they describe the imagination, or what one might risk calling "pathepistemia" or "felt thinking." Man becomes truly human, a part of humanity, in this interchange with what is deeply interfused in nature. Man's response to nature, his giving and taking, are part of nature. Their medium of communication, "the language of the sense," leads to "purest thoughts" (line 110) in "purer mind" (line 30): thus, after the "coarser pleasures" of boyhood and the "dizzy raptures" of youth, the thinking, reflective, imaginative man can serenely and morally dwell in his now-formed mind, which is still a dependent and reciprocal part of nature. In the quietly didactic mood that follows on the gentle euphoria of conviction, the poet can draw a simple summary conclusion:

Therefore am I still
A lover of the meadows and the woods,
And mountains; and of all that we behold
From this green earth; of all the mighty world
Of eye and ear, both what they half-create,
And what perceive; well pleased to recognize
In nature and the language of the sense,
The anchor of my purest thoughts, the nurse,
The guide, the guardian of my heart, and soul
Of all my moral being.

Man is the child of kind and fruitful nature, but he also possesses his maturing faculty of "thought" while he still depends upon nature; even his eye and ear at least half-create something inward and human from the direct impressions made upon them from outside. So in this poem and the revelatory conviction it expresses we find operative not only nature in the external though impressive sense but also the maturing faculty innate in man that makes him both at one and equal with nature—all by his own choice and through his indispensable volition or ready openness. Nature is the ground of man's being in childhood and maturity, yet man can be both a part of it and a freely choosing communicant or rebel. God is not here, nor are the gods, not even a creator is envisioned. To say that nature has become god or in some way divine is to impose upon the poem. To ascribe argued doctrinal pantheism to the poem is to pervert it too conveniently into a prepared category derived from notions of a Romantic *Zeitgeist*. The notion of *Zeitgeist* is useful but runs the danger of becoming itself metaphorically pantheistic; indeed, *Zeitgeist* seems often the phlogiston of intellectual history.

In the last long paragraph, Wordsworth, instead of preaching a system, or drawing moral lessons for everyday use, or proclaiming a universal revelation, turns naturally and humanly to his sister, of whose presence only now are we aware. She has been the silent and unwitting audience to his deeply personal meditation. She is like his former self, which he now understands as something in process that should in good time ripen to maturity. And he can now depend on her for the unreflective closeness to nature he has necessarily given up, though with "abundant recompense." If he did not feel that way, he would no longer allow his "genial spirits," the spirits of "thoughtless youth," to subside or "decay."

> Nor, perchance,
> If I were not thus taught, should I the more
> Suffer my genial spirits to decay:
> For thou art with me, upon the banks
> Of this fair river; thou, my dearest Friend,
> My dear, dear Friend, and in thy voice I catch
> The language of my former heart, and read
> My former pleasures in the shooting lights
> Of thy wild eyes. Oh! yet a little while
> May I behold in thee what I was once,
> My dear, dear Sister!

The circle is complete: the genial spirits must subside if knowledge, or self-consciousness, or imagination, or thought is to reach a mature and individual creativity; communion with the past, however, remains vicariously possible in the "wild eyes" of his sister. For her, as it once was for him, the eyes directly take in nature and she is content with immediate perception. For him now, as it will be for her, the "wild eyes" of the unreflectingly naïve convey the familiar, now only remembered experience to the reflectingly mature by their "shooting lights." What was lost and what was gained are incommensurable, and yet maturity, fully accepted, has its consolation. Then in a prayer he affirms his belief in the abundance of blessings (even in the presence of human viciousness) derived from nature, which "never did betray / The heart that loved her." Even in self-reflexive maturity nature "can so inform / The mind that is within us, so impress / With quietness and beauty, and so feed / With lofty thoughts" that we are protected and sustained. Again the process leads from unconscious "informing" and "impressing" to the "feeding" of "thoughts" that are called "lofty" (recalling earlier "elevated thoughts," "purest thoughts") to enhance the element of feeling that infuses reflective ratiocination. In such a mood of confidence he foresees that she too will live through these essentially solitary "wild ecstasies" until her mind and memory are "informed" and fitted for "all lovely forms" and for "all sweet sounds and harmonies." Indeed, in the midst of later pain she will remember and then be reflectively conscious of what he calls "these my exhortations." And once again, with a modesty and hesitation, as before, which undercut his "exhortations," he expresses hope that she will remember this time and him if he should be absent or dead.

> Nor, perchance,
> If I should be where I no more can hear
> Thy voice, nor catch from thy wild eyes these gleams
> Of past existence, wilt thou then forget . . .

Memory is the saving grace of maturity: it can knowingly preserve and integrate "past experience," which is *not* to be taken in any sense derived from the "Intimations" ode. In fact, she will be witness then that he came there unwearied in nature's service:

> rather say
> With warmer love, oh! with far deeper zeal
> Of holier love.

And he closes with the vision of her witness that "these steep woods and lofty cliffs" (the sublime and haunting aspects of nature) "And this green pastoral landscape" (the gentle presence of man living in nature as a part of nature)

> were to me
> More dear, both for themselves, and for thy sake.

The quiet simplicity and utter lack of presumption in these last lines should help us remember the absence of any systematic doctrine in the whole poem.

Here there is no sketch of a thoroughgoing pantheism, no portent of a creator, no overt or emphatic stress on pre-existence or the afterlife, and no drawing of self-righteous moral lessons. Indeed the hesitancy of so many colloquial turns of phrase, the repeated "nor perchance," the achieved serenity of the whole occasion—all should prevent us from going beyond this self-contained poem and trying to impose some cosmic and apocalyptic system of pantheistic religion for Wordsworth. If there is any sort of "religion" here it would be more like the *familial* and immanently natural religion of the ancient Romans without mythology and with only the simple cultivation of *pietas*. In this sense we can say that, just as Lomonosov expressed his own complex view in terms somewhat related to deism, so Wordsworth creates here for himself and for his sister a kind of peculiar *religio familiaris* founded on his own experience of nature and his modest and tentative inclusion here and there in the poem of "humanity" and the "*pastoral* landscape." I would again stress that there is no mention of God or the divine and that the terms of the poem are not overtly religious in the orthodox sense. What Wordsworth leaves out in this poem should not be foisted on it. His later adhesion to the Church of England is too far in the future to interest us in the reading of this poem. His philosophical Neoplatonic and quasi-religious musings in the "Intimations" ode (1802–7) are still to come. We have in "Lines" a calmly pondered rendering of the poet's transcendent experience of maturing in immanent nature and his modest profession of a familial piety searchingly set forth as the best there is for him, and perhaps for others.

Whatever vagueness or indefiniteness we encounter in the poem is not a doctrinal deficiency on the part of Wordsworth, but rather a means of simple yet profound eloquence such as may be found nowhere else in English poetry. This noble poem, composed in the mind and written down on walking into Bristol, set up and printed as the last poem in the *Lyrical Ballads*, is both an end and a beginning: it is ripe and mature on its own terms, it really satisfies canons of style that Wordsworth awkwardly expressed in his notion of the speech of "rustic" or "rural" men, and its natural eloquence is independent of what comes later, however much it is a stage on Wordsworth's way. It is, perhaps, his finest poetic "spot of time."

A Measure of Infinity

The landscape and its inhabitants, for the early Leopardi, consisted in the town of Recanati, just inland from the Adriatic and south of the port city of Ancona, set in a backward hilly region of the Papal State, with no particular history other than immemorial settlement and remote connection with great events. As with Wordsworth in the Lake Country or the valley of the Wye, town and country here were hardly separable in daily life: the vendors were country folk, townhouses depended on their farms, servants and peasants were of the same stock. Besides, a view of the landscape from the town was immediately there. In one of the better early poems, "La sera del dì di festa" (mid-1820), Leopardi sets the scene so familiar to his readers:

> Dolce e chiara è la notte e senza vento,
> E queta sovra i tetti e in mezzo agli orti
> Posa la luna, e di lontan rivela
> Serena ogni montagna. O donna mia,
> Già tace ogni sentiero, e pei balconi
> Rara traluce la notturna lampa.

(The night is soft and bright and windless, and the moon rests quietly above the roofs and in the gardens, and in the distance it reveals each mountain serene. O my lady, every pathway is now silent, and along the balconies the lamp of night sparsely glimmers.)

Roofs, kitchen gardens, mountains, paths, balconies are all lit by the same moon and seen by the same observer. Short of discussing the whole poem, I simply posit this setting as "typical" for Leopardi and refer divergences to it. The thoughts that occur to the speaker in this poem concern his

childhood when after the longed-for holiday he lay awake at night listening
to a song from the pathways and feeling a tug at his heart, just as now
hopelessness assails him as he thinks of a girl, heedless of him, calmly
sleeping nearby. He contemplates the sky that seems so benign and also
nature that has destined him for inner turmoil.

> Tu dormi: io questo ciel, che sì benigno
> Appare in vista, a salutar m'affaccio,
> E l'antica natura onnipossente,
> Che mi fece all'affanno.

(You are sleeping: I look out to greet this sky that seèms in aspect
so benign, and ancient all-powerful nature that made me for travail.)

That ancient and all-powerful nature, speaking directly, then tells him that
even hope is not for him and that his eyes will shine only from tears. This
is one kind of nature that pursued him all his life: like an ever-present
malignant stepmother she is sovereign and beyond appeal. To understand
that view of nature and the other views that occur in Leopardi, a brief
sketch of his development, before and after "L'Infinito" (composed in its
first version in September 1819), will be useful, not to indulge in
biographical speculation but to help evaluate the context of the poem and
appreciate the momentary balance it achieves.

Giacomo's father, Count Monaldo Leopardi, had succeeded in nearly
ruining his patrimony through speculation while at the same time amassing
a considerable library of eighteenth-century erudition and ideology. His
character rested on the dogmas and prejudices of the Enlightenment as
perceived by a provincial dilettante and observant son of the church, and on
his stern wife who took over the management of the family and its fortune.
From priestly tutors, from his father, and by his independent labors,
Giacomo learned enough to make his father's library wholly accessible to
him. His earliest works were academic exercises, compilations, translations, and imitations that reflected the enormous prestige of classical
philology in a neo-Alexandrian vein and of French culture of the Enlightenment as represented most famously in Voltaire, Rousseau, and Fon-
tenelle. His precocious studies were unremitting and broadly European in
their classicizing and old-fashioned scope. Such learning and skeptical
philosophy occupied his mind to the detriment of his frail body. Until he first
realized his desire, so passionately entertained in the summer of 1819, to

leave home for the first time (1822–23, for Rome), he continued to live at Recanati through changing stages of awareness in an atmosphere of household severity and bookish imagination. His first original poems were understandably traditional: patriotic *canzoni* in the line of Petrarch and in a style that is often stiff and hortatory; solemn odes on death and on abstract or conventional love; and a few perfunctory Christian hymns that betoken mere religiosity. Stylistically he was recapitulating the learned line of Latin and Italian poetry and also the more recent sentimental or "pre-Romantic" modes found, for example, in Vincenzo Monti and Melchiorre Cesarotti's translation of Ossian. Ideologically, he was attempting to sort out for his own worldview inherited notions of reason, nature, and religion as related to progress, happiness, and belief—all in the fashion of the later eighteenth century. In his poetry, which can be quite accurately dated, in his vast and miscellaneous notebook, the *Zibaldone* (meaning something like "gallimaufry"), and in his expressive correspondence, we can follow the twists and turns of his interests and thoughts, which he had some hope of ordering into what could have amounted to a mature existential philosophy based upon materialism and what Schopenhauer in 1844 called his "pessimism." Attempts have been made to systematize his thought for him, though clearly he has no standing among true and original philosophers. Many more attempts have been made to construct a Leopardian worldview based upon a mixture of biographical, ideological, and poetic elements, which, when synthesized, is used to speculate back upon his fictive works and inner biography. In both cases the procedure is most often methodologically wrong: Leopardi's thinking or meditation on the human condition underwent a gradual evolution that hardly admits of total synthesis or of reading more mature views back into his earlier work. The trajectory of his dominant mood evolved gradually from a bittersweet innocence caught between yearning and disillusionment, still hopeful in the face of disappointment and deeply sympathetic to the harmless creatures of nature, through a kind of sardonic intensity that could range between cold anger and sad irony, to a final attitude of controlled and vigilant pessimism that sees men at common war with vengeful nature and, only if thus banded together, able to live in some decency and rectitude among the humbler creatures that are also objects of nature's malevolence.

The meaning of "nature" can thus range, in Leopardi's usage, from the whole of the universe in either an eighteenth-century deistic or a scientific sense, to the gentle and harmless aspects of life, to the personified malignant destroyer even worse when seemingly indifferent, to a secular abstraction that seems to stand for an evil god. Rather summarily, one may say that Leopardi, while at times mingling such views, went from an early state of superficial acceptance of either a vaguely orthodox or a vaguely deistic nature, through various states of doubt and indignation on philosophical and rational grounds, to a state of stoic pessimism. Concomitantly, those states are tinged with a range of emotions that seem to evolve from guarded hope, to hope against hope, to stoic absence of hope. These views in process may be discerned in his disparate writings. Confining the matter to fictive works, I would hazard to say that Leopardi found a first provisional balance in "L'Infinito," in which potentially dangerous depths are exhilarating; a second provisional balance in some of the great *Operette morali* in which a moving and gentle irony plays about the encounter between hopeful innocent man and the cruel or indifferent limits arbitrarily placed on him; and a third provisional balance in some of the last poems (including "La Ginestra") in which memory of innocence and pleasure or sympathy with the gentle and lowly seem, in somber thought, an acceptable consolation for mortality and indifferent fate.

As one sees even in the early poem "La sera del dì di festa," there are, along with hopelessness and vehemence against fate, elements of natural beauty and innocence preserved by hope and joy. The moon is quietly shining, the girl perhaps is dreaming of those she liked and those who liked her, a solitary workman sings as he walks home late at night. The speaker's thoughts of fate, transience, and suffering as a child after the holiday is over and now as a young man in hopeless love, are muted by sympathy and sentiment—and also by the simple comparison of the song heard now and that heard long ago:

> ed alla tarda notte
> Un canto che s'udia per li sentieri
> Lontanando morire a poco a poco,
> Già similmente mi stringeva il core.

(and late at night a song that was heard along the paths, fading in the distance little by little, now likewise was tugging at my heart.)

But there is also in the poem some posturing and self-pity in the evocation of nature as a cruel stepmother and in the outburst against fate provoked by his thought that the girl had opened a wound in his breast yet surely would not count him among those she liked.

These themes open into Leopardi's future. But to go back about a year, let us consider his first great poem, "L'Infinito," which is a break with the stilted immediate past and a precocious provisional balance as he entered on his true career as a poet. Out of the density of archaizing diction and forensic tone of his earlier poetry emerges this little poem of purely subjective meditation, so seemingly simple and so immediately natural in setting and expression. Here there is no oblique relationship between nature and God, so deeply felt by the speaker in Lomonosov's "Evening Meditation." Nor is there here any humble affirmation of faith in immanent nature made by the speaker in his own name and that of his sister and "future" witness, as in Wordsworth's "Lines." Rather, we find the speaker in a familiar everyday setting, truly alone, expatiating outward just to the edge of fear or the sublime and simultaneously inward to the depth of thought—all ending in pleasurable breathless oblivion.

A reading of these fifteen hendecasyllabic lines gives an impression of unusual richness and smoothness.

> Sempre caro mi fu quest'ermo colle,
> E questa siepe, che da tanta parte
> Dell'ultimo orizzonte il guardo esclude.
> Ma sedendo e mirando, interminati
> Spazi di là da quella, e sovrumani
> Silenzi, e profondissima quiete
> Io nel pensier mi fingo; ove per poco
> Il cor non si spaura. E come il vento
> Odo stormir tra queste piante, io quello
> Infinito silenzio a questa voce
> Vo comparando: e mi sovvien l'eterno,
> E le morte stagioni, e la presente
> E viva, e il suon di lei. Così tra questa
> Immensità s'annega il pensier mio:
> E il naufragar m'è dolce in questo mare.

(This lonely hill was always dear to me, and this hedgerow that shuts out the view from so great a portion of the last horizon. But sitting and looking, I fashion in thought unending spaces beyond it [the hedgerow] and suprahuman silences and the deepest quiet: at which my heart almost takes fright. And as I hear the wind rustling among these plants, I find myself likening that infinite silence to this voice: and I recall eternity and the dead seasons and the present and living one, and its sound. Thus, in the midst of this immeasurableness my thought drowns: and foundering in this sea is sweet to me.)

We may perhaps be surprised, as after reading Tennyson's "Tears," to see that there is no rime. That impression of richness can partially be explained, I think, by four objective features of sound: the relatively high frequency of sibilants; the absence of double-stop consonants (tt, dd, gg); the unsystematic presence of assonantal rime (interminati/sovrumani; vento/quello/eterno; quiete/presente; parte/mare); and the very high incidence of enjambement (depending on criteria, from ten to twelve of the fifteen lines). "L'Infinito" thus stands in prosodic contrast to "Evening Meditation," whose end-stopped lines may give an impression of measure and exactitude and whose few run-on lines have unusual dramatic effect. It even goes beyond the freedom of Wordsworth's subtly sustained blank verse in its much briefer and admittedly unsustainable effect. Yet the onrushing impression is checked somewhat by the weak syntactical pauses within lines and by the pervasive aura of assonance.

These effects of sound are consonant with the meaning of the poem, and it is for that reason that I call attention to them: not to make mere murmurs of "musicality." Both in sound and in sense the poem sets out from a fixed point and, making a vast trajectory through evocation of the senses of sight and sound, ends in all and nothing. Through the imagination, or through "thought" in the imaginative sense ("pensiero," as Leopardi uses it), the audacious and self-induced plunge into measurelessness is aesthetically successful. The poet somehow knows that the infinite cannot be imaginatively, that is, humanly, rendered without some means of measurement and comparison. The terms of spatial measurement are the point and the line, of temporal measurement the sequence of time in subjective experience of moments and in the progression of the daily and yearly cycles. The mutually defining terms of comparison are between space and non-space, sight and invisibility, sound and silence. All the terms must somehow coexist and reciprocally define or locate or characterize each other; otherwise, as in unbroken silence, the situation would become inhuman, a perversion of experience, an utter alienation. Tone also is crucial in a poem that deals with extremes of experience; it is the result of psychic distancing and expressive control over immediacy and ultimate unknowability. The poet must communicate through the medium of chosen words and syntax both to himself and to the reader. In "L'Infinito" the extreme subjectivity, the almost total concentration of self, is mitigated by seemingly casual urbanity. The reader's role is barely activated by the poem, and yet the candor of confessionalism and the potential universality of the experience rendered make the reader essential as witness to be aesthetically convinced.

In the first line a tone is established of casual intimacy. The syntactical inversion is disarmingly conversational and even the word "sempre" seems only to convey colloquial exaggeration. The hill is deserted or barren, perhaps, but more likely the unusual word "ermo" still retains from Greek and Latin the aura of hermit and hermitage once possessed by English and French "desert." Not only was *this* hill always dear to him, but also *this* hedgerow that cuts off sight of so great a part of the farthest horizon. We are already in a defined place, contemplating with the speaker the hedgerow that, by limiting, suggests the beyond that is actually there though unseen. Psychologically and aesthetically the mere mention of the hedgerow is of the greatest importance: it is particular, familiar, defining; at the same time, it is continuous and suggestive beyond what can be seen of it. In the fourth line the adversative "ma" indicates contrast: the scene is familiar and defined, *but* thinking or thought ("pensiero") creates or toys with the uncanny and the immeasurable. It is only a seeming paradox, though nonetheless dramatic: the imaginings of the mind expatiate in ways that could lead to ultimate issues of ratiocination and belief. The words appear casual and even ordinary. "Pensiero" is capacious enough, like "thought" in Wordsworth's sense; it is a comprehensive creative and imaginative faculty that will be taxed in the poem to its utmost.

> Ma sedendo e mirando, interminati
> Spazi di là da quella, e sovrumani
> Silenzi, e profondissima quiete
> Io nel pensier mi fingo.

Just sitting and looking, the speaker creates or imagines for himself (ambiguities of this favorite word "fingersi") unended spaces beyond the hedgerow, and suprahuman silences, and the deepest quiet. Are they somehow *there* in the sense that the hill and hedgerow are *there*, or does thought overcharge itself and create or re-create its own universe? It is a heady enterprise

                              ove per poco
                 Il cor no si spaura:

at which, we may interpret, the heart barely misses taking fright. The
vague connection "ove" is here put to tantalizing use: its locative sense is
attenuated and a temporal sense is implied; it can serve thereby a
diplomatically ambiguous function, indicating that there is in all this the
danger of panic. But at once we are back in immediate nature among *these*
plants, *this* landscape:

                        e mi sovvien l'eterno,
                 E le morte stagioni, e la presente
                 E viva, e il suon di lei.

The voice recalls first the eternal in general—a word not negative in
formation like "in-terminati" or "in-finito" and not relative to the human as
"sovrumani," but rather serenely indicating (from Latin *aetas* and *aeternum*)
a state beyond time. Though the past is evoked in passing by the "dead
seasons" (in Italian *stagione* is, it happens, related to "standing" or "stages,"
not "sowing" [*sationem*] as in French and English), it is the present season
or stage that is immediate in the experience and alive in its very sound as
well as sight.

The moment has been evoked along with the past that helps define it.
But we and the speaker are not encouraged to dwell on the past or the
future, which for that matter is not mentioned in human terms; rather, we
find the present moment, as it were, infinitely expandable or, by implication, even repeatable. Onrushing thought and thoughts—in effect, the
imagination and what arouses it in nature—come to a climax that is not
ideological, though it is introduced by a modulating, almost didactic "thus,"
but rather irrational and experiential, in which the mind, while skirting
danger, can achieve its own eternity through exhaustion, surrender, and
ambiguous annihilation.

                              Così tra questa
                 Immensità s'annega il pensier mio:
                 E il naufragar m'è dolce in questo mare.

Thus—we may interpret—in this measurelessness his "thought" drowns,
and the foundering or *shipwreck* is sweet to him in this sea. The mind is

literally overwhelmed and must go under. That experience, by implication, as I say, even repeatable, is a sweet release or dissolution in which the one who drowns somehow paradoxically (as with other Romantics) survives *to know what it is like*. Knowing, in this context, means hardly expressible memory; "what it is *like*"—that profoundly casual phrase—means the making of comparisons, similes, and metaphors, or the imaginative faculty of "pensiero" that survives its own destruction. Why then is the ground of metaphor changed at the end of the poem from land to sea? Because "pensiero" has that power: it is both the means of transition and the medium itself; the earthly world is absorbed and transformed in it and by it. The mind founders and sinks into itself.

"L'Infinito" is a poem in precarious balance, poised between imagination and ratiocination and infused with "pensiero" in which those otherwise distinguishable faculties are not dangerously divided against each other. There are other dangerous possibilities within the cosmos of the poem, some alluded to and others always part of the human condition. How would things be in terms of human relationships in such a cosmos? Are questions to be raised about causality, creation, responsibility, boredom, death? The balance remains perilous, though inclusiveness would be utterly destructive to the poem and its mood. Facile solutions are shunned, as in the poems of Lomonosov and Wordsworth, and no easy synthesis is presented. The achieved poem is the momentarily sufficient resolution. It is a moving aesthetic achievement precisely about becoming itself. Successfully to create something fictively in the mind ("fingersi nel pensiero") may be as much true wisdom and consolation as the poet can conceive for himself in this life.

Concluding Reflections

Here, then, are three poems discussed according to their set of ideas and emotions, their immediate biographical circumstances, and their literary achievement. The primary requisite of this triadic essay is to understand the poems in their inward intense complex of words. By the inescapable reference of words outward from subjectivity to communicability, meaning radiates to the point that its boundaries may threaten to dissolve. Are there any aesthetic controls that may properly apply without resolving these or other poems into ideology or biography or history or capricious linguistic play? We may answer hesitantly that there are: the poem itself as a system of interrelated or "intersubjective" norms; the whole imaginative poetic production of the poet who can be considered as somehow evolving his own mode or style; the language conceived in terms of a rigorous historical semantics; and the striking formulations of doctrine within a tradition of thought and expression to which judicious reference must be made. All are interconnected so subtly that dealing with such controls may seem too difficult or best left to the understanding of the optimum reader. Yet some defense is needed to mitigate what may otherwise seem mere arbitrary choice: three poems I like or three poems on "immensity" or just three poems in three different languages.

To consider the poems first as three intelligible works of art, I would stress that they are all interesting and good, that they are meditations that purport deep experience, that they deal with intense relationships between the most concrete and the most universal, and that they represent in their national traditions significant departures or inventions in poetic method. Their linguistic and metrical medium involves a theory of poetic language and its relation to ordinary and erudite speech. Rhetorically, the relationship among speaker, object addressed, and reader differs from poem to poem but in an arguably evolutionary fashion. In Lomonosov's poem private meditiation seeks a public audience in the sages who are more or less Leibnizian deists, yet the poet stops short of transforming his poetry into argument or taking the familiar eighteenth-century pose of generic apostrophe: observable phenomena in all their particularity and strangeness are in the foreground and their vital connection with general significance and private feeling is maintained. In Wordsworth's "Lines" the poet addresses himself and the river Wye as he puts past experience into perspective and renders his life whole. Then toward the end his internal audience, his sister, is invoked as future verifying witness and also as a means of corroborating his hesitant generalizing of his own experience. The public or ceremonial mode has receded even farther than in "Evening Meditation," while the *general* level of discourse hovers even closer to the chosen particulars. In Leopardi's poem the extreme tension between the particular and the general becomes the subject, and the reader and "object addressed" become one and are relegated to near-absorption in the speaker's climatically inward movement: throughout the poem the reader is kept vigilant by the intensely indicative use of "this"—from "quest'ermo colle," which exists in the poem, to "questo mare," which exists only in the mind or *is* the mind. Here, then, is one set of relationships between the three poems aesthetically considered. It is also a set of relationships that has some developmental historical relevance in the life of literature.

Within each poet's oeuvre we can discern these poems as being aesthetically crucial. For Lomonosov the poem is his greatest literary achievement, almost isolated, but nonetheless early and exemplary. In Wordsworth we find in "Lines" his first great achievement in what Keats (making a sole exception for Wordsworth when he wrote of the "chameleon" poet) called the "egotistical sublime." For his immediate predecessors in English meditative poetry, the tension between the particular and the general had been broken by what might be called mechanical or stereotyped afflatus. Wordsworth, in returning to the humble and ordinary and private for his subject matter, created a new connection with the sublime, conceptually less lofty than in Lomonosov, as well as many other eighteenth-century poets, and therefore more able to remain in tension with the lowly. The mode for *The Prelude* was set. Leopardi's poem is a liberation from the pompous, "aulic," public, or generically solemn and at times sentimental poetry of his early youth and of his immediate predecessors: in language and subject it is an innovation for the poet and for Italian poetry. Yet much is left out of the poem or lies only in the potential danger of upsetting balance or marring subjective experience; his loftier poetry, which would generate stronger human and social tensions, rather than personal and cosmic, came about as a kind of aesthetic synthesis of the early "public" and the newly discovered "personal" modes of expression. All three poems, then, are crucial within the oeuvre of each poet and, we may add, crucial in the history of their native poetic traditions, and somewhat more than merely symptomatic of the development of European poetry during a possibly arbitrary period between 1740 and 1820.

Thorough study of key words in their historical semantic evolution needs to take into account usage in all linguistic contexts and to determine their range of contextual meaning. Certain words have been so studied with great profit (in the manner of A. O. Lovejoy, Leo Spitzer, C. S. Lewis, and Fritz Schalk) to ascertain shades of meaning often obscured for the modern reader by current usage. Such studies are closely related to the more frequent and traditional studies of concepts, often embodied in key words but not limited to them. I have suggested ways, while discussing these three poems, in which the words "mysl'," "thought," and "pensiero" are closely related in their contemporary meaning and how they are related much more closely than now to notions like imagination or creativity or the vaguer notion of feeling. At this point we encounter a temptation to overconceptualize or induce systematic doctrine or rigor where it does not belong. Matters of philosophical or cosmological doctrine, or of theology in a traditional orthodox sense, should be only very delicately touched in reference to the poems. Indeed, the whole point is that these poems are in their several ways paradoctrinal or even predoctrinal. Lomonosov in some way goes beyond Leibnizian or Wolffian deism, not back to Orthodoxy or pre-Rationalism but to a state of renewed wonderment and questioning at "divine majesty" and the "Great Creator" and the mystery of nature's "laws." Wordsworth bypasses traditional Christianity entirely and rests upon an existential faith based on immanent natural mysticism, though hardly pantheistic, which suffices abundantly for him and his sister, and perhaps others. Leopardi rests upon his mind alone and glories as his self-annihilator and self-creator through an overt secular mysticism that is the least systematic or doctrinal of the three kinds of experience.

In the whole process of artistically rendering experience through "thought," we need not abrogate the right, both in aesthetic and in libertarian terms, to employ abstractions for their own poetic purposes whose "resolution" is not to be imposed from any outside ideology or from their biography and later development. It is significant (but how significant remains a question) that the poems are all by quite young men in a more than usually heightened state and at some sort of turning point. Their "ideology" or "doctrine" or "thought content" is provisional and hesitant. At the very least we must recognize the poems as somehow youthful; their authors were not good gray poets in uniform editions.

Biographical, historical, and ideological material, properly used, can provide a kind of screen of protection against capricious or tendentious interpretation. Differences between man's poetic activity and his other ethical and practical activities—to use Crocean terms—must be upheld even in the heat of explanation, classification, and historical placement. We return to the poems themselves and their own connections with the past and with the real world. As optimum readers we must imaginatively submit to *their* terms, and we should as always know enough and learn enough to discern what those terms are.

Bibliographical Notes

My views on all three poets and poems are partly in reaction to the attempt to systematize their often idiosyncratic and casual "philosophy." By narrowing chronological matters and by giving biographical circumstances where necessary, I hope to have made my points without entering into what I consider other debates. Of general books I find most useful A. O. Lovejoy's *The Great Chain of Being* (Cambridge: Harvard University Press, 1936), Joseph Warren Beach's *The Concept of Nature in Nineteenth-Century Poetry* (New York: Macmillan, 1936), and Marjorie Hope Nicholson's *Mountain Gloom and Mountain Glory: The Development of the Mathematics of the Infinite* (Ithaca: Cornell University Press, 1959). The work of Helmut Rehder, *Die Philosophie der unendlichen Landschaft: ein Beitrag zur Geschichte der romantischen Weltanschauung* (Halle: Niemeyer, 1932), while suggestive, is pitched at so high a level of philosophical generality that its usefulness for literary purposes is compromised; the subject it attempts to define remains nonetheless cogent. Karl Kroeber's *The Artifice of Reality* (Madison: University of Wisconsin Press, 1964) undertakes to treat both English and Italian Romantic poets ("Poetic Style in Wordsworth, Foscolo, Keats, and Leopardi" is the subtitle) and makes interesting parallels and generalizations. His reading of "L'Infinito" is somewhat vitiated by misunderstandings of the text: "siepe" he translates as "thicket," "stormire" as "storming," and "la presente [stagione] e viva" as "the living present."

To sort out real and apparent debts and anticipations in the scholarship on Wordsworth would be disproportionate here. For careful and useful commentary I have consulted in particular the edition of the *Lyrical Ballads* by R. L. Brett and A. R. Jones (London: Methuen, 1963) and that by Derek Roper (London: Collins, 1968); I have also collated the poem with the original printing of 1798. Among the numerous critical accounts of "Lines," that of Albert O. Wlecke, *Wordsworth and the Sublime* (Berkeley and Los Angeles: University of California Press, 1973), is one of the best. I have respectfully bypassed accounts of Wordsworth that deal heavily in the sublime, the transcendent, and the unconscious.

For Lomonosov I rely primarily on the complete Academy edition, *Polnoe sobranie sochinenij* (Moscow; gen. ed. S. I. Vavilov), vol. 8 (1959), ed. V. V. Vinogradov, A. I. Andreev, and G. P. Blok, as well as the derivative and reliable *Izbrannie proizvedenija* in the Biblioteka poèta, ed. A. A. Morozov (Moscow, 1965), with an informative introduction. A fairly circumstantial biography in English is B. N. Menshutkin, *Russia's Chemist-Courtier-Physicist-Poet Lomonosov* (Princeton: Princeton University Press, 1952), translated by J. Eyre and E. J. Webster. Dimitri Obolensky's brief comment and "plain prose" translation are to be found in his *Penguin Book of Russian Verse* (Harmondsworth: Penguin, 1962). In a fine essay, "Zu den Quellen von Lomonosovs 'Kosmologischer Lyrik'" (*Zeitschrift für slavische Philologie* 34 [1969], 225–53), Walter Schamschula argues interestingly, sensitively, and convincingly that Lomonosov was much influenced by Barthold Heinrich Brockes (1680–1747), a member of Christian Wolff's circle in Hamburg and author of poems collected as *Irdisches Vergnügen in Gott, bestehend in Physikalisch- und Moralischen Gedichten* (nine volumes published from 1721 to 1748). The parallels in subject matter and verbal expression are impressive. In effect they establish an anterior filiation deriving from Baroque pietism. The essential artistic originality and achievement of Lomonosov remain unshaken, though now set with greater subtlety and precision in their European literary and ideological context.

For critical appraisal of Leopardi one begins with the literary history of Francesco De Sanctis and continues almost ad infinitum. In the *Compendio di storia della letteratura italiana* of Natalino Sapegno, vol. 3 (Florence: La Nuova Italia; rev. ed. 1965), there is a wise and balanced account for which I am grateful. The seven-volume edition of *Tutte le opere* by Francesco Flora (Milan: Mondadori, 1937–49) is standard, though now rivaled by the edition of Walter Binni bearing the same title (Florence: Sansoni, 1969, 2 vols.). A good commented edition of the *Canti* is that of Alberto Frattini (Brescia: La Scuola, 1960; 2d ed., 1964); somewhat more readily available is that edited by Niccolò Gallo and Cesare Gàrboli (Turin: Einaudi, 5th ed. 1972). For a general study in English one may turn to Iris Origo's *Leopardi: A Study in Solitude* (London: Oxford University Press, 1953) and J. H. Whitfield's *Giacomo Leopardi* (Oxford, 1954). Of special interest for Leopardi's literary self-awareness within the tradition, as he conceived it, of Italian poetry is the anthology he compiled after his anthology of prose had had some success. It has been edited by Giuseppe Savoca as Giacomo Leopardi, *Crestomazia italiana: la poesia* (Turin: Einaudi, 1968). A fuller and also somewhat duplicative study is my own "Leopardi's 'L'Infinito'" in *Studi in onore di Natalino Sapegno*, ed. Walter Binni et al. (Rome: Bulzoni, 1974; vol. 4); there in the notes I deal more extensively with Leopardi's use of "pensiero" and "fingersi," as well as with Italian commentary on the poem.

12

LEOPARDI FIRST AND LAST

Since the great efflorescence of Italian literature in the late Middle Ages and the Renaissance, when the incumbency of tradition from classical antiquity and Provensal was established, Italian poets have felt the pressure of the past at increasingly complex levels. Perhaps one of the reasons for the neglect of Dante until the later eighteenth century was that the example of the *Divine Comedy* was too momentous to cope with: a cosmic poem in intricate verse whose language was as much a creation as any of the other aspects of the poem; a poem overwhelmingly exemplary, self-consistent, complex, and complete; a poem intensely personal and idiosyncratic, and yet so public as to be the literate reader's total possession. Even Dante's lyric poetry took on the character of private-public autobiography (the *Canzoniere* as well as *La Vita nuova*) in so systematic a way as almost to exclude imitation or rivalry on its own terms.

Petrarch's poetry is, of course, another matter. In the *Canzoniere*, which we may properly call, with precise Petrarchan casualness, his *Rime sparse*, there is indeed a scheme; but it is quite new in encompassing both randomness and intensity, expressed in a new sort of language, and in creating a new tension between the private and the public. The scheme is variable and capacious, with many spaces for the reader to conjecture in and no grand necessity to march on or to adduce the next piece of evidence to fit into the all-sufficing whole. Moreover, the language, despite the fact that it is somewhat artificial, seems spoken and intimate—occasionally solemn, but meditatively rather than forensically so. And in point of autobiography and the reader's fictive identification, obviously Petrarch's world is more immediately engaging than Dante's in its direct concern with the fluctuant fortunes of earthly love and its familiar sentiment and pathos.

Though inadequate, such terms of comparison between Dante and Petrarch give some basis for explaining the distant, brooding presence of Dante in later Italian poetry and the immediate, intimate, and pervasive influence of Petrarch. Or, to put it better, succeeding Italian poets underwent an *experience* of Dante and an *experience* of Petrarch in ways that were obligatory and complex; yet it was the experience of Petrarch that in Italian poetry (not to mention European) was the more continuous and far-reaching. For centuries it was at the school of Petrarch that the novice Italian poet learned his lessons, and Leopardi was no exception.[1]

Leopardi did not make his public start as an amorous Petrarchan sonneteer, but rather as the author of two patriotic *canzoni* reminiscent, naturally, of Petrarch's "Italia mia," not to mention classical antiquity, Dante, and seventeenth- and eighteenth-century Italian poetry. This is not the place to recapitulate the long history of Italian patriotic poetry that kept the very idea of an integral Italy alive. Yet some account of the place within that tradition of Leopardi's "All'Italia" (with some minor reference to the so-called twin *canzone* "Sopra il monumento di Dante") will serve to characterize that poem of his early youth and thus to provide, perhaps, some useful points of comparison and contrast with Leopardi's last poem, "La Ginestra," which is the major subject of this essay.

It is my purpose here glancingly to evoke the traditions of Italian poetry within which two relatively "public" poems of Leopardi stand and to deal with each poem in some detail. Clearly, I cannot do proper justice to the full complexity of the traditions, in particular to the Italian "pre-Romantic" poetry now so much discussed by scholars; but I wish primarily to do some justice to Leopardi's two poems, first and last, without becoming mired in the humus of antecedents, including Leopardi's own juvenilia, and the vast and disproportionate attention sometimes given the *Zibaldone,* the *Pensieri,* and the second-rate poetry.

Any discussion of the patriotic and hortatory (commonly referred to in

Italian criticism as "paraenetic") elements of Italian poetic tradition must begin with Dante. His most famous and effective apostrophe to Italia occurs in *Purgatory*, canto 6, 76–151, on the occasion of Virgil meeting Sordello; both of them were natives of Mantua and poets in "la lingua nostra," that startling and moving conception of Romania and the whole Latin and Neo-Latin tradition of culture. The very gladness and courtesy of their encounter are the occasion for an ironic and sarcastic diatribe against the warring factions of Italy and the weak Holy Roman emperors (Albert of Hapsburg, in particular), who have not established secular authority able to "accompany" or counterbalance the papacy. For our purposes, what is important is not only the impassioned tone but also the personification of Italia as servile woman, no mistress of provinces but madam of a brothel in which the lust is blood-lust. Yet that personification does not function fully and consistently; rather, it gives way to Rome as "vedova e sola" ("widow and alone") and finally to Florence as a sick woman tossing on a feather bed.

By way of contrast, the personification of Italia in Petrarch's poem is elaborated more fully and consistently.[2] Italia is seen as a wounded body, yet a body that is also the topographical map of Italy, hence an allegorical figure with great latitude between signifier and signified. Indeed, the poet feels free to turn directly to his real audience, the local warring lords who should make peace and unite against the Teutonic invaders in defense of the *patria:* the female figure Italia has easily merged into the more generic patria and at the end, in the envoi, the audience is now the *canzone* itself that is sent off as message and messenger to plead for safe-conduct:

> di' lor: "Chi m'assicura?
> I' vo gridando: Pace, pace, pace."

> (Say to them: "Who will pledge my safety?
> I go crying 'peace, peace, peace.'")

In effect, then, Petrarch has written, in a form most often associated with love-poetry, a circumspect diplomatic *démarche* to the political leaders of an imaginary nation.

Without going into the different political circumstances that conditioned Dante and Petrarch in their apostrophes, and without recapitulating the confused post-Napoleonic and pre-Risorgimental situation of Leopardi in 1818, we can still make certain claims for Leopardi's patriotic poem as a poetic novelty of some success. Motifs that he uses are, of course, to be found in Alfieri and Foscolo, not to mention a whole tribe of minor poets and poetasters. Among the latter is Vincenzo Da Filicaia (1642–1707), whose most lasting fame is the fact that he has a tomb in Santa Croce in Florence.[3] In a truly turgid *canzone*, "All'Italia," and in a set of six sonnets under the same title, Italia is indeed personified. Yet only in the fifth sonnet ("Quando giú dai gran monti bruna bruna / Cade l'ombra") is there a hint of dramatic pathos, as Italia is directly addressed:

> E in così buie tenebre non vedi
> L'alto incendio di guerra, onde tutt'ardi?
> E non credi al tuo mal, se agli occhi credi?
> Ma se tue stragi col soffrir ritardi,
> Soffri, misera, soffri; indi a te chiedi
> Se sia forse vittoria il perder tardi.

> (And in such gloomy darkness do you not see the high conflagration of war from which you are all afire? And do you not believe your ill fortune if you believe your eyes? But if by suffering you delay your slaughters, suffer, poor wretch, suffer; then ask of yourself if losing late may perhaps be victory.)

There is some tepid pathos in this. Though parallels are sometimes drawn to Leopardi's *canzone* from elsewhere in Filicaia's poetry (the poems on the Siege of Vienna and on Sobieski), they seem weak and generic or to have a common source in Homer or Virgil.

More to the point is a poem by the good minor Baroque poet Fulvio Testi (1593–1646) whose epistolary poem "Sopra l'Italia" Leopardi includes in his *Chrestomathy*.[4] It is a meditation on the ruins of Rome (in a lineage familiar from Hildebert of Lavardin to Castiglione to Du Bellay and beyond), which lie amid plowed fields and pastures as witness to the Roman corruption through Eastern luxuries, and as a portent that unless Italia rouses herself she may be invaded and occupied even by Persians and Thracians, traditional enemies more properly of Greece than of Rome. Enough remains, perhaps, of ruined Rome to inspirit the modern, divided Italians if they were at all worthy.

> Ben molt' archi e colonne in più d'un segno
> Serban del valor prisco alta memoria;
> Ma non si vede già, per propria gloria
> Chi d'archi e di colonne ora sia degno.

(A great many arches and columns in more than a trace preserve the exalted memory of ancient valor; but no longer is there to be seen anyone who through his own glory might be worthy of arches and columns.)

Again Italia is personified:

> E non t'avvedi, misera, e non senti
> Che i lauri tuoi degeneraro in mirti?

(But do you not realize, poor wretch, and do you not sense that your laurels have degenerated into myrtles?)

The customary pathos is there, as well as the inevitably appropriate images of arches and columns, of which the iconography in poetry and painting is vast. Testi is also author of a full-blown poetic prosopopeia, "L'Italia," whose pathos is undercut by its practical purpose of exalting the martial valor of the then duke of Savoy.

In regard to patriotic poetry just preceding Leopardi, at least some mention should be made of the ingratiating tergiversator and copious poetaster, Vincenzo Monti, who in 1805 composed a sort of "vision" on the occasion of Napoleon's coronation as king of Italy, "Il Beneficio."[5] In his vision the poet creates a highly sentimental figure of Italia holding on to her ragged dignity and reminding the nations she was once their queen. Her sons, in response to her call for help, turn their swords on each other. Who should appear but Napoleon, like Zeus from Olympus. The rest, with Dante appearing and speaking some of his own lines, is bombasted fustian.

These, then, are some of the texts known to the nineteen-year-old Leopardi. Apart from the generally ennobling example of Dante and Petrarch, and more indirectly in this particular case, of Alfieri and Foscolo, they could afford him small reason for emulation and only weak precedent in the matter of conception. A truly effective combination of consistent and vivid personification, pathos, the Greek as well as the Roman model, and the figure of the poeta-vates is left to Leopardi's "All'Italia," which is inevitably and fruitfully conscious of the tradition that evokes it, and which achieves a precocious and quite successful originality.

In contrast to the companion poem, "Sopra il monumento di Dante," which, in its unrelieved hortatory and grandiloquent posturing, is what one might expect of a gifted adolescent, "All'Italia" creates, by selective detail and precise, dramatically conceived episodes, a nobly modulated evocation of Italia, past, present, and in perspective. After centuries of invasion, occupation, and division into small states, and after the upheavals of Napoleonic imperialism that provoked so many abortive allegiances and cruel proscriptions, Italy in Leopardi's youth seemed set in the divisions imposed and sanctioned by the Treaty of Vienna (1815): in brief, the states of Piedmont, Tuscany, Modena, the Kingdom of the Two Sicilies, the Papal States, and Austrian occupation of northeastern Italy. Not only were Italian patriots conscious of invidious division and weakness (though, of course, "unification" was hardly a universal desire among the enormously diverse regions and the inarticulate masses), but they were also burdened with the recent memory of Italians fighting in foreign wars for an infinity of motives and by simple coercion.

All the more effective, then, the evocation in 1817 of the figure of Simonides, poet-celebrant of the Hellenes, for once all united against a common invading enemy, the Persians. Obviously, it was precisely the illusory hopes aroused by Napoleon's unprecedented state-making and unmaking during the years from 1796 to 1815, and the solemn atmosphere of rhetorical heroicizing, that could sanction and revivify, with an urgent if only imaginative calculus of possibilities, the age-old notion of a unified Italy. In the relative calm of Leopardi's day, a new perspective seems to have been possible: a new modulation of fervor and lament, a new hope derived from the vast historical scope that Leopardi must have learned poetically from Foscolo in the *Sepolcri,* not from the stale laudations or lamentations of the glorious past evoked in pedantic imitation of classical Roman poetry.

Granted, it is difficult to distinguish generically between the earnest, learned allusiveness and the classicizing language of Foscolo on the one hand, and the corresponding mechanical paraenesis of a Da Filicaia or a Monti on the other. Within Leopardi's work that represents a problem too: the distinction between the stiff, conventional elevated style with contorted syntax and archaisms, and the still conventional elevated style whose success may seem to come from nearly the same means. Why not, indeed, say that it is a central problem in the whole history of Italian poetry since Dante? The critic is at some disadvantage here, in that to make his points convincingly he must or should induce in the less experienced reader a numbing knowledge of the traditional, mediocre verse in the elevated line, from out of the echo chamber of *aulicità* or grandiloquence.

To give some example from the early Leopardi, we may cite and inspect the beginning of "Sopra il monumento di Dante":

Perché le nostre genti
pace sotto le bianche ali raccolga,
non fien da' lacci sciolte
dell'antico sopor l'itale menti
s'ai patrii esempi della prisca etade
questa terra fatal non si rivolga.
O Italia, a cor ti stia
far ai passati onor; che d'altrettali
oggi vedove son le tue contrade,
né v'è chi d'onorar ti si convegna.

(While peace may gather our peoples under its white wings, Italic minds will not be loosened from the bonds of ancient somnolence if this fated land does not confront again the patriotic examples of the primeval age. O Italy, may you take it to heart to do honor to [our] forebears; for your regions are now widowed of such as they, nor is there anyone whom it would be fitting for you to honor.)

It is perhaps not so much that contorted syntax and archaisms are present here, but that they abound, clamoring all at once for attention, as the reader performing the text puts each in a provisional niche with an urgent marker. Then he must transpose or somehow translate, and in doing so arrives at a simple sense that almost renders both the poet's and the reader's effort vain: though the Restoration effected in 1815 has brought peace to the Italian people, their minds will not awaken unless they think back on the good old Roman times.

Some of the crabbedness of the verse doubtless derives from a sort of *trobar clus* against the censor, but that is no aesthetic excuse or redeeming poetic value in this case: the closet-patriot is hardly a fit celebrant of soldierly self-sacrifice. This poem shows how hard it was to compose a good and brave poem in an often meretricious genre. Leopardi's other poem, "All'Italia," shows in what ways the difficulty can be met with surprising success, how the burden of the past can be borne with some grace and strength.

It is, then, within the hortatory patriotic tradition, the tradition of *aulicità* and paraenesis, that we are constrained to approach the poem. What we find at the beginning is a rapid panorama of the imposing ruins, not for the purpose of sentimentally evoking past grandeur and making the usual explicit and obvious comparisons to the pusillanimous, inglorious present or merely the solemnly corrosive passage of time, nor for the sake of a genre-scene of flocks amid crumbling ramparts, in the evocative style of Piranesi or Canaletto. Instead, we encounter a fervent speaker who sees at a glance what is there and what is missing. "Erme" in "erme torri degli avi nostri" is, as one of Leopardi's favorite words, a sparing touch of pathos.

> O patria mia, vedo le mura e gli archi
> e le colonne e i simulacri e l'erme
> torri degli avi nostri
> ma la gloria non vedo . . .

(O my fatherland, I see the walls and the arches and the columns and the images and the desolate towers of our forefathers, but glory I do not see . . .)

The objects are seen in a hurried catalogue whose paratactic sweep is all the more impressive if we think that each would serve a conventional poet to pursue forced inspiration through *amplificatio*. And the speaker is there, unaided and *in propria persona*, not one of a crowd of well-meaning mourners. Rather than the usual clutter of symbolic plants and weapons, we encounter the laurel and the iron with which the forehead and the breast of Italia are no longer girded.

> . . . non vedo il lauro e il ferro ond'eran carchi
> i nostri padri antichi. Or fatta inerme,
> nuda la fronte e nudo il petto mostri.

(. . . I do not see the laurel and the iron with which our ancient fathers were laden. Now made defenseless, you show your forehead naked and naked your breast.)

The prosopopeia of Italia that follows is certainly a familiar device, though here it is freshened by an unblenching description of her face abjectly between her knees, and by the consistency of the personification that seems to call out for chivalrous rescue. Fortunately, though, she says nothing in her own voice (far from speaking rancorously like a once-fashionable grande dame, as in Monti's poem), nor does she appear suddenly as a topographical map of Italy in uneasy Neopetrarchan allegory. Instead, the poet becomes aroused to speak as her impassioned advocate and to call on Heaven and earth to answer his anguished question, "chi la ridusse a tale?" ("who brought her to this pass?"); and in effective passion he calls out for arms:

> nessun pugna per te? non ti difende
> nessun de' tuoi? L'armi, qua l'armi: io solo
> combatterò, procomberò sol io.

(No one battles for you? None of your own defends you? Arms, arms here! I alone shall fight, alone shall I fall prostrate for you.)

His blood may become fire in "italici petti"—a conventional phrase, a bit pompous perhaps, but far preferable in its Foscolian sonority to "itale menti," "itali pregi," and "itali ingegni," which clutter the poem on Dante's monument. Why is there no one else to do battle? It is not simply a deplorable decline in martial valor among the moderns (the usual moralizing and tiresome reproach), but the hard, sad fact that Italians are forced to fight for others and against others' enemies. The poet hears and seems to see the somber foreign battles he tersely and impressively describes. Those Italian soldiers cannot say on dying "alma terra natia, / la vita che mi desti ecco ti rendo" ("nourishing native land, the life you gave me I here return"), as could the ancient Hellenes, for once united against the invading barbarian.

With considerable power, the scene is set for a prototype or archetype of the poet-celebrant to appear: not the blind Homer only *foreseen* by Cassandra in Foscolo's *Sepolcri,* but the poet Simonides, contemporaneous singer of the Hellenic wars against the Persians. With bardic solemnity (which owes something to Ossian) Simonides mounts the heights above Thermopylae and, looking out on the sky, the sea, and the land, sings his impassioned tribute to the dead at that forlorn battleground that served to warn the Hellenes and challenged the surge of Xerxes and his army. Not only is the courage of the young band of Greek soldiers stressed but also their grace:

> Parea ch'a danza e non a morte andasse
> ciascun de' vostri, o splendido convito:
> ma v'attendea lo scuro
> Tartaro, e l'onda morta . . .

(It seemed as if each of you were going to a dance or to a
resplendent feast and not to death; but awaiting you was dark
Tartarus and the dead wave)

The tone here is one of hortatory pathos kept in check by understatement
and concrete description that well convey an early Greek in contrast to an
oratorical Roman tone or, in more precise terms, a tone that suggests
Virgilian battle, Foscolian Hellenism, and indeed certain fragments of
Simonides himself.[6]

The range of the poem is expansive both geographically and historically,
and also in the poetic resonances that echo from so bold an entry into the
lists of a long tradition. The scene of battle is evoked and described in the
present tense with considerable force and concision. At the end the Greek
warriors, finally overcome by their wounds, fall one upon the other, and the
poet cheers them with "Oh viva, oh viva" ("Evviva, evviva" in the first
version), which Leopardi defends in a note that claims such colloquial
exclamations were not considered indecorous by the ancients. Such a
poetic self-defense against his potential critics underscores the success
with which he hoped to go, and indeed did go, however cautiously, beyond
the frigid proprieties of his time.

The poem ends in calm reverence for the dead warrior-patriots, as the
poem's Simonides declares their immortal fame and wishes that his own
blood might have soaked the same earth—a conventional sentiment which,
in its direct simplicity, occasions no embarrassment. But since that sacrifice
is not for him, at least the gods may grant that his modest fame will last as
long as theirs.

> Deh foss'io pur con voi qui sotto, e molle
> fosse del sangue mio quest'alma terra.
> Che se il fato è diverso, e non consente
> ch'io per la Grecia i moribondi lumi
> chiuda prostrato in guerra,
> così la vereconda
> fama del vostro vate appo i futuri
> possa, volendo i numi,
> tanto durar quanto la vostra duri.

(Ah would that I too were with you down under here and that this
nourishing earth were soft with my own blood. But if fate is contrary

and grants not that I, struck down in war, close my dying eyes for
Greece, so may the modest fame of your bard among those to
come, the gods willing, last as long as yours may last.)

It is a poet's hope expressed with proper modesty: their fame is clearly
great and he, the poet, has rightly celebrated it. "Quanto la vostra [fama]"
is therefore not a weak reference but one that must again be taken as
understatement, which so often has the force of eloquence in Greek poetry.

Naturally, the author of this poem, "All'Italia," is wholly bound up in the
figure of his own creation, Simonides, just as the fate of Greek patriotism
is, by cultural or learned tradition, bound up with that of the Italians. The
full set of possible parallels is left for the reader's meditation, as the poem,
ending in Simonides' words (indeed, almost half given over to his role),
seems to invite the reader to return to the beginning "O patria mia"; for
ancient Greece is Leopardi's cultural patrimony almost as intensely as Italy
and the whole Latin tradition are his immediate *patria*. Ancient Greece, the
ruins of Rome, the modern pitiable state of Italia, and the paralyzing
dilemma of the patriot with no effective battle to fight for liberty of the
fatherland—all are rendered vividly and as parts of some undetailed
argument or plan of action. The lack of a program and an explicit moral is
part of the honesty of the poem, whose tensions are unresolved and
unresolvable. The distancing through the ancient Greek example, the
alternation of sustained and decorous pathos, vivid though vain action, and
understatement, create not so much a portentous and paraenetic sermon
as a dramatic and noble meditation on the fate of Italy, with no foreclosure
of hope for the future yet with somber uncertainty.

"All'Italia" begins Leopardi's career as a poet but, if we may be allowed
to discount his other patriotic and satirical verse, he therewith paid a kind
of tribute to a national poetic tradition and thereafter went his own
personal, at times almost solipsistic, way as a poet of solitary meditation
and remembrance up to his final poem, "La Ginestra." A brief sketch of that
momentous poetic career between his first and last poems (excluding
juvenilian exercises) can only suggest some reasons why a comparison of
first and last need not be a useless or meretricious telescoping.

Continuing in various versions of the celebratory Greco-Roman style,
Leopardi composed several poems balancing life, accomplishment, fame,
and death (even stoical suicide): "A un vincitore nel pallone" (1821), "Bruto
Minore" (1821), and "Ultimo canto di Saffo" (1822). Their varying tones of
evanescent triumph, clear-sighted regret, and nobility in contemplation of

death, are rendered in terms of calm, circumstantial pathos, far from the youthful, committed fervor of "All'Italia."

More important artistically are the so-called first idylls: the unexampled little poem of secular ecstasy, "L'Infinito" (1819), and the more elaborated genre scenes of tender hope and melancholy, "La sera del dì di festa," "Alla luna," "Il sogno," and "La vita solitaria" (1820–21). Later gusts of poetic inspiration in the 1820s created such masterpieces of remembrance and regret as "A Silvia" (1828) and "Le ricordanze" (1829), as well as other genre pieces, "Il sabato del villaggio" and "La quiete dopo la tempesta" (both 1829), in which tenderness skirts the edge of sentimentality and the universal moral that death cures all cares threatens, however understated, to become too insistent and repetitive.

It was in the mid-1820s, mostly in 1824, that Leopardi composed his best essays and dialogues, which he called *Operette morali*. At times they are tinged with Lucianic satire and diatribe, but most often—as in "Federico Ruysch e le sue mummie," "Storia del genere umano," and "Torquato Tasso e il suo genio familiare"—they are poised between disillusionment and ingenuous hope—or better, a kind of hoping for hope that is quintessentially Leopardian. The poem that best reflects that poise is "Canto notturno di un pastore errante dell'Asia," which shares with many of the *Operette morali* in dialogue form, an artistically salutary distancing and a making-strange in the Russian sense of *ostranenïe*.

A lonely, wandering shepherd in the limitless wilderness of nature asks of the distant but seemingly companionable moon all the simple questions about the purpose of life. We are *toto caelo* removed from conventional apostrophes to the moon's beauty and evocations of pleasurable moods in gardens or quiet towns, not to mention allusions to classical moon myths—all of which Leopardi had shown he could manage well, and even brilliantly. With a sort of ingenuous generosity, the shepherd answers for the silent moon:

> Ma tu per certo,
> giovinetta immortal, conosci il tutto.

(But you, immortal girl, surely know all.)

As for himself, he knows and senses that all the eternal movements of the universe may bring contentment to someone else, but to him life is suffering:

Questo io conosco e sento,
che degli eterni giri,
che dell'esser mio frale,
qualche bene o contento
avrà fors'altri; a me la vita è male.

He turns to his flock and artlessly asks how their rest can be restorative
and tranquil while he, if he lies down, is tormented by tedium and vexation:

perché giacendo
a bell'agio, ozioso,
s'appaga ogni animale;
me, s'io giaccio in riposo, il tedio assale?

At the end he imagines that if he had wings he might be happy in that
freedom of flight; but then, perhaps all creatures of whatsoever kind, are
born to misfortune: "forse . . . è funesto a chi nasce il dì natale." Again,
the danger of a flatly pessimistic moral is barely averted by the ingenuous
tone successfully sustained throughout and by that finally hesitant and
moving *forse*.

In this regard, and in contrast to the "Canto notturno," it is relevant to
mention two late poems in which the interrogative mode is superseded
rather harshly by direct and crushing answers. "A se stesso" (1833) is a
brief, bleak call for death and a declaration of nature's ugly malevolence and
"l'infinita vanità del tutto." In "Il tramonto della luna" (1836) even the
nocturnal light of the moon fades; though day comes again, lost youth can
have no further dawn and age has only the tomb. With such despondency
Leopardi might well have ended his actual wracked life and his poetic career
with the word *sepoltura*.

Leaving aside much paraenetic, occasional, argumentative, and satirical
verse that has been, along with his best works, so much and too often
undiscriminatingly discussed, and simply on the basis of those works
mentioned so far and briefly characterized and evaluated, let us turn to
Leopardi's last major poem, "La Ginestra," in order to put it in the
perspective of his earlier literary achievement and to judge it on its literary
merits.[7]

In my discussion I have been sparing in citation of the literary and
ideological traditions that were inherent and incumbent in Leopardi's time:
the Enlightenment and its aftermath, from Voltaire and the *philosophes* to

Rousseau and beyond. By intention I have avoided what I consider a misleading and confusionary temptation to posit a system of thought on Leopardi's part and to make selective and supposedly conclusive references to the farrago of the enormous and intriguing notebook he compiled between 1817 and 1829 (with a few last entries up to 1832). Leopardi was not a systematic thinker, though his occasional reflections and jottings are sometimes striking. His notebook, the *Zibaldone,* serves best as a quarry for his intellectual biography, his critical views, and his taste, and now and then as a clue to his method of composition; yet surely it cannot substitute for what is or is not in the poems themselves. To the fact that he read and speculated widely over a period of twelve years or so we have testimony in the *Zibaldone.* But that his poetic utterance is somehow controlled or determined by his notebook or that he stuck to certain positions sketched at various times therein, without regard to the fluctuations of memory and poetic imagination, is a notion that cannot be plausibly sustained. We run the risk, in submitting our judgment to whatever jotting may seem related in those 4,500 manuscript pages, of misreading or overreading the individual poems. A philosophical system cannot be summed up in a lyric. Indeed, the danger is that in lyric form an explicit worldview may lose conceptual and necessarily discursive nuance and end up as a banality of commonplaces.

For a sympathetic reading and evaluation of "La Ginestra" it would seem proper to lay stress not on the philosophical or ideological propositions (which are, in summary, hardly original or intellectually compelling) but rather on the poetic texture and structure, the diction and sound, the varying syntax and tone, the role of the reader in response to his fictive role as it is written in the poem itself. On the other hand, it is, of course, entirely legitimate to note parallels and antecedents in Leopardi's own previous poetry, and even to posit some scheme of smooth development or "inevitable" unity after the fact (the fact of the poet's death and thus the completion of his work, which then we may view as a whole).

But there are excesses and disadvantages and distortions to be incurred along that line as well. I take only a partial risk by stressing first and last—mostly the differences which seem illuminating—and by lightly referring to the "great" and the "first" idylls. It does not serve my purpose, if it is legitimate, to deal here with the poems I leave out, for example, "Palinodia," "Il pensiero dominante," "Aspasia," the two sepulchral poems, and the "Paralipomeni della Batracomiomachia." By leaving them out, I stress that the two poems I deal with most fully can stand usefully as independent and as contrasting with each other—all by way of illuminating

Leopardi the major poet (both *major* poet and major *poet*). What I earnestly wish to avoid are false claims, misplaced erudition, and the veiled apology for supposed failure that Leopardi himself so scornfully disdained.

Seven strophes, seven movements of mood, constitute the poem and interplay in ways that would take inordinately long to explicate in this context; thus a simpler, linear account would seem preferable here, an account that tries to discuss the poem as performed, or more punctiliously as performance, after the fact of first reading. For convenience, the movements or strophes are: one (lines 1–51); two (lines 52–86); three (lines 87–157); four (lines 158–201); five (lines 202–36); six (lines 237–96); seven (lines 297–317). All are clearly indicated by pauses in the text and by individual inner consistency. Throughout the poem is the speaking voice of the poet, generally alone in a point of vantage, meditating, as in the "idylls," and on occasion hortatory, in distant echo of "All'Italia," but then also peremptory and derisive in a new and disconcerting tone for Leopardi's major poetry. Always we are "here" with the poet:

> Qui su l'arida schiena
> del formidabil monte
> sterminator Vesevo . . .

(Here on the parched back of the fearful, destroying mountain Vesuvius . . .)

Present danger, the mindless cruelty of Natura,[8] the indifference of age-old existence, past eruptions attested by the petrified lava—all seem somehow balanced by the humble endurance, the selfless beauty, and the unaccountably generous scent of the ginestra that alone grows in this hostile place, as it does in the countryside around decayed Rome. Once here were pleasant farms and grainfields, but now only the ginestra, "contenta dei deserti," as we are told at the beginning, seems to live through it all, as if out of compassion for all-encompassing ruin.

> Or tutto intorno
> una ruina involve,
> dove tu siedi, o fior gentile, e quasi
> i danni altrui commiserando, al cielo
> di dolcissimo odor mandi un profumo,
> che il deserto consola

(Now one ruin encompasses all about, where you reside, O gentle flower, and as if pitying the harms of others, you send to heaven a scent of sweetest smell that consoles the wilderness)

The casual wanderer may soberly take note.

But then, suddenly, comes a burst of scorn for those who exalt man's estate in the bosom of "loving" Natura, calling on them to come and see what a slight or slightly stronger movement can senselessly do to destroy. Here Leopardi addresses not the vulgarized Leibnizians (as did Voltaire in *Candide ou l'Optimisme*), but rather the neoteric Rousseauvians and the armchair primitivists who, as Lois Whitney has shown,[9] could also entertain, without a sense of contradiction, aspirations to infinite human progress—in the banal and modish phrase taken from his cousin Terenzio Mamiani and mockingly quoted here: "le magnifiche sorti e progressive" (in effect, "the ever-grander fortunes of mankind"). The moral is drawn abruptly, didactically, scornfully; and to read the poem we must put up with the sudden vehemence.

Indeed, the poem itself becomes something like a lava flow and inundates the next two sections, issuing from an eruption comparable to Dante's famous sudden and lengthy invective, already cited, against "serva Italia" (*Purgatory,* canto 6,76ff.). Our expectations for the *canzone* form and for Leopardi's previous use of it hardly prepare us for this torrent. Only in the high-mindedly dramatic "All'Italia" is there anything like it in Leopardi; it is the tradition of *saeva indignatio* from Persius and Juvenal to Swift and Voltaire that gives it some literary sanction. Yet Leopardi's naked scorn and mockery in *canzone* form may still seem new, upsetting, perhaps excessive, and artistically even an embarrassment.

Be that as it may, for a time we shall follow the crushing flow. Again, it is *this* place (*qui*), but here the present age must see itself mirrored, the age that falsely turns away from the rational thought and civility achieved by the Renaissance to again enslave free thought in brutish illusions. Addressing the present age, the poet says, in paraphrase: the bright wits whom ill-luck made you their father, fawn on your childish antics, though at times they vapidly mock you. But the poet Leopardi will not die without openly declaring his contempt even if he risks oblivion as a mocker of his own time.

The watchword of the modish is *libertà,* yet they wish thought (*pensiero,* which often in Leopardi means "imagination") to be their slave. In other words, liberty has become a cant-word (attrition partly of the Napoleonic illusions and disillusions); it has become a slogan that hides the truth of our existence in dogmas of infinite social progress and happiness (all based on an erroneous belief in the benignity of human nature and Natura); whereas true liberty and freedom of thought must acknowledge that man is puny and Natura indifferent or cruel. Man is really nothing in the vastness of the cosmos, and can find wisdom only by recognizing his littleness. It is only civility, or civilization (*civiltà*), that can guide the people's destinies (*i pubblici fati*) toward something better.

Civiltà takes on great richness, especially when one realizes that the poem acknowledges no real father (as in *patria*) or real mother (as in sentimental, "romantic" nature). What remains is a kind of civil brotherhood and the honest, hard truth of man's real fate to endure in decency till death. But the age does not accept such a view, caught as it is between "soft" primitivism and prideful progress.

> Cosí ti spiacque il vero
> dell'aspra sorte e del depresso loco
> che natura ci dié . . .

(Thus you disliked the truth about harsh fortune and the depressed place that Natura gave us)

Again the cowardly age has turned its back on the light that reveals the harsh truth:

> Per questo il tergo
> vigliaccamente rivolgesti al lume
> che il fe' palese . . .

Here we hark back to the epigraph at the beginning of the poem, which is quoted in Greek from John 3:19: "But men preferred darkness to light." The verse continues, "because their deeds were evil." At all events, the scriptural phrase is ironically made to refer to the light of eighteenth-century rationalism and stoicism, not to that of supernatural revelation or the comfort of an afterlife. (Of his great contemporaries, Leopardi often seems most in tune with the later Byron.) The age reserves the epithet *magnanimous* only for those knaves and fools who exalt the human condition up beyond the stars:

> magnanimo colui
> che se schernendo o gli altri, astuto o folle,
> fin sopra gli astri il mortal grado estolle.

Throughout this movement, then, the crabbedness and sputtering scorn, in their apparently confused vehemence, would seem to stem from the vastly confused variety of optimistic views held at the time in horrendous colloidal suspension—later to be precipitated out in the meliorists, religious revivalists, progressivists, utopians, social prophets, positivists, and so on indefinitely.

After this invective, this scattering of scorn and vituperation, comes the third movement with its still impassioned but more reasoned account of human failings and pretensions. While the truly high and noble spirit acknowledges his human limitations, those who are falsely high-minded scribble absurd claims and promises that natural disasters habitually obliterate. Nature in a humanly noble sense, and in reference to humble, harmless things, stands in utter contrast to Natura, the inhuman cosmos that cruelly and indifferently prevails around us.

> Nobil natura è quella
> che a sollevar s'ardisce
> gli occhi mortali incontra
> al comun fato, e che con franca lingua,
> nulla al ver detraendo,
> confessa il mal che ci fu dato in sorte,
> e il basso stato e frale . . .

(Noble nature is that which dares to raise its mortal eyes up to meet the common fate, and which with honest tongue, subtracting nothing from the truth, professes the evil that was given as our lot and the low and frail condition . . .)

The other "nature," which I distinguish as Natura, is the true guilty party:

> che de' mortali
> madre è di parto e di voler matrigna.

(who is mother of mortals by parturition and stepmother by desire.)

It is she who is the real enemy of mankind (*l'umana compagnia*), who must band together in fraternal love, giving aid in the common war (*guerra comune*) we are forced to wage against our "natural" enemy, stepmother Natura. But then, men carry battle to their own camp, forgetful of the true enemy, and fight rabidly among themselves. There is yet some hope, however, that once again the truth will be understood by the common folk (*il volgo*), after the vaunted delusions of omnipotent human progress and the notion of gentle, nursing nature are dispelled; people will then be able to return to the root of the matter through wisdom (*verace sapere*), frank and upright relationships ("l'onesto e il retto / conversar cittadino"), justness (*giustizia*), and pious concern (*pietade* in the Roman sense).

All these words have their richness in a simple morality derived from no religion, no higher calling, no categorical imperative, but rather from lowly prudence (*probità*) purged of prideful illusions (*superbe fole*). At first men were drawn together in *social catena* by horror at impious Natura; now rational, humble truth has been revealed (though pretentiously rejected by mongers of progress and optimism), and men may again turn away from their folly and return to making the best of things as they really are. Against the frenzy of foolish progress, meaningless wars for false causes, religious and patriotic delusions, the poet sets a gentler, humbler, though still somber hope. Invective against the vainglorious age subsides gradually into a meager but reasonable vision of simple people living in decency and prudent concord: a great comedown from grandiose pretensions; poetically, an extremely difficult and perhaps unsuccessful modulation from high and violent indignation to a sort of Horatian or Wordsworthian *mediocritas*.

After these two violent and argumentative movements, barely controlled or contained, we return to the place where the speaker views outward nature in its calm nocturnal beauty. The cosmic meditation and anguish are not stilled by the scene: what gradually happens through the rest of the poem is that the fullness of nature-Natura's indifferent beauty and terror, and the inexorable fate of man, whatever his momentary feelings and thoughts, are brought into some equilibrium based on acknowledgment and clear-sighted acceptance, movingly symbolized in the ginestra.

But first the poet searches the night sky and the vast view of the bay of Naples from his point of vantage, for some measure of infinity. It is night and he is sitting in a somber landscape of solidified lava. The stars flaming in the sky and reflected in the sea seem to be the world, the universe (*il mondo*). They are mere points to the eye, yet they are immense, as we know from *il vero* or the rational science of truth; just as to the stars the earth and sky are only a point in their midst, and just as man is nothing on this earthly globe. Then there are the nebulae, those stellar mists to which our stars, our "universe," are nothing. For the early Leopardi of "L'Infinito" such reflections might lead to a "sweet foundering" in the sea of his own imagination. But that ecstatic possibility is long since past. He is now facing the consequences of the infinitesimal, the infinite in reverse, of man and his world: at best a "point of nebulous light." The whole passage is eloquent and intricate, deriving its power from a nearly overwhelming concatenation of comparisons. All man's fables of his own identity and importance, the myths of divine epiphanies and interventions on earth, the new myths of "progress," are vanity of vanities. Indeed, the new notions are superstition like the old. Overpowered, we are caught between derision and pity:

> qual moto allora,
> mortal prole infelice, o qual pensiero
> verso te finalmente il cor m'assale?
> Non so se il riso o la pietà prevale.

(What emotion then, unhappy mortal race, or what thought toward you at last assails my heart? I know not whether laughter or pity prevails.)

So the poem fluctuates, almost unbearably, almost inartistically, between the two emotions: cosmic pessimism and unavailing compassion. Mockery or satire, urbanely modulated, might have been a poetic strategy, as with Persius or Swift; but Leopardi had tried that mode in 1835, in his "Palinodia al marchese Gino Capponi," and had verbosely and awkwardly failed.

Thus, Leopardi rejects the vastness of new Romantic myth in the grand manner of Foscolo, not to mention Hölderlin and Keats, who of course based themselves on ancient literary tradition; or the manner of Goethe and Shelley, not to mention Blake, who created a modern cosmic mythology with man still at the center. All that range of myth and assumption Leopardi rejected, doubtless in part because it was beyond him, but also, and most important, because for him it was hopelessly vain. There are no gods, they do not visit earth, the whole imaginable pantheon is a figment of man on this tiny earth, this little grain of sand ("questo oscuro / granel di sabbia"). Nor is the grand egocentricity of Rousseau or the "egotistical sublime" of Wordsworth, whose own minds seemed to them so momentous in the universe, for him. No, Leopardi, from his fearful cosmic vision of nullity and vanity, can only turn to see disaster in indifferent flux; it matters little whether among the nebulae, among the gods, or in an anthill.

In the fifth movement Leopardi makes the obvious comparison between a colony of ants crushed by a little apple that drops out of mere inevitable ripeness, and the tremendous explosion of a volcano that just as indifferently, but to our senses "infinitely" more momentously, snuffs out human life. In neither case is the disaster ennobling or remediable. But the comparison is made in grand Homeric fashion, conjoining small to great, for a torrential length of twenty-eight lines. It is partly the Homeric precedent and partly the previous tenor of the poem that should help dispose us to accept the seeming incongruity. After the terrible, destroying flood of lava seems to inundate the slender lines of the *canzone,* we confront head-on the hard moral that Natura has no special preference for men over ants, but that man lies somewhat less in the way of destruction only because his lineage is less fecund and widespread. The eruption is described in all its violence, but it is not particularized in this movement as the most famous and destructive eruption of A.D. 79 that buried Pompeii and the surrounding countryside. Yet the suddenness and violence of the description give it a poetically convincing air that it would not have had if it were simply another set-piece, like Voltaire's or Varano's poems on the Lisbon earthquake of 1756. After the shock of that description, the poet can then return to the fully particularized setting on the side of the ominous volcano and, in simple, homely terms, evoke the contemporary scene of the ruined countryside, the humble peasants who struggle to live there, and again the grand panorama of land and sea—all under the unpredictable menace of destruction.

In this sixth strophe the scale is reduced: the menace now is not so much another general explosion as the imminent possibility of a local burst of lava that could at any time destroy a little family and all its possessions. After nearly eighteen hundred years, the *villanello,* or humble peasant tending his vines, still raises his fearful gaze to the death-dealing peak:

> ancor leva lo sguardo
> sospettoso alla vetta
> fatal . . .

And at night he may lie awake, jumping up now and then to keep a fearful eye on the course of lava that may boil up from the unexhausted womb and suddenly light up the vast region from Capri to the port of Naples and

Mergellina. If he should hear it approaching, signaled by the seething of the water in his well, he will waken his children and wife and flee, perhaps to look back and see all that he owns covered by the burning flow.

These humble folk are more pathetic than the rich palaces of Pompeii now being excavated, like buried skeletons, for greed or historical "piety." The wandering tourist may see the broken colonnades and the still-smoking double peak and so contemplate the ruins of empire. The ruined scene may, in fact, still be lit up by the lava.

> E nell'orror della secreta notte
> per li vacui teatri,
> per li templi deformi e per le rotte
> case, ove i parti il pipistrello asconde,
> come sinistra face
> che per vòti palagi atra s'aggiri,
> corre il baglior della funerea lava,
> che di lontan per l'ombre
> rosseggia e i lochi intorno intorno tinge.

(And in the horror of the secret night, by the deserted theaters, by the disfigured temples and by the broken houses where the bat hides its young, like a sinister torch that gloomily might stray through empty palaces, runs the glow of the funereal lava, which at a distance reddens through the shadows and stains the places round about.)

Rather than sudden terror, this is a scene of continuing sinister presence, superficially reminiscent of the graveyard and the *upupa* of Foscolo, not to mention other lurid descriptions in so-called pre-Romantic poetry. But one must allow that Vesuvius, with its numerous eruptions of greater and lesser intensity, its continual menace, and the then newly exposed ruins of Pompeii, Stabia, and Herculaneum, is something historically and actually more concrete and impressive than a merely imaginatively conjured scene of bubbling lava and deserted ruins with an ornamental bat.

In other words, the closeness of the mimesis of reality, the historical actuality, and the descriptive force, all confer on the passage something beyond conventional "gothic" or "pre-Romantic" sensationalism. Once again we are not permitted to miss the lesson, but it comes in muted form:

our idea of antiquity is nothing in the eternal process of nature, and nature there, ironically, is always green:

> sta natura ognor verde, anzi procede
> per sí lungo cammino
> che sembra star.

(Nature stays at all times green, rather she proceeds by so long a road she seems to stay still.)

Leopardi takes his casual word *sta* and then elaborates that nature "stays" or "stands" but only seems to stand because in truth she proceeds by an unimaginably long road: empires fall, cultures disappear, and she sees nothing to hold her interest. Yet man arrogates to himself the boast of eternity:

> ella nol vede:
> e l'uom d'eternità s'arroga il vanto.

So in this, the sixth movement, we have returned to the pathos of the humble human (as in some of the "idylls") and of the unprotected innocent. There is no grand lament for past glories and magnificence, no vaunting of the *patria* as heir to antiquity, no salvation through national political means of governance, state, or martial heroism. Humility and endurance are the prime virtues, and there is no sanction from myth or religion or other vanities and illusions. The poem has, in its widely modulating moods, made all that scorchingly and glaringly clear. The paraenetic rhetoric of impassioned declamation in some of Leopardi's earliest poems, the fervor and despair of some of the middle poems, the gentle pathos here and there, are somehow brought together under the aegis of a sovereign pessimism, meaning expectation of the irremediable worst. There can be no appeal to a sentient, omniscient, purposive power because there is none. Ultimately, despite appearances, nature and Natura are one.

In the face of the unappealable and inconsolable, the true measure and example cannot be religion, the political state, the ancients, the self-perpetuating poetic-patriotic-religious tradition. Only the ginestra, the true and only nature we humanly perceive as opposed to cruel, cosmic Natura, can be a true measure and example in its humble endurance free from cowardice or frenzied pride, stronger and wiser for that than man. Here,

Leopardi shows himself to be a "hard" primitivist and anti-progressivist, a true pessimist (as Schopenhauer was later to testify) who can only mingle scorn with pity and who knows there is no appeal.

At the end of this poem, then, the poet addresses the humble plant tenderly:

> E tu, lenta ginestra
> che di selve odorate
> queste campagne dispogliate adorni,
> anche tu presto alla crudel possanza
> soccomberai del sotterraneo foco
> che ritornando al loco
> già noto, stenderà l'avaro lembo
> su tue molli foreste.

(And you, slow ginestra, who adorn with your fragrant woods these despoiled fields, you too will soon succumb to the cruel sway of the subterranean fire which, returning to the already familiar place, will spread its greedy edge over your pliant forests.)

Selve and *foreste* may seem out of proportion to a small yellow-flowering shrub, yet the poem has had much to say about proportions. When the lava comes once again, the ginestra will bend its head before the overwhelmingly deadly mass, but not in cowardly and useless supplication. It will, by its very gentleness, avoid the extremes of being madly erect or utterly supine before its future oppressor. It is wiser and less infirm than man in not thinking its frail stems immortal either by decree of some fate or by its own deluded belief:

> ma più saggia, ma tanto
> meno inferma dell'uom, quanto le frali
> tue stirpi non credesti
> o dal fato o da te fatte immortali.

So the poem ends in humble, hopeless finality but with a lowly dignity—or rather wisdom. The plant is the paragon of wisdom; it *is* wisdom. We are not invited to return to our egos (as often occurs in Romantic poets who use flowers or the landscape as ego-projections); if anything, we should leave them and ask for nothing, no satisfaction, no comfort, but simply endure like the flower of the wilderness, the "fiore del deserto" of the title. It is not its prosopopeia but the ginestra itself that is in focus at the end.

This disturbing poem is unbalanced between its extremes of harsh rhetoric and the tender quasi-personified plant, between the addresses to self-deluded man in his pride and to the lowly plant that asks nothing. Yet the alternatives Leopardi might have taken are safer and tamer. It could have been a somber, stoical meditation, a final affirmation of specifically religious consolation for man's hard fate, a simple moral exhortation to be somehow like a plant, or a scornful, mocking satire against mankind or deified Natura. That it is not quite any of these may well give us a sense of unease. The poet, however, chooses to advocate no consolation; he chooses instead to advocate the cold light of reason and the minimal virtue of endurance amid unremitting and mindless disaster—cold comfort indeed. Because reasonable arguments go unheeded in this age, he must utterly expose human vanity and pride. In doing so he imitates, in effect, the molten force of the all-consuming lava and the rough, barren, craggy aspect of its petrified waves and ridges, now grown cold but still witness to the prospect of further burning disaster. The contradiction between malevolent Natura and the gentle creatures of nature remains unresolved: there is no pretense at resolving it. Exegetes who for sentimental or rationalistic motives wish to do the resolving for Leopardi expose themselves to his scorn and mockery from beyond the grave. The second part of Goethe's *Faust* and Hugo's *La Légende des siècles* would surely have appalled him, though one can imagine him being in sympathy with *In Memoriam* and a good deal of twentieth-century poetry.

"La Ginestra" is a solemn poem that exceeds the bounds of the traditional *canzone,* even in the paraenetic mode we have earlier sketched, from Petrarch to "All'Italia." Its lesson is hard and shorn of habitual hopes and illusions. Its respites are piercingly poignant. All in all, a terrible, terrifying vision. Probably the poem is a grand failure. We, as readers, also fail in often not reading it whole, in often not wanting to read it whole. But there it is, with its crabbed scorn, its mocking anger, its gentle despair, and its hard, unphilosophically stoic beauty. We turn elsewhere in Leopardi (to "All'Italia" and the "idylls") and to Foscolo's *Sepolcri,* as well as to Petrarch, the presiding *numen* of language, in order to know what Leopardi here forthrightly and almost pitilessly rejects and denies to both himself and us. Would that it were otherwise, we may think. But it is not. There it is.

Notes

1. I use the word *experience* instead of the usual *influence* with its hydraulic or astral overtones, because a poet has an idiosyncratic, active, and selective experience of reading another poet. It is implausible, even subliminally, to think of poets as passive receptacles.

2. Poem no. 128 in *Le rime*, ed. Ferdinando Neri, in the Riccardo Ricciardi series: Francesco Petrarca, *Rime, trionfi, e poesie latine* (Milan, 1951), 183–88.

3. The texts cited from Da Filicaia and Testi are in Carlo Calcaterra, *I lirici del seicento e dell'Arcadia* (Milan: Rizzoli, 1936).

4. *Crestomazia italiana poetica* (Milan: Stella, 1828). See my Bibliographical Notes for reference to Savoca's edition.

5. For the text, see Vincenzo Monti, *Tragedie, poemetti, liriche*, ed. Gino Francesco Gobbi (Milan: Hoepli, 1927), 458–70.

6. See the two fragments translated by Leopardi in 1823–24 from, as he seems to have known, Simonides of Amorgos—not, apparently, Simonides of Ceos. They are included in the *Canti*, ed. Niccolò Gallo and Cesare Gàrboli, 5th. ed. (Turin: Einaudi, 1972), 311–18. Generically about the inevitable passage of time, neither of them is appropriate or useful in regard to "All'Italia." The real Simonides of Ceos is the one whose martial fragments Leopardi has in mind.

7. *Ginestra* is a plant woodier than heather or furze, called in English "broom" (hence the small article of domestic utility). For obvious reasons, I prefer to use the word *ginestra* even in an English context when referring to the plant outside the poem's title. On similar problems of translation, see Mario Praz's fine essay "Nomi di fiori," in *Machiavelli in Inghilterra ed altri saggi*, 2d ed. (Rome: Tumminelli, 1943), 329–44.

8. Leopardi's use of the word *natura* may cause confusion. Mainly it has four senses: nature as all of existence; human nature; nature as benign flora and fauna, at times including man; and Natura as a malevolent or indifferent presiding deity or cosmic force. Only the last two senses directly concern us here. The benign sense, I translate as "nature"; the malign sense I capitalize and leave latinate as "Natura." In a strange way the two can even blend.

9. See Lois Whitney, *Primitivism and the Idea of Progress* (Baltimore: The Johns Hopkins University Press, 1934), passim.

Bibliographical Notes

The most convenient, complete, and up-to-date edition of Giacomo Leopardi is still *Tutte le opere*, edited by Walter Binni with the collaboration of Enrico Ghidetti, in two volumes (Florence: Sansoni, 1969). There the reader will find all the texts responsibly presented with a long introduction, a bibliography, and thorough analytic indexes. Still very useful are the editions of Francesco Flora (Milan: Mondadori, 1937–49) and the truly critical one (in the textual sense) of the poems and the *Operette morali* by Francesco Moroncini (Bologna, 1927–29). Mario Fubini's old, commented edition of the *Canti* (Turin: UTET, 1930) is still useful. Currently, the most convenient and informative commented edition of the *Canti* is that of Niccolò Gallo and Cesare Gàrboli in the Nuova Universale Einaudi series (Turin, 1972): the notes and apparatus are reliable and informative; only the occasional critical comments may seem flimsy or overblown.

Fortunately there exists a good account of Leopardi's critical fortune so far as the *Canti* are concerned: Alberto Frattini, *Critica e fortuna dei "Canti" di G. Leopardi* (Brescia: La Scuola Editrice, 1957; rev. ed., 1964). To the same author we owe the best brief general introduction readily available in Italian: *Giacomo Leopardi* (Rocca San Casciano: Cappelli, 1969). Also useful is Emilio Bigi's historical and bibliographical survey of criticism in *I classici italiani nella storia della critica,* ed. Walter Binni (Florence: La Nuova Italia, 1967), 2:353–407. An excellent sketch of Leopardi's whole career is to be found in Natalino Sapegno's *Compendio di storia della letteratura italiana* (Florence: La Nuova Italia, 1947; rev. 1965), 3:202–56. Also informative are his *Dispense, Storia della poesia di Leopardi* (Facoltà di Lettere, Università degli Studi di Roma, academic year 1953–54), in two volumes, mainly for Leopardi's early intellectual and poetic development.

Francesco De Sanctis's great *Storia della letteratura italiana* (1870–71; ed. Benedetto Croce [Bari: Laterza, 1912, and often reissued]) does not reach so far as Leopardi; but he left essays and the major portion of a book on Leopardi, which are both impassioned and quite sound (in *Opere complete,* gen. ed. Carlo Muscetta, vol. 3, ed. Walter Binni [Bari: Laterza, 1953]). De Sanctis's love for the early patriotic poems of Leopardi stems from the high patriotic fervor of his own time (the Neapolitan ferment from about 1830 to 1848 and beyond); he is an excellent critic of the "idylls" but he never came to terms with "La Ginestra." Not many others have. Certainly not Croce, whose whole theory of *poesia* would predispose him against the "didactic" and paraenetic in much of Leopardi's poetry: see the characteristic short essays on Leopardi in *Poesia e non poesia* (Bari: Laterza, 1922) and in *Poesia antica e moderna: interpretazioni* (Bari: Laterza, 1940). Later Italian critics have often been stung or embarrassed by Croce's occasionally derogatory remarks. They could, if they would, take comfort from his odd praise of the poet Vigny, who too often seems didactic, without verve, and a bit dowdy now.

In the welter of books and articles on Leopardi recently published, one notes the insistent claims, *pace* Croce, for Leopardi's greatness not only as poet but as linguist, existentialist, and philosopher—or at least *philosophe.* Such claims often seem lacking both in critical preciseness and proper international perspective. The studies in which they are set forth may simply be exercises within the assumed parameters of Italian academic expectations and performance: a phenomenon familiar in most countries as part of a general inflation and overproduction of critical, academic discourse.

Also, one notes a growing, perhaps overgrowing, interest in eighteenth-century intellectual and literary "background," in pre-Romanticism, however that may be defined. It is certainly a great gain that scholars like Mario Fubini and Franco Venturi have explored and expounded so well the intense and interesting activity of eighteenth-century ideologues and *littérateurs,* establishing the high level of native culture and seeing it in its proper international perspective. Recently, however, there has been a tendency to claim too much originality for the Italian settecento. As far as Leopardi is concerned, the first hefty volume of the *acta* of the Centro Nazionale di Studi Leopardiani (Florence: Olschki, 1964) contains some good essays but a great deal of unproportioned ballast.

A sometimes good, sometimes merely hortatory critic whose great claims for Leopardi have aroused emulation is Walter Binni, whose fine edition has been mentioned and whose *La nuova poetica leopardiana* (Florence: Sansoni, 1971, a new and enlarged edition of a work first issued in 1947) is quite important but disappointing in its imprecise formulation and its idiom of Italian academic jargon, which defies brief exemplification. At least Binni devotes a whole chapter to "La Ginestra" and is thus one of the few critics to confront the poem extensively; the results are rather fuzzy, however. As for "background" in poetry of the eighteenth century, the best thing of all is the volume, edited by Bruno Meier, with a fine, long introduction by Mario Fubini, in the Riccardo Ricciardi series: *Lirici del settecento* (Milan, 1959). Fubini's bibliographic note, with its strictures on Binni's "isms," is also a valuable contribution to that volume. A good specialized study on Italian eighteenth- and nineteenth-century taste, which takes proper account of Leopardi in the last section, is Renzo Negri, *Gusto e poesia delle rovine in Italia fra il sette e l'ottocento* (Milan: Ceschina, 1965), a commendably well-informed and generally well-written book on the subject in its full European context.

As for volcanoes, and Vesuvius in particular, perhaps the best reference as a start is the article in the *Enciclopedia italiana*. For other indications, see the excellent essay by G. M. Matthews, "A Volcano's Voice in Shelley," *ELH* 24 (1957), 191–228. Also the Leopardian volcanologist should look up the numerous references to current earthquakes and eruptions in Italy to be found in *Antologia* (1821–33), the great magazine which surely was a source of multifarious information for many men of letters, including Leopardi, to whom later scholars attribute an often unrealistic degree of "firsthand" erudition. In point of both ruins and volcanoes, not to mention the Lisbon earthquake, it would seem disproportionate to attempt a particular array of "sources" for Leopardi beyond the common literary and historical tradition and the undeniable assumption that Leopardi read Voltaire, Bettinelli, and Baretti (all with well-known texts on Lisbon), Rousseau and Ossian, Foscolo, and whomever else a well-read genius would plausibly have read and known.

For his reading, one must of course refer to the *Zibaldone* for the years he kept it and also to the two chrestomathies of verse and prose that he compiled and published. See the *Crestomazia italiana: la poesia* (Turin: Einaudi, 1968), well edited by Giuseppe Savoca. Finally, perhaps the best long account of Leopardi's intellectual setting is *L'Ideologia letteraria di Giacomo Leopardi* (Naples: Liguori, 1968) by the distinguished and wide-ranging scholar Salvatore Battaglia.

In English, J. H. Whitfield's *Giacomo Leopardi* (Oxford, 1954) is informative. The best general introduction to his life in any language is *Leopardi: A Study in Solitude* (London, rev. ed. 1953) by the admirable Marchesa Iris Origo. Interesting confrontations are to be found in Karl Kroeber's *The Artifice of Reality: Poetic Style in Wordsworth, Foscolo, Keats, and Leopardi* (Madison: University of Wisconsin Press, 1964). *A Leopardi Reader,* edited by Ottavio M. Casale (Urbana: University of Illinois Press, 1981), is a deftly conscientious selection and guide for the Anglophone.

Citation could go on indefinitely as the critical corpus is vast and always growing. If in my essay I do not engage other critics of these poems in some sort of fraternal dialogue, it is because I must honestly conclude that there are few real debts I owe.

13

BAUDELAIRE AND VIRGIL

A Reading of "Le Cygne"

Baudelaire's evocation of an episode from the *Aeneid* in his poem "Le Cygne" is an excellent example of what we may call with special emphasis *literary* allusion. It is quite common in literature for one work to allude to another. An obvious case is direct translation or paraphrase. Byron in *Don Juan*, for example, felicitously renders the beginning of *Purgatory*, canto 8, and a fragment of Sappho for the purpose of enhancing his own description of the twilight hour.[1] But the allusion is limited. Nothing in Byron's context allows the reference to Dante's *Purgatory* to echo and expand. And he simply incorporates Sappho's fragment whole. A more complex sort of literary allusion occurs when the whole range of association in the work or passage cited is relevant to its new context. The modern master of such allusion is T. S. Eliot. To choose a familiar instance, at the beginning of the second part of *The Waste Land* the rich neurotic lady in her heavily luxurious surroundings is described in terms borrowed from Shakespeare and Milton. As usual with Eliot, the allusions work ironically and sardonically to contrast, in this instance, the empty present of the lady with the heroic past of Cleopatra and the idyllic past of a paradise since lost.

Still more complex is Baudelaire's allusion in "Le Cygne," where he not only borrows words and phrases from the *Aeneid*, but incorporates all the resonance of the episode to which he alludes into his own poem. The episode is Aeneas's encounter with Andromache and Helenus.[2]

Books 2 and 3 of the *Aeneid* constitute a flashback; Aeneas is bidden by Dido to recount the fall of Troy, his escape, and his wanderings. Throughout his account, and indeed throughout the *Aeneid*, the reader is never allowed to forget that Aeneas is in the process of fulfilling his fate. It is his high destiny, set by Fate and Jupiter, to found the race that, long after his death, will build a city to last eternally. In comparison with Aeneas and his supremely fateful enterprise, all those he encounters on his journey—Dido, Polydorus, Andromache, Helenus, and all the dead in Avernus—seem pathetic and unfulfilled, abandoned and cut off. Aeneas is beset by toil and suffering; he is kept long years from reaching his fated goal: "tantae molis erat Romanam condere gentem." Yet he is engaged in the business of living importantly, working out the significant essence that will finally be realized at his death.

Virgil's lower world contains, fixed for eternity, those who have already realized their essence. His scheme embraces, according to later commentators, nine circles or categories of the dead (Dante's clear point of departure)—among them the souls of the untimely dead ("quos dulcis vitae exsortis et ab ubere raptos / abstulit atra dies et funere mersit acerbo," 6, 428–29), the suicides, the lovers ("quos durus amor crudeli tabe peredit," 6, 442), the warriors, the tortured inhabitants of Tartarus, and the blessed inhabitants of Elysium. Even the last are described with a kind of pathos (Aeneas speaks of his father's "tristis imago," 6, 695); for they are no longer in a state of becoming, but have reached the end where nothing further can add to their essence. Except for those who will be granted purgation and forgetfulness and be reborn, they have perforce taken up their stance to all eternity, exiled from the process of life.

Even more pathetic are the living whose lives are over and who can only live them out in repetition or stasis. This is the condition of Andromache and Helenus in book 3, lines 294–505. After the heroic grandeur and important suffering of the Trojan War, life for most of those who were unlucky enough to survive it meant exile, humiliation, and emptiness. When Andromache's husband, Hector, was killed by Achilles and when Troy was finally taken, she, now a slave, fell to the lot of Pyrrhus (Neoptolemus), the son of Achilles. Pyrrhus begot children on her and then gave her over to Helenus, a son of Priam and now a slave himself, when he conceived a passion for Hermione, daughter of Helen and Menelaus and bride of Orestes. In his familiar role as avenger, Orestes overtook Pyrrhus and slew him. For some reason or other, part of Pyrrhus's inheritance went to Helenus—a remote land on the coast of Epirus which he named Chaonia after a man from Troy.

Aeneas, in his wanderings, hears the "incredible" news that Helenus rules over "Greek cities." Inflamed by a strange longing to see the hero and to know his adventures, Aeneas heads for Epirus. There, in a grove outside the city, by the waters of a mock Simoïs ("falsi Simoëntis ad undam"), he encounters the tearful Andromache invoking and placating the shade of Hector at the empty tomb she has constructed ("Hectoreum ad tumulum, viridi quem caespite inanem . . ."). She faints at the sight of him. When she recovers, she asks, in effect, whether he is a phantom and, if he is, where then is Hector. In her living death, the distinction is not really important; she had consummated her essence in the great life she had with Hector in Troy; her life now is stasis, meaningful only in communion with the past and with the dead. She goes on to recount her sad life since the Trojan War, in much the same way the souls in the lower world describe the point of their lives. But then she breaks off, as there is really nothing more to tell, and asks about Aeneas's fate and the fate of his son Ascanius, of the same age as her dead child Astyanax. Helenus approaches and, after greetings, leads Aeneas to his city, a little replica of Troy ("parvam Troiam"). Such is the place he has built in the remote land of Epirus. It is "simulata," made to look like the great Troy, with its own river Xanthus, a pathetic dry creek:

> procedo et parvam Troiam simulataque magnis
> Pergama et arentem Xanthi cognomine rivum
> agnosco . . .

Here, in relative splendor, Aeneas is entertained for an indefinitely long time ("iamque dies alterque dies processit"), till the winds of fate begin again to swell his sails. He then approaches Helenus, who has fame as a seer, and asks his advice on his future course:

> quae prima pericula vito?
> quidve sequens tantos possim superare labores?

Helenus tells him that his suffering and wandering are not ended, but that in time he will reach the Lavinian shores and will find the place where Rome will be founded: "is locus urbis erit, requies ea certa laborum." There is something ironic and peculiarly Virgilian about "that certain rest from travail." After all, Rome will not be founded for generations; the whole enterprise will not be completed in Aeneas's lifetime; besides, we know, having read the poem, that he will encounter war and all manner of dangers when he lands. That emphatic *requies* means, more than anything, a significant death; it certainly does not mean suburban ease. Virgilian melancholy or gentle despair also encompasses Aeneas, for he too is an exile. Helenus's prophecy now becomes more circumstantial: Aeneas must avoid Scylla and Charybdis; he must appease Juno; he must consult the Sibyl at Cumae and descend into Avernus. Then, at Aeneas's departure, the already accomplished fate of Andromache and Helenus is given its last and strongest stress.

Following the ancient custom, Helenus presents Aeneas and his band with gifts. Andromache, not to be outdone, brings precious garments of her own making as a gift for Ascanius. She says to him:

> accipe et haec, manuum tibi quae monimenta mearum
> sint, puer, et longum Andromachae testentur amorem,
> coniugis Hectoreae.

They are *monimenta,* formal memorials, a pathetic means of associating herself with a high destiny as yet unfulfilled. In the formality of her presentation she names herself and adds, in apposition, "coniugis Hectoreae," for it was in that role (curiously stressed by the adjectival form of Hector's name) that she achieved all that was important to her earthly essence. The final touch is her pathetic likening of Ascanius to her own dead son:

> cape dona extrema tuorum,
> o mihi sola mei super Astyanactis imago.
> sic oculos, sic ille manus, sic ora ferebat;
> et nunc aequali tecum pubesceret aevo.

In her sadly desperate imagination Ascanius has served, along with the false Simoïs, the dry Xanthus, and the little Troy, as a temporary means of restoring the old days. Her cult of the past is, as it were, an instinctive recognition that she is now among the living dead.

All the more ironic and pathetic, then, is Aeneas's valediction:

> vivite felices, quibus est fortuna peracta
> iam sua: nos alia ex aliis in fata vocamur.
> vobis parta quies.

On one level the "vivite felices" is merely a conventional formula like "good-bye." But surely the words are charged with compassionate irony: for Andromache and Helenus, living is over and done with and their chance of happiness and fulfillment is long since past. Indeed, Aeneas goes on to console them gently. Their fortune, for better or worse, has already run its course ("peracta"). While Aeneas and his followers are called upon to meet the vicissitudes of continuing destiny, they now have achieved rest:

> vobis parta quies: nullum maris aequor arandum,
> arva neque Ausoniae semper cedentia retro
> quaerenda.

They have their "effigiem Xanthi Troiamque" made by their own labor under, Aeneas hopes, better auspices than the old Troy and less in the way of the Greeks. Aeneas then promises that, when he reaches the Tiber (emphatically repeated as a river parallel to the others named), he will join the two regions, Italy and Epirus, as they have a common origin and a common lot. But the joining will be in the mind and spirit:

> si quando Thybrim vicinaque Thybridis arva
> intraro gentique meae data moenia cernam,
> cognatas urbes olim populosque propinquos,
> Epiro Hesperiam (quibus idem Dardanus auctor
> atque idem casus), unam faciemus utramque
> Troiam animis: maneat nostros ea cura nepotes.

By now the cities have multiplied: the original Troy, now razed, the "little Troy" of Helenus and Andromache, the future Troy that will be Rome, and a Troy of the mind. That is some consolation for the past and some hope for the future. But it is a future beyond the participation and control of Andromache and Helenus. Even Aeneas, who significantly changes to the first-person plural ("faciemus"), will not live to see it. There is a suggestion here of almost infinite alienation; the sack of Troy and the exile of the surviving Trojans is very much like the expulsion from a paradise that then continues to haunt men like an irrecoverable dream.

Such a reading of the passage is, I think, implied by Baudelaire's evocation of it in "Le Cygne."[3] His major theme in the poem is exile, to be taken in the widest range of meanings: isolation, deprivation, abandonment, exclusion, inadequacy, and more. His main audience and prime symbol is Andromache:

> Andromaque, je pense à vous!

And he is thinking of her just as Virgil describes her:

> Ce petit fleuve,
> Pauvre et triste miroir où jadis resplendit
> L'immense majesté de vos douleurs de veuve,
> Ce Simoïs menteur qui par vos pleurs grandit,
>
> A fécondé soudain ma mémoire fertile,
> Comme je traversais le nouveau Carrousel.

Already certain identifications are made. The "falsus Simoïs" has suffered a further remove—it is now also the Seine. Paris has become another, even less real, "parva Troia." The poet imagines this storied river as having long ago reflected like a mirror the sorrows of widowed Andromache. The pathos is enhanced by the contrast between the river, "pauvre et triste," and the "immense majesté" of Andromache; but then, with fitting irony, her tears are the source whereby the poor sad river grows to its present deceptive size, now doubly "menteur." Again ironically, her salt tears have had the power suddenly to "fecundate" his already all-too-fertile memory. Here the metaphor of springs and streams as sources of poetic inspiration is revitalized by the concrete implication of the river bringing water to irrigate the land and cause it to bloom. On one metaphorical level what blooms from the brackish water are sadly nostalgic memories. Still, the scene here is urban and in the poem cities represent change and evanescence:

> Le vieux Paris n'est plus (la forme d'une ville
> Change plus vite, hélas! que le cœur d'un mortel).

An archetypal memory is about to be invoked, a memory associated with the old Paris and set with precision in the old Place du Carrousel, which in the old days had been a jumble of ancient buildings between the Louvre and the Tuileries.

Je ne vois qu'en esprit tout ce camp de baraques,
Ces tas de chapiteaux ébauchés et de fûts,
Les herbes, les gros blocs verdis par l'eau des flaques,

Et brillant aux carreaux, le bric-à-brac confus.

The old Paris is now only a city of the mind; and the part of it evoked here was a kind of city within a city. Not only that, it was a mock city. The poet sets it only in his mind's eye: it was a campground of hovels and booths (as in a market or a fair), transient and half-dismantled. There were heaps of roughly hewn or vaguely painted capitals and shafts, perhaps, by implication, on a flat surface like stage scenery. They were not even whole columns, but only the separate pieces. Weeds had grown up and large rough blocks of building material had become moss-covered lying in puddles; even in the past the scene was largely of random and discarded objects, though gleaming ironically on the windowpanes.

In this, the most concretely topographical of his poems, Baudelaire alludes in general to the "urban renewal" under Napoleon III and in particular to the demolition of buildings that before 1852 had stood between the Louvre and the Tuileries. In his *Nouveau dictionnaire historique de Paris*,[4] Gustave Pessard quotes without giving the source an illuminating description of the old quarter:

> Vers cette époque, la *place du Carrousel*, très mal éclairée par quelques rares lanternes à l'huile et formant un dédale inextricable de petites rues était un véritable coupe-gorge quand arrivait la nuit, de sorte que c'est à peine si les passants osaient s'y hasarder seuls à cause des sinistres habitués des bouges environnants. Le jour, les baraques de brocanteurs, de bouquinistes, de marchands d'oiseaux installés contre des palissades en bois avaient envahi les moindres espaces laissés vides, l'herbe poussait entre le pavés disjoints et pour compléter le déplorable état de cette place, un large égout nauséabond s'engouffrait au pied des palissades vermoulues placées de tous côtés.

Another witness is Balzac's description in *La Cousine Bette* of Mme. Marneffe's residence on the rue du Doyenné. Indeed, from guide books and other sources it is possible to gather much testimony to the squalor and antiquity of the district.[5]

It would be just such a place (dear, of course, to Baudelaire's heart) where amid the hovels and the sordid booths of shady merchants, a traveling menagerie might camp.

> Là s'étalait jadis une ménagerie,
> Là je vis, un matin, à l'heure où sous les cieux
> Froids et clairs le Travail s'éveille, où la voirie
> Pousse un sombre ouragan dans l'air silencieux,
>
> Un cygne . . .

It is early morning, cold and clear, the time when the squalor of the place would be most harshly visible. The workers, or better, the "work force" awaken and set about, in abstract depersonalized form, doing their anonymous tasks; they too are alien to other people's rubbish and litter. "Le Travail" represents both the laborers and, by its very abstraction, the whole concept or condition of inescapable daily work. Already the street cleaners have begun to raise an unnatural and therefore exotic and foreign "hurricane" of dust and debris, now "sombre" in the daylight. Their splashing of water and raising of dust is as unnatural in the environment as a typhoon. In this harsh setting the swan appears, having gained its ironic freedom:

> Là je vis . . .
>
> Un cygne qui s'était évadé de sa cage,
> Et, de ses pieds palmés frottant le pavé sec,
> Sur le sol raboteux traînait son blanc plumage.
> Près d'un ruisseau sans eau la bête ouvrant le bec
>
> Baignait nerveusement ses ailes dans la poudre,
> Et disait, le cœur plein de son beau lac natal:
> "Eau, quand donc pleuvras-tu? quand tonneras-tu, foudre?"
> Je vois ce malheureux, mythe étrange et fatal,
>
> Vers le ciel quelquefois, comme l'homme d'Ovide,
> Vers le ciel ironique et cruellement bleu,
> Sur son cou convulsif tendant sa tête avide,
> Comme s'il adressait des reproches à Dieu!

The "fecundating" memory of Andromache has brought to the poet's mind the image of the swan, for their plights are parallel in many ways.

Both are ironically free: Andromache is no longer in bondage, the swan is no longer confined in its cage. But what use is freedom? Andromache has constructed with Helenus a little Troy that serves as a cage to imprison her in the past. The swan has escaped, not to its "beau lac natal," but to new confinement in a hostile environment: a harsh dry street, rough ground, a waterless stream. Ironically, it attempts to bathe its white wings in the dust. The "sombre ouragan" was a parody of nature. Now the swan, "mythe étrange et fatal," is imagined as invoking the natural, the fecundating processes of nature—rain, or even merely the presage of thunder. It is still a further irony that, just as Andromache's simulated Troy could not bring back the past, so the rain the swan invokes could not restore it to its natural element. She is exiled in her city in Epirus, and the swan is exiled in the city of Paris. For both the fair weather is ironic. Andromache's days are in a sense serene, for she has achieved rest; as Aeneas says to her and Helenus, "vobis parta quies." For the swan the sky, "ironique et cruellement bleu," is a source of despair for the possibility of alleviation. Its longing head is stretched upward by its convulsive neck like the version of newly created man in Ovid; but the literary allusion is again ironic.

At the beginning of the *Metamorphoses* Ovid, in his generally optimistic celebration of the natural world and its continual processes, asserts that some god ("quisquis fuit ille deorum") gave man an upright countenance and bade him turn his eyes skyward:

> Pronaque cum spectent animalia cetera terram,
> [deus] os homini sublime dedit caelumque videre
> iussit et erectos ad sidera tollere vultus.
>
> (1, 84–86)

In several ways the allusion is ironic. The swan is a swan; by an effort of its supple neck it can turn its head upward to the sky; but no help, no communion, no relief seems to come from there. Much more, then, according to the Ovidian text, should a man be able to express his nobility and importance by gazing skyward in the expectation of help or recognition. But still the sky remains ironically and cruelly blue. Indeed, the swan, quite unlike Ovid's man, seems even to be casting reproaches at God. In such a way the swan can become a symbol of man's condition without the poet having to resort to a moral too obviously drawn as in "L'Albatros" ("Le Poëte est semblable au prince des nuées"). Even Ovid himself is drawn into the context, as he of all men is the archetype of the exiled poet.[6] By indirection we are reminded also that the whole poem is, like others in the "Tableaux parisiens," dedicated to Victor Hugo, now exiled under the dictatorship of Napoleon III, the "renewer" of the old Paris. It may seem, however, that Baudelaire is personifying too directly and too circumstantially in his image of the swan. After all, swans do not talk. Besides, Baudelaire does not elsewhere personify animals nearly so intensely; he certainly does not have them speak. But the way is prepared by the parallel with Andromache and even by the human suggestion in the technical term "pieds palmés." Most important, swans do traditionally sing at the approach of death and poetically they are presented as "talking" in extremis. The citation of Ovid's man cannot but carry the relevant aura of metamorphosis. The swan is, in fact, a neo-Ovidian "mythe étrange et fatal."

Through Andromache's memory of old Troy and the swan's memory of its "beau lac natal" comes the transition to the second part of the poem. Here, in a kind of desperate and pathetic catalogue, the poet directs our attention not to complex actions and detailed "tableaux," but rather to figures caught for the rest of their lives in repetitive and futile situations. Their stance has been fixed in actuality and in memory by irrevocable and irremediable circumstance. The city, or cities, may change. And change is at least something. But memory preserves and resists; it carries the burden of the unconsolable past over into the alien present.

> Paris change! mais rien dans ma mélancolie
> N'a bougé! palais neufs, échafaudages, blocs,
> Vieux faubourgs, tout pour moi devient allégorie,
> Et mes chers souvenirs sont plus lourds que des rocs.

Even the old faubourgs partake of the changing new and become part of an allegory—they represent unsubstantially something other than themselves. The irony basically derives from the assertion that the poet's sardonically "dear" memories are weightier than rocks or than the buildings, whether they be under construction or newly built or even old. The changing city, and not the mind, represents, ironically, the transience and irrevocability of life.

The reader emerges into a vivid present tense and into a precise location: "Aussi devant ce Louvre une image m'opprime." The effect of "ce" is presumably to concretize, even though there is only one Louvre. In the light of the previous stanza, the effect of the verb "opprime" (eventually from "ob" and "premere") is also to concretize; its meaning is not merely "oppresses," in the usual French and English sense, but primarily "presses down" or "weighs upon." The "image" is precisely that of the swan elaborated in the first part of the poem. Here is a sort of memory within memory; the poem recalls its earlier self.

> Je pense à mon grand cygne, avec ses gestes fous,
> Comme les exilés, ridicule et sublime,
> Et rongé d'un désir sans trêve! . . .

The figure of the swan has now become one of the several archetypes to be evoked as in a ceremonial roll call. They are all archetypes of the exiled or alienated, so out of harmony with their surroundings (people, places, even the "sol raboteux") that they are "ridicules" and yet so nobly or tenaciously assertive of their essence that they are, in the several senses of the word (including the Ovidian), "sublimes." The same sort of internal reference recurs when the poet evokes again, in summary fashion, the image of Andromache:

> et puis [je pense] à vous,

> Andromaque, des bras d'un grand époux tombée,
> Vil bétail, sous la main du superbe Pyrrhus,
> Auprès d'un tombeau vide en extase courbée;
> Veuve d'Hector, hélas! et femme d'Hélénus!

Here is her life *in parvo*, presented now with telescoped brevity; she is "tombée" directly beside the "tombeau." She has fallen from the arms of her great husband (one recalls their memorable embrace in the parting scene in the *Iliad*) and has come, like a lowly chattel, even "cattle," under the sway of the proud Pyrrhus. There is almost a further corroboration of her likeness to the swan; she, a human being (which implies a certain dignity, an "os sublime"), has become, by harsh metamorphosis, a "vil bétail." She has had to exchange the encompassing and plural arms for submission to the threatening and singular hand. Though now she is finally free from servitude to Pyrrhus, she is still seen, in this final archetypal image we have of her, as *bent* over the empty tomb of Hector; for she is still in bondage which no "freedom" can annul. The word "extase" derives richness from its Greek origin. Though fixed for life in a kind of stasis, she finds, in mourning for Hector, some ironic movement and transcendence of time into the timeless. But, in reality, the timeless is simply the irrecoverable past; her "ecstasy" is far from the ecstasy of carefree bliss. We are brought back to the "real" present of the poem by the now-weighty line:

Veuve d'Hector, hélas! et femme d'Hélénus!

At this point, by multiple evocation of memory, the great archetypes of Andromache and the swan have been elaborated and fixed in their stance. The circle, wide by implication, can now expand by example.

One does not need to know that Jeanne Duval is "la négresse" of the next stanza. Yet perhaps the implication for those who know something of Baudelaire's biography enhances the concreteness we found in the precise references to places in Paris. The vivid contrast between the exile and the environment is still strongly drawn, however, without that knowledge.

> Je pense à la négresse, amaigrie et phtisique,
> Piétinant dans la boue, et cherchant, l'œil hagard,
> Les cocotiers absents de la superbe Afrique
> Derrière la muraille immense du brouillard.

In a northern city she is clearly out of place—"exiled" from Africa and "exiled" in the city for being a "négresse." With awkward animal gestures like the swan, she tramples in the city mud, seeking through the city fog, with her wild eyes, the coconut trees of Africa. The incongruity is heightened by the contrast between the mud of the city and the desirable, exotic coconut trees of proud (that is, noble and unbowed) Africa. Moreover, the pathos of her futile search is expressed in the taut phrase "Les cocotiers absents"; she is seeking things that by definition are absent. Vainly, she is seeking them behind an immense wall of fog. The city walls are confining enough, but they are at least real and obviously ineluctable; the wall of fog is insubstantial and therefore ironically enticing. Yet the wall of fog is, in the emphasis of the passage, the more cruel and pervasive; because it deceptively seems eventually penetrable, it is even more of a wall than real walls. In ironic contrast to Andromache, "la négresse," instead of constructing walls or building a sort of African oasis in the midst of the city, is trying to free herself from the cage of walls and the circumambient wall of fog. But neither is physically in bondage nor yet spiritually free.

These are not rare instances of "exile." There are many in the human condition. In the last two stanzas of the poem the poet generalizes them into category after category, finally stressing the endlessness of the list in the final phrase: "[je pense] à bien d'autres encor!" He thinks

> A quiconque a perdu ce qui ne se retrouve
> Jamais, jamais! à ceux qui s'abreuvent de pleurs

Et tettent la Douleur comme une bonne louve!
Aux maigres orphelins séchant comme des fleurs!

The category of those who have lost the irrecoverable is the largest of all—it
includes all the others in the poem, more particularly those who ironically
"quench" their thirst on their own salt tears and suckle Sorrow as if it were a
kindly wolf. The ironies are many. One is suggested in the relation between
man and nature. Sorrow reduces one to a kind of animal state as implied
perhaps by the word "s'abreuvent" and of course by the "bonne *louve.*" Then,
too, there is an ironic reference in the image of the suckling wolf, the
counterpart of the wolf that suckled Romulus and Remus. In the old legend
Remus is slain for jumping over the little walls of Romulus's little Rome.[7] But
of course that Rome had a future. It would become the new Troy *rediviva,*
more glorious than the old; it would become the archetype of cities. But in the
poem we know what cities have been since the prime archetype, Troy, was
sacked and since that "paradise" was lost. So the "bonne louve" brought forth
more sorrow than joy; in the perspective of latter days the wolf can serve as
a complex ironic symbol. The implied image of Romulus and Remus, orphans
exposed, suggests also those orphans who have not even a "bonne louve."
They are "exiles" in life, forever deprived of their natural element (their "beau
lac natal" or their "superbe Afrique"); inevitably, then, they wither, pathetically, like flowers (again, an ironic image of nature) and, by implication, like
flowers cut from their parental roots.
    Still further categories are enumerated in the final stanza.

Ainsi dans la forêt où mon esprit s'exile
Un vieux Souvenir sonne à plein souffle du cor!
Je pense aux matelots oubliés dans une île,
Aux captifs, aux vaincus! . . . à bien d'autres encor!

The culminating "ainsi" refers not merely to the previous stanza but to the
poem as a whole; this is a summary or even a didactic statement, stressing
the universality of these archetypal exiles. The mind of the poet, who has
so emphatically placed his point of observation in the city, can "exile itself"
in a mental forest—exile in the city and, within the city, exile in a forest of
the mind. An old memory resounds like a full-breathed hunting horn,
nostalgic and searching, haunting and hunting. It is *the* memory the poem
is about, the whole complex of memories which by association, as the poem
shows, elaborate themselves one by one and coalesce as a single chain and

a single capitalized "Souvenir." The poem, then, is in some way circular.
Andromache has led to the swan and to the "négresse" and to all the other
kinds of exile. Each memory evokes the others; they are all, in fact, *the*
memory.

What Baudelaire has accomplished is a survey of human sorrow and
alienation throughout history. The plight of all those with sensibility is
universal. Part of that universality derives from the complex multiplication
of cities. Taking his point of departure from Virgil's already rich example, he
carries it even further, perhaps consciously influenced by the medieval
partiality to Troy and the widespread harking back to a Trojan founder. It
may echo in the reader's mind that Ronsard in his *Franciade* had
resurrected Astyanax under the name of Francion and made him the
refounder of Troy whose task was to "bastir les grans murs de Paris." In
Virgil there is the original Troy, the little Troy of Andromache and Helenus,
the future Troy of Rome, and the Troy of the mind. In Baudelaire the
contemporary Paris that he evokes becomes a little Troy too; but in the
past there had been a slightly more nearly original Troy in "le vieux Paris,"
which contained a kind of mock city within it, the "camp de baraques." Most
important is the Troy of the mind, the never-never city that haunts the
memory and that represents a kind of unsuccessful exile from the present,
either into the paradisiacal past or into the impossible future. Memory, then,
is both liberation from the present and at the same time, ironically, bondage to
the past—just as the country of the mind is escape from the city of the mind,
and also a kind of mirage which imprisons the mind in illusion. The human
condition is one of inescapable exile. A sensitive spirit can never be "dans le
vrai." One of the great ironies of the poem is that people can be exiles, as the
poet is (he perhaps most pitiable of all), in their own native place. It is not so
much an urban alienation from nature as it is the self-reflexive curse of
mankind. Nature, even a mental landscape, is not a refuge or native
element—nor is history, in the sense of return to a golden age.

"Le Cygne" is a remarkable fusing of literary allusion and originality.
Baudelaire borrows directly from Virgil, yet in borrowing he implies his own
interpretation of the text (the correct one, I think) by his very elaboration of
it. He not only achieves a marvelous fusion of incident and theme and a deep
general sympathy with a congenial poetic sensibility in the remote past, but
also in his language manages to find the discreet and delicately adjusted
medium for that fusion. Suffice it to mention again the rich Latinisms "superbe"
and "sublime." Perhaps it is not too much to suggest also that Baudelaire's
characteristic use of vague and capacious adjectives like "grand," "triste,"

"beau," and "immense" is a reflection of Latin style. These words seem to have "empty spaces in them, in which, when the right word comes near them, they can suddenly generate a new and often unexpected meaning."[8] Certainly, they allow the particular to expand resonantly into the general; they act as a means of mediation between the two and so reflect one of the main thematic urges of the poem. Perhaps that is its main success; starting from the particulars of a classical allusion and the consequence of "urban renewal" in the Paris of Napoleon III, the poem succeeds through its own concrete reference in elaborating a vision of "l'humaine condition."

Notes

1. Canto 3, stanzas 107 and 108.

2. Baudelaire's "source" is emphatically not Racine's *Andromaque*. A number of commentators (for example, Albert Feuillerat, "L'Architecture des *Fleurs du Mal*," *Yale Romanic Studies* 18 [1941], 84–85) err in carrying over their memory of Racine. Though Racine in his prefaces to *Andromaque* avows a single source (with the exception of a mere touch from Euripides) in the third *Aeneid*, we should note that he deals with Andromache while she is still the slave of Pyrrhus (Helenus does not appear in the tragedy), that he takes the liberty of setting the action in Epirus, and that he permits Astyanax to survive the sack of Troy. There are of course general resemblances between Virgil's and Racine's Andromache; still, in Baudelaire, only Virgil can be discerned. I should mention that Baudelaire set as an epigraph to the first publication of his poem a phrase from the Andromache episode in Virgil: "falsi Simoentis ad undam."

3. I cite the text in Baudelaire's *Oeuvres complètes*, 2 vols., ed. Claude Pichois (Paris: Gallimard, 1975), vol. 1, 85–87 (notes, 1003–9). The text was originally published in the 22 January 1860 issue of *La Causerie*. The commentaries and notes in J.-D. Hubert's *L'Esthétique des* "Fleurs du Mal" (Geneva, 1953) and in *Les Fleurs du Mal*, ed. Jacques Crépet and Georges Blin (Paris, 1942), are in different ways helpful. Robert-Benoit Chérix, in his *Essai d'une critique intégrale: Commentaire des "Fleurs du Mal"* (Geneva, 1949), is not particularly illuminating. Much could be made of the school exercise in Latin verse (1837) which its editor has entitled "L'exile" (Charles Baudelaire, *Vers latins*, ed. Jules Mouquet, 2d ed. [Paris: Mercure de France, 1933, 57–61], also in *Oeuvres Complètes*, ed. Pichois, vol. 1, 228–31). It concerns an exile from the Terror who is expelled across the Rhine as "non Gallus," only to return at night. The final lines are suggestive of later Baudelairean alienation:

> "Parva sed ingentis restant solatia casus,
> Quod circum patriam vecti notumque per amnem,
> Obscurosque procul colles dilectaque patrum
> Ejecti castella vident, auraque fruuntur
> Quae forsan patriis flores libavit in hortis."

I should mention also that certain phrases in "Le Cygne" are to be found elsewhere in the *Fleurs du Mal*: in "La Chevelure," "L'Irréparable," "Moesta et errabunda," "À une passante," and "Le Voyage" (sec. 2).

4. Gustave Pessard, *Nouveau Dictionnaire historique de Paris* (Paris: Eugène Rey, 1904), 261.

5. Compare, for instance, the maps and descriptions in two issues of *Galignani's New Paris Guide*: that of 1848 (155) and that of 1854 (170). See also David H. Pinkney, *Napoleon III and the Rebuilding of Paris* (Princeton: Princeton University Press, 1958), especially plates 12, 13, 14.

6. As witness this stanza from "Horreur sympathique":

> "—Insatiablement avide
> De l'obscur et de l'incertain,
> Je ne geindrai pas comme Ovide
> Chassé du paradis latin."

7. One might note that Romulus and Remus, born of a violated vestal virgin, Rhea Silvia, who named Mars as her ravisher, were set adrift in a basket on the swollen Tiber which then receded, leaving them on dry land. See Livy I, iv. For the two versions of Remus's death, see Livy I, vii.

8. W. F. Jackson Knight, *Roman Vergil* (London: Faber, 1944), 192.

Bibliographical Notes

Since this essay was first published in 1961 nothing has appeared that would challenge its discoveries or conclusions. There are some still who assume that somehow Andromache has to do with Racine or who are quite unaware of the existence before Napoleon III of the Vieux Carrousel.

In his edition of *Les Fleurs du mal* in the Classiques Garnier series (Paris, 1961), which came to my attention after my essay was submitted, Antoine Adam mentions in general terms the episode from the *Aeneid*, refers to the former aspect of the place du Carrousel without giving the full circumstances of its transformation, and notes that Jacques Crépet identified the proper reference in Ovid (citing its evocation in *Fusées*). More recent notes to the poem such as those in Marcel A. Ruff's l'Intégrale edition of the *Oeuvres complètes* (Paris, 1968) follow suit. The irrelevance of Racine's *Andromaque* and some awareness of the matter of "urban renewal" seem now accepted in a general way. With the exception of an article by Victor Brombert (which speaks of my dealing with "échos virgiliens," for which I claim of course much more than "echoes": "'Le Cygne' de Baudelaire: Douleur, Souvenir, Travail," *Etudes baudelairiennes* 3 [1973], 254–61), I have not encountered extensive treatment of the poem in the vast array of publication on Baudelaire. Within its rhetorical concerns there are good remarks in the book of Sandro Genovali, *Baudelaire o della dissonanza* (Florence: La Nuova Italia, 1971). This book, which stresses catachresis and levels of style, is worthy to be set alongside that of J. D. Hubert cited in note 3.

One can find views of the district of the old Carrousel in Claude Pichois, *Baudelaire à Paris* (Paris: Hachette, 1967), items 71, 72, and 73. A full, rich, and interesting book is Pierre Citron, *La poésie de Paris dans la littérature française de Rousseau à Baudelaire*, 2 vols. (Paris: Minuit, 1961). Vol. 2, chapter 25, "Les noctambules de la Bohème et Nerval," has matter concerning the old Carrousel and Doyenné. In chapter 26, "La poésie du Paris de Baudelaire," Citron rightly observes that Baudelaire in his poetry rarely names precise places: "Reste un seul poème dont le cadre soit précisé: *Le Cygne*, où sont nommés le Carrousel et le Louvre" (vol. 2, 358).

14

TRANSLATIO LAURI

Ivanov's Translations of Petrarch

[As epigraph I set here Vyacheslav Ivanov's sonnet on translation. He himself translated not only Petrarch but also Aeschylus, Novalis, and Dante, and knew that a translation of a poem should also be a poem. I brazenly tempt his muse and mine by englishing his wittily sardonic sonnet.]

Переводчику

Будь жаворонок нив и пажитей—Вергилий,
Иль альбатрос Бодлэр, иль соловей Верлэн
Твоей ловитвою,—все в чужеземный плен
Не заманить тебе птиц вольных без усилий,

Мой милый птицелов,—и, верно, без насилий
Не обойдешься ты, поэт, и без измен,
Хотя б ты другом был всех девяти Камен,
И зла ботаником, и пастырем идиллий.

Затем, что стих чужой—что скользкий бог Протей:
Не улучить его охватом ни отвагой.
Ты держишь рыбий хвост, а он текучей влагой

Струится и бежит из немощных сетей.
С Протеем будь Протей, вторь каждой маске—маской!
Милей досужий люд своей забавить сказкой.

To the Translator

Lark Virgil of the fields and meadowlands,
Albatross Baudelaire, or nightingale
Verlaine ensnared? Surely alien hands
Cannot entice free birds without travail,

My dear birdcatcher—even though you may refuse,
As poet, to betray, to force amain,
Or though you be the friend of every Muse
And evil's botanist and idyll's swain—

Because it's not your poem; in slippery jet
God Proteus, despite your pluck and flail,
Can flee by flowing through your feeble net

And leave you holding a mere fish's tail.
Be Proteus to Proteus, set mask to mask!
Or else amusing idlers is your proper task.
                    (Translated by Lowry Nelson, Jr.—brazenly
                                        by way of epigraph.)

Both Francesco Petrarch and Vyacheslav Ivanov were passionate poets, passionate scholars, and passionate believers. Yet both men disciplined themselves through form, through history, and through religion. The positive tensions generated by their individual modes of conceiving and living their lives were, in both, the source and the means of their poetic expression. Parallels could be drawn between their views of scholarship: in the most general terms, they set out to know the past, to understand it, and to retrieve it in some way for the present. For Petrarch, the past was largely ancient Rome and the barely knowable barbarism that succeeded it. For Ivanov—Hellenist, Latinist, historian, and philosopher—the past was naturally much vaster and the range of reference incalculably greater. Yet both found their alpha and omega and their center in eternal Rome, and both as exiles: Petrarch was born in Arezzo in familial exile from Florence and grew up near the exiled Roman Church in Avignon; Ivanov, born in the "third Rome," Moscow, became for the last twenty-five years of his life, an exile in the first and only Rome. It is tempting to dwell on the differences and the ironies of their destinies, but my purpose here is merely to suggest that a large-scale comparison is not incongruous or unfruitful. What brings them together in history is poetry. Though of vastly disparate provenience in time, place, and culture, they share a skill that each practiced in such a way that I am not shy of calling them both great poets. Here, then, are my precise terms of comparison: we have the unusual case of one great lyric poet translating another great lyric poet, and doing so across a gap of some 570 years. My comments and generalizations leave entirely out of account epic and dramatic and didactic poetry, not to mention epyllia, epistles, and the rest: I am concerned with lyric poetry and its translation into lyric poetry. Both the greatness of the poets Petrarch and Ivanov and the greatness of the gap of time are thus to me unusual and remarkable.

As the first lyric poet to be translated Petrarch has had an extraordinary impact on the whole enterprise of poetic translation itself. When did it begin? Almost automatically one thinks of Catullus's translation-with-a-difference of Sappho, but can one think of any other lyric instances before the Renaissance? It is one of those obvious questions that no one I know of has before now even asked. Implicit in the question itself is the need to define "translation," as distinct from "version," "imitation," and "reelaboration," not to mention matters like form, content, influence, and whatever else enters into this kind of intertextuality. But I arbitrarily invoke, for my present purposes, the rule of rigor, with enough play to make the game interesting. If it be granted that there is such a thing as translation and that it properly aspires to fidelity, the questions that seem central are these: Who does it and how? Who reads it and why? And, What relation does it bear to its original? I would say, simply, that it takes a poet to translate a poem, that the poet-translator must know the language from which he is translating, and that equivalent or reasonably modified formal patterns should be observed. These are of course sticking points, since Ezra Pound's example, for Anglo-American aspirants who all too often take ego-trips on another poet's ticket, usually in a now-dated modernistic vein, but now and then also in the old fake-antique vein. The question of *how* translators do it may for the moment be deferred or perhaps reverently referred to their several muses. It is an act of craft or art. The first readers are naturally the poet-translators themselves, who must sense an affinity, a challenge, and a peculiar sort of inspiration. Translations of lyrics, though, are usually offered to a readership without a knowledge of the original in its own native idiom. On the most pragmatic level, the translation is supposed to give a feeling (notion-emotion) of what the original is *like*. That is a modest and proper goal. English idiom is here peculiar, and differs from any other language I know: What is it like? is the form of a question we ask on all sorts of occasions. Not *How is it?* But *What is it like?* We are asking for a comparison, a simulacrum, a simile, a metaphor perhaps, or even a symbol. And what could be more challenging to our powers of equivalence and analogy or to our poetic imaginations? In ordinary speech our responses are often trite, but in formal verse translation the tension between fidelity and equivalence is acutely focused. A successful translator should be able to say to the reader, in effect, This is *not* the original, this is not a plain-prose rendering, this is not an imitation or a version or a set of variations, but simply, That is what it's like. Granted then that there is an original poem and a poetic translation of it into another language, my last general question is, What relation do the two texts bear to each other? First, they are both poems and can be read and enjoyed and evaluated quite separately. Their separateness is, for better or worse, one of the staple assumptions of national literary histories. The versions or translations of Petrarch produced by, say, Sir Thomas Wyatt or Joachim du Bellay are sometimes not even acknowledged as such or if they are so acknowledged they are seldom compared with their originals. Such a comparison might seem merely the province of a pedant or a comparatist. That there is something positive about this I would not deny: the translations are correctly, however partially, viewed as poems in their own right.

Currently there is a general linguistic and practical concern with translation within various contexts: comparative syntax and contrastive grammar; construction of computerized translating machines; and official political and diplomatic conventions of equivalence. In the West there has been only sporadic concern with theory of translation as related to practice; some major monuments would be the essays of Friedrich and August Wilhelm Schlegel on Ludwig Tieck's translation of *Don Quixote,* the pronouncements and practice of Ezra Pound, the volumes *The Craft and Context of Translation* (1961) edited by William Arrowsmith and Roger Shattuck and *On Translation* (1966) edited by Reuben Brower, the views of Vladimir Nabokov as elaborated in his multifarious edition of Pushkin's *Evgenij Onegin,* and such a specialized yet theoretically grounded work as Anna Kay France's *Boris Pasternak's Translations of Shakespeare* (1978). Elsewhere, especially in the Soviet Union, unusual attention has been paid to the theory of literary translation by such notable practitioners as Korney Chukovsky and Efim Etkind, who not only theorize, but also minutely and interestingly evaluate and often masterly exemplify. I know of no attempt, however, to consider and evaluate Ivanov's translations of Petrarch. In my own sketch of a theory, I first fix boundaries of definition by setting apart the otherwise estimable enterprises of paraphrase, imitation, reelaboration, and parody (sacred or profane). Poetic translation, in my view, attempts to transmute into the target language as much of the content and the form of the original as a translator possibly can. His task is literally a kind of re-presentation or, in terms of painting, a copying of the original. The ruling principle is fidelity. The operational principle is equivalence. In translation, as distinct from other forms of intertextuality, a sonnet should be rendered as a sonnet, an ode as an ode, a rimed poem as a rimed poem. The level of language should be matched. But it would be quite unreasonable to demand that in some mechanical way nouns should be rendered as nouns or adjectives as adjectives or verbs as verbs, even within the Indo-European family of languages. Casting a Petrarchan sonnet in a Shakespearean mold seems to me within the bounds of fidelity. Where a poem has marked alliteration, marked assonance may do. For a hendeca-syllabic line a pentameter may be more natural. A general pattern of caesura or enjambement may be honored generally. My principles might well be denounced as too binding and prescriptive, yet a free-for-all is not translation: it can go its own way to find another label.

Because I shall make judgments as to success or value, I should be explicit in naming possible, even actual dilemmas. It has been wittily observed that a good poem that is a translation of a poor poem is by that fact a poor translation: it has violated the principle of fidelity. Balmont's brilliant translations of Edgar Allan Poe are, then, failures as much as is Baudelaire's ridiculous "Peace Pipe" extract from Longfellow's *Song of Hiawatha*. The usual situation is, of course, quite different: the translator aims at approximating an impossible target and may, with luck, come close; he could only succeed under J. L. Borges's dispensation for the utterly unique Louis Ménard. More to the point is the following pedestrian scheme of permutations: a good translation of a good poem; a poor translation of a good poem; a good translation of a poor poem; a poor translation of a poor poem. Fortunately these extreme and schematic possibilities are narrowed by my insistence that both Petrarch and Ivanov are great poets, not day in and day out perhaps, but the level is high. Ivanov, in his translations, always plays the game of translating Petrarch according to the rules and definitions I have proposed. If he falls short as translator, he does so on his and our terms.

Writing a poem of one's own is a remarkably complex process: it involves language with a history, a tradition of usage, a host of predecessors, an awareness and multiple sorts of self-awareness, a gift of craft, a flash or flashes of inspiration, and hard labor. Poets almost always revise and rework and even recast. Every change reverberates through the whole poem; every change requires adjustment of other elements, or, alternatively, the other elements conspire to force the change. Besides, the result may be more likely poor than good. In translating someone else's poem a writer must necessarily adopt some sort of allegiance or fidelity to an *original* and in doing so he naturally restricts his range of choices. Revising and recasting, which for an "original" poet can be sources of fresh, unexpected inspiration, are for the translator like the feats of a straitjacketed escape artist. He can of course give up approximating the target and settle for a version, an imitation, or a parody—but that becomes a different matter. Yet I would insist that the translator is also a poet with his own linguistic historical repertory. Before examining the nature of Ivanov's translations and versions of Petrarch I shall attempt briefly to characterize the peculiar, native, free-valenced lyrical strain in each one.

Petrarch has, in my view, great limitations as a poet. His range, though spanning life and eternity, is nonetheless rather narrow in its moods and insights. He is a poet of love and conscience, of sensuousness and asceticism, of political passion and spiritual anxiety. Generally he qualifies and mutes his contrasts and outbursts. He is incapable, at one extreme, of solemn grandeur and, at the other extreme, of playful wit or humor. He is never sublime or witty. Yet he can evoke both pathos and joy. Though he often laments to the point of querulousness, he is at times successful in expressing quietly a moving irony. This irony, this understated plaint or elation is, I think, his greatest gift of expression. He can indeed compose a masterpiece, though there are not 366 masterpieces in his *Canzoniere*. No poet has ever had that luck. Perhaps also no poet has ever so boldly challenged the reader to savor and judge quality as did Petrarch in stringing so many poems into an ambiguous continuity and equality of setting. As inheritor and progenitor of the most durable lyric strain in history, he caught up in his work aspects of Provensal and Siculo-Tuscan poetry and became himself the model and motive for about three succeeding centuries. For the lyric his place is as crucial as Virgil's is for the epic. On the bad side, he unwittingly spawned a school of tyros and poetasters as well as emulators and reactors. That Russian literature had no Renaissance such as in the West was in some ways a blessing as well as a handicap. Ivanov, scholar-poet, could set out on his own to recover in an original way an older past that, unlike the Enlightenment and Romanticism, never really happened in Russia.

Ivanov had, however, the resources of Old Slavonic and the language and example of Derzhavin and Pushkin, as well as the fully ripened fruits of Western European poetry since Dante and Petrarch. (Obviously, for my limited purpose, I leave out any consideration of Ivanov's profound involvement with ancient Greece.) Long before he published in 1915 his translations of 27 sonnets from Petrarch's *Canzoniere*, Ivanov had mastered the sonnet to a degree and in a plenitude far surpassing any previous Russian poet. *Pilot Stars (Kormchie zvezdy,* 1903) and *Transparency (Prozrachnost',* 1904)—his first two collections of poetry which in the complete edition occupy 275 ample pages—contain 49 sonnets in various thematic groupings in the midst of other poems of the greatest formal variety. *Cor Ardens* (1911)—more than 300 pages in the complete edition—contains in its vastness all of 98 sonnets, again in groupings. Indeed, book 4 of *Cor Ardens* is called "Life and Death" and has as its epigraph a passage from Petrarch's first *canzone* on Laura's death: the parallel is thus explicit between Laura and Lydia Dmitrievna Zinovieva-Annibal. All this original sonneteering precedes the translations from Petrarch, and of course does not bring to an end Ivanov's mastery of the sonnet, as witness his greatest examples of that form in *Evening Light (Svet Vechernij,* 1962), his final and posthumous volume of poems. Quite early, it would seem, Ivanov fashioned for himself a range of style that is astonishing in its suppleness and variety. Much of his poetry is difficult for its compression of grammatically linked words and phrases more than for any syntactical participial involution. In other terms, he takes more artistic advantage of prefixes and suffixes than of periodic sentence structure. Yet in his versification he follows, naturally, the established tradition of Russian syllabotonic poetry, strict in observance of line-length and rime-pattern. This is indeed in considerable contrast to Petrarch's native freedom in the use of apocopation, elision, and synalepha. Oftentimes in Petrarch the sense and sound vie with each other for prominence, as in the sonnet of twenty-three rivers (no. 148) in which their exotic names flow fluvially into each other. Perhaps the two poets are equal in their syntatic prowess, that is, in the difficulty, the *aesthetic* difficulty, they often present on first reading. Lexically they are at once equal and different: equal, in the sense that they both draw on various levels of style and use what may be perceived as unusual, exotic, or archaic words; different, in the sense that Petrarch for us is often truly archaic with respect to modern Italian, while Ivanov often uses words and forms that are Slavonic or obsolete or even dialectal. A finer parallel could be drawn between the two poets and their lexicon, but I save that for my examples instead of generalizing here.

Ivanov's style is perhaps more learned than Petrarch's, yet its tonal range is broader. Seldom is Petrarch in the *Canzoniere* hieratically solemn, however insistently contrite and weary of the earthly world. He can be serious, intimate, tender, laconically ironic, and quietly joyful. Ivanov, in his original poetry, stretches the range of Petrarch greatly, from the mystical and rhapsodic at one extreme, to the playfully witty at the other. Both took poetry seriously enough to covet in earnest the laurel or the thyrsis. For the Augustinian Petrarch, heir of a Christianized Plato and cultivator of the moral Romans, lyric poetry was eschatologically *vanitas*. For the Hellenic Catholic Ivanov, heir to Byzantium and cultivator of Mnemosyne and Dionysus, poetry, as nature, was immanently divine and earthly love and its poetic memorials were *realia* empowered to lead to *realiora*. Hence a difference in mission and in cultivation of verse. As child of his time, Petrarch wrote his poems within a figural view of fulfillment of life in the life after death. For Ivanov, symbolist-realist, this earthly life is infused and inanimated with divinity, and this life and the life to come, in their individual embodiment, exist in a fusion for which the term "symbol" was the most potently descriptive. Though different in "manner, person and style" they share enough traits to make their compresence on Ivanov's writing-table congenial and momentous. Both were *vates*.

After so many centuries and between two so diverse tongues, equivalence in key vocabulary becomes a prime criterion for *re*-presentation. So much of Petrarch's lexicon had become trite, especially at the hands of his latter-day heirs, the Romantics: beautiful, dear, sweet, pale, weary; eyes, mouth, hair; love, sorrow, joy, virtue—not to mention the objects of external nature, such as birds, meadows, rivers, sun, stars, and moon. But such signifiers are, of course, the continuing givens of our experience. How to freshen, vary, recast, or adapt them without traducing sense and subject? Petrarch himself faced up to this in often avoiding the Provensal-isms and Siculisms of his immediate predecessors. For Ivanov what must have been a besetting preoccupation was to avoid the shopworn words and formulas of *his* immediate predecessors in their lyrics of love and death, nature and introspection, earthly and celestial forms of common experience—ever new in individuals but ever obsolescing in expression. Nothing like a computer lexicon will do. Love is not love in all cases of *amore* or *ljubov'*. The Christian words in the Vulgate—*caritas* and *dilectio*—became one with pagan Latin *amor*, first in Provensal and then in Italian. But Petrarch inherited both traditions in his poetry and uses *amore* in ways that Ivanov carefully distinguishes by using not only *ljubov'* but also *amur* or *bog* or *bog ljubvi* or on one occasion *kumir* and, on another, omitting translation. That wide-ranging word *dolore*, and its cognates *duolo* and *doglia*, are variously rendered by *bol'* (most commonly) and *skorb'*. I think I detect here a strong tendency to avoid the nouns *gore, pechal'*, and *grust'*, as well as *tomlenie* and *toska* (used once each) and of course *skuka*, as well as their adjectival derivatives. Petrarch's emblematic word *pensero* (modern form, *pensiero*) is rendered either as *dukh* or less commonly as *dumy*. *Smorto* and *impallidire* are inevitably some form of *blednyj*, just as *stanco* is usually *ustalyj*, though once *iznemog*, and once omitted. *Dolce* is almost always forthrightly *sladkij* or (I must say, understandably) either omitted or paraphrased, as in the case where Petrarch contrasts *alcun dolce* with *tanti amari* (57) and Ivanov writes *mëd skupoj* contrasted with *ne sladok pozdnij mëd*. It surely is significant that for *dolce* we seldom find either *milyj* or *nezhnyj* (though in other connections these words do rarely appear). Such instances as these could be multiplied, yet to do so would run the risk of distorting the translator's task, which is of course not simply to render noun by noun and adjective by adjective. What I hope to have shown in this preliminary comparison is that Ivanov has taken some care to break out of conventionalized nineteenth-century equivalencies like those familiar to English-readers in versions of Rossetti and his epigones working in the wake of the great English Romantics.

It should come as no surprise that Ivanov does not equally succeed in all of his twenty-seven translations from Petrarch. In a more ample context it would be a worthy and enlightening enterprise to take up each sonnet in turn and mark their qualities, deficiencies, remodelings, and misses. I feel my own understanding and enjoyment of both poets have been greatly enhanced by my private and fairly exhaustive study of these texts. What I propose, within narrower public bounds, is to choose—I trust not tendentiously—a few whole poems and passages for the purpose of showing high achievement, honorable failure, local triumphs, some free variations, and a few clashes of sensibility.

First I consider Ivanov's translation of Sonnet 156, which in the original has a certain sustained rapture and gentle solemnity but which in Russian takes on something like a Rossettian or early Yeatsian, indeed a Pre-Raphaelite, portentousness. Petrarch, in this sonnet, celebrates the harmony of his beloved's demeanor on earth that reflected her heavenly origin and destination. Terrestrial nature was so hushed by the harmonious heavens that not a leaf stirred. The first quatrain goes thus:

I' vidi in terra angelici costumi
e celesti bellezze al mondo sole,
tal che di rimembrar mi giova e dole,
ché quant'io miro par sogni, ombre e fumi.

(I saw on earth angelic ways and heavenly beauties unique in the
world, such that remembering pleases and pains me, for whatever
I look upon seems dreams, shadows and vapors [smokes].)

Ivanov singles out for his exordium the sense of the word "dole" (which is
coupled in the original with its antithesis "giova") and makes from the
attributive "angelici" an actual substantivized angel twice mentioned in the
first three lines. "Celesti bellezze" is omitted; "dreams" become "a dream";
"shadows" become "a cloud of charms"; and "fumi" or "vapors" are either
subsumed by "cloud" or are simply omitted. (One learns by the way what
a trial to the poet is the English word "smoke" and its plural.) The classical
echo of phrases like "pulvis et umbra" or "umbra, cinis, nihil" is lost in the
selective questioning: was it a dream? or a cloud?

Ja litsezrel nebesnuju pechal',
Grust' angela v edinstvennom javlen'e.
To son li byl? No angela mne zhal'.
Il' oblak char? No sladko umilen'e.

(I beheld heavenly sorrow, an angel's sadness in a singular vision.
Was it a dream? But I grieved for the angel. Or a cloud of charms?
But sweet was the emotion.)

I should mention that there is a variant reading for "char": "gar," meaning
something like smoking embers. One must wait for the definitive edition
under way. And the manner continues, as in the second pair of lines in the
second quatrain. Petrarch's words are simple and his hyperbole traditional:

e udi' sospirando dir parole
che farian gire i monti e stare i fiumi.

(And I heard words spoken sighing that would make mountains
move and rivers stay.)

In considerable contrast, Ivanov, with languorous elaboration, adds and ornaments:

> Krotkikh ust molen'e,
> chto val skovat' moglo b i sdvinut' dal',—
> iznemoglo, istajalo v tomlen'e.

(The supplication of her gentle lips, which could fetter the billow and shift distance, grew faint, melted with lassitude.)

Perhaps in an effort to shun triteness and at the same time to fulfill his uncharacteristic scheme of easy, mostly grammatical, rimes, Ivanov chooses to be consistent in his fin-de-siècle and mannered rendition. Petrarch ends his poem with great artistic control, describing the stillness of heaven and earth in which "no leaf on a bough could be *seen* to move." In Ivanov we read:

> i vozdukh byl raznezhen eju—stol',
> chto ni listka v vetviakh ne shelokhnulos'.

Petrarch's breathless silence and immobility suggest, inappropriately, to Ivanov all those Romantic rustlings and murmurings we *hear* with crashing frequency in his immediate and earlier predecessors.

For the reasons I have given, Sonnet 156 in its Russian vesture is a fascinating failure. It is a good example of what many poets of Ivanov's generation, both in Russia and elsewhere in Europe and in America, coped with in their practice and in some splendid instances—Yeats, Pound, Rilke, Blok, and Ivanov—overcame on their way to a less edulcorated new style that we may now call modernism. It is also a good example of Ivanov's own independence, however willful in confronting and transmuting his brother poet. There are notable examples of intriguing failures of fidelity also in a few translations that in effect "out-Petrarch" Petrarch at his most mannered. In one of Petrarch's most imitated sonnets (199) he addresses with fancy fervor that most metonymically coveted appendage, the female hand:

> O bella man che mi destringi 'l core
> e 'n poco spazio la mia vita chiudi . . .

(O beautiful hand that grips my heart and encloses my life in such little space . . .)

That hand is an artwork on which nature and heaven have lavished every
skill. The fingers are orient pearls that, naked, can "enrich" when they are
not probing love's wounds. Even the white glove that covers the coveted
hand is dear as a token he has snatched; it makes him wish he had also
some of her veil. But such is the inconstancy of life that this is theft and he
must be deprived. One might irreverently call this a pretty poem and
wonder idly about the *other* hand. It is trivial and at the same time a bit
solemn, a combination that had enormous and continuous vogue for five or
six centuries: let me call it "proto-baroco-rococo." Ivanov cannot resist
further prettifying the poem, but to his credit he adds a touch of sly drama
and humor of which Petrarch was temperamentally incapable. Reference to
the inconstancy of life is simply dropped and supplanted with an airy
exclamation "In vain! The brief delight is over: the culprit must return his
booty":

> Votshche! Nastal konets uslady kratkoj:
> Vernut' dobychu dolzhen likhodej.

Even this slight poem in its Russian version is a worthy cultural appropriation: it contains and emblematizes with inventive grace a whole long
European tradition of coy clever poetry from the Alexandrians to Petrarch
and his imitators down to polished album verse of the nineteenth century.
Suffice it to cite, along that way, Romeo's words of wonder:

> See how she leans her cheek upon her hand!
> O that I were a glove upon that hand,
> That I might touch that cheek!

But to follow this would conjure up the *blason* and all its precious
body-parts.

A considerable achievement of Petrarch in the sonnet was to make its
slender and articulated form capable of dramatized passion. His means are
often visions, some dialogue, and understatement or Petrarchan irony.
Sonnet 336 is an especially interesting example in that the dialogue goes on
inside his own mind, in that the vision is presented as a memory and not an
outward fiction or allegory, and in that the crushing reality of Laura's death
takes the form of the dry, spare, precise citation of its hour and date. In
paraphrase the poem goes thus:

She returns to my mind (whence Lethe cannot banish her) just as I saw her in flower lit up with the rays of her star. I see her as in our first meeting, pure, lovely, solitary, and demure. I cry, "It is she, still alive!" and beg the gift of her sweet speech. Sometimes she answers, sometimes not. As if coming to my senses I tell my mind, "You are deceived; you know that her blessed soul left her body at the first hour on April 6, 1348."

It is something of a stroke of genius to versify the calendar. Ivanov shows in his fine translation that he deeply respects the tone and modality of Petrarch's poem, occasionally heightening and condensing, yet observing essential fidelity. The solemnity of Petrarch's interruptive parenthesis on Lethe in the first quatrain is naturalized in a normal flow of syntax and rendered forceful by the word *neprestannoj*. The sequence of typical adjectives in the second quatrain is summarized creatively:

> dushoju obajannoj
> Lovlju v chertakh zastenchivost' priveta.

(In my captivated mind I catch in her features a shyness in greeting.)

The word "greeting" does not occur in the original, but it is latent in Petrarch's world of the beloved's momentous *saluto-salute*. And she does speak later, most mysteriously, as would a memory: "Talor risponde e talor non fa motto" (at times she answers and at times says not a word). Ivanov here heightens the necessarily imprecise memory: "Poroj molchit,— poroju . . ." (at times she is silent, at times . . .). The phrase falters movingly. Again, in this first tercet, Ivanov condenses the lightly sententious lines of Petrarch,

> i', come uom ch'erra e poi più dritto estima
> dico a la mente mia . . .

(I, like one who errs and then reckons more justly, say to my mind . . .),

into a heightening of the mental state from a wandering brought back along the straight and narrow path to a raptness or even intoxication followed by regaining sober consciousness. Ivanov invents the phrase "Serdtsu dorog / Takoj vostorg" and continues:

> A posle, kak ot khmelja
> Ochnuvshijsja, skazhu: "Znaj, obmanula
> Tebja mechta."

"The dream-vision has deceived you" as compared to Petrarch's phrase, "I say to my mind: thou art deceived." The final lines in Petrarch would translate: "You know that in 1348, the sixth day of April, at the first hour, that blessed soul issued from the body":

> Sai che 'n mille trecento quarantotto,
> il dì sesto d'aprile, in l'ora prima,
> del corpo uscìo quell'anima beata.

To put that into another language without sounding like a bureaucrat or anchorman is a greater achievement than may seem plausible to those who have not had the often hopeless and thankless experience of a poet-translator. Ivanov manages to naturalize that dry direct simplicity, using the customary three rimes in the sestet: dorog/sorok, khmelja/aprelja, and obmanula/usnula. The last sentence reads:

> V tysjacha trista sorok
> Os'mom godu, v chas pervyj, v den' aprelja
> Shestyj—mezh nas blazhennaja usnula.

This is the sort of triumph a translator must keep to himself or share only with those in the know. As a whole this sonnet radiates and resonates authentically and artistically in its Russian glow and echo.

At times, between these two systems of texts, there is something like an antiphonal correspondence from two corners: dissonance that resolves into harmony; a musical "third" that rings true; a coincidence of perfect pitch; or even a cadence that improves. In tone, as I have said, Ivanov's range is wider than Petrarch's: he can be more intensely passionate and truly witty; he can more easily avoid insistent complaint and near-bathos. For example, Petrarch's lovely Sonnet 190, "Una candida cerva sopra l'erba / verde"—also well known from Wyatt's very free adaptation "Whoso list to hunt, I know where is an hind"—relates the appearance of a golden-horned doe with a necklace inscribed in diamonds and topazes: "Let no one touch me; it pleased Caesar to set me free." After so dazzling a vision and so enigmatic a motto, the poet fell into the water and the doe disappeared:

> Et era 'l sol già volto al mezzo giorno,
> gli occhi miei stanchi di mirar, non sazi,
> quand'io caddi ne l'acqua, et ella sparve.

This is very close to bathos, if I am not mistaken, though the poet's sudden plunge, presumably in full dress, can be of course attenuated by pious commentary. Ivanov in his translation shows great discretion. *His* poet is said to "forget all" in his enchantment and a hint of danger or violence is added in the phrase "Ne ran'!" that follows the canonical "Ne tron' menja!" Besides, the doe is called a "splendid-headed wanderer on magical shores," whose "collar of diamantine words was sparkling on her neck." By such added enhancement Ivanov suffuses a fairy-tale atmosphere. The fall thus can become delicately mythic as it is circumstantial in the last lines:

> No ne byl syt moj vzor, kogda v rechnye
> Zatony ja upal—i skrylas' lan'.

(But my gaze was not sated when into the river eddies I fell, and the doe vanished.)

Yet on the other hand some fine touches of Petrarch's laconic irony go unacknowledged in the Russian texts of these poems. In Sonnet 285 Petrarch celebrates the tender and solicitous tutelage he receives from his beloved in heaven to keep him on the right path, and he does so with a continuous rhetorical sweep that leads up to the climactic last line:

> E sol quant'ella parla ò pace o tregua.

(And only so long as she speaks do I have peace or truce.)

The word "tregua" (truce) is more than a pleonasm or afterthought; it gently or ironically reminds us that on earth peace is never a permanent state. Ivanov chooses to render "l'alma," which has in Petrarch its religious

sense, as both "dukh" and "serdtse," and expands the single Italian line to
two:

> I mir mne dan s molitvoj legkokryloj,
> kogda svjataja serdtsu govorit.

(And peace is given me with light-winged prayer when the blessed
one speaks to my heart.)

In this otherwise admirable and welcome rendition the most delicate effect
is, for whatever reason of craft, lost. Likewise in Sonnet 364, which comes
just before the last sonnet and the final *canzone* directed in prayer to the
Virgin, the humble supplication to God in the conclusion undergoes in the
Russian version a change in tone. Indeed Ivanov heightens the mood of
repentance throughout the poem. Petrarch's final lines are thus:

> Signor che 'n questo carcer m'ài rinchiuso
> tramene salvo da li eterni danni,
> chi' i' conosco 'l mio fallo e non lo scuso.

(Lord who hast enclosed me in this prison, draw me from it safe
from eternal ills, for I know my guilt and do not excuse it.)

It is late contrition, end of the whole drama of the *Canzoniere,* for which he
tallies his sins and waits in hope for God's absolving grace. In Russian,
however, it takes on a rather Dostoevskian tone or, perhaps more
accurately, a Davidian tone echoing the Book of Psalms, and thus more Old
than New Testament:

> k tebe moj vopl' iz sej temnitsy strastnoj,
> gde ty menja zamknul, i chrez ogni
> vvedi v Svoj raj tropoju bezopasnoj!

(But mark my cry to Thee from this suffering prison where Thou
enclosed me, and through fires lead me to Thy paradise by a safe
way!)

Petrarch's tone of utter humility, which cannot of course in any way *demand*
God's grace, becomes a cry *de profundis,* with almost a touch of Christo-

pher Marlowe's Doctor Faustus, for safe-conduct through Purgatory to Paradise. Here there is a notable dissonance of tone between the two poems. To put it more positively, these are two poems whose differences are as interesting as their resemblances.

A true chiming of both poets occurs with Sonnet 312, my last example. In a long enumeration of the attractive shows of nature and of mortal life, Petrarch leads up to the sad reality that the beloved has buried them all for him, because she was his light and mirror. The last three lines are movingly measured in the understated irony he found consolatory.

> Noia m'è 'l viver sì gravosa e lunga
> ch' i' chiamo il fine per lo gran desire
> di riveder cui non veder fu 'l meglio.

> (For me living is an anguish so burdensome and prolonged that I call out for the end in my great desire to see her again, *not* seeing whom had been best.)

The sense is not easy to render exactly; it is, with its own emotional exactitude, appropriately *uneasy*. (Latin usage, in proverbial and sententious utterances, is the model here.) In his beautiful translation Ivanov achieves true artistic fidelity and yet retains a measure of creative independence, as exemplified here in his final tercet:

> Zhizn' odnozvuchna. Zrelishche unylo.
> Lish' v smerti vnov' uvizhu to, chego
> Mne luchshe b nikogda ne videt' bylo.

> (Life is monotonous. Its pageant is melancholy. Only in death will I see again that which it would have been better for me never to see.)

English idiom allows this slightly uncommon rendering of the tenses. The present in the past is normal in Russian, and gives a fairly close approximation of the original Italian. Petrarch is not saying flatly that it would have been better if he had never seen his beloved at all. He is, in classical idiom, stressing the pain of loss sustained over so many years and the even-greater desire to see her, if possible, again and forever. "Noia" suggested to Ivanov not its true archaic meaning of "anguish" but rather its modern meaning of "boredom" or "nuisance." Yet he chose the right word by his lights: "odnozvuchna." The usual modern equivalence, "skuchna," would have perhaps inappropriately evoked shades of Pechorin and Onegin. "Zrelishche unylo," though not exact, is proper in the context of the whole poem. Petrarch's "gran desire" goes unrendered, but it is there implicitly. Most important of all, the sense and tone live viably in the Russian words. When free, as in other places I have not mentioned, Ivanov's version has its own further function as a mediation of traditions. But that is a very complex matter for which neither the present context nor the present writer is adequate.

Ivanov as Russian Petrarchist came far too late to found a lineage. Yet he succeeded in showing once again, in these twenty-seven Russified sonnets from the Tuscan master, how vital his sense of poetic mission was: to retain and renew memory and make Mnemosyne, mother of the Muses, respond to his artful, mediated invocations. The scholar-historian reconstructs and interprets the past, recovering it from dormancy and oblivion and freshening it for new contemplation. The poet or poet-translator weaves himself a pattern from and among the patterns already in the fabric of memory and so changes and reorders it, however slightly. Both Petrarch and Ivanov as profoundly religious men were, above all, concerned with anagoge, the eschatological way to God; but that way can pass by and through poetry and can be known through presage and memory. For Ivanov, Petrarch's "cult" of the laurel was "revolutionary." It was something of which Petrarch himself was in no way aware. To quote from Ivanov's essay on "Il lauro nella poesia del Petrarca" (1933):

> [In Petrarch's love poetry] for the first time Parnassus is completely separated from religion, for never in the ancient world was it set up in opposition as a sovereign, independent, intellectualist realm, nor had the separatism of art ever been previously so radically asserted. No reaction [such as Petrarch made] could any longer deprive humanism of its charter of freedoms, its privilege of having, on the same footing as any religion, a paradise of its own.

Perhaps there is a touch of mischief in Ivanov's summation: it is a high tribute in the name of poetry and secular learning, but it might well have given Petrarch, so pious and yet so anxious to become *laureatus,* both pang and pleasure and made him burn in ice and freeze in fire. Both poets are now, we trust, in the same true Paradise, beyond all passion and repentance, beyond earthly schism and syncretism. For us, the heirs of

their common humanism, it is, I hope, an instructive pleasure to overhear their Parnassian colloquy in these sonnets in the paradisiacal region of our own memorial poetic minds.

Note

The works of Vyacheslav Ivanovich Ivanov are being published for the first time in a collected edition, *Sobranie Sochinenii*, ed. D. V. Ivanov and O. Deschartes (Brussels: Foyer Oriental Chrétien, 1971–). Four volumes have appeared so far. For a general discussion of theory and practice with many examples, see Lowry Nelson, Jr., "Literary Translation," *Translation Review* (published by the American Literary Translators Association [ALTA]), no. 29 (1989), 17–30.

Sonnets Cited

156

I' vidi in terra angelici costumi
e celesti bellezze al mondo sole,
tal che di rimembrar mi giova e dole,
ché quant'io miro par sogni, ombre e fumi;

e vidi lagrimar que' duo bei lumi
ch'àn fatto mille volte invidia al sole,
et udi' sospirando dir parole
che farian gire i monti e stare i fiumi.

Amor, senno, valor, pietate e doglia
facean piangendo un più dolce concento
d'ogni altro che nel mondo udir si soglia,

ed era il cielo a l'armonia sì intento,
che non se vedea in ramo mover foglia:
tanta dolcezza avea pien l'aere e'l vento!

199

O bella man che mi destringi 'l core
e 'n poco spazio la mia vita chiudi,
man ov' ogni arte e tutti loro studi
poser natura e 'l ciel per farsi onore;

di cinque perle oriental colore,
e sol ne le mie piaghe acerbi e crudi,
diti schietti soavi, a tempo ignudi,
consente or voi, per arricchirme, Amore.

Candido, leggiadretto e caro guanto,
che copria netto avorio e fresche rose,
chi vide al mondo mai sì dolci spoglie?

Così avess' io del bel velo altrettanto!
O inconstanzia de l' umane cose:
pur questo è farto, e vien ch' i' me ne spoglie.

156

Я лицезрел небесную печаль,
Грусть ангела в единственном явленье.
То сон ли был? Но ангела мне жаль.
Иль облак гар? Но сладко умиленье.

Затмили слезы двух светил хрусталь
Светлейший Солнца. Кротких уст моленье,
Что вал сковать могло б и сдвинуть даль,—
Изнемогло, истаяло в томленье.

Все—добродетель, мудрость, нежность, боль—
В единую гармонию сомкнулось,
Какой земля не слышала дотоль.

И ближе небо, внемля ей, нагнулось;
И воздух был разнежен ею—столь,
Что ни листка в ветвях не шелохнулось.

199

Прекрасная рука! Разжала ты
И держишь сердце на ладони тесной.
Я на тебя гляжу, дивясь небесной
Художнице столь строгой красоты.

Продолговато-вежные персты
Прозрачней перлов Индии чудесной,
Вершители моей судьбины крестной,
Я вижу вас в сиянье наготы.

Я завладел ревнивою перчаткой!
Кто, победитель, лучший взял трофей?
Хвала, Амур! А ныне ты ж украдкой

Фату похить иль облаком развей!..
Вотще! Настал конец услады краткой:
Вернуть добычу должен лиходей.

336

Tornami a mente, anzi v' è dentro, quella
ch' indi per Lete esser non po sbandita,
qual io la vidi in su l' età fiorita
tutta accesa de' raggi di sua stella;

sì nel mio primo occorso onesta e bella
veggiola, in sé raccolta e sì romita,
ch' i' grido: «Ell' è ben dessa, ancor è in vita»,
e 'n don le cheggio sua dolce favella.

Talor risponde e talor non fa motto;
i', come uom ch' erra e poi più dritto estima,
dico a la mente mia: «Tu se' 'ngannata:

sai che 'n mille trecento quarantotto,
il dì sesto d' aprile, in l' ora prima,
del corpo uscìo quell' anima beata».

190

Una candida cerva sopra l' erba
verde m' apparve, con duo corna d' oro,
fra due riviere, all' ombra d' un alloro,
levando 'l sole a la stagione acerba.

Era sua vista sì dolce superba
ch' i' lasciai per seguirla ogni lavoro,
come l'avaro che 'n cercar tesoro
con diletto l' affanno disacerba.

«Nessun mi tocchi» al bel collo d' intorno
scritto avea di diamanti e di topazi,
«libera farmi al mio Cesare parve».

Et era 'l sol già volto al mezzo giorno;
gli occhi miei stanchi di mirar, non sazi,
quand'io caddi ne l' acqua, et ella sparve.

336

Я мыслию лелею непрестанной
Ее, чью тень отнять бессильна Лета,
И вижу вновь ее в красе расцвета,
Родной звезды восходом осиянной.

Как в первый день, душою обаянной
Ловлю в чертах застенчивость привета.
«Она жива,—кричу,—как в оны лета!»
И дара слов молю из уст желанной.

Порой молчит,—порою... Сердцу дорог
Такой восторг!.. А после, как от хмеля
Очнувшийся, скажу: «Знай, обманула

Тебя мечта! В тысяча триста сорок
Осьмом году, в час первый, в день апреля
Шестый—меж нас блаженная уснула».

190

Лань белая на зелени лугов,
В час утренний, порою года новой,
Промеж двух рек, под сению лавровой,
Несла, гордясь, убор златых рогов.

Я все забыл, и не стремить шагов
Не мог (скупец, на все труды готовый,
Чтоб клад добыть!)—за ней, пышноголовой
Скиталицей волшебных берегов.

Сверкала вязь алмазных слов на вые:
«Я Кесарем в луга заповедные
Отпущена. Не тронь меня! Не рань!..»

Полдневная встречала Феба грань;
Но не был сыт мой взор, когда в речные
Затоны я упал—и скрылась лань.

285

Né mai pietosa madre al caro figlio
né donna accesa al suo sposo diletto
diè con tanti sospir, con tal sospetto,
in dubbio stato sì fedel consiglio,

come a me quella che 'l mio grave esiglio
mirando dal suo eterno alto ricetto
spesso a me torna co l' usato affetto,
e di doppia pietate ornata il ciglio,

or di madre or d' amante; or teme or arde
d'onesto foco, e nel parlar mi mostra
quel che 'n questo viaggio fugga o segua,

contando i casi de la vita nostra,
pregando ch' a levar l' alma non tarde:
e sol quant'ella parla ò pace o tregua.

364

Tennemi Amor anni ventuno ardendo
lieto nel foco e nel duol pien di speme;
poi che Madonna e 'l mio cor seco inseme
saliro al ciel, dieci altri anni piangendo;

omai son stanco e mia vita reprendo
di tanto error, che di vertute il seme
à quasi spento, e le mie parti estreme,
alto Dio, a te devotamente rendo,

pentito e tristo de' miei sì spesi anni:
che spender si deveano in miglior uso,
in cercar pace ed in fuggir affanni.

Signor che 'n questo carcer m'ài rinchiuso
Tramene salvo da li eterni danni,
ch' i' conosco 'l mio fallo e non lo scuso.

285

Не слышал сын от матери родной,
Ни муж любимый от супруги нежной
С такой заботой, зоркой и прилежной,
Преподанных советов: злой виной

Не омрачать судьбы своей земной,—
Какие, малодушный и мятежный,
Приемлю я от той, что, в белоснежный
Одета свет, витает надо мной

В двойном обличье: матери и милой.
Она трепещет, молит и горит,
К стезе добра влечет и нудит силой,—

И, ей подвигнут, вольный дух парит;
И мир мне дан с молитвой легкокрылой,
Когда святая сердцу говорит.

364

Лет трижды семъ повинен был гореть я,
Амуров раб, ликуя на костре.
Она ушла,—я дух вознес горе.
Продлится ль плач за грань десятилетья?

Страстей меня опутавшую сеть я
Влачить устал. Подумать о добре
Давно пора. Твоей, господь, заре
Я старости вручаю перволетья!

Зачем я жил? На что растратил дни?
Бежал ли я змеи греха ужасной?
Искал ли я Тебя? Но помяни

К Тебе мой вопль из сей темницы страстной,
Где Ты меня замкнул, и чрез огни
Введи в Свой рай тропою безопасной!

312

Né per sereno ciel ir vaghe stelle
né per tranquillo mar legni spalmati
né per campagne cavalieri armati
né per bei boschi allegre fere e snelle,

né d' aspettato ben fresche novelle
né dir d' amore in stili alti ed ornati
né tra chiare fontane e verdi prati
dolce cantare oneste donne e belle,

né altro sarà mai ch' al cor m' aggiunga:
sì seco il seppe quella seppellire
che sola agli occhi miei fu lume e speglio.

Noia m' è 'l viver sì gravosa e lunga
ch' i' chiamo il fine per lo gran desire
di riveder cui non veder fu 'l meglio.

312

Ни ясных звезд блуждающие станы,
Ни полные на взморье паруса,
Ни с пестрым зверем темные леса,
Ни всадники в доспехах средь поляны,

Ни гости, с вестью про чужие страны,
Ни рифм лубовных сладкая краса,
Ни милых жен поющих голоса
Во мгле садов, где шепчутся фонтаны,—

Ничто не тронет сердца моего.
Все погребло с собой мое светило,
Что сердцу было зеркалом всего.

Жизнь однозвучна. Зрелище уныло.
Лишь в смерти вновь увижу то, чего
Мне лучше б никогда не видеть было.

15

THE FICTIVE READER
AND
LITERARY
SELF-REFLEXIVENESS

If it be taken as hypothesis that any work of literary art is in some way a communication—that is, making common or mutual an aesthetic experience—then not only the author's intentions and actual performance, not only the objective text to be interpreted and judged from age to age, but also the reader, to whom the communication is directed, can become in his individuality as well as commonality collaborator or accomplice in the whole process. It is the reader's contractual duty in the very act of reading to assume provisionally a fictive role, not as outsider but as a communicant, willing to suspend his disbelief. Coleridge's formulation here alluded to may seem merely negative or indulgent as a suspension of truth, reality, and common sense. Obviously one cannot wholly exist in a fictional world and still cope with actual quotidian needs. Yet in accepting and evaluating an artistic communication the reader must dispose himself to the special and indeed prescriptive demands of a fictional world which in a truly aesthetic sense patterns his impulses deriving from his own experience of real life and also from his notions of what another real life might or could be. Given and having accepted his role, the reader must to some extent be drawn into the fiction as if it were true, as if it were entirely normative, as if it were for the time his full commitment. To what extent the suspension of disbelief is willing would depend naturally on experience, disposition, and what might be called aesthetic ambivalence, that is, the ability of mind to be actor and self-observer, participant and judge, at one and the same time.

We realize that the observer is himself observed in advance, that the reader is aware of being guided and manipulated by the text, which he must both accept and eventually judge, that the fictionality could well, by analogy to real life, be otherwise; nonetheless, as readers we voluntarily enter into an imagined cosmos not properly as escapists or dupes but as provisional believers and hopeful collaborators; we enter into the world of the "as if," the simulacrum of reality, as self-aware questioners of what reality is.

It is still a puzzling question as to what Aristotle meant by "mimesis." We can, however, be quite sure that he was intrigued by the central question of what the relation could possibly be between story or myth and, on the other hand, exact truth or historicity. He must in fact have felt some of the same ambivalence, or even embarrassment, as his master Plato. Yet he did have the sort of mind to venture upon resolving dubieties into categories and syllogisms, as means of taxonomic observation and seeming certitude. One of his central conceptions is of course a dramatic involvement of the audience or readership in a "purgative" experience during the actual performance or, by analogy and extension, reading. Originally and properly the experience of ancient as well as modern drama was time-bound, both visual and aural, immediate in ways that are distinguishable from the experience of later poetry and narrative. In modern terms the *reader,* while experiencing in time, can return, dwell at leisure, skip, or otherwise manipulate the flow or sequence of discourse. He has then a certain control over the rate of flow of his own aesthetic experience, at least when reading printed texts. Horace, in his *Epistula ad Pisones,* comes closer to common modern assumptions that blur the distinction between spectator and reader, between dramatic and literary critic, though indeed the notion of the play as poem need not be programmatically rejected as irrelevant even to the notion of the "living theater." If, in regard to the involvement of the literary communicant, Horace's criterion of applause be taken as a sign of artistic success or accomplishment, then of course a false democracy of approval by poll-count usurps the right of spectator and reader to argue the premises of their response and judgment. Involvement of the reader or spectator as collaborators is essential in the curious situation of artistic communication. Any categorical notion of the "active" writer and the "passive" reader, conceived as entirely independent roles, would of course contravene the *contrat littéraire* between communicator and communicant, creator and collaborator, perpetrator and accomplice.

Such reflections are not essentially novel, in that essential novelty is rare in literary criticism. Yet one may argue that matters of systematic aesthetic constructions, with their play of emphasis and inventiveness in conceptualization, are at least relatively of the essence. In *Baroque Lyric Poetry* (New Haven, 1961) I have written of what I called the rhetorical situation: the interaction or collaboration of the speaker, the person or object addressed or presented, and the reader. By way of emphasis, if not novelty, I should like to stress the role of the reader as accomplice (literally after the fact) whose responses are written into the literary work itself which then becomes normative for any individual performance. Each work requires in its integrity what I would call by way of emphasis an *optimum* reader, initially well disposed, fully competent in "historical semantics," in the sense Leo Spitzer gave the phrase, and free from irrelevant associations of the sort I. A. Richards exposed and analyzed. These would be some of the basic qualifications of the optimum reader. His role is as ambivalent as that of a dramatic actor in being both performer aware of his real self and collaborator within the fiction. In seeming contrast to the fictive reader is the fact that in many works of literature one finds an inward-turning self-reflexiveness: the poem commenting on itself, first in the process of composition and then in the reading or performance of it. Yet one may argue that both the fictive role of the reader and the self-reflexiveness of the work have in common a playing with the reality of the fiction or, more strongly, the exposure of the fiction to the end, paradoxically, of reinforcing it.

Of the many ways in which the reader is granted his fictive role, perhaps the most elementary is the direct address to him, for instance by conventional dedication, as in Ariosto's apostrophe to Ippolito d'Este at the beginning of *Orlando Furioso* or Cervantes's Prologues to the "desocupado lector" in Part 1 and to the "lector ilustre" in Part 2. A further elementary and obvious means of reminding the reader of his role is direct mention of him within the fictional body of the work: here examples are numerous from Cervantes to Henry James. Fielding's *Tom Jones* is a particularly rich instance. The novel is conceived as a direct dialogue between narrator and reader as collaborators in observing actions of the characters within the "true" fiction. Not only the intercalated chapters of discursive commentary and speculation, and the occasional exposure of the puppets' strings, but also the direct address to the reader ("my reader may please to remember") contribute to a fictional collaboration expressed in the first-person singular and plural. Other, indeed many other, examples come readily to mind.

Involvement of the reader in the fiction by such elementary means can obviously serve to heighten the "truth" of the fiction provided the fiction is skillful enough to draw the reader into his fictive role and create for him a successful ambivalence between his real and fictionally disposed self. One of the most effective uses, on a more complex level, of the address to the reader is found in the first of Baudelaire's *Les fleurs du mal,* "Au lecteur." As the poem begins, and continuing almost to the end, we find no direct address, only a pervasive reference to the first-person plural:

> La sottise, l'erreur, le péché, la lésine,
> Occupent nos esprits et travaillent nos corps,
> Et nous alimentons nos aimables remords,
> Comme les mendiants nourrissent leur vermine.

The reader is drawn into the poem at least provisionally and collaborates with it in an equilibrium of aesthetic ambivalence. Yet in the second to the last stanza and the first two lines of the last he is given, as it were, some respite: even though there is reference immediately before to "la ménagerie infâme de nos vices," no direct use of the first-person plural is made.

> Il en est un plus laid, plus méchant, plus immonde!
> Quoiqu'il ne pousse ni grands gestes ni grands cris,
> Il ferait volontiers de la terre un débris
> Et dans un bâillement avalerait le monde;
>
> C'est l'Ennui!—l'œil chargé d'un pleur involontaire,
> Il rêve d'échafauds en fumant son houka.

In the last two lines of the poem, however, something sudden, direct, and even shocking occurs: a frontal implication and accusation of the reader as accomplice, as exposed fellow sinner and sufferer:

> Tu le connais, lecteur, ce monstre délicat,
> —Hypocrite lecteur,—mon semblable,—mon frère!

It amounts almost to an unmasking of the reader's balanced ambivalence. The unexpected direct address in the intimate form of the second-person singular implicates him much more deeply in what has gone on before; his acquiescence, provisional until now, becomes a heightening of his involvement and an aesthetically necessary complicity with the speaker of the poem.

In such terms, as well as others, can be explained the force of those lines. That the last line should become for T. S. Eliot an Arnoldian "touchstone" in *The Waste Land* is not surprising. Still, the point must be emphasized that the line derives its force from the poem sequentially read or performed—in commoner terms, from the total context. Matthew Arnold's notion of the touchstone has of course been criticized before, most eloquently by Robert Penn Warren in his essay "Pure and Impure Poetry." Yet in defense of Arnold and certainly of Eliot one should perhaps assume that the single lines culled from this or that masterpiece are meant to evoke their total setting. Here it is the task of the reader to be or to make himself optimum. The allusions in the poetry of Eliot have provided a reading list for generations of readers who then can reread with more awareness and less bafflement and finally proceed to inherit their heritage and expect enriched futures in the future.

It is a descent from the eloquence, control, and "dramaticality" of Baudelaire's poem, yet as a further instance, perhaps a limiting one, of the role of the fictive reader it might be useful to consider a poem often derided, Wordsworth's "The Thorn." It is a work that was harshly treated not only by Francis Jeffrey in his essay "Crabbe's Poems" (1808), but also by Coleridge in chapter 17 of *Biographia Literaria* (1817). Their strictures are of interest in this context. To quote Jeffrey, who is parodying Wordsworth's somewhat defensive description of the speaker of his poem as a retired sea captain living on an annuity in "some village or country town, of which he was not a native, or in which he had not been accustomed to live": "Of this piece the reader will necessarily form a very erroneous judgment unless he is apprised that it was written by a pale man in a green coat—sitting cross-legged on an oaken stool—with a scratch on his nose, and a spelling dictionary on the table." Coleridge, giving qualified exception to the Nurse in *Romeo and Juliet,* notes that "it is not possible to imitate truly a dull and garrulous discourser, without repeating the effects of dullness and garrulity." Yet he does go on to commend certain passages of the poem, while compromising his commendation by writing that with the exception of certain passages others "are felt by many unprejudiced and

unsophisticated hearts, as sudden and unpleasant sinkings from the height
to which the poet had previously lifted them, and to which he again
re-elevates both himself and his reader." Perhaps a casual passage in
Dorothy Wordsworth's *Grasmere Journal* (1801), though written of course
after the poem, can provide a general and mitigating clue. She attempts at
one point to reproduce the accent of a local native girl: "She says: 'ye may
say what ye will, but there's naething like a gay auld man for behaving weel
to a young wife. Ye may laugh, but this wind blows no [favour] and where
there's no love there's no favour.'" Are we not then confronted in "The
Thorn" with an essentially dialectal monologue produced in standard
English form? Robert Burns faced the artistic dilemma by resolving it both
ways, by standard and by dialectal spelling, as well as by both ways in the
same poem (e.g., "The Cotter's Saturday Night"). The problem of the
fictive reader, then, is to gauge his responsibility in reading or, better,
performing such poetry as "The Thorn."

It would be indeed troublesome to defend "The Thorn" as a successful
poem. Nonetheless, if granted its proper hearing by the performing reader,
it could undefensively be regarded as portraying the dramatically garrulous
maundering of a simple man who, like the Ancient Mariner, recites his
obsessive experience. It is a revealing contrast to attempt first to read the
poem aloud in a North Country accent and then in standard literate speech,
whether English or American. The latter rendition can easily evoke
derisory mirth and quick critical dismissal. But the former may well have
the effect of reinforcing the reader's admiration for Wordsworth's artistic
integrity even in so mediocre an example of his art. The third stanza may
serve as a tryout:

> High on a mountain's highest ridge,
> Where oft the stormy winter gale
> Cuts like a scythe, while through the clouds
> It sweeps from vale to vale;
> Not five yards from the mountain path,
> This Thorn you on your left espy;
> And to the left, three yards beyond,
> You see a little muddy Pond
> Of water never dry;
> I've measured it from side to side:
> 'Tis three feet long, and two feet wide.

Though this is perhaps the most banal stanza of the poem, one might hope that a dialectal performance might help to quell the qualms not only of Wordsworth's admirers, but also of ready scoffers. It is not a matter of renouncing critical evaluation; it is a matter of fair and normative performance inherent in the text and justified historically. The author's imperfect intentions are not so much at stake as the imaginative and historically grounded awareness of the reader-performer who should be *optimus inter impares*. True, "The Thorn" is something of a limiting case, and any defense of it need not extend in principle to "The Idiot Boy" or to the tediously short and insipid "We are Seven." Yet the fictive reader's role surely demands first sympathetic and imaginative understanding, then "ambivalent" involvement, and finally the valid critical evaluation that is the reader's ultimate duty. A poem conceived as dramatic monologue should perhaps supply to the reader the sorts of direction common in musical compositions. There are very few among all who know the tune of the first aria in Handel's *Xerxes* (commonly known as the "Largo") who are also acquainted with the words and the condition of the king awakening from a Persian bout of drunkenness.

Special roles are assigned the fictive reader in the first-person novel and in the epistolary novel as well. To take the former first, let us assume that there is a gamut running from a novel like *The Brothers Karamazov* to *Lazarillo de Tormes*. It may come as a surprise to someone with a more or less distant recollection of his last reading of Dostoevsky's novel that it is, however faintly, cast as a first-person narrative. Yet in the very first sentence both the first-person singular and the first-person plural appear to the end of establishing the almost confessional veracity of the narrative about to unfold. The narrator thus identifies himself as a local witness of the notorious events that occurred in his native village: we are thus prepared for a full account from his point of observation. But soon the first-person observer dissolves into the narrative "we" of the omniscient narrator who is privileged to know what goes on in the secret minds of the characters he is creating: the single outside observer almost imperceptibly melts into the all-knowing narrator, only rarely to reemerge in his role as local witness, particularly, as it happens, at the trial where he is "realistically" able to describe the atmosphere, the jurymen, and the behavior of those in the courtroom audience and those called to the witness stand. He manages also, with no little embarrassment, to reveal to us the name of his village: Skotoprigonevsk; meaning something like a "stockyard." The first-person witness, then, is a latent resource whose usefulness is apparent and whose

inconsistent presence is attenuated by the overwhelmingly vivid presentation of the omniscient narrator.

Still within the technique of the first-person novel we may consider
toward the other end of the gamut *Lazarillo de Tormes,* that flawed but
primordial exemplar of the picaresque novel. To begin with, there is the
usual conventional or, most likely, parodistic prologue which ends in a
supplicatory dedication to an unnamed man of wealth and of course a
potential patron. What follows are seven chapters ("tratados") of unequal
length and fictional merit. Though the novel is purportedly addressed to the
hoped-for patron, it is of course the optimum reader who is called upon to
allow himself to enter into the fiction presented as a confessional first-
person narrative. The reader encounters a world of cruelty and uncertainty
enhanced by squalid atmosphere and crude humor. Finally Lazarillo, whose
vicissitudes could become so repetitive as to try the patience of the most
willingly fictive reader, accepts the offer of the archpriest of San Salvador
to marry one of his servant girls. Up to this point the autobiographical
narrative has placed no particular strain on the reader's direct collaboration:
everything has seemed straightforward and consistent in presentation. But
then Lázaro, as he is now known, learns from "evil tongues" or "friends"
that his wife has continued to frequent the house of the archpriest and that
she had allegedly given birth three times before marrying him. Still he
accepts the professions of innocence both from the archpriest and from his
wife. If anyone thereafter should allude to the matter, he would say: "Look,
if you're my friend, say nothing that would make me suffer, since I hold no
one my friend who makes me suffer. . . . Why, I'll swear by the conse-
crated Host that she is as good a woman as lives within the gates of Toledo.
Whoever would say anything else, I'll fight him to the death. And so they
say nothing to me and I have peace in my house." What is the fictive reader,
having faithfully followed the fictional veracity of the first-person narrator,
to make of this? He is now on his own and left balancing the evidence as
given and evaluated by his first-person fictional collaborator, who happens
under the circumstances to be his only source.

Similar situations occur throughout the tradition of the picaresque novel.
In the Simplicissimus cycle of Grimmelshausen most of the main characters
are self-servers or dupes whose actions are presented either with authorial
"objectivity" or with first-person self-defensiveness. It is often left to the
knowing reader who is cast as a scamp drawn into the fiction to play his
provisional role while, at the same time, reserving and accumulating his
brief for an elusive final judgment. Daniel Defoe, in *Moll Flanders,*

confronts the fictive reader with a first-person account of a life of crime (whoredom, theft, incest, and canny calculation) which ends, according to Moll, in marriage, respectability, and repentance. Having one witness, Moll herself, how are we to take this? Though it may seem a moot matter, I would suggest that Moll is again self-serving and self-defensive, that she enacts a parody of sincere confessionalism common enough in the Christian era, in particular in Defoe's own time and country, and that her affluent and agreeable settlement at the end represents a gilded conscience and self-satisfaction that cause the sympathetic reader, duped or ambivalently fictive, deep doubts concerning her veracity about herself and the validity of what might be called her final smugness. The fictive reader may seem to be left hanging in a limbo of irony created by the author behind the scenes and his first-person narrator who gives us all the surface *données*. Toward the end of the novel Moll, amid her protestations of repentance, declares: "I could fill a larger history than this with the evidences of this truth [that is, her husband's repentance], and but [*sic*] that I doubt that part of the story will not be equally diverting as the wicked part." It seems to me that here, as elsewhere in the novel, there exists a sort of contractual understanding between author and reader that transcends the self-knowledge of Moll and the fictional sincerity, as she nears the age of seventy, of her remorse. At all events, the fictive reader is cast in the role of wary rather than gullible witness and participant.

The fictive reader's role is even more complex in the epistolary novel. In Richardson's novels, Choderlos de Laclos's *Les Liaisons dangereuses,* and Smollett's *Humphrey Clinker*—to name a few notable examples—it is the reader who must weigh and adjudicate the motives and veracity of the fictional writer or writers of the letters. The result is a deep involvement of the reader as, so to say, reconstructive historian in accepting his commitment as fictive collaborator with the author. A particularly suggestive instance of the epistolary form of fiction is Goethe's *Die Leiden des jungen Werther.* About two-thirds of the novel consists of letters sent to Werther's intimate friend Wilhelm to whom he tells all: by the all-pervasive and unself-serving mode of sincerity and confidence the reader in his fictive role is bound to accept the veracity of Werther's sufferings. One might be tempted to say that distance lends sincerity, in the sense that Werther shows he has nothing to hide and everything, from his point of view, to confide. The essential theme of distance and fictional sincerity is asserted in the very first sentence of the epistolary part of the novel: "Wie froh bin ich, dass ich weg bin!" His letters to Wilhelm, as well as to Albert and

Lotte, and also his intimate diary confirm the fictional necessity of the reader's accepting what is vouchsafed him as the authentic and unquestionable truth of the protagonist. It is a duty of the reader to learn and fictively embrace the code of feeling in any work of any age by the contractual exercise of his historical imagination—the reader being properly as much of a chameleon, in Keats's sense, as the author himself. Throughout *Werther* we are induced to dwell in a state of feeling memorably expressed in a passage alluding to a certain prince:

> Auch schätzt er meinen Verstand und meine Talente mehr als dies Herz, das doch mein einziger Stolz ist, das ganz allein die Quelle von allem ist, aller Kraft, aller Seligkeit und alles Elendes. Ach, was ich weiss, kann jeder wissen—mein Herz habe ich allein.

Besides its use of intense fictional sincerity, to which the fictive reader should contractually submit, the novel gains authenticity from the documentary mode of the last part. Werther has demonstrated his depth of feeling by committing suicide with the pistols lent by Albert and cleaned by Lotte for a purported hunting expedition. It could have been left at that. But Goethe had the genius to close with a section entitled "Der Herausgeber an den Leser," thus stressing the reader's role and the authenticity of the account. In the course of the last part of the novel the "editor" by his circumstantiality draws the willing fictive reader into a fictional credence or acquiescence, indeed an acceptance of the truth of the fiction. In startling contrast to the outpourings of Werther, the novel ends with a terse objective description of the burial in the manner of a newspaper dispatch:

> Um zwölf mittags starb er. Die Gegenwart des Amtmannes und seine Anstalten tuschten einen Auflauf. Nachts gegen elf liess er ihn an die Stätte begraben, die er sich erwählt hatte. Der Alte folgte der Leiche und die Söhne, Albert vermocht's nicht. Man fürchtete für Lottens Leben. Handwerker trugen ihn. Kein Geistlicher hat ihn begleitet.

Until the last "editorial" section the reader has been cast in the role of being his own editor or at least the master of his own collaborative surmises. It is in the last section that he finds himself "objectively" informed, corroborated, and ineluctably controlled in accepting the final fictional truth and his final fictive role.

In seeming contrast to the "active" role of the reader as directly and willingly involved in the literary work is the emphasis of some works, either pervasive or sporadic, on their inner self-awareness or self-reflexiveness. In the realistic novel of, say, Balzac, Flaubert, or Tolstoy, the reader is in some degree kept at a distance: he is more of a witness, along with the chronicler-narrator, than a directly "invited" participant or collaborator; at all events, his fictive involvement requires more strenuous efforts on his part to assess and play his role. I do not wish to suggest anything approaching an absolute contrast, but merely to suggest the important aesthetic difference between the confessional and conversational mode, on the one hand, and, on the other, the direct, seemingly impersonal or formal, presentation of fiction. In imaginative discourse, as distinct from "scientific" discourse, *impassibilité* is ultimately impossible. It is of course a matter of degree and coloring, but they are literarily of the essence. That the children of Mme. Aubain in "Un cœur simple" are named Paul and Virginie may be taken perhaps as a laggingly provincial and culturally pretentious allusion to Bernardin's sentimental novel; while naming the central character, the pathetic drudge, Félicité (a name within the bounds of common historical plausibility) must, however underplayed, involve the reader in her touchingly ironic fate. Flaubert cannot be accused here of coyness; he may even be commended for restraint or understatement.

Such tension for the fictive reader inheres in the role cast for him in the *Divine Comedy*. Here the rhetorical situation is extraordinarily complex. The Dante within the poem is both the individual and self-engrossed Christian pilgrim and also, at the same time, the representative wayfaring soul in search of certainty through extraordinary but exemplary revelation. At the very beginning of the introductory canto such meaningful ambivalence, the individual implicit in the general, the concrete circumstances implicit in the human condition, is set forth subtly by the use of a seemingly casual first-person plural adjective and by the concrete description of an actual first-person experience:

> Nel mezzo del cammin di nostra vita
> Mi ritrovai per una selva oscura . . .

The sudden appearance of Virgil, in the midst of "Dante's" danger of being devoured by the objectified beasts of his own sinfulness, and the further narrative of the unique *Bildung* of the Dante in the poem could have the effect of a rather distanced adventure tale in which the reader's involvement is rarely invited by direct appeal. Who else is there who has been offered such imagined or imaginative grace? Who else is there who has been granted such distinguished guides (Virgil, Beatrice, Piccarda, Saint Bernard), and most portentously, who else is there who has been granted the special dispensation of traversing as a mortal all the regions of the afterlife? In his extraordinary pilgrim's progress, the Dante of the poem can allow himself a whole "personal" range from denunciation, human susceptibility, humble acquiescence, and joyous acceptance of a provisionally final revelation. Furthermore, the question of plausibility or fictional veracity is poised in as teetering an equilibrium as the reader finds himself, vacillating between his fictive roles, along with his moral, anagogical, and allegorical belief. Here the fictive reader of any age or persuasion finds himself stretched along a gamut of literal acceptance (which, in orthodoxy, cannot always be accepted), interpretative or allegorical "truth" (which may lead to orthodox conviction), provisional acquiescence in the moral and religious relevance of the narrative, imaginative and critical acceptance of the poem after granting its premises, and finally, at the extreme, literal rejection of the unprovable pretensions of the narrative. It is here that the properly sympathetic, imaginative, aesthetically provisional, and self-enrolled fictive reader can hope to aspire to be the optimum reader. His task is demanding. He must, in the face of possible truth, fictively grant his willing suspension of disbelief; he must go beyond the fictional world of, say, Ariosto and somehow balance an awareness of the fiction and a willingness, or even desire, to believe in its ultimate truth in both imaginative and perhaps substantive senses.

On a direct and literal level the reader is often reminded of his role in varying intensities and in varying relations of the self-reflexiveness of the work: if instances were counted, whose evaluation would carry us to untoward length, the sum would be that direct address to the reader occurs five times in the *Inferno,* seven times in the *Purgatorio,* and four times in the *Paradiso,* quite a large number in a work of any age. Yet our conclusion may well be that Dante, as author, is managing to maintain an aesthetically perilous, though successful, balance between fictive involvement of the reader and artistically inward self-reflexiveness. There lies a certain danger in such balance for the unhistorical fictive reader: he may willfully be tempted to rebel against the role cast for him by the text. Perhaps the surest test is the reading of the *Inferno.* The Dante in the poem reveals his own subjective susceptibilities: when he enters Hell and sees the uncompromising words "Lasciate ogni speranza voi che entrate," he says to Virgil,

"Il senso lor m'è duro"; and when he hears Francesca's moving yet unrepentant words he, at the end of the canto, says, "E caddi come corpo morto cade." Indeed, we as readers sympathetically encounter, particularly in the *Inferno,* an uncertainty of fictive role, along with the fictional protagonist. Often when we think of Dante's Hell in retrospect we recall most vividly those figures who were great and unrepentant in being evil in a sense that is objective within the poem: those figures who have taken a stand in spite of all, including God, and who, in a word or a gesture, express their archetypal essence. We may think, for instance, of Francesca, of Farinata, of Guido da Montefeltro, of Ulysses. Perhaps, we might provisionally think, Dante succeeded all too well; perhaps we would rather dwell with the great sinners than with the righteous who may seem to lose their sharp identity in attuning their wills to God's. But we must reflect that it is easier to portray vice than virtue and that the fictive reader must stand responsibly on his own recognizance. Though vice may be, as the Baron de Charlus called it, a vicious circle, it still may seem to have the complicating movement and the charming devilishness that virtue may seem to lack. But after all, Dante is writing his notion of the afterlife with himself as provisional protagonist, and as he keeps reminding us in our own imaginary journey from Hell to Purgatory to Heaven, things are not the same beyond as they are here. Our imaginations as fictive readers are stretched almost beyond compass in being led to conceive in some way what it is like to exist in a state of not four dimensions (including time) but, as we would say in our paltry earthbound language, of either nullity or infinity of dimensions. As Dante writes in the first canto of the *Paradiso:*

> Trasumanar significar *per verba*
> non si porìa; però l' essemplo basti
> a cui esperïenza grazia serba.

Toward the end of the last *cantica,* after the revelation of the Divine Vision, the reader is drawn in as collaborator with the speaker in a supremely inevitable failure to express the unexpressible. Dante's poem, with the masterly self-reflexiveness of his art, turns in upon itself and implicates, or literally enfolds, the reader. It is not only a poem about the writing of itself; it is a poem about the impossibility of its ever having been written.

It is Dante himself who, by his subject, means, and self-awareness, requires of a critic so intensely paradoxical a cryptic summation. Many other literary works can successfully maintain a viable balance between the role required of the fictive reader and their own self-reflexiveness: the "contract" between reader and work is astonishingly kept. It might be well, in lesser compass, to consider briefly a poem that has fascinated and teased the minds of countless readers, Coleridge's "Kubla Khan." Written in irregular but persistent rime and in syllabic length ranging from six to eleven—from which it formally derives a sort of primitive, dithyrambic, or spontaneously authentic force—the poem has often seemed to readers an intriguing, perpetually "cliff-hanging" fragment. It was originally published with the title "Kubla Khan; or a Vision in a Dream" and was preceded by a circumstantial account of its composition, "Of the Fragment of Kubla Khan." Here we are introduced to the famous or egregious "person on business from Porlock," who purportedly dispelled the remaining pregnant vapors of vision. It may seem presumptuous on my part and on the part of others before, but the poem, as we have it, can on arguable grounds be considered a whole, and indeed an impressive whole, that may serve as an instance of the tension, aesthetically productive, between fictive reader and self-reflexive work. In the first eleven lines the reader enters an exotic and mysterious setting in which the artifact of the "stately pleasure-dome" and the weirdly natural "sacred river" and "sunless sea" seem both to strain and assuage the reader's credulity almost simultaneously. In its wild course the "fountain" with the intermittent force of the river Alph unpredictably throws up "huge fragments vaulted like rebounding hail." For five miles the "sacred river" meandered through a normal landscape,

> Then reached the caverns measureless to man,
> And sank in tumult to a lifeless ocean:
> And 'mid this tumult Kubla heard from far
> Ancestral voices prophesying war!

By their very semblance of historicity and particular location ("In Xanadu . . . ," "Where Alph, the sacred river, ran . . ."), by their mingling of the familiarly natural and strangely artificial and unnatural, the first thirty-six lines of the poem engage the reader in his fictive and collaborative role. He may even have an inkling that the combination of natural and unnatural (or perhaps supernatural) succeeds in rendering the river potently symbolic. But symbolic of what? Adverting proleptically to the latter part of the poem, I would suggest that the river in its "mazy motion" at least foreshadows a symbolic function as representing creative inspiration, that mysterious and gratuitous human experience sacred since the oracle at Delphi. What does Kubla Khan hear after decreeing his pleasure-dome but "Ancestral voices prophesying war"? Inspiration, prophecy, and poetry are in ancient terms barely separable. In "Kubla Khan" we have, I think, an imaginative presentation of the tradition of antiquity in such matters, including the wellspring, the "mighty fountain," reinterpreted, especially in the last eighteen lines:

> A damsel with a dulcimer
> In a vision once I saw:
> It was an Abyssinian maid,
> And on her dulcimer she played,
> Singing of Mount Abora.
> Could I revive within me
> Her symphony and song,
> To such a deep delight 'twould win me,
> That with music loud and long,
> I would build that dome in air,
> That sunny dome! those caves of ice!
> And all who heard should see them there,
> And all should cry, Beware! Beware!
> His flashing eyes, his floating hair!
> Weave a circle round him thrice,
> And close your eyes with holy dread,
> For he on honey-dew hath fed,
> And drunk the milk of Paradise.

It might be asserted at first blush that these lines are discontinuous with the previous and longer part of the poem, a kind of break in rhetorical address and subject matter. But that I think is, *pace* Coleridge himself, a mistaken interpretation of a remarkably cohesive poem. True, there is something of a gap: a certain reflexive distancing supervenes, along with a direct first-person assertion of the speaker of the poem. The previous past narration gradually gives way to the conditional and then to the imperative mood. In the earlier part of the poem we are presented, not with a vision described as such, but with an "actuality," a *donnée*, described in historical "eyewitness" terms. In the latter and far shorter part of the poem the fictive reader is distanced as collaborative witness of what has gone on before, evoked in fictional frustration at the impossibility of poetically re-creating "that sunny dome," "those caves of ice." He becomes sympathetically drawn into what may seem a hopeless effort of the imagination. But, almost paradoxically, has not that effort already succeeded in the earlier part of the poem? Has not the reader already been involved in what has already been accomplished? The poem, in the "truth" of its fiction, looks back upon itself and becomes thereby self-reflexive and complete. It is the fictive reader who is thus fully activated and charged with the imaginative task of successfully making a whole of the self-reflexive poem.

Here we have in "Kubla Khan" what may serve as a final, if not necessarily culminating, example of the particularly intimate aesthetic collaboration between speaker and reader, "script" and performer, author and audience. The sharpest point is, I hope, clear: first, that the literary work of art is a communication and that the communicant is thereby guided and controlled, though not coerced, by its totality. In the aesthetic experience of literature I suggest that there exists a distinction between the fictional creation of the author and the implicit, nay obligatory, fictive or participating role of the reader. I have in effect distinguished between "fictive" and "fictional" in an attempt to stress the reader's double role as believer and agnostic and, on the other hand, the author's double role as contriver and communicator. In the process the permutations and combinations of the acts of writing and reading are wonderfully complicated and engrossingly complex. We, if I may be permitted to involve my own reader, have here traipsed and trespassed through a galaxy of genres toward a hypothetical conclusion: that the role of the reader is an intrinsic part of the fiction of literature and that the fictive reader must provisionally obey the contractual norms before rendering his incumbent verdict *in sede critica.* Every critic, by etymology and tradition, must be judge according to his fullest knowledge and awareness. But first of all he must be fictive participant, accomplice, collaborator, and amicus curiae in the literary court—roles which may render him something of a hippogryph which, Ariosto assures us, is at least half true.

That my examples, drawn from hither and yon, may give to some readers the impression of a tourist among sacred and inviolable sanctuaries does not weigh heavily on my sense of literature and criticism, as *nihil litterarum alienum me puto.* I would like, however, to stress my belief that general or theoretical questions in literary criticism can be illustrated from our common legacy without regard, in such a pursuit, to time, place, or language. Needless to say, time, place, and language are also and equally, depending on the chosen context and emphasis, of the essence. If my own reader looks back to my shifting terminology, my rhetoric of critical ineffability, it may seem indiosyncratic, perhaps even inevitable, to end up with a welter of words: accomplice, communicant, collaborator, real, fictive, fictional, self-reflexive. Yet I plead the extenuating circumstance of nuance. Such terms are not strictly synonymous because there are no true synonyms; such terms may responsibly be used in an attempt to express shades of meaning directed toward what we hope is actually there at a center that we may convincingly approximate but never quite reach. The fictive reader and the self-reflexive work seem to be strangely parallel and, on occasion, even more strangely, to intersect. Is that not all emblematic in the word "mimesis"?

INDEX